GEGE AKUTAMI

NO TAX!

GEGE AKUTAMI published a few short works before starting *Jujutsu Kaisen*, which began serialization in *Weekly Shonen Jump* in 2018.

JUJUTSU KAISEN

VOLUME 16
SHONEN JUMP EDITION

BY GEGE AKUTAMI

TRANSLATION John Werry
TOUCH-UP ART & LETTERING Snir Aharon
DESIGN Joy Zhang
EDITOR John Bae
CONSULTING EDITOR Erika Onabe

Printed in Italy

Published by VIZ Media, LLC
P.O. Box 77010
San Francisco, CA 94107

10 9 8 7 6 5 4 3 2
First printing, June 2022
Second printing, June 2022

VIZ MEDIA
viz.com

SHONEN JUMP

ratings.viz.com
RATED T+ OLDER TEEN

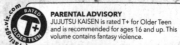

PARENTAL ADVISORY
JUJUTSU KAISEN is rated T+ for Older Teen and is recommended for ages 16 and up. This volume contains fantasy violence.

JUJUTSU KAISEN

16

THE SHIBUYA INCIDENT
—GATE CLOSED—

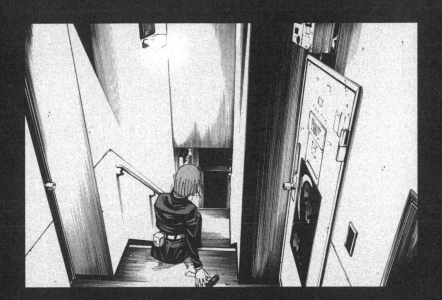

STORY AND ART BY GEGE AKUTAMI

JUJUTSU KAISEN CAST OF CHARACTERS

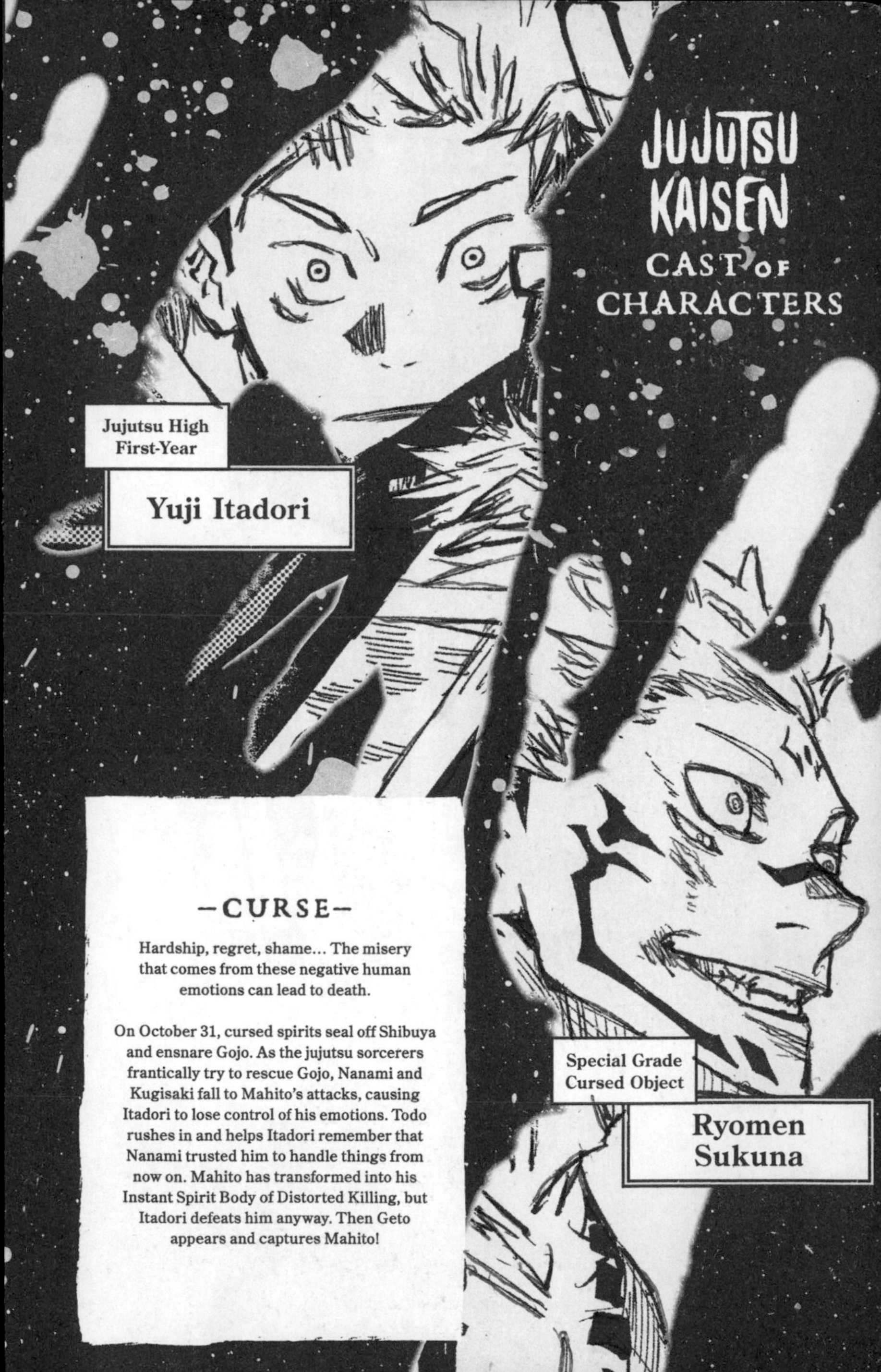
Jujutsu High First-Year
Yuji Itadori
Special Grade Cursed Object
Ryomen Sukuna

—CURSE—

Hardship, regret, shame... The misery that comes from these negative human emotions can lead to death.

On October 31, cursed spirits seal off Shibuya and ensnare Gojo. As the jujutsu sorcerers frantically try to rescue Gojo, Nanami and Kugisaki fall to Mahito's attacks, causing Itadori to lose control of his emotions. Todo rushes in and helps Itadori remember that Nanami trusted him to handle things from now on. Mahito has transformed into his Instant Spirit Body of Distorted Killing, but Itadori defeats him anyway. Then Geto appears and captures Mahito!

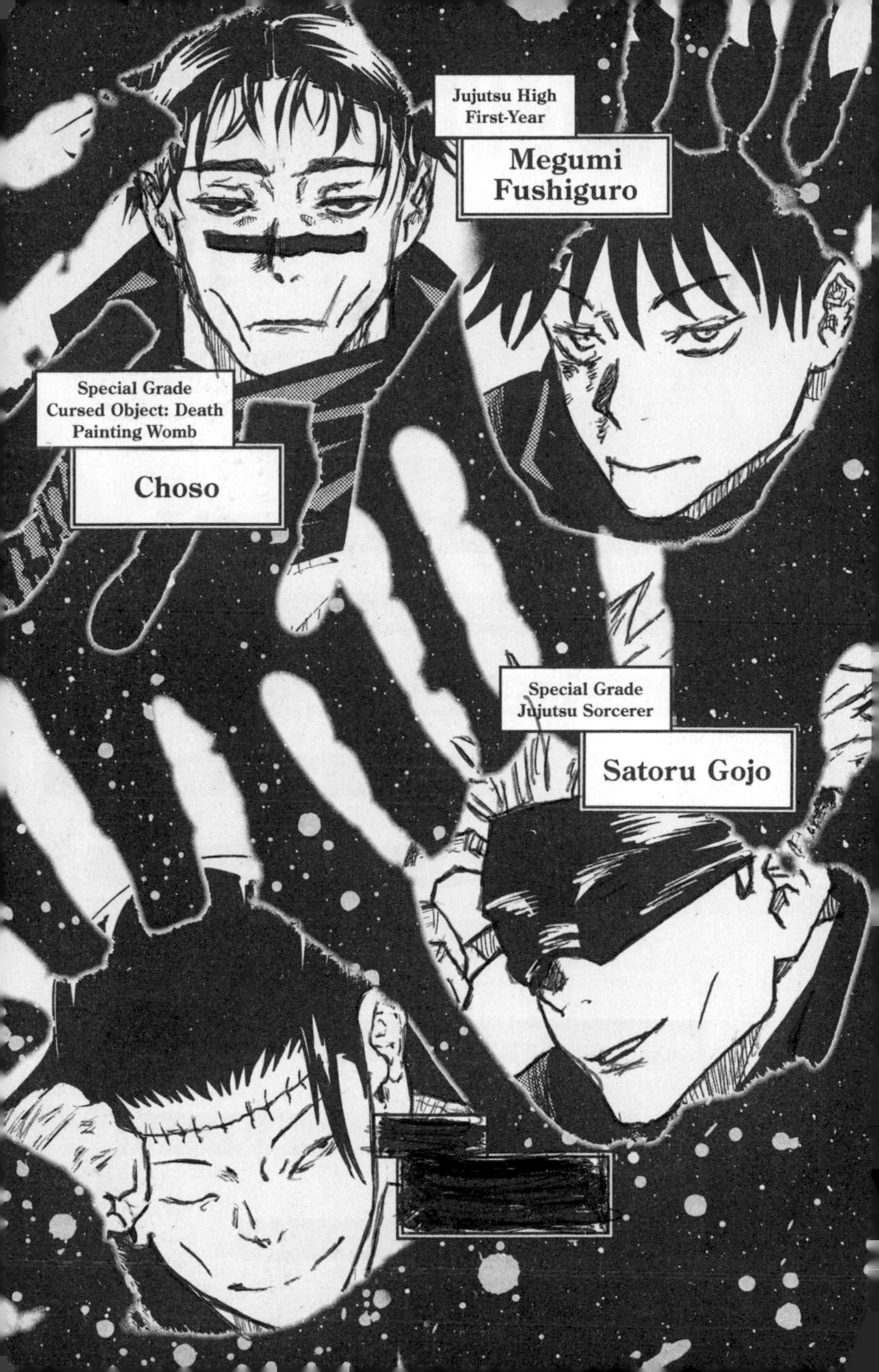
Jujutsu High First-Year
Megumi Fushiguro
Special Grade Cursed Object: Death Painting Womb
Choso
Special Grade Jujutsu Sorcerer
Satoru Gojo
[redacted]

JUJUTSU KAISEN

16

THE SHIBUYA INCIDENT
—GATE CLOSED—

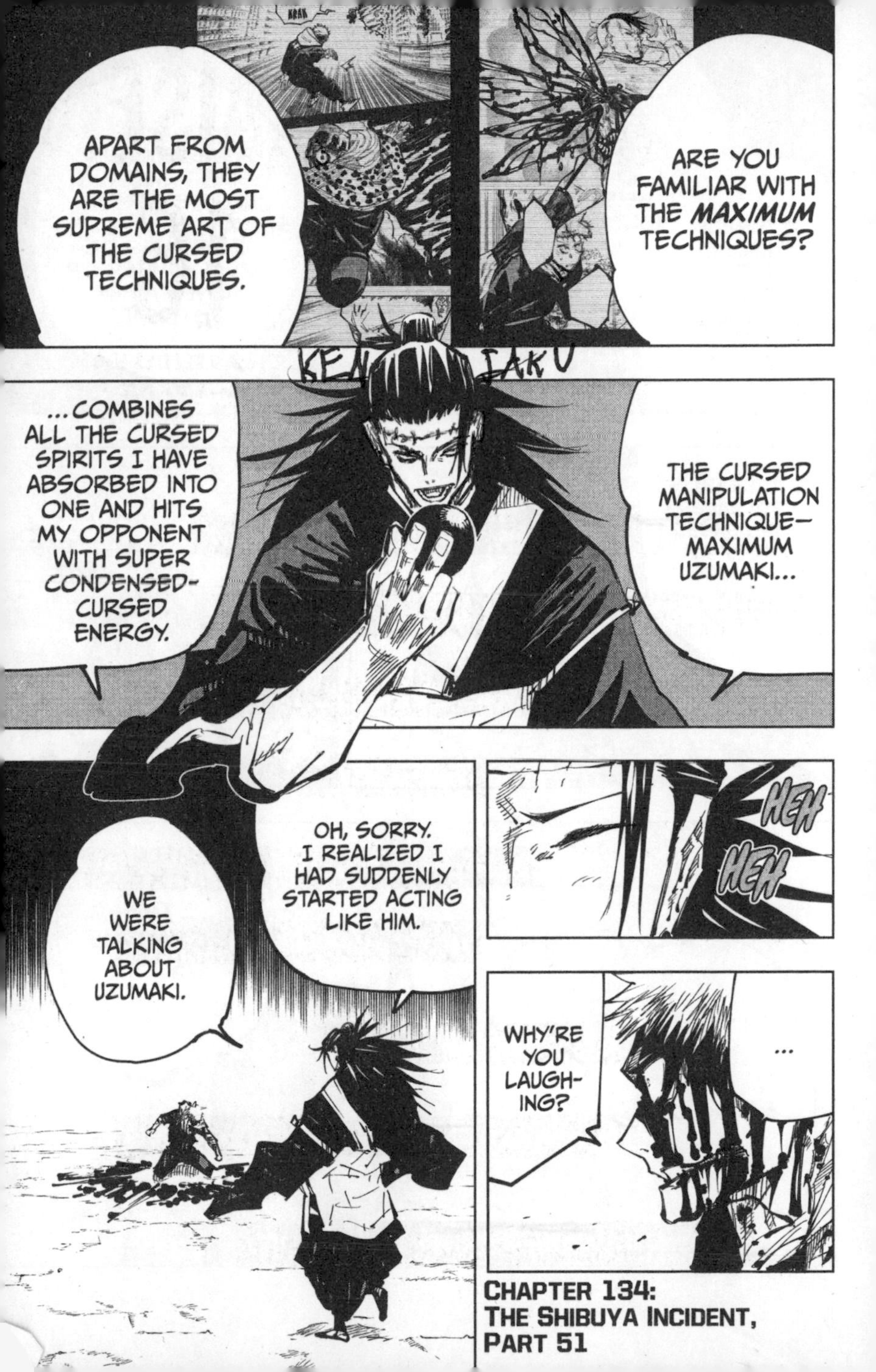
ARE YOU FAMILIAR WITH THE *MAXIMUM* TECHNIQUES?
KRAK
APART FROM DOMAINS, THEY ARE THE MOST SUPREME ART OF THE CURSED TECHNIQUES.
KENJAKU
THE CURSED MANIPULATION TECHNIQUE—MAXIMUM UZUMAKI...
...COMBINES ALL THE CURSED SPIRITS I HAVE ABSORBED INTO ONE AND HITS MY OPPONENT WITH SUPER CONDENSED-CURSED ENERGY.
HEH
HEH
...
WHY'RE YOU LAUGHING?
OH, SORRY. I REALIZED I HAD SUDDENLY STARTED ACTING LIKE HIM.
WE WERE TALKING ABOUT UZUMAKI.

CHAPTER 134: THE SHIBUYA INCIDENT, PART 51

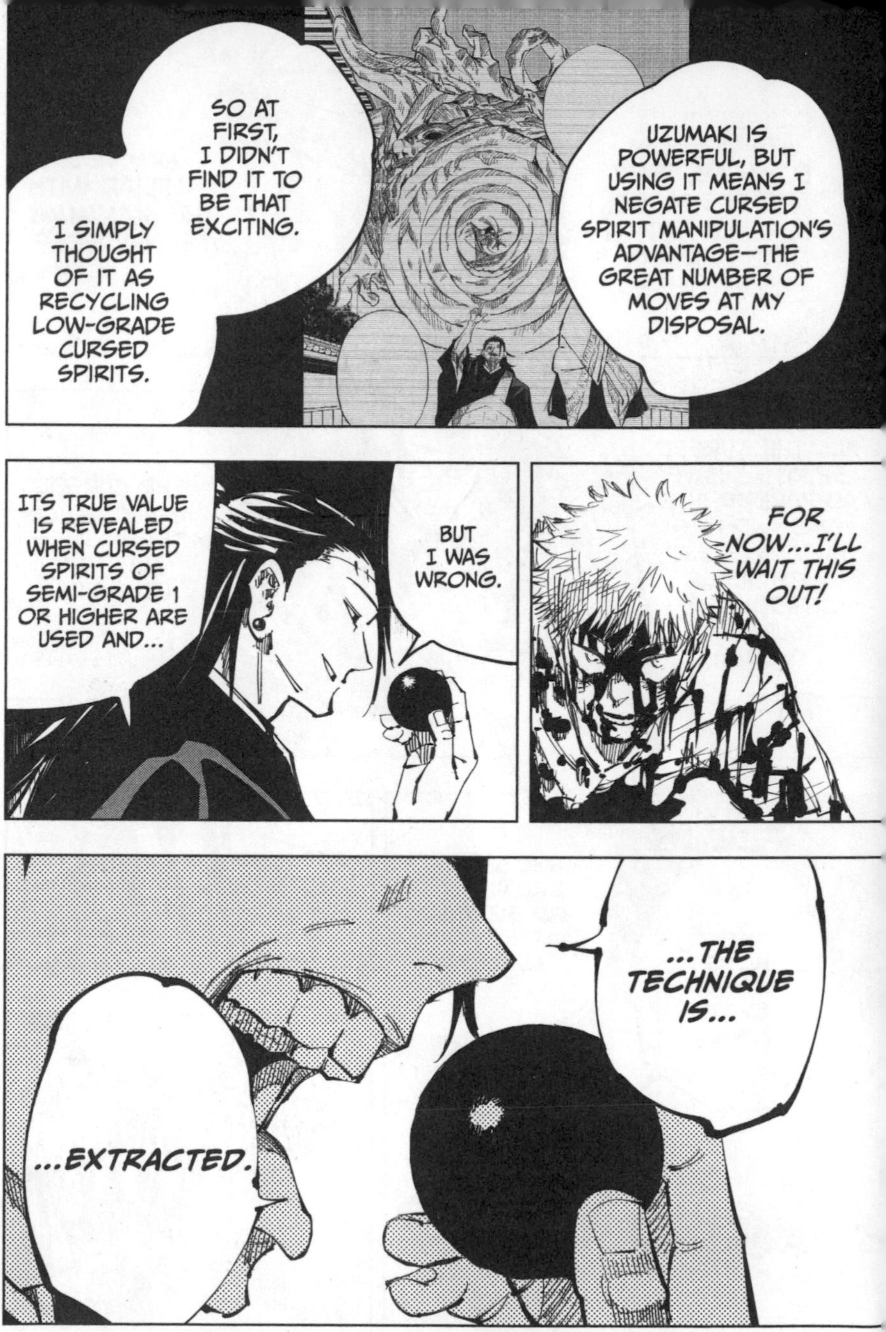
UZUMAKI IS POWERFUL, BUT USING IT MEANS I NEGATE CURSED SPIRIT MANIPULATION'S ADVANTAGE—THE GREAT NUMBER OF MOVES AT MY DISPOSAL.
SO AT FIRST, I DIDN'T FIND IT TO BE THAT EXCITING.
I SIMPLY THOUGHT OF IT AS RECYCLING LOW-GRADE CURSED SPIRITS.
FOR NOW...I'LL WAIT THIS OUT!
BUT I WAS WRONG.
ITS TRUE VALUE IS REVEALED WHEN CURSED SPIRITS OF SEMI-GRADE 1 OR HIGHER ARE USED AND...
...THE TECHNIQUE IS...
...EXTRACTED.

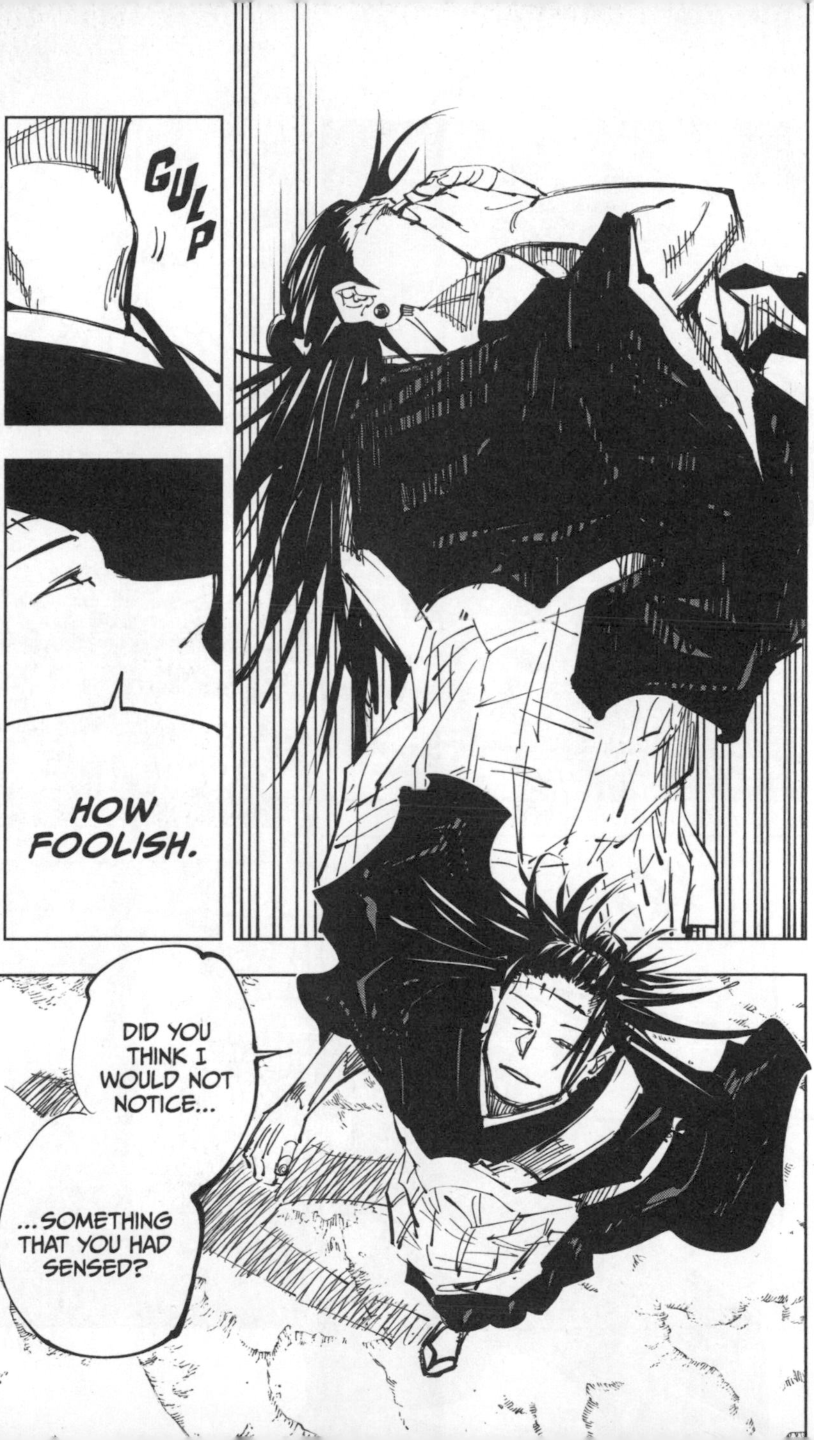
GULP
HOW FOOLISH.
DID YOU THINK I WOULD NOT NOTICE...
...SOMETHING THAT YOU HAD SENSED?

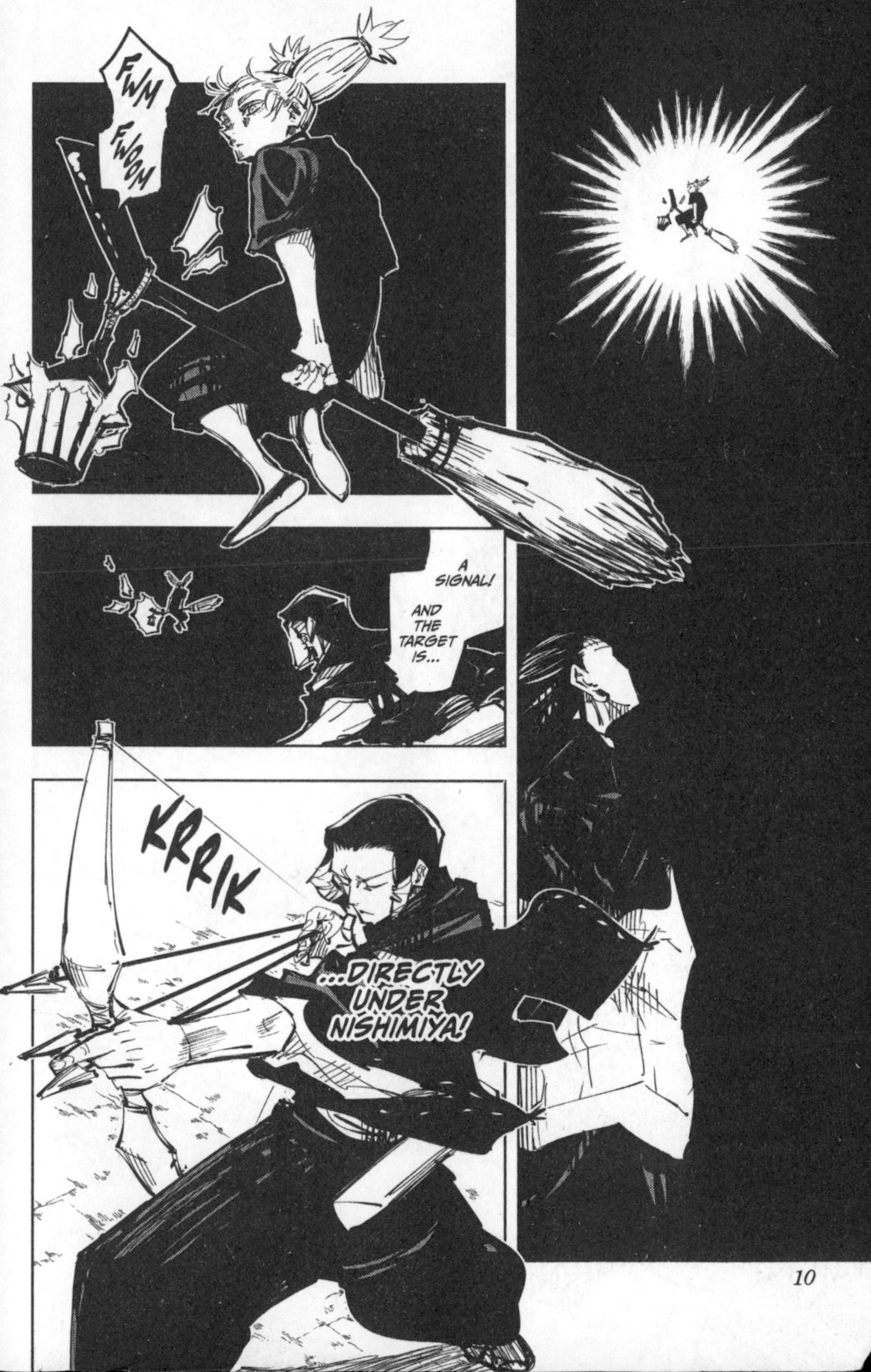
FWM FWOOM
A SIGNAL!
AND THE TARGET IS...
KRRIK
...DIRECTLY UNDER NISHIMIYA!

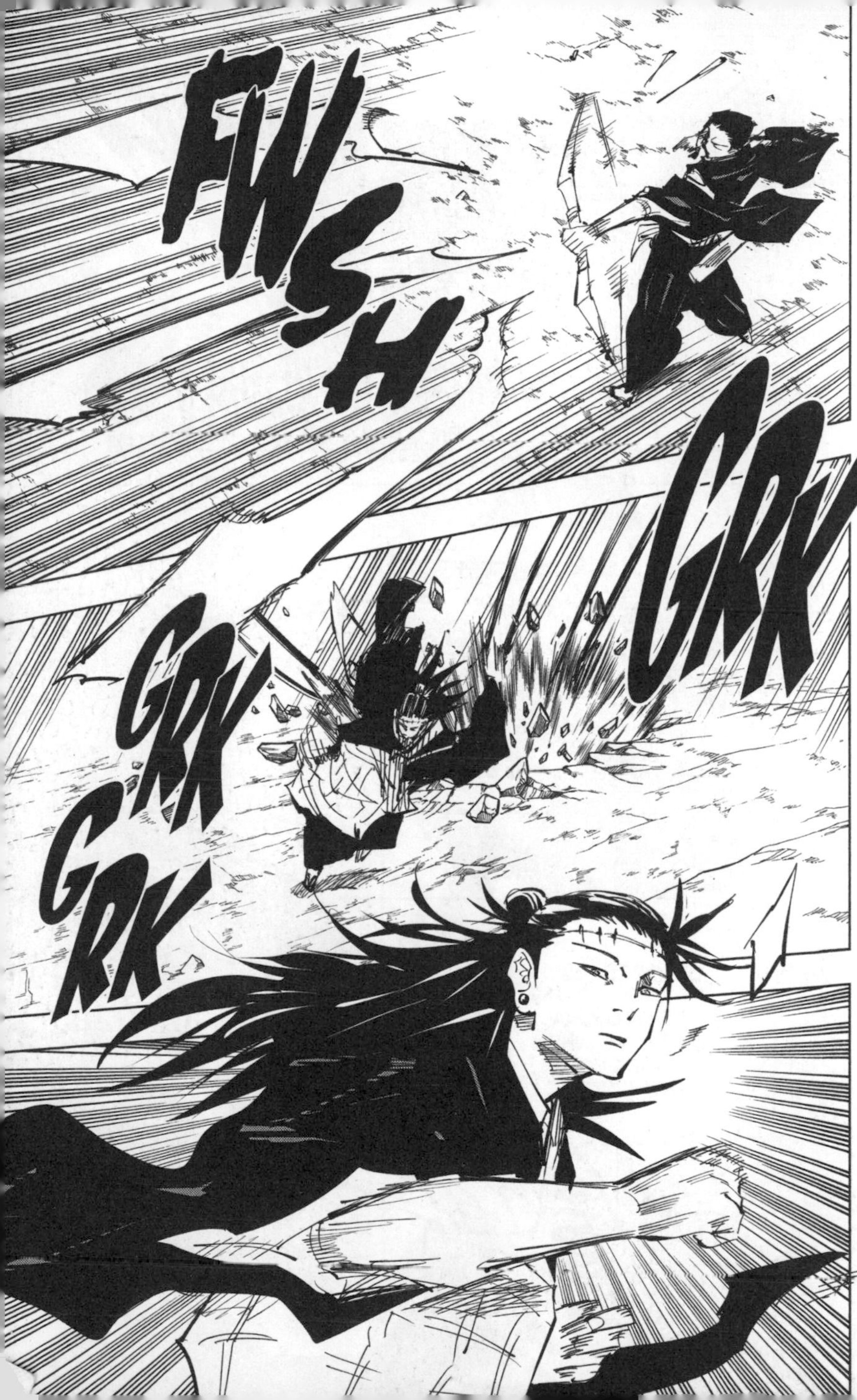
FWSH
GRK
GRK
GRK

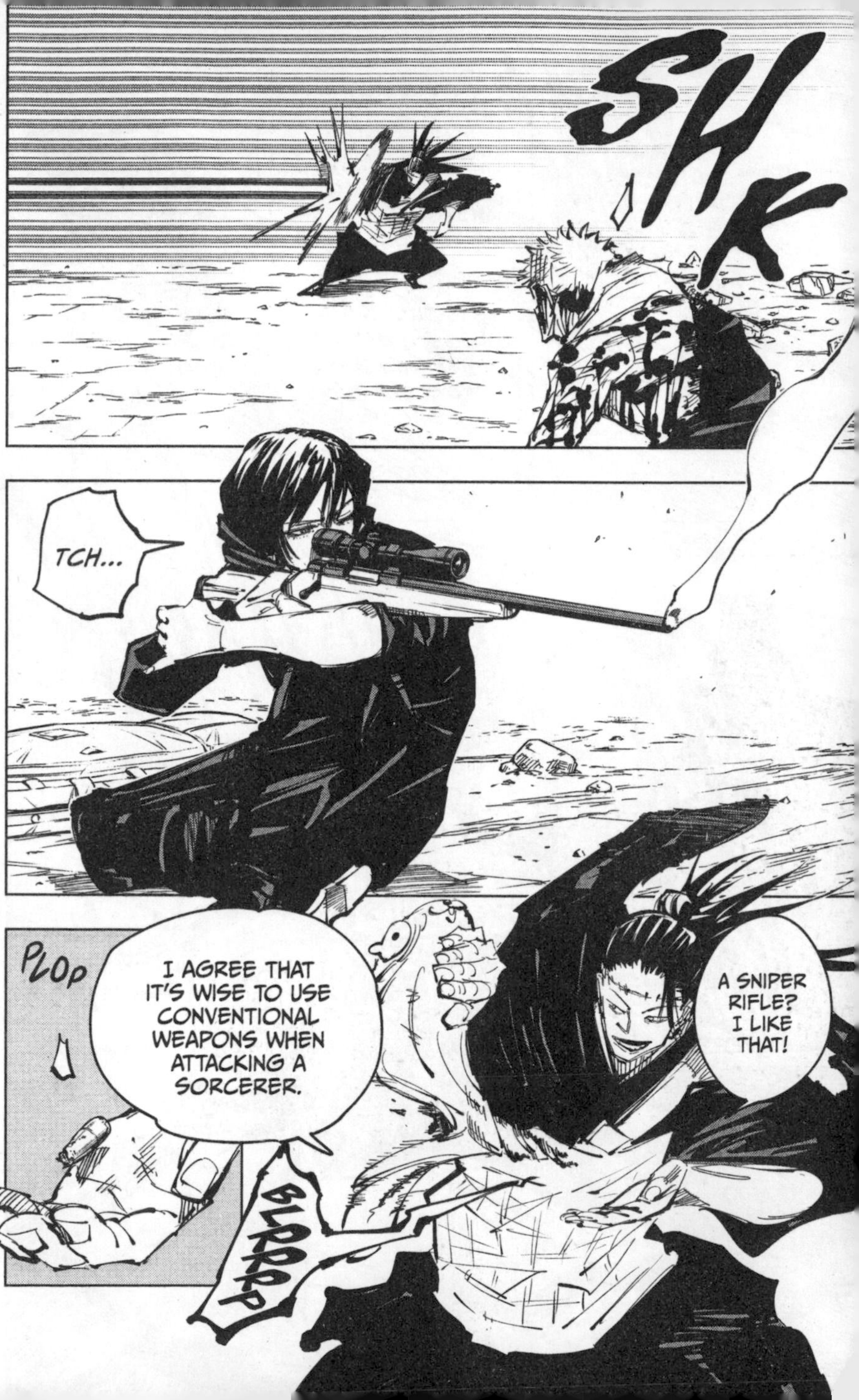
SHK
TCH...
A SNIPER RIFLE? I LIKE THAT!
I AGREE THAT IT'S WISE TO USE CONVENTIONAL WEAPONS WHEN ATTACKING A SORCERER.
PLOP
BLRRRP

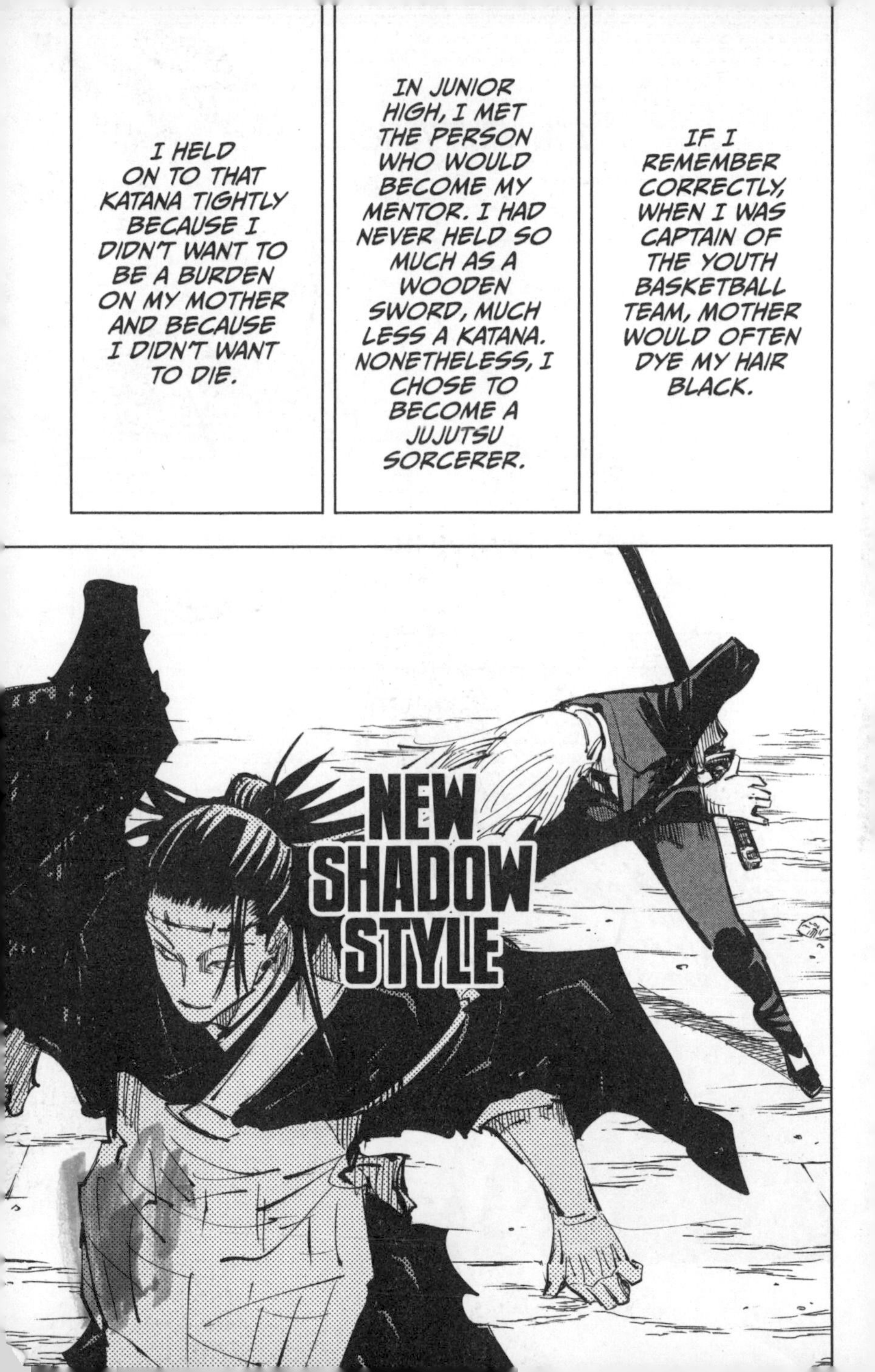
IF I REMEMBER CORRECTLY, WHEN I WAS CAPTAIN OF THE YOUTH BASKETBALL TEAM, MOTHER WOULD OFTEN DYE MY HAIR BLACK.
IN JUNIOR HIGH, I MET THE PERSON WHO WOULD BECOME MY MENTOR. I HAD NEVER HELD SO MUCH AS A WOODEN SWORD, MUCH LESS A KATANA. NONETHELESS, I CHOSE TO BECOME A JUJUTSU SORCERER.
I HELD ON TO THAT KATANA TIGHTLY BECAUSE I DIDN'T WANT TO BE A BURDEN ON MY MOTHER AND BECAUSE I DIDN'T WANT TO DIE.
NEW SHADOW STYLE

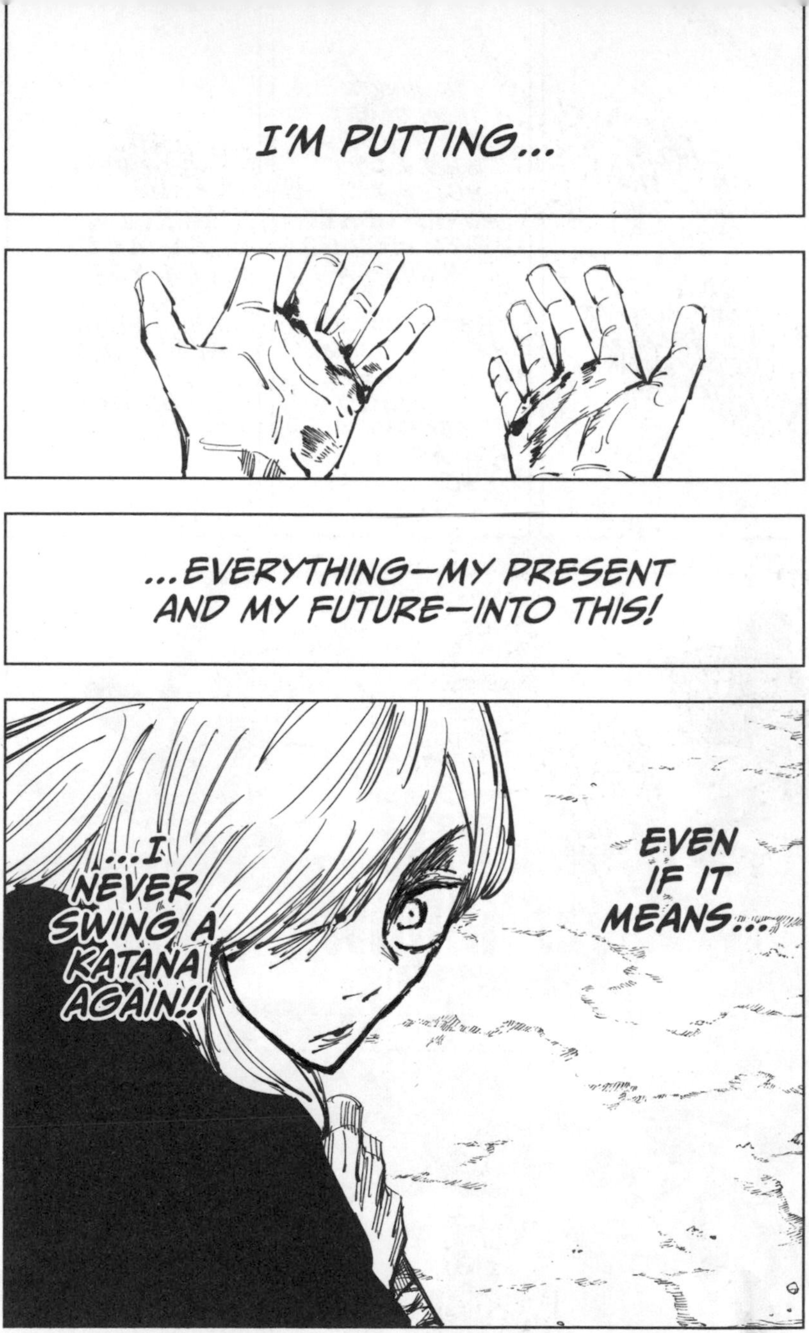
I'M PUTTING...
...EVERYTHING—MY PRESENT AND MY FUTURE—INTO THIS!
EVEN IF IT MEANS...
...I NEVER SWING A KATANA AGAIN!!

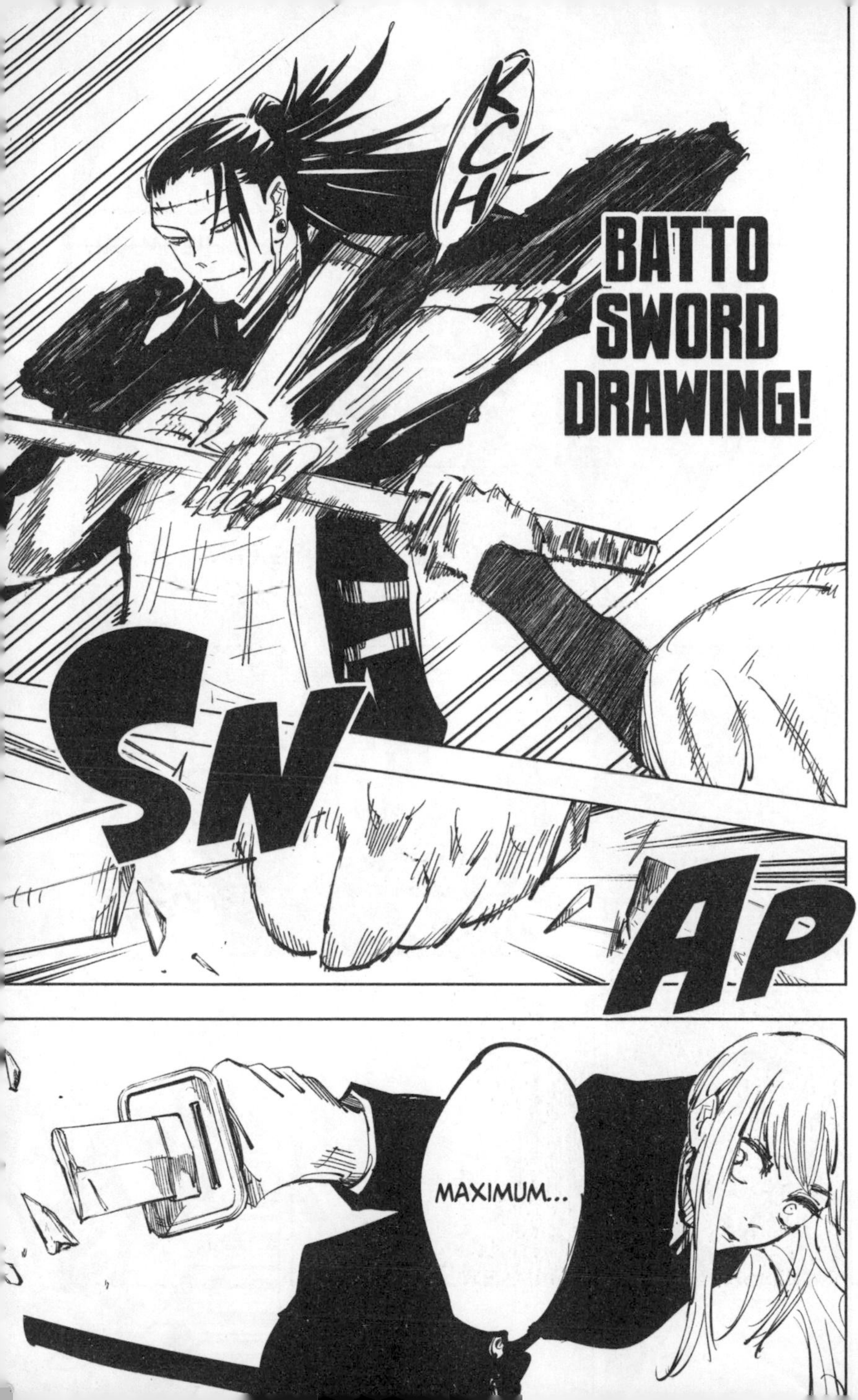
KCH
BATTO SWORD DRAWING!
SNAP
MAXIMUM...

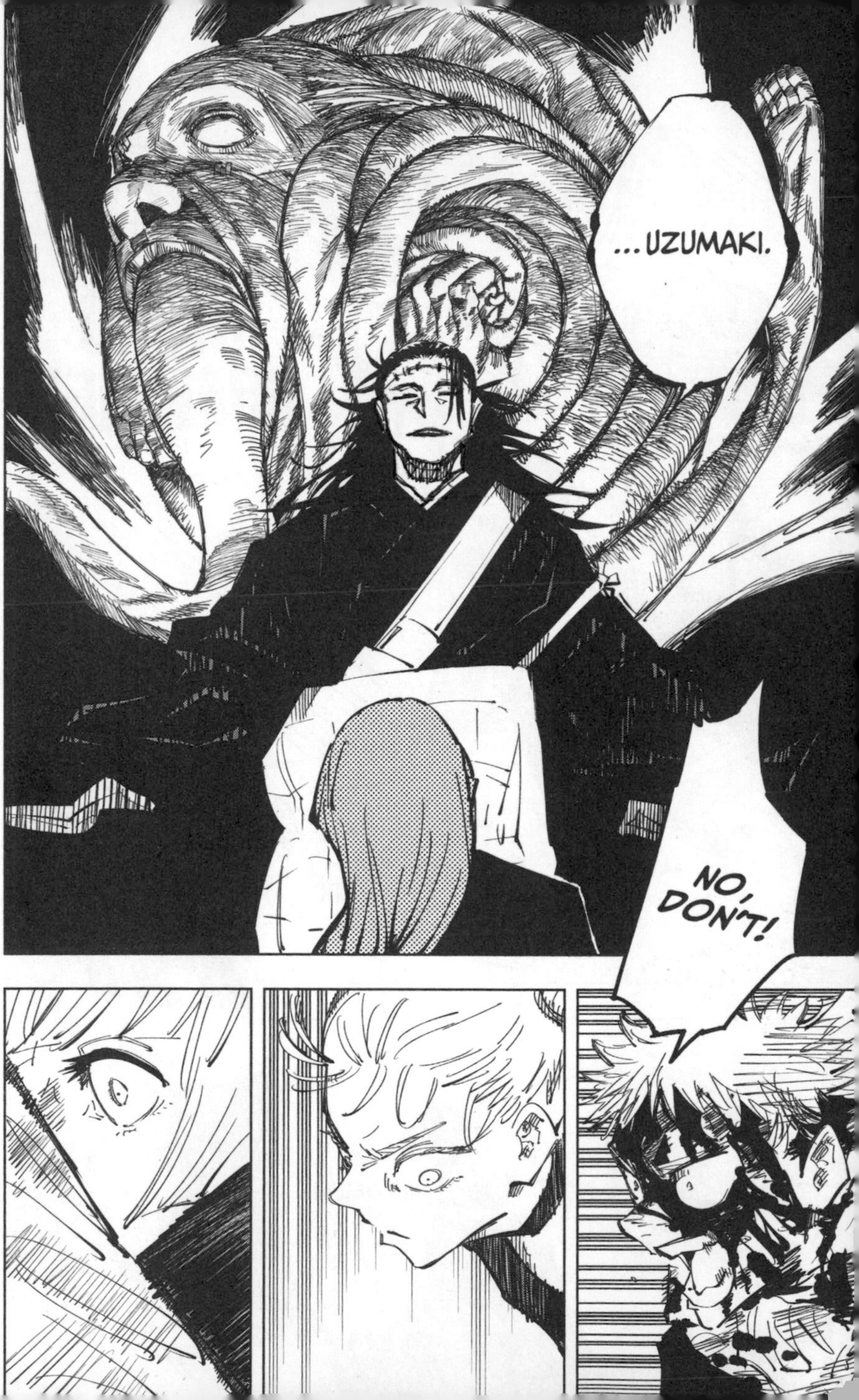
...UZUMAKI.
NO, DON'T!

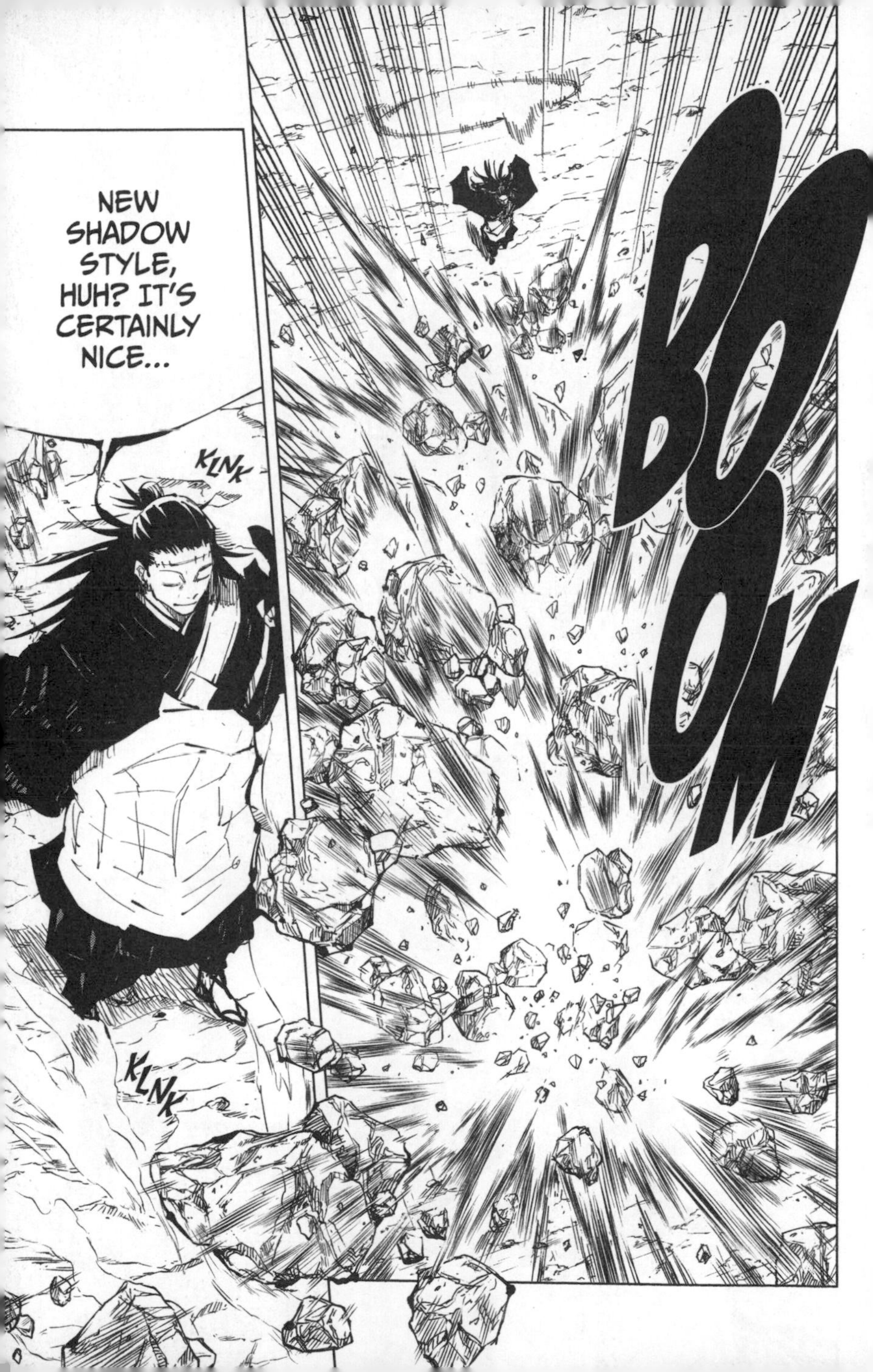
BOOM
NEW SHADOW STYLE, HUH? IT'S CERTAINLY NICE...
KLNK
KLNK

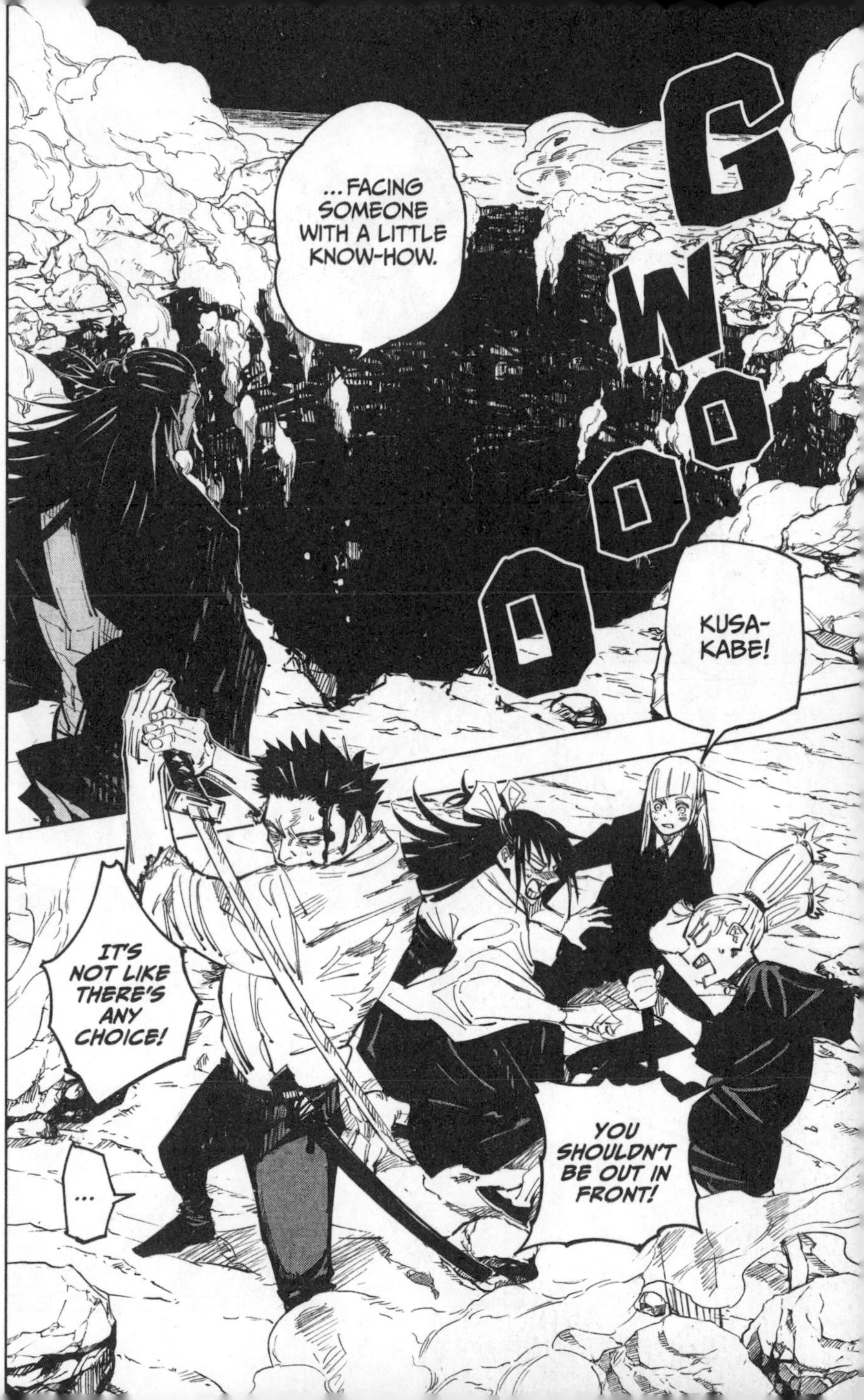
GWOOO
...FACING SOMEONE WITH A LITTLE KNOW-HOW.
KUSA-KABE!
YOU SHOULDN'T BE OUT IN FRONT!
IT'S NOT LIKE THERE'S ANY CHOICE!
...

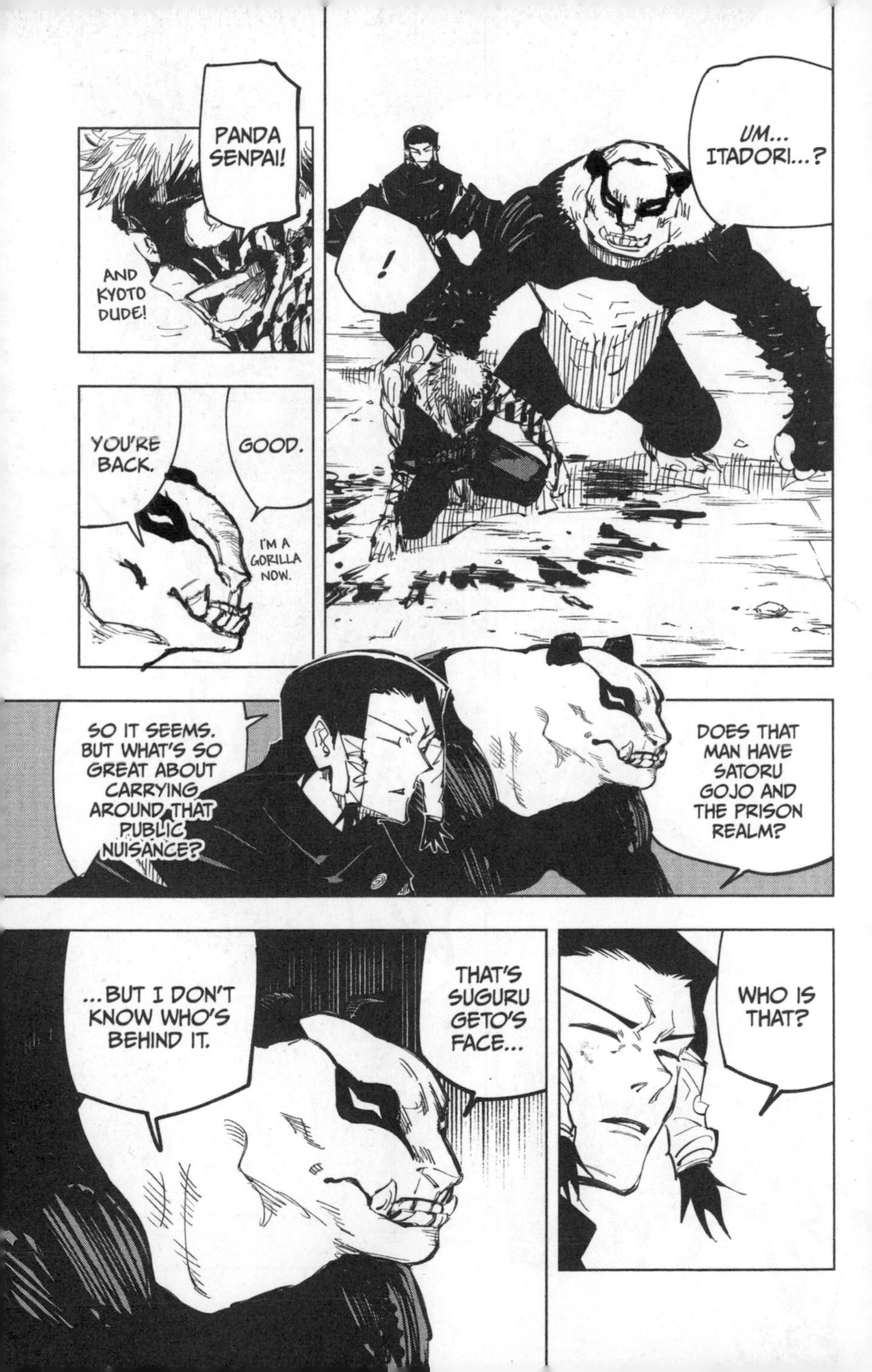
UM... ITADORI...?
!
PANDA SENPAI!
AND KYOTO DUDE!
GOOD.
YOU'RE BACK.
I'M A GORILLA NOW.
DOES THAT MAN HAVE SATORU GOJO AND THE PRISON REALM?
SO IT SEEMS. BUT WHAT'S SO GREAT ABOUT CARRYING AROUND THAT PUBLIC NUISANCE?
WHO IS THAT?
THAT'S SUGURU GETO'S FACE...
...BUT I DON'T KNOW WHO'S BEHIND IT.

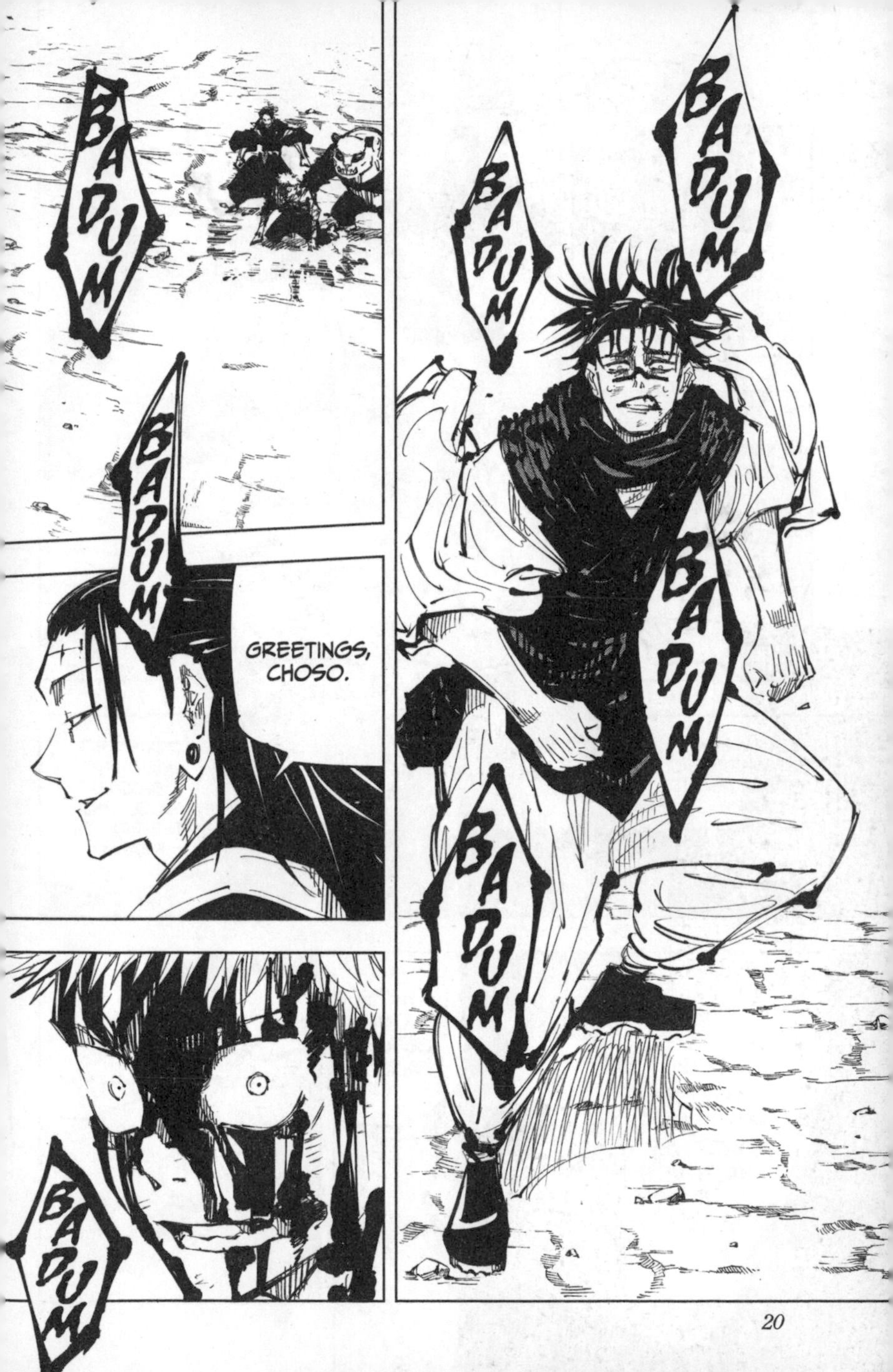
BADUM
BADUM
BADUM
BADUM
BADUM
BADUM
GREETINGS, CHOSO.
BADUM

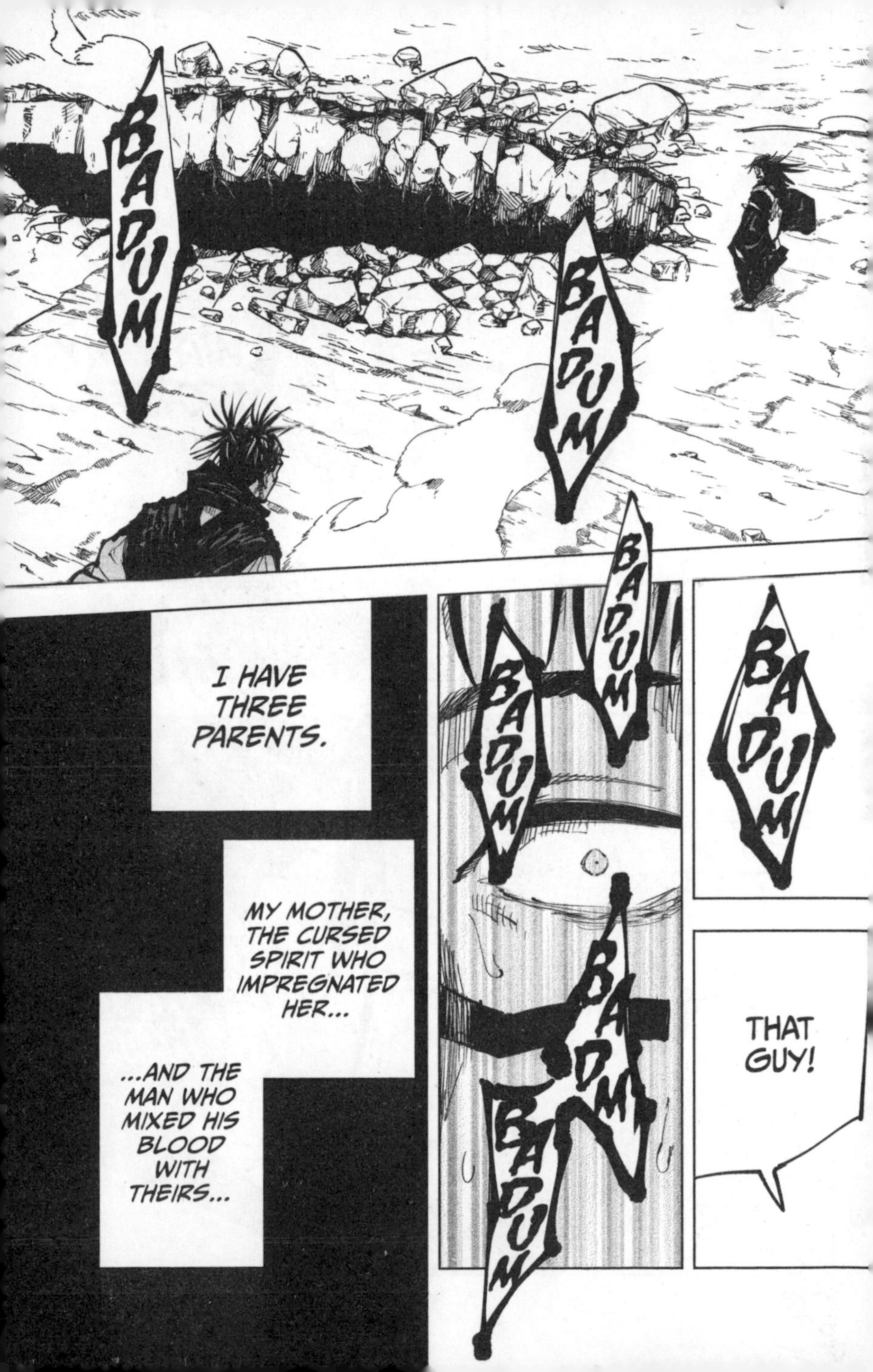
BADUM
BADUM
BADUM
THAT GUY!
BADUM
BADUM
BADUM
BADUM
I HAVE THREE PARENTS.
MY MOTHER, THE CURSED SPIRIT WHO IMPREGNATED HER...
...AND THE MAN WHO MIXED HIS BLOOD WITH THEIRS...

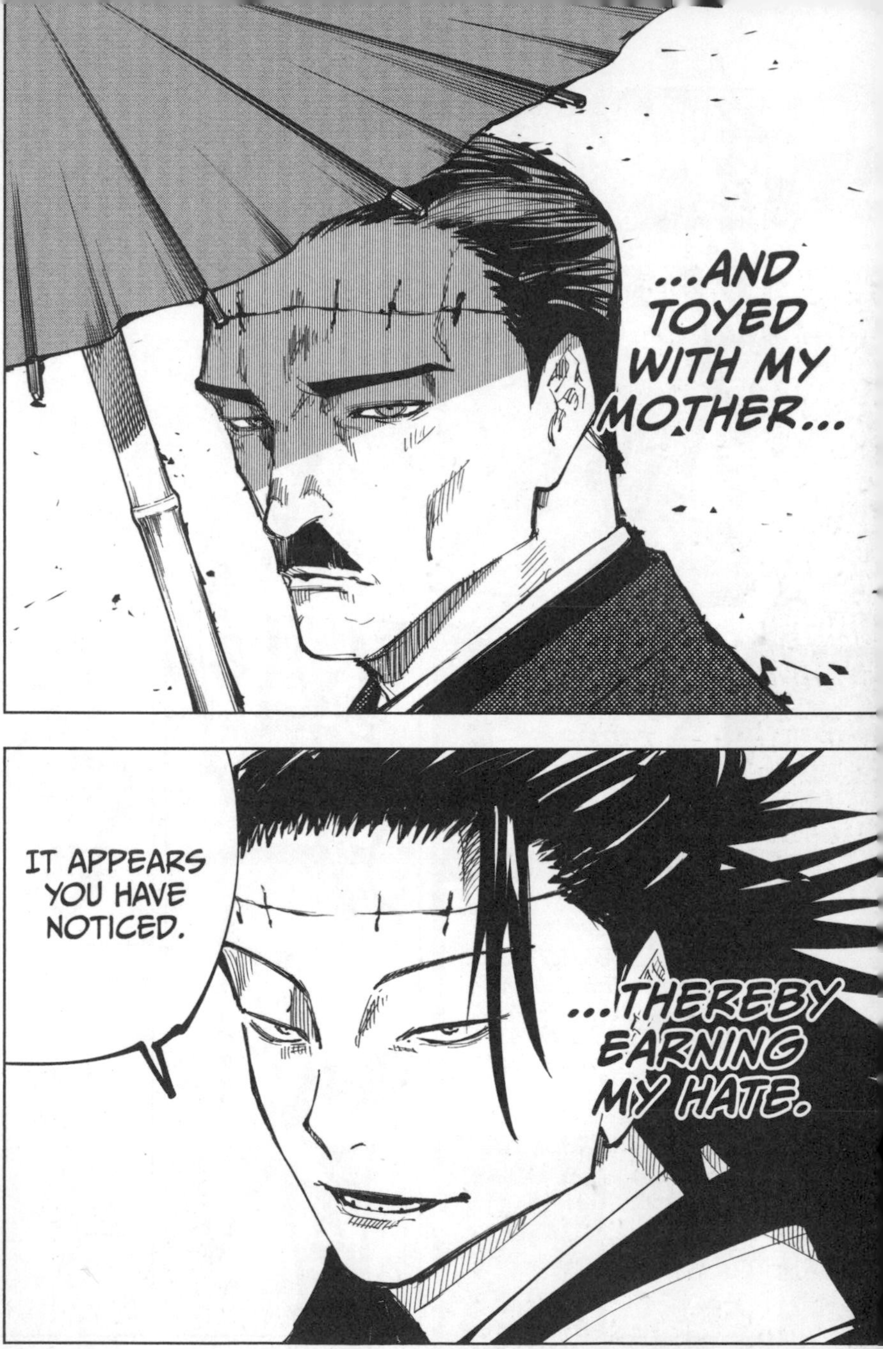
...AND TOYED WITH MY MOTHER...
...THEREBY EARNING MY HATE.
IT APPEARS YOU HAVE NOTICED.

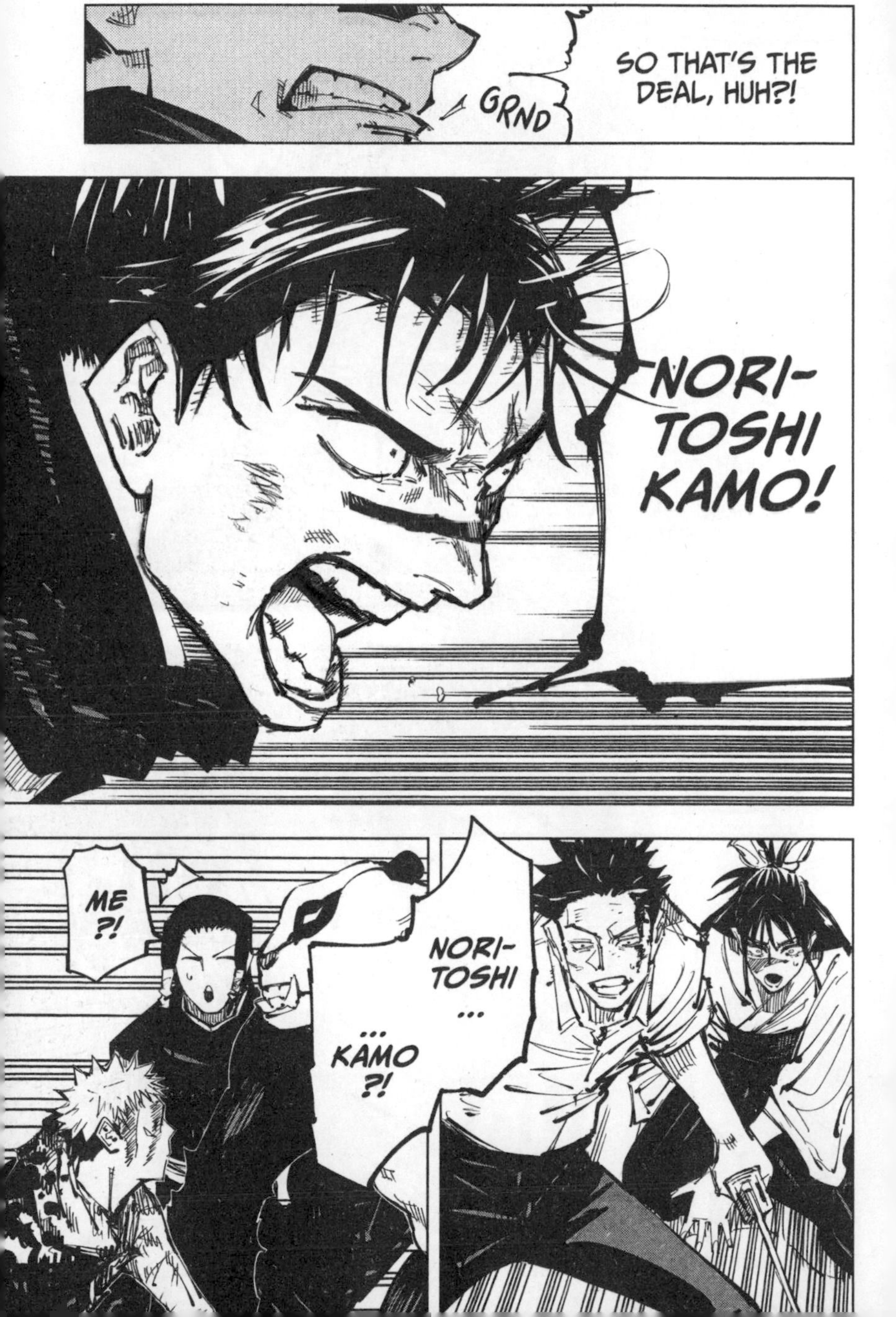
SO THAT'S THE DEAL, HUH?!
GRND
NORI-TOSHI KAMO!
NORI-TOSHI ...
... KAMO ?!
ME ?!

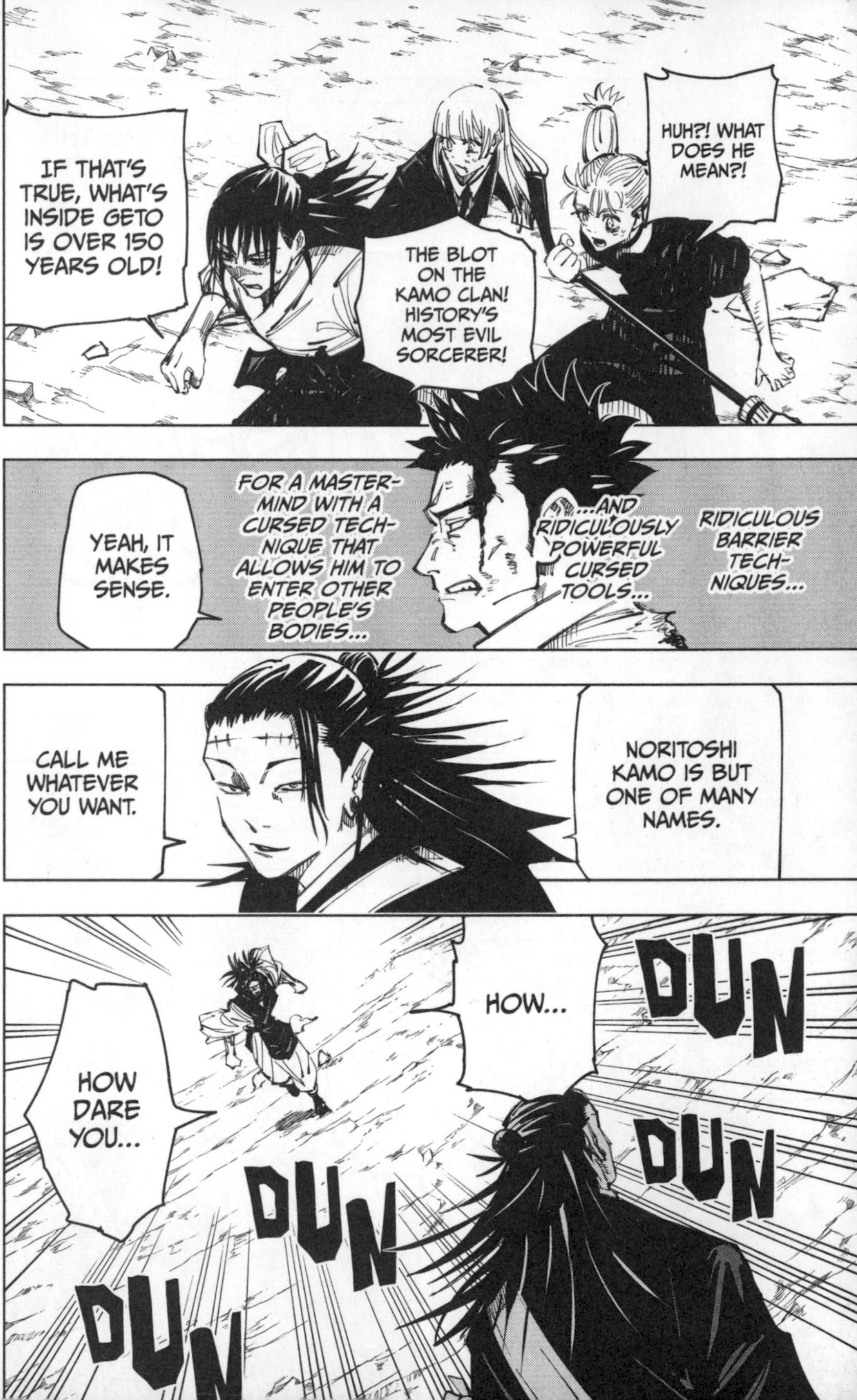

HUH?! WHAT DOES HE MEAN?!
THE BLOT ON THE KAMO CLAN! HISTORY'S MOST EVIL SORCERER!
IF THAT'S TRUE, WHAT'S INSIDE GETO IS OVER 150 YEARS OLD!
RIDICULOUS BARRIER TECHNIQUES...
...AND RIDICULOUSLY POWERFUL CURSED TOOLS...
FOR A MASTERMIND WITH A CURSED TECHNIQUE THAT ALLOWS HIM TO ENTER OTHER PEOPLE'S BODIES...
YEAH, IT MAKES SENSE.
NORITOSHI KAMO IS BUT ONE OF MANY NAMES.
CALL ME WHATEVER YOU WANT.
DUN
DUN
HOW...
HOW DARE YOU...
DUN
DUN

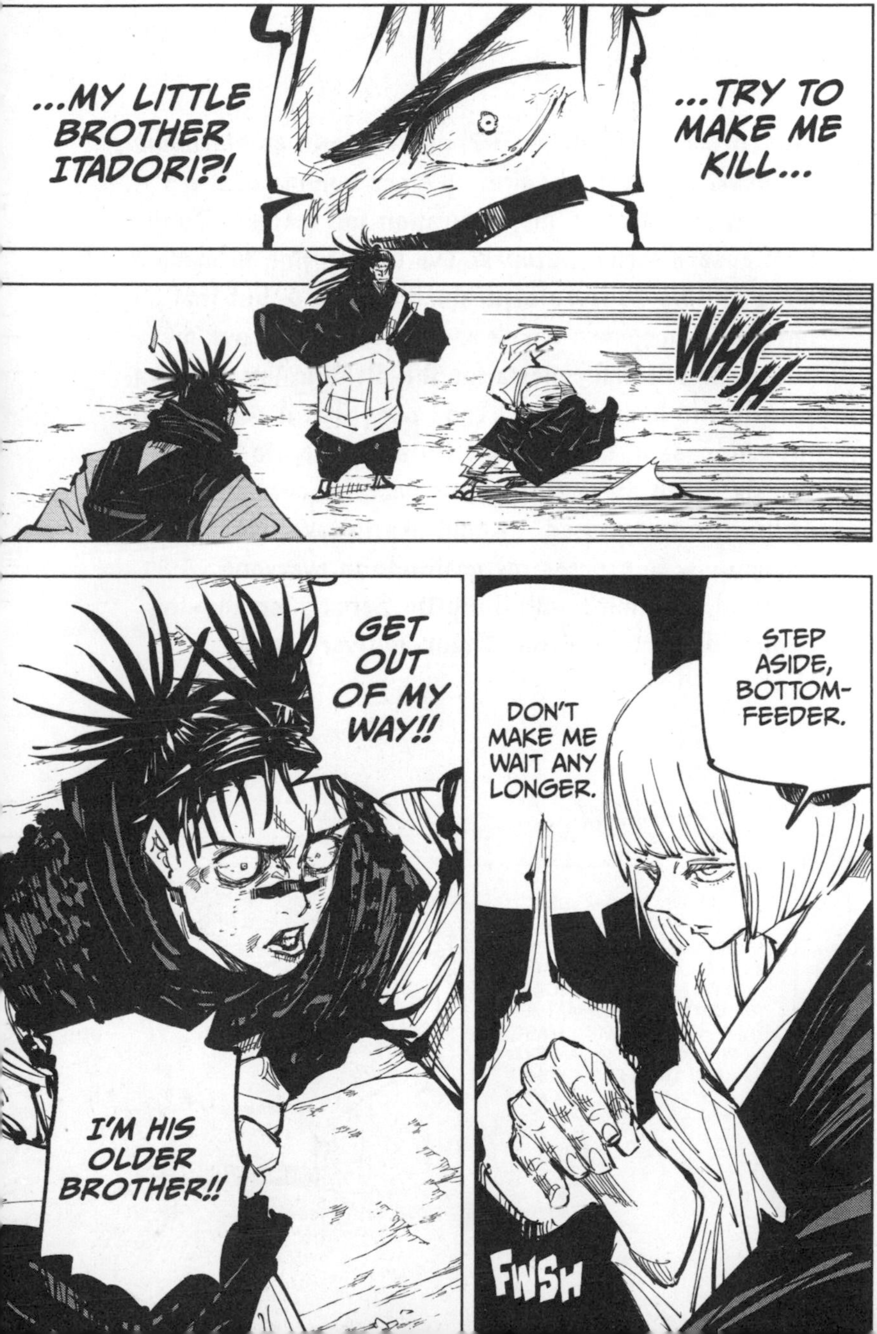
...TRY TO MAKE ME KILL...
...MY LITTLE BROTHER ITADORI?!
WHSH
STEP ASIDE, BOTTOM-FEEDER.
DON'T MAKE ME WAIT ANY LONGER.
FWSH
GET OUT OF MY WAY!!
I'M HIS OLDER BROTHER!!

The cursed manipulation technique known as *Maximum Uzumaki* has been showing up since volume 0. If it's not obvious already, the inspiration for that was Junji Ito Sensei's series *Uzumaki*. I've been trying to make it more like Ito Sensei's style since volume 0, but that horrific atmosphere wasn't easy to convey. I have my own clear internal criteria for the dividing line between parody and homage, but I can't deny that it depends on the kindness of many people (in this case, Ito Sensei). Weekly series move at a frantic pace, so even though some time has passed, I would like to take this opportunity to express my gratitude to everyone involved, beginning with Junji Ito Sensei, for allowing depictions such as these. Thank you very much!

I LOVE "NAGAI YUME," ("LONG DREAM") WHICH APPEARS IN VOLUME 9 OF HIS COLLECTED MASTERPIECES! THERE ARE DIGITAL VERSIONS OF BOTH THE *UZUMAKI* SERIES AND HIS COLLECTED MASTER-PIECES, SO YOU CAN EVEN BUY THEM FROM HOME!

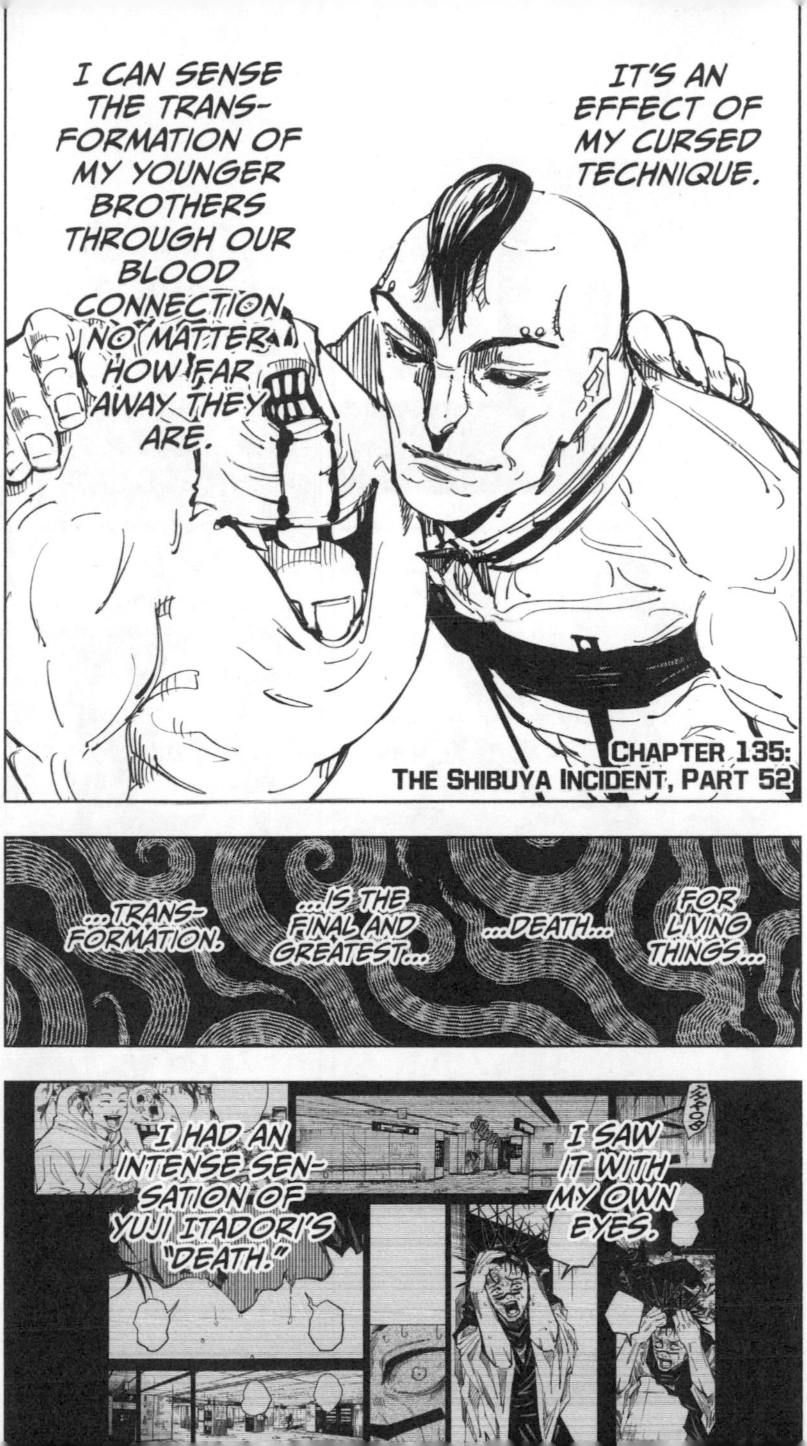
IT'S AN EFFECT OF MY CURSED TECHNIQUE.
I CAN SENSE THE TRANSFORMATION OF MY YOUNGER BROTHERS THROUGH OUR BLOOD CONNECTION NO MATTER HOW FAR AWAY THEY ARE.
CHAPTER 135: THE SHIBUYA INCIDENT, PART 52
FOR LIVING THINGS...
...DEATH...
...IS THE FINAL AND GREATEST...
...TRANSFORMATION.
I SAW IT WITH MY OWN EYES.
I HAD AN INTENSE SENSATION OF YUJI ITADORI'S "DEATH."

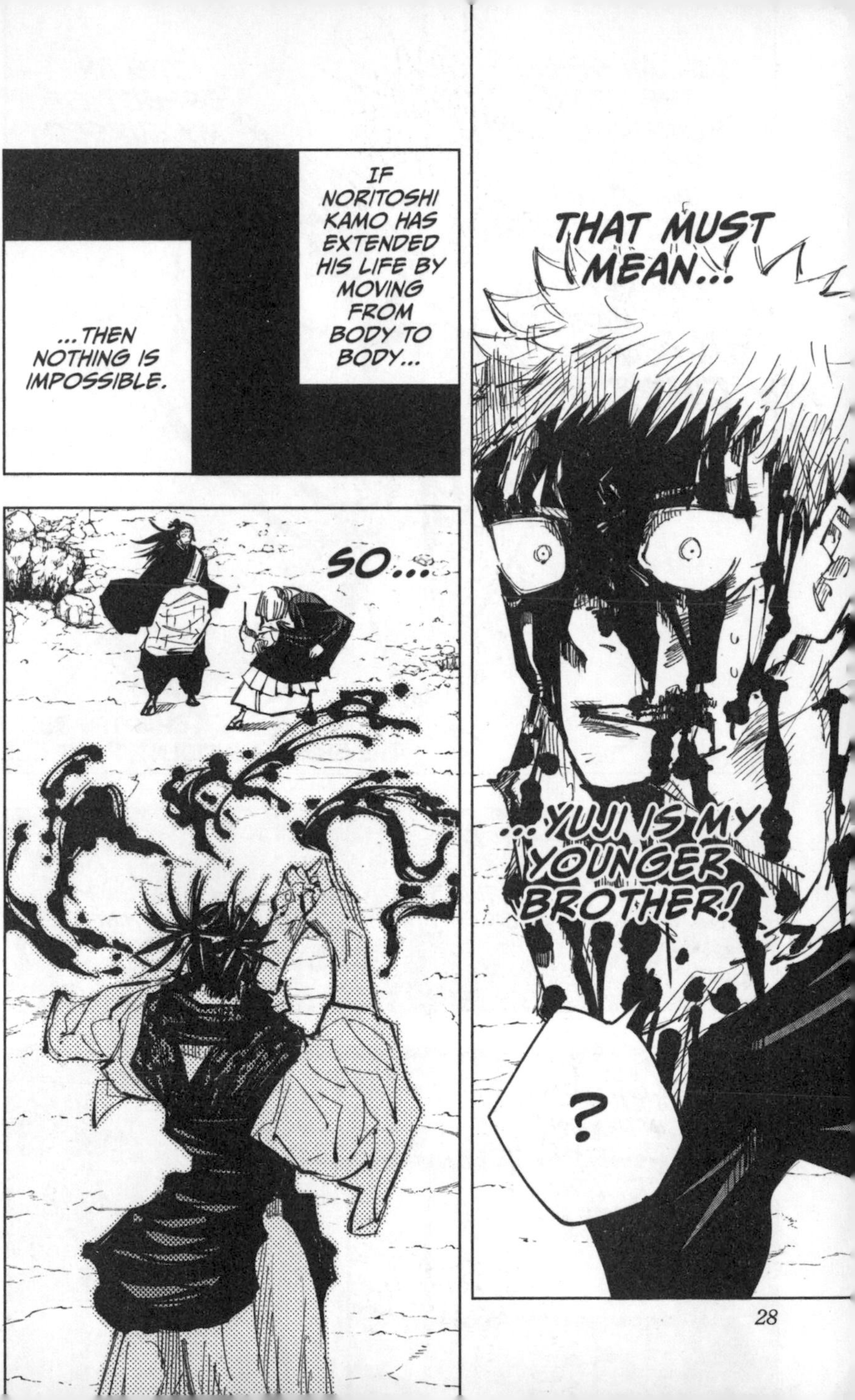
IF NORITOSHI KAMO HAS EXTENDED HIS LIFE BY MOVING FROM BODY TO BODY...
...THEN NOTHING IS IMPOSSIBLE.
SO...
THAT MUST MEAN...!
...YUJI IS MY YOUNGER BROTHER!
?

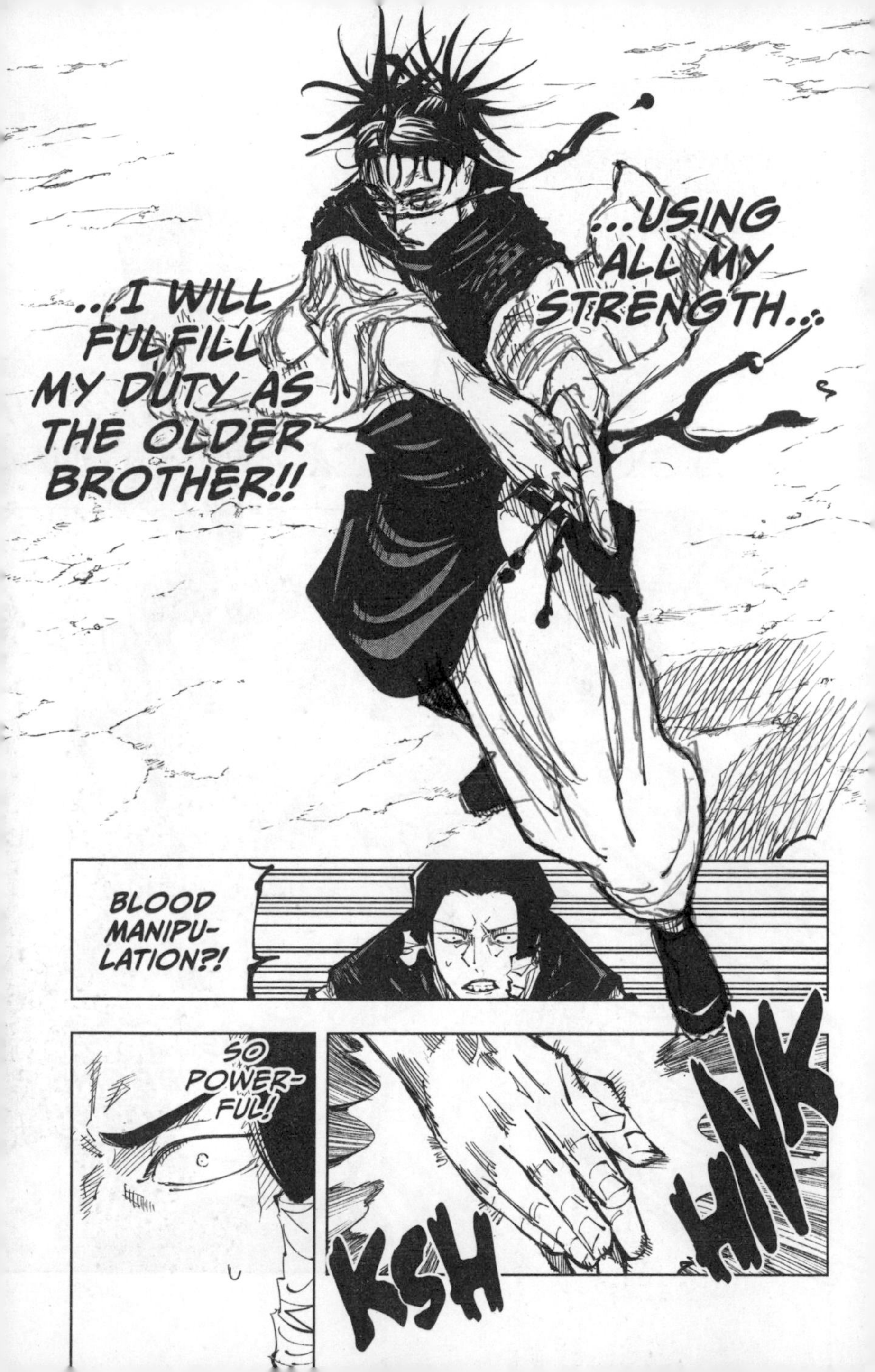
...USING ALL MY STRENGTH...
...I WILL FULFILL MY DUTY AS THE OLDER BROTHER!!
BLOOD MANIPU-LATION?!
KSH
HNK
SO POWER-FUL!

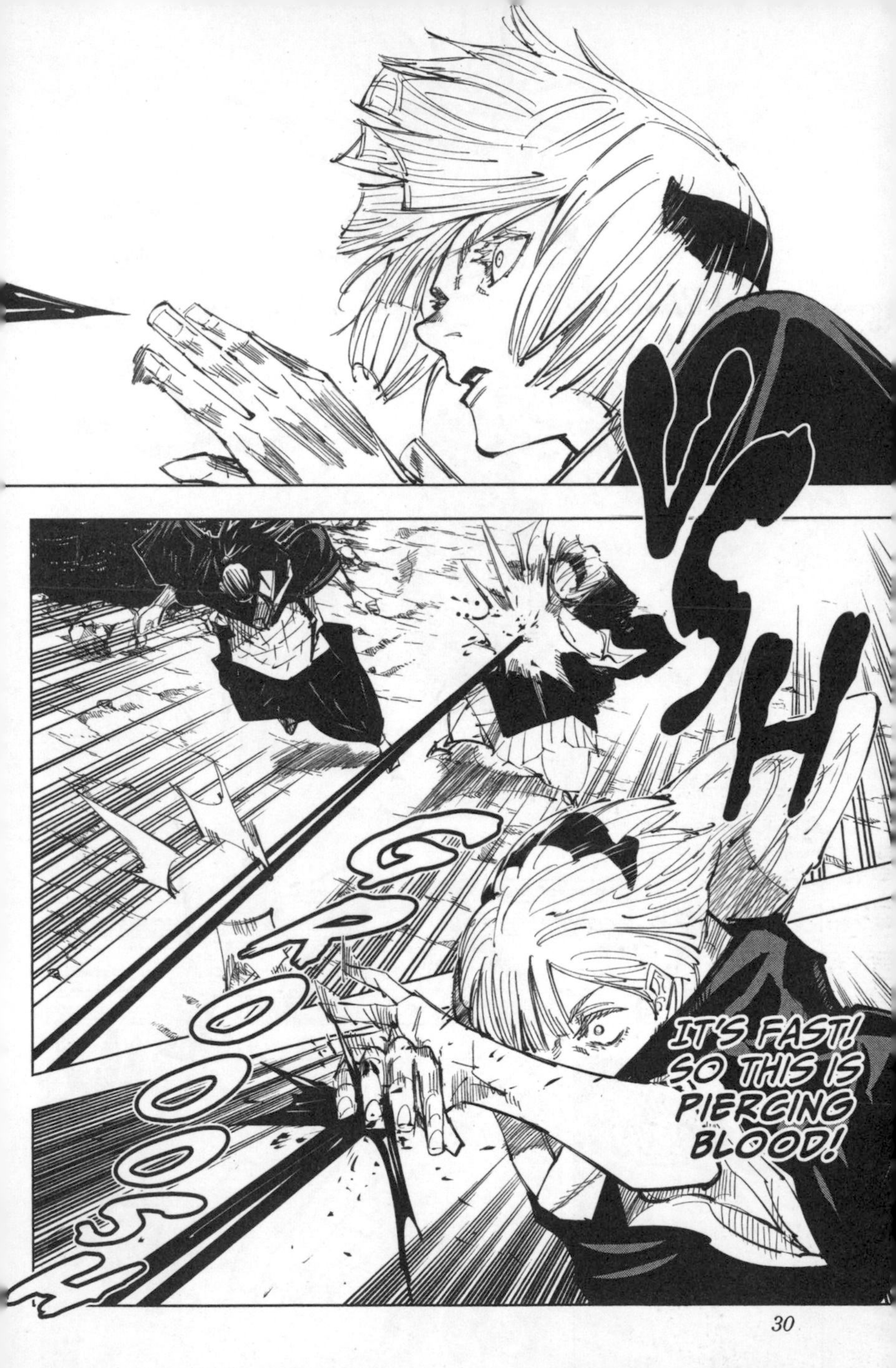
VSH
IT'S FAST! SO THIS IS PIERCING BLOOD!

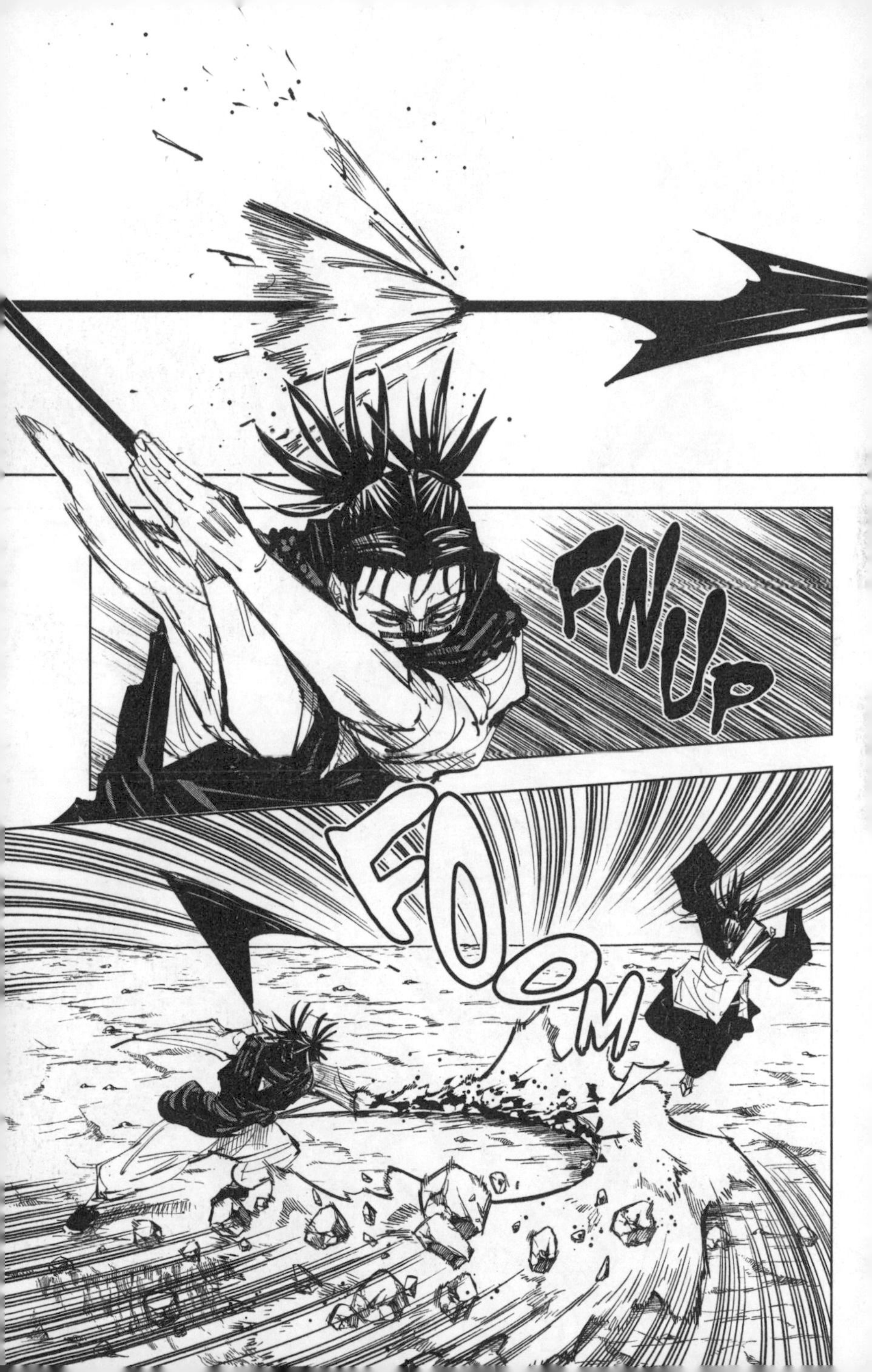
FWUP
FOOM

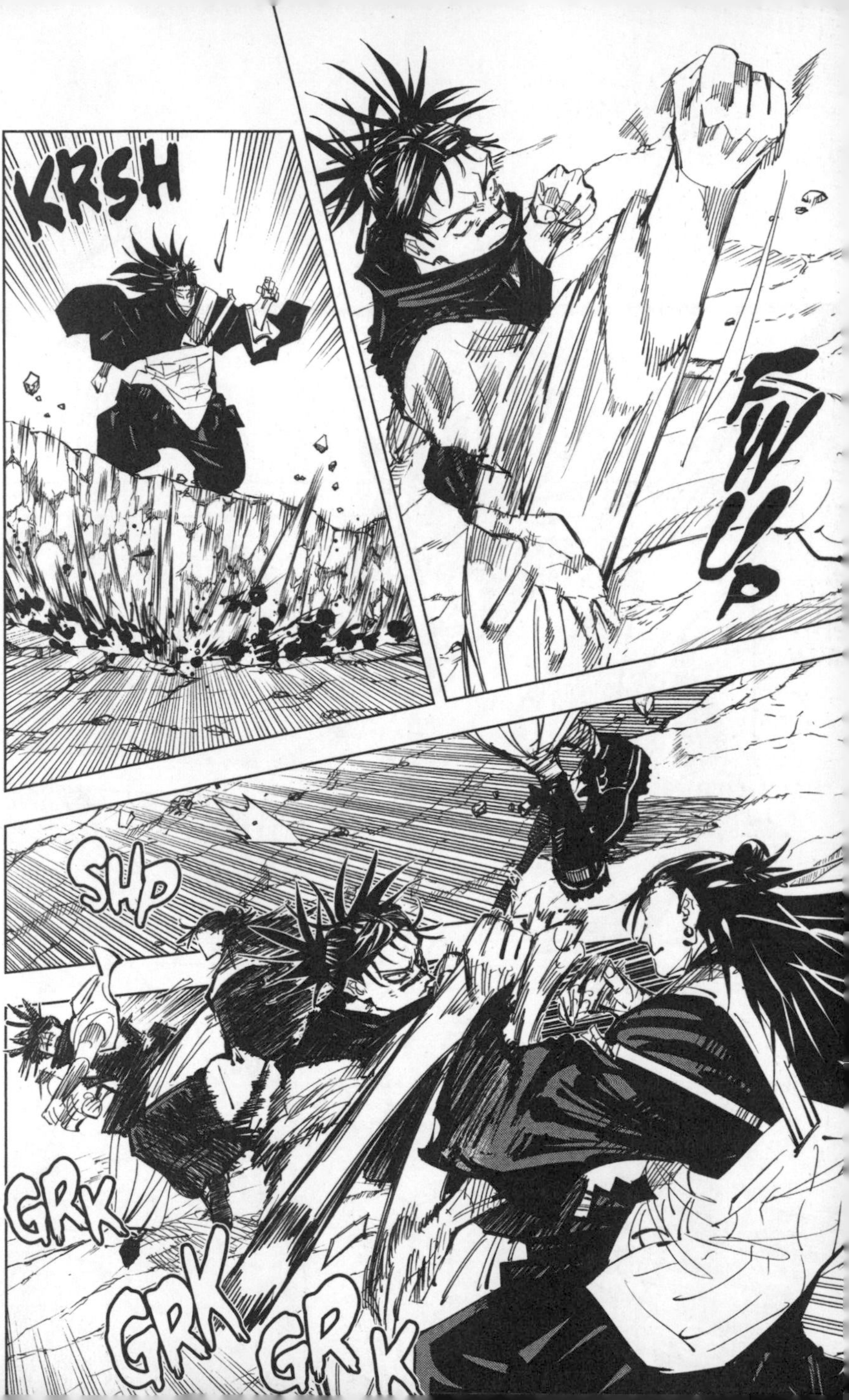
FWUP
KRSH
SHP
GRK
GRK
GRK

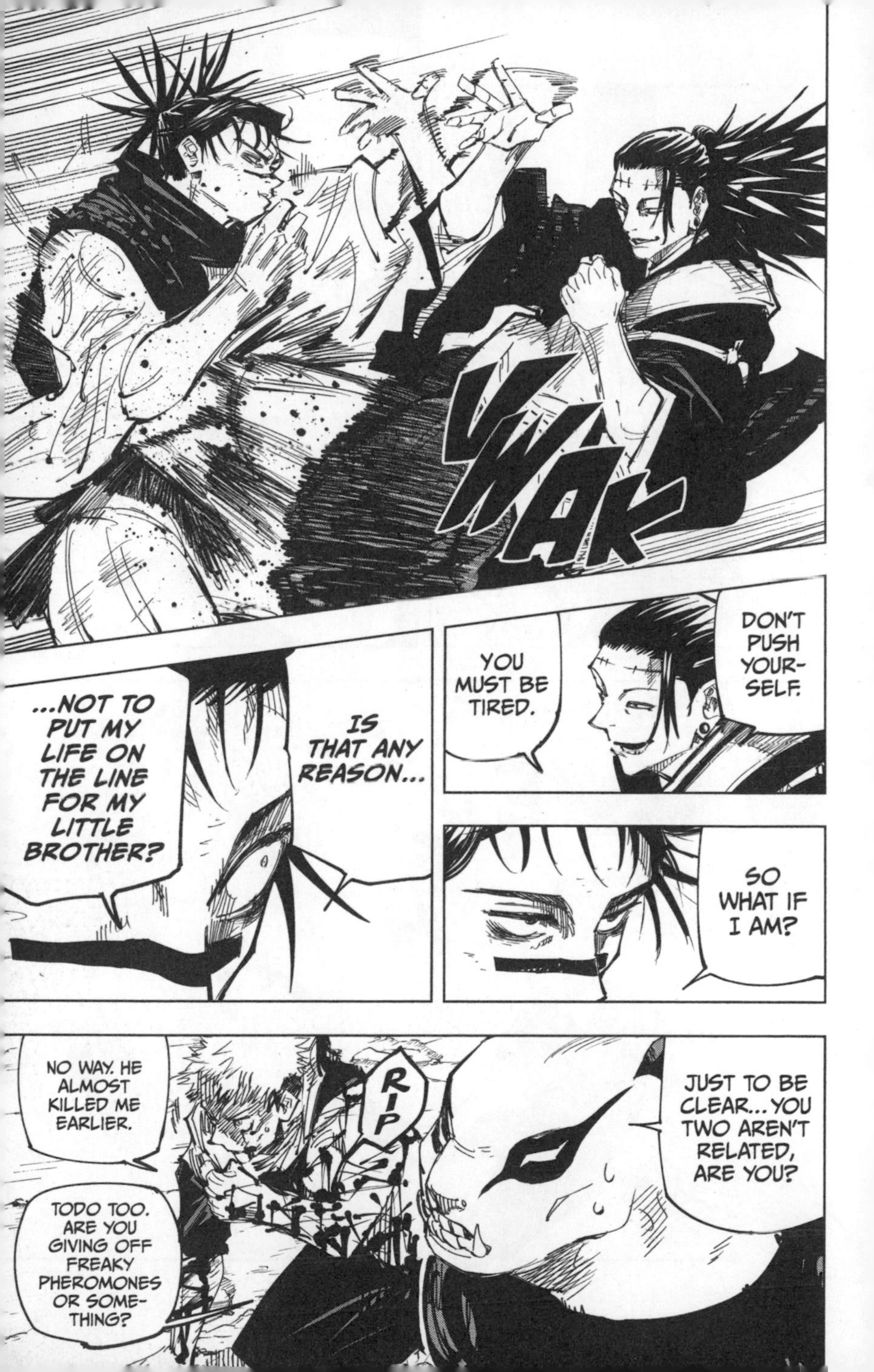
WAK
DON'T PUSH YOURSELF.
YOU MUST BE TIRED.
SO WHAT IF I AM?
IS THAT ANY REASON...
...NOT TO PUT MY LIFE ON THE LINE FOR MY LITTLE BROTHER?
JUST TO BE CLEAR... YOU TWO AREN'T RELATED, ARE YOU?
RIP
NO WAY. HE ALMOST KILLED ME EARLIER.
TODO TOO. ARE YOU GIVING OFF FREAKY PHEROMONES OR SOME-THING?

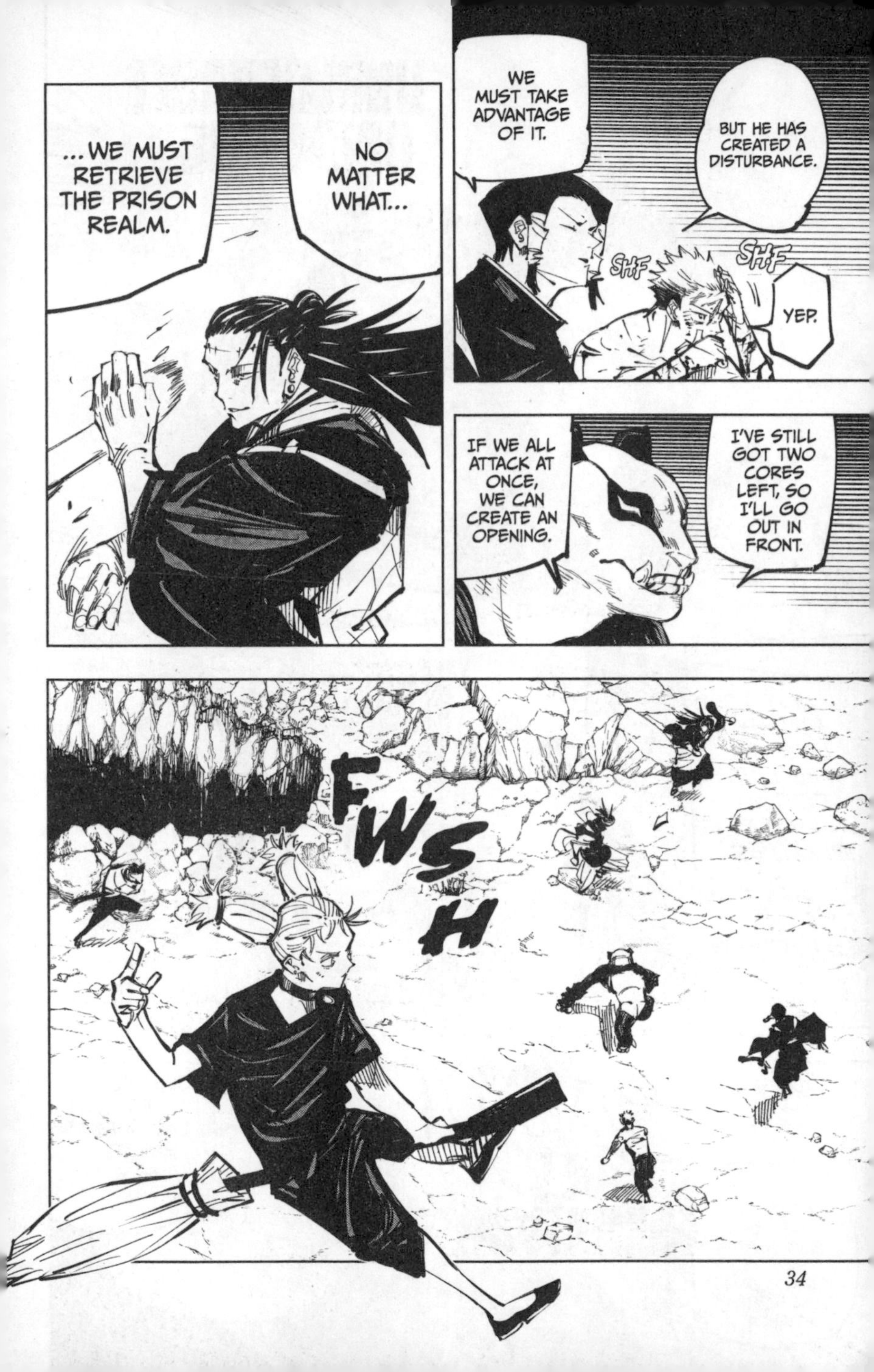
BUT HE HAS CREATED A DISTURBANCE.
WE MUST TAKE ADVANTAGE OF IT.
SHF
SHF
YEP.
I'VE STILL GOT TWO CORES LEFT, SO I'LL GO OUT IN FRONT.
IF WE ALL ATTACK AT ONCE, WE CAN CREATE AN OPENING.
NO MATTER WHAT...
...WE MUST RETRIEVE THE PRISON REALM.
FWSH

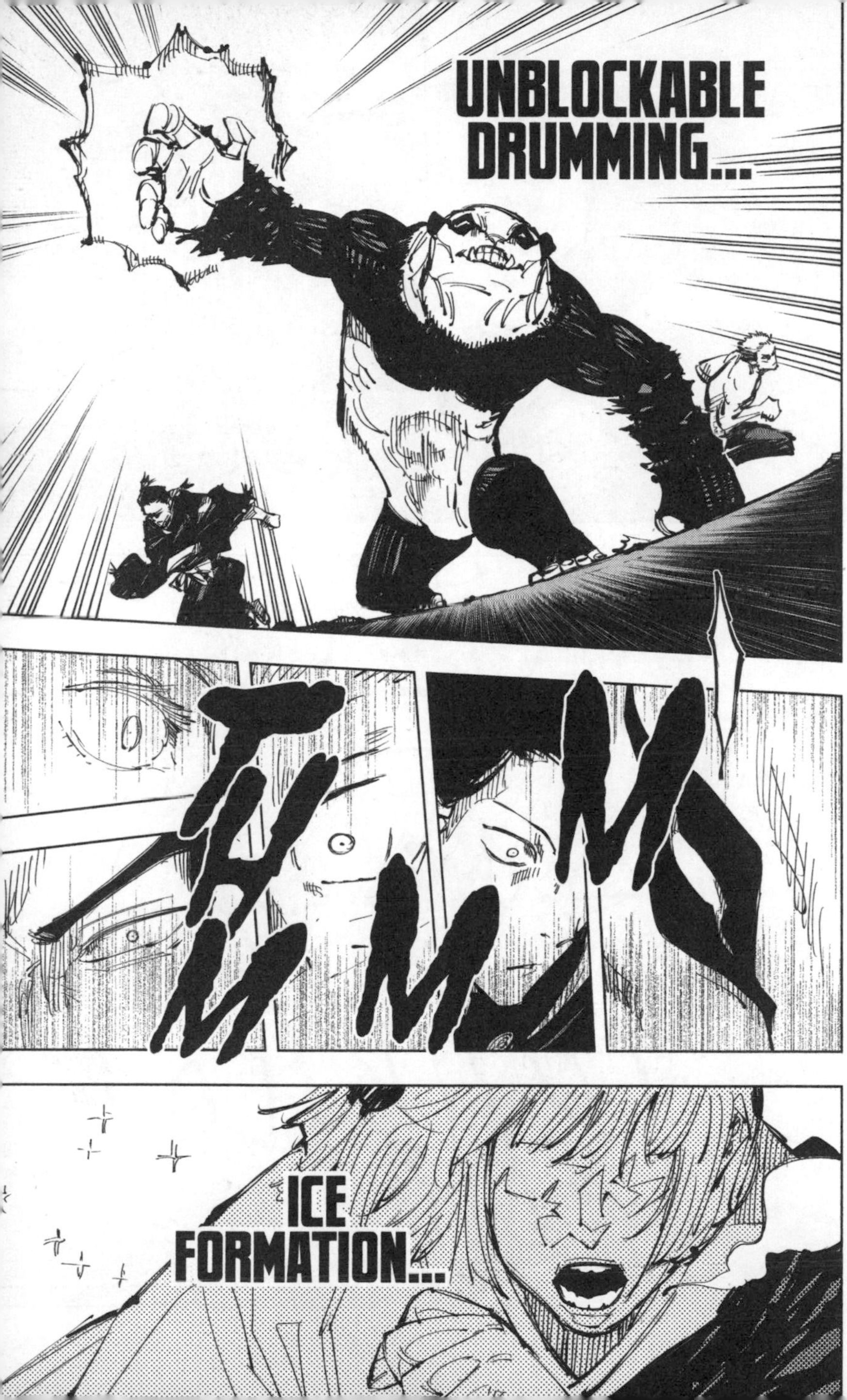
UNBLOCKABLE DRUMMING...
FWMM
ICE FORMATION...

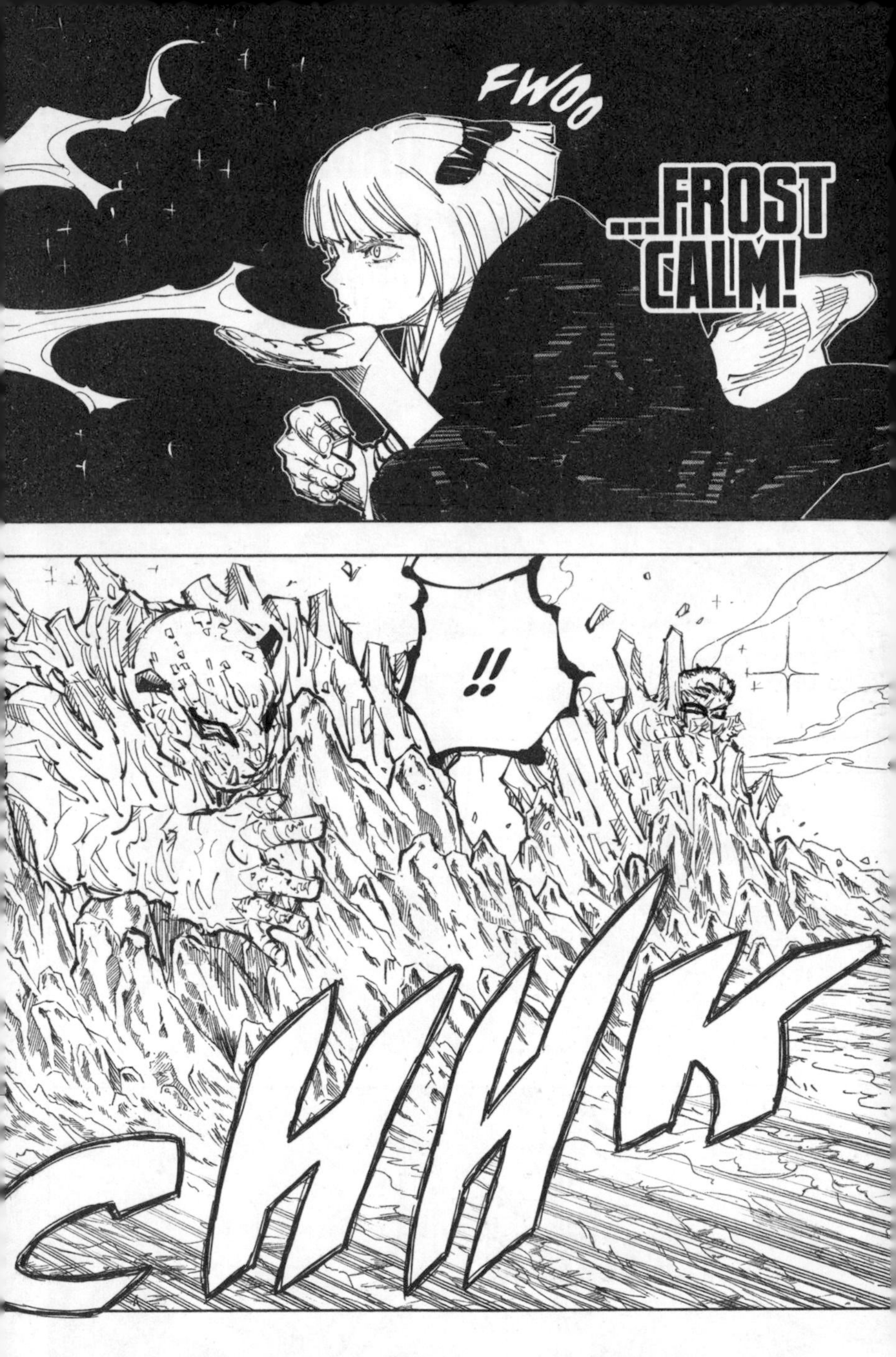
FWOO
...FROST CALM!
!!
CHHK

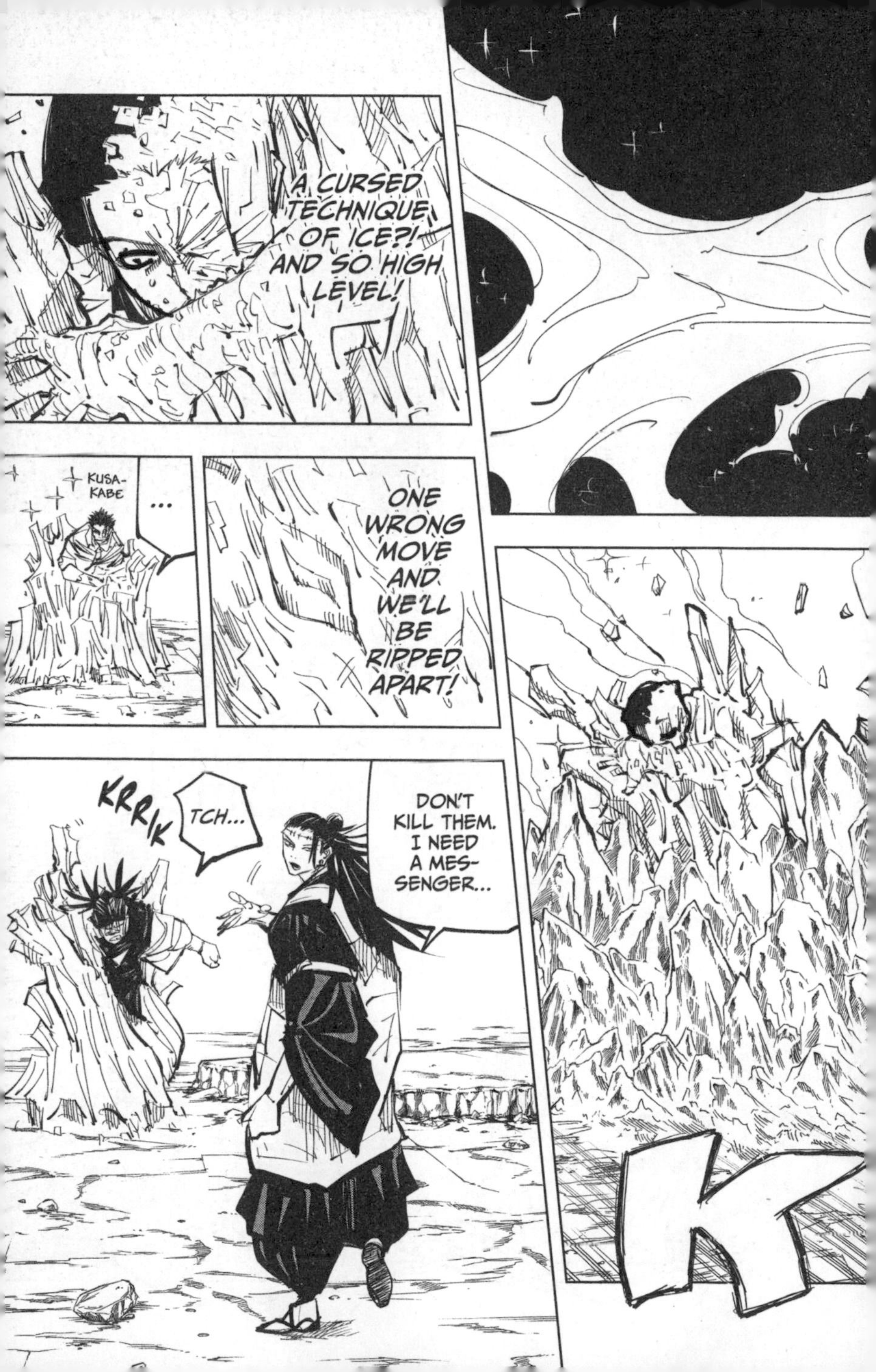
A CURSED TECHNIQUE OF ICE?! AND SO HIGH LEVEL!
K
ONE WRONG MOVE AND WE'LL BE RIPPED APART!
KUSA-KABE
...
DON'T KILL THEM. I NEED A MES-SENGER...
TCH...
KRRIK

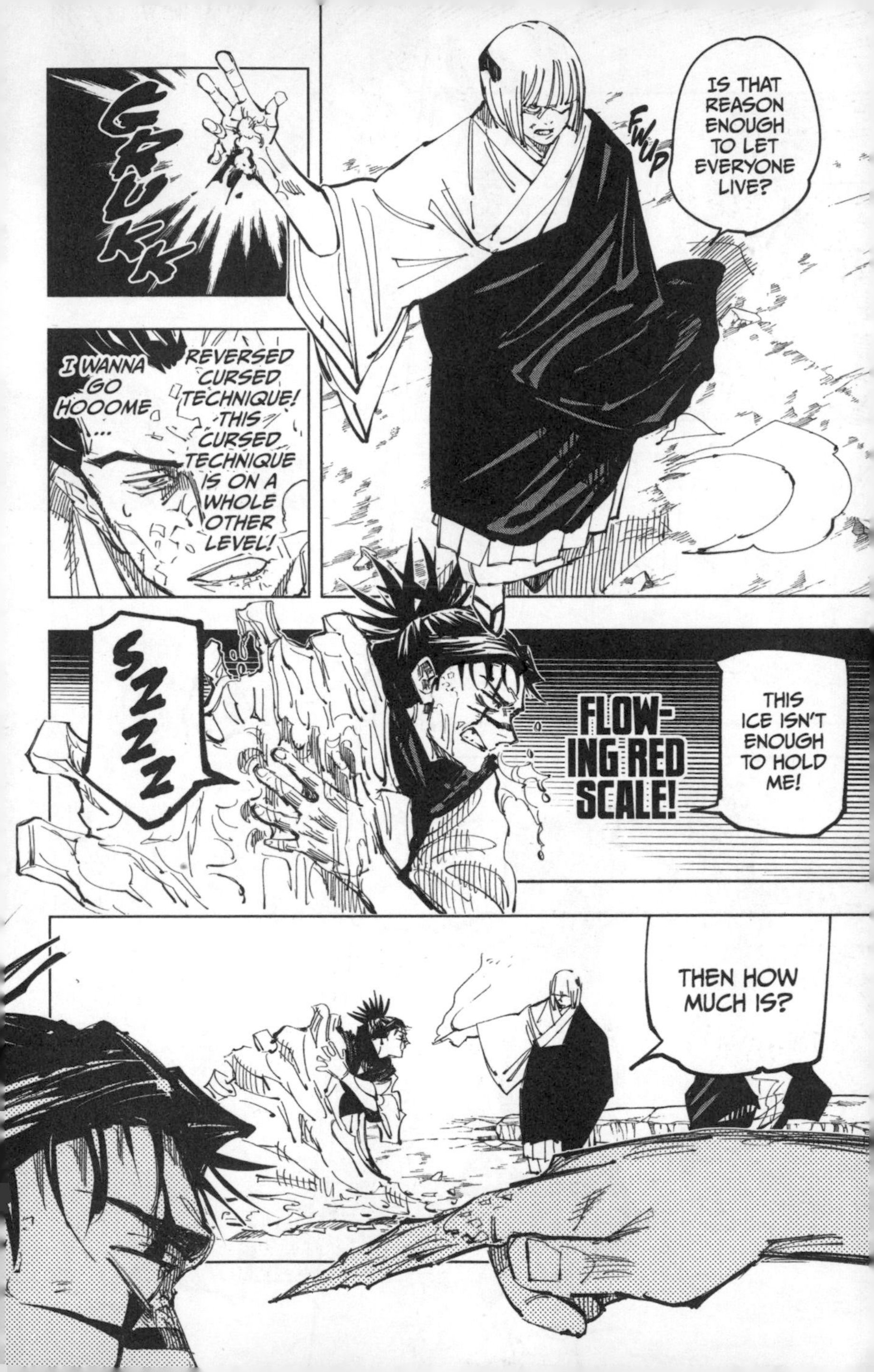
FWUP
IS THAT REASON ENOUGH TO LET EVERYONE LIVE?
GRUKK
REVERSED CURSED TECHNIQUE! THIS CURSED TECHNIQUE IS ON A WHOLE OTHER LEVEL!
I WANNA GO HOOOME...
THIS ICE ISN'T ENOUGH TO HOLD ME!
FLOWING RED SCALE!
SZZZZ
THEN HOW MUCH IS?

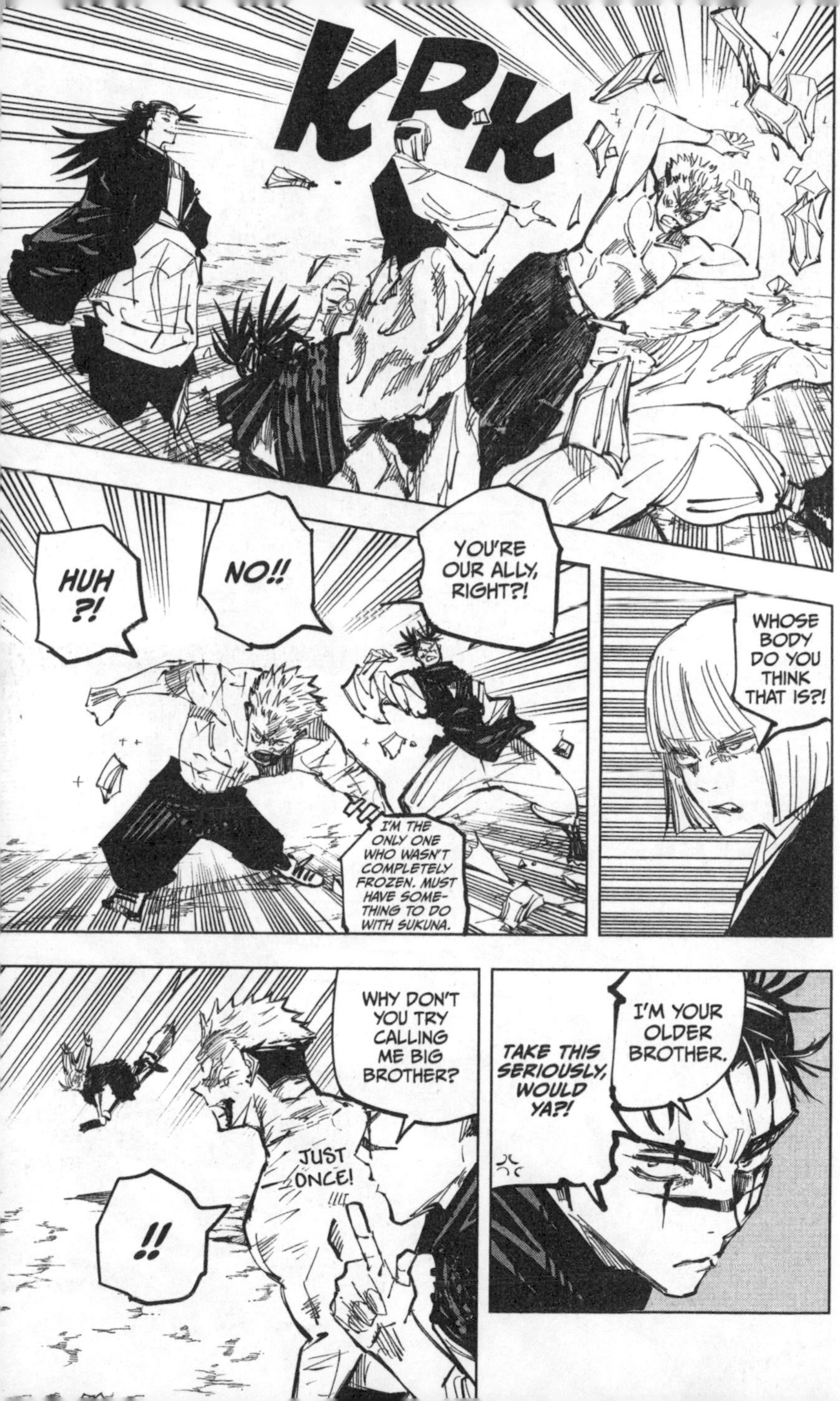
KRK
WHOSE BODY DO YOU THINK THAT IS?!
YOU'RE OUR ALLY, RIGHT?!
NO!!
HUH ?!
I'M THE ONLY ONE WHO WASN'T COMPLETELY FROZEN. MUST HAVE SOME-THING TO DO WITH SUKUNA.
I'M YOUR OLDER BROTHER.
TAKE THIS SERIOUSLY, WOULD YA?!
WHY DON'T YOU TRY CALLING ME BIG BROTHER?
JUST ONCE!
!!

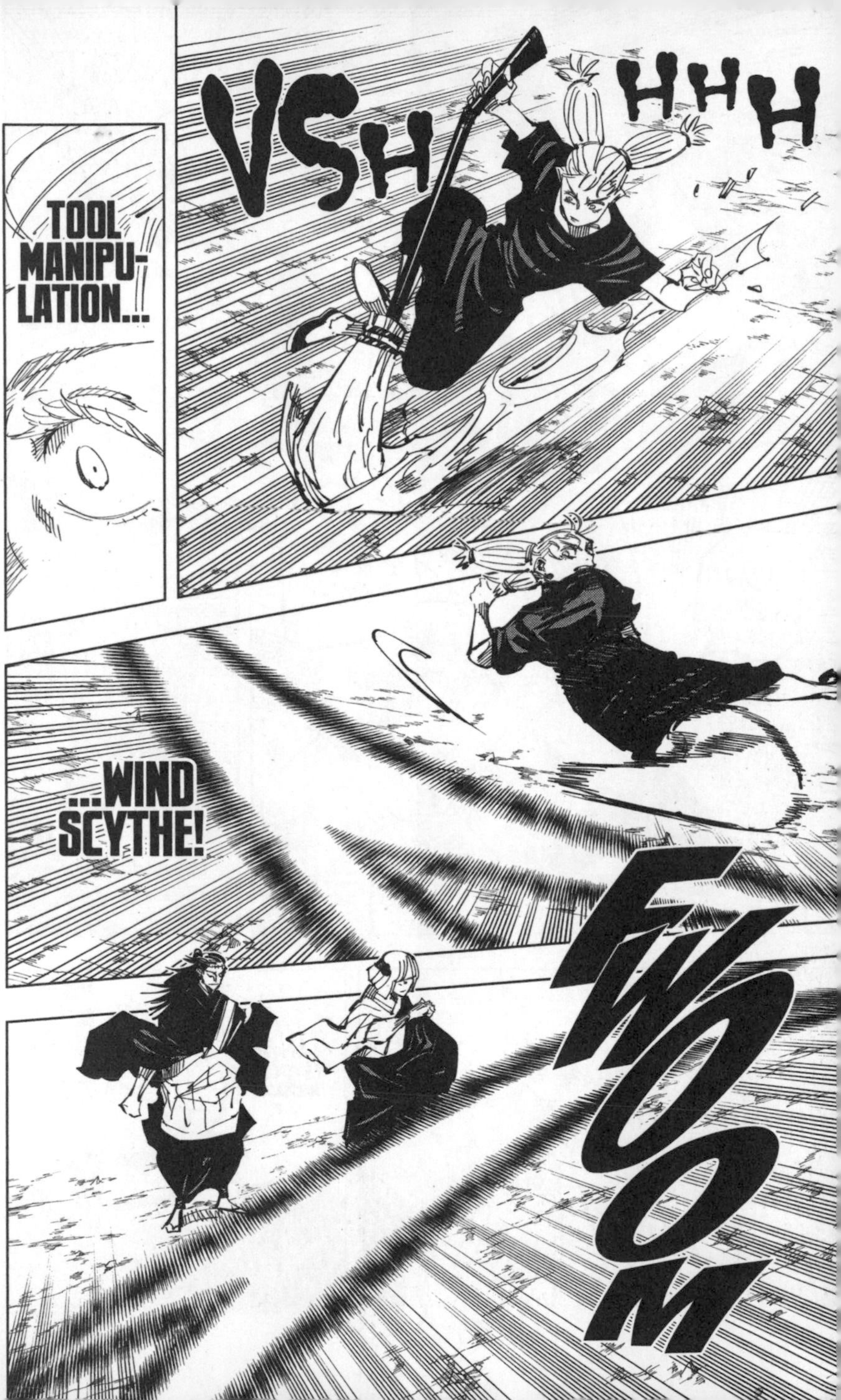
VSHHHH
TOOL MANIPU-LATION...!
...WIND SCYTHE!
FWOOM

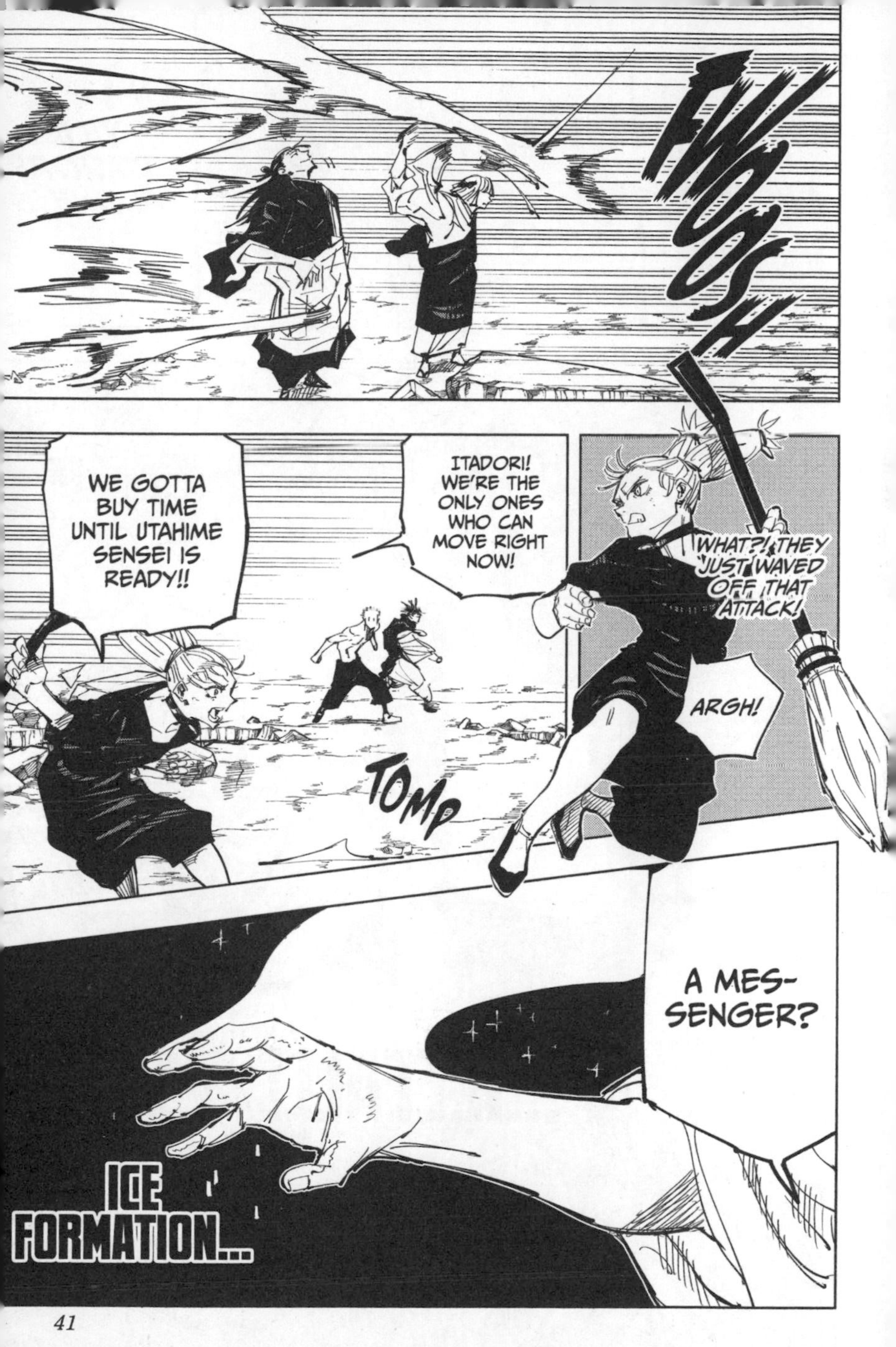
FWOOSH
WHAT?! THEY JUST WAVED OFF THAT ATTACK!
ARGH!
ITADORI! WE'RE THE ONLY ONES WHO CAN MOVE RIGHT NOW!
WE GOTTA BUY TIME UNTIL UTAHIME SENSEI IS READY!!
TOMP
A MES-SENGER?
ICE FORMATION...

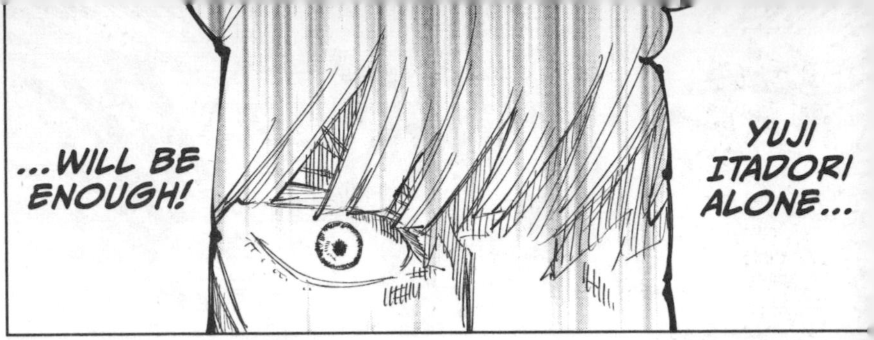
YUJI ITADORI ALONE...
...WILL BE ENOUGH!

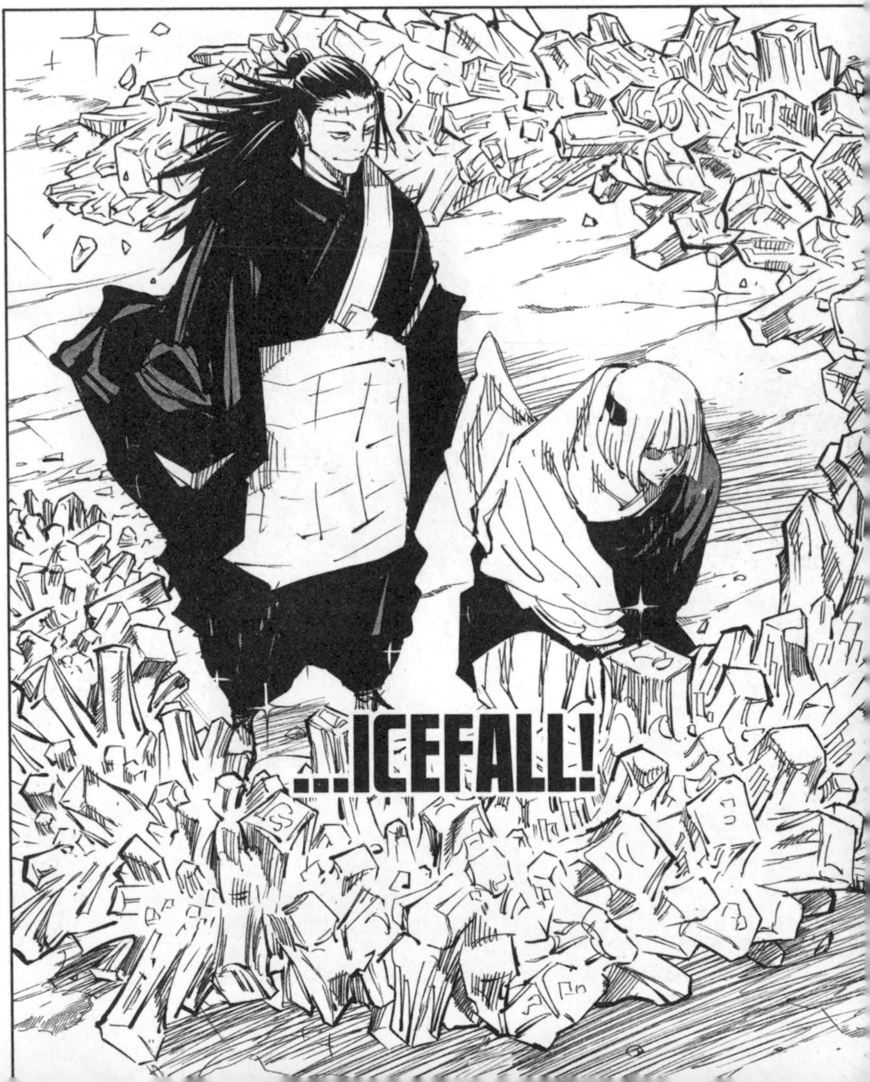
...ICEFALL!

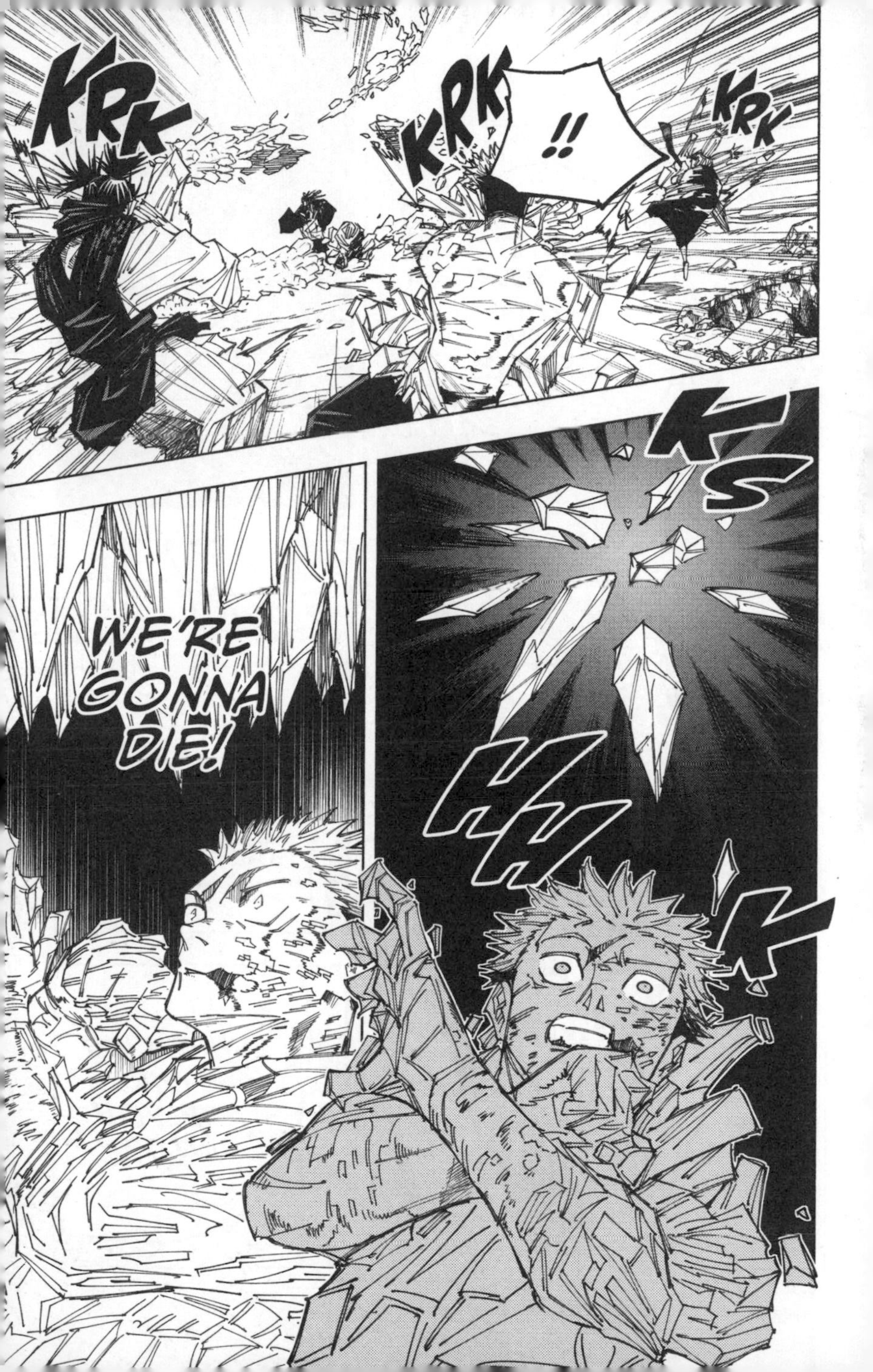
KRK
!!
KRK
KRK
KS
HH
K
WE'RE GONNA DIE!

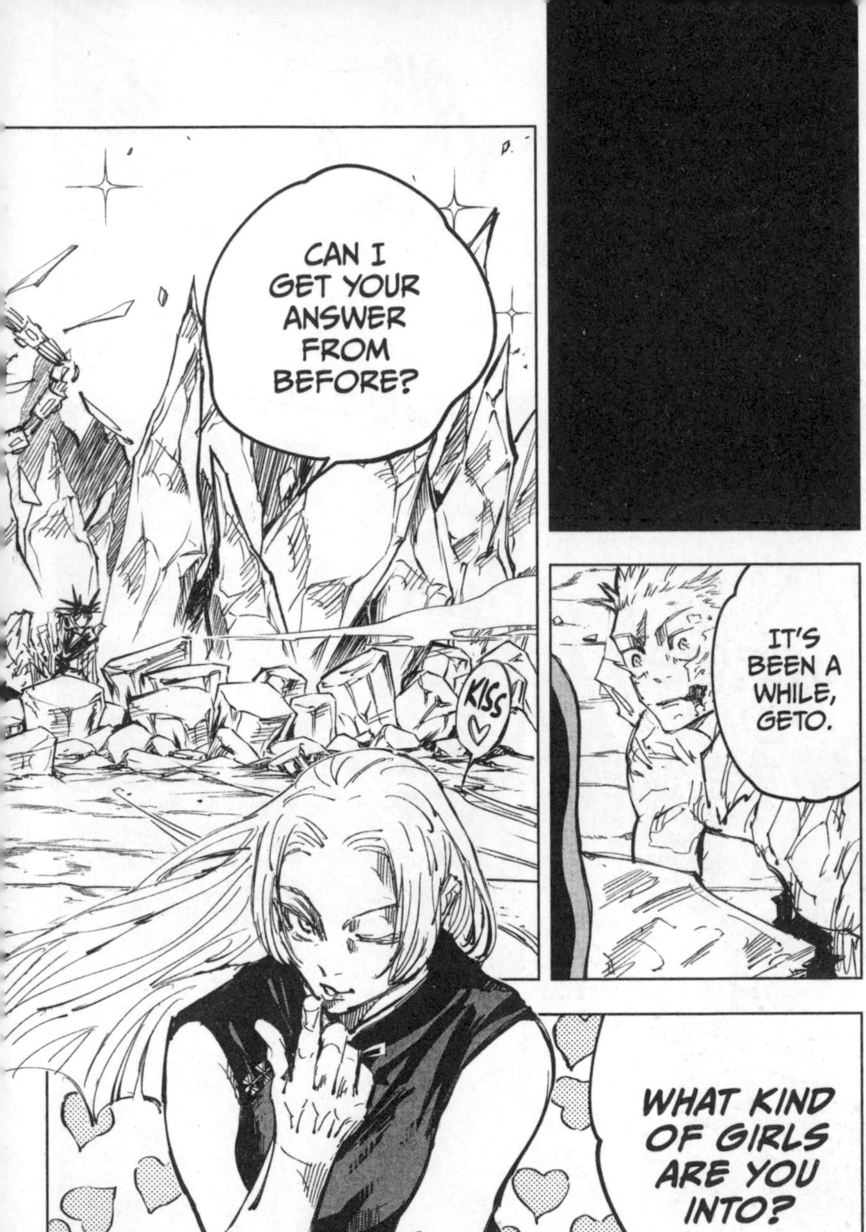
IT'S BEEN A WHILE, GETO.
CAN I GET YOUR ANSWER FROM BEFORE?
KISS ♡
WHAT KIND OF GIRLS ARE YOU INTO?

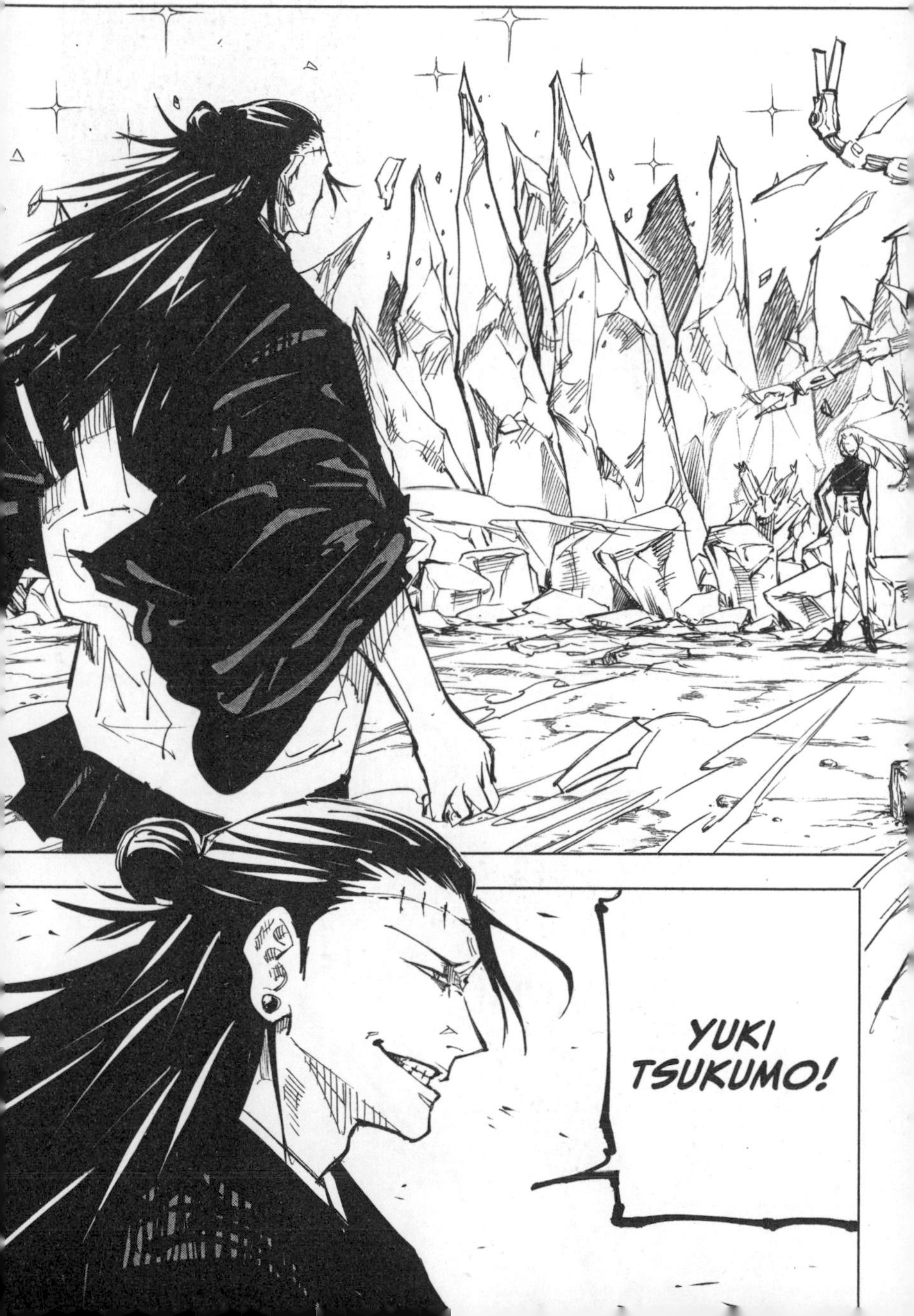
YUKI
TSUKUMO!

URAUME

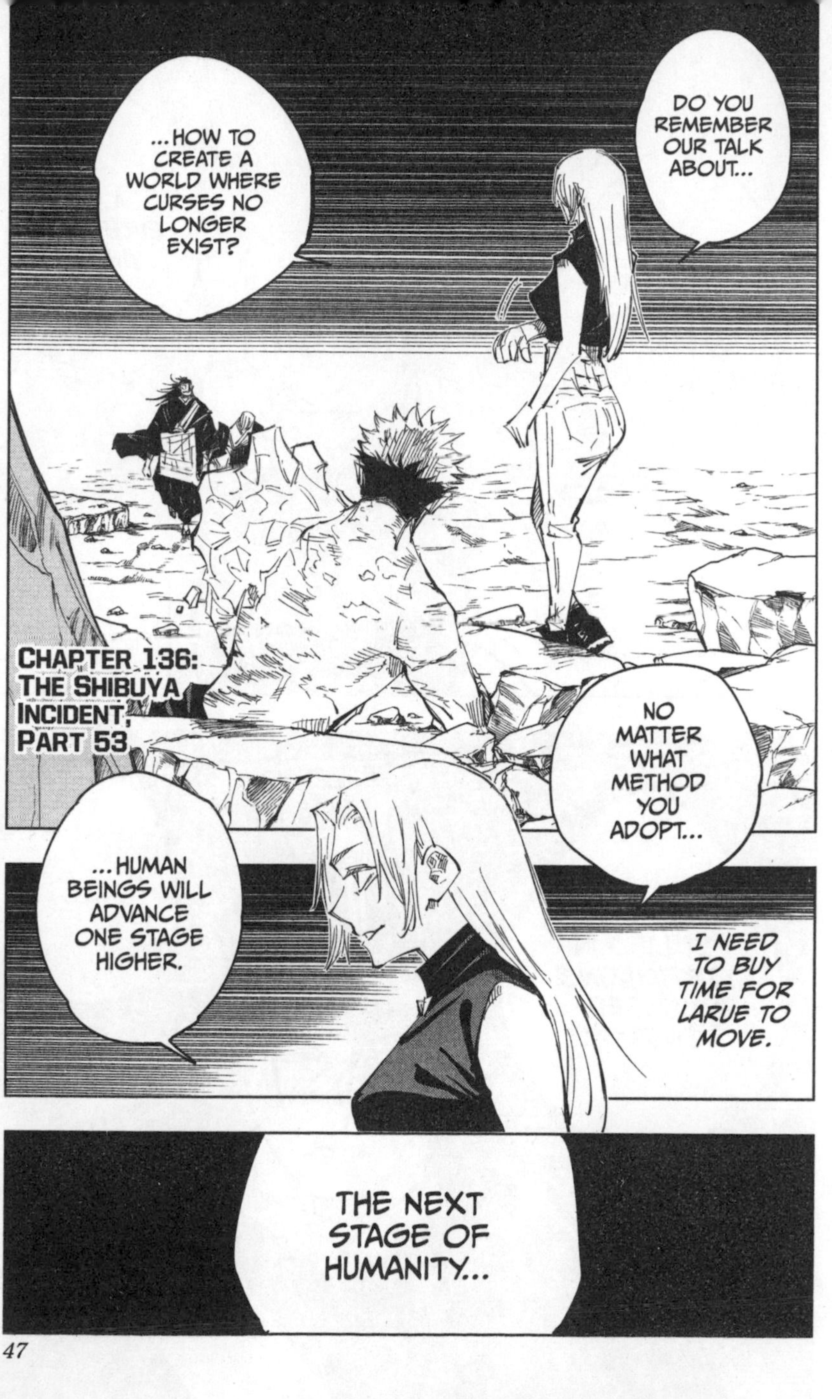
DO YOU REMEMBER OUR TALK ABOUT...
...HOW TO CREATE A WORLD WHERE CURSES NO LONGER EXIST?
CHAPTER 136: THE SHIBUYA INCIDENT, PART 53
NO MATTER WHAT METHOD YOU ADOPT...
...HUMAN BEINGS WILL ADVANCE ONE STAGE HIGHER.
I NEED TO BUY TIME FOR LARUE TO MOVE.
THE NEXT STAGE OF HUMANITY...

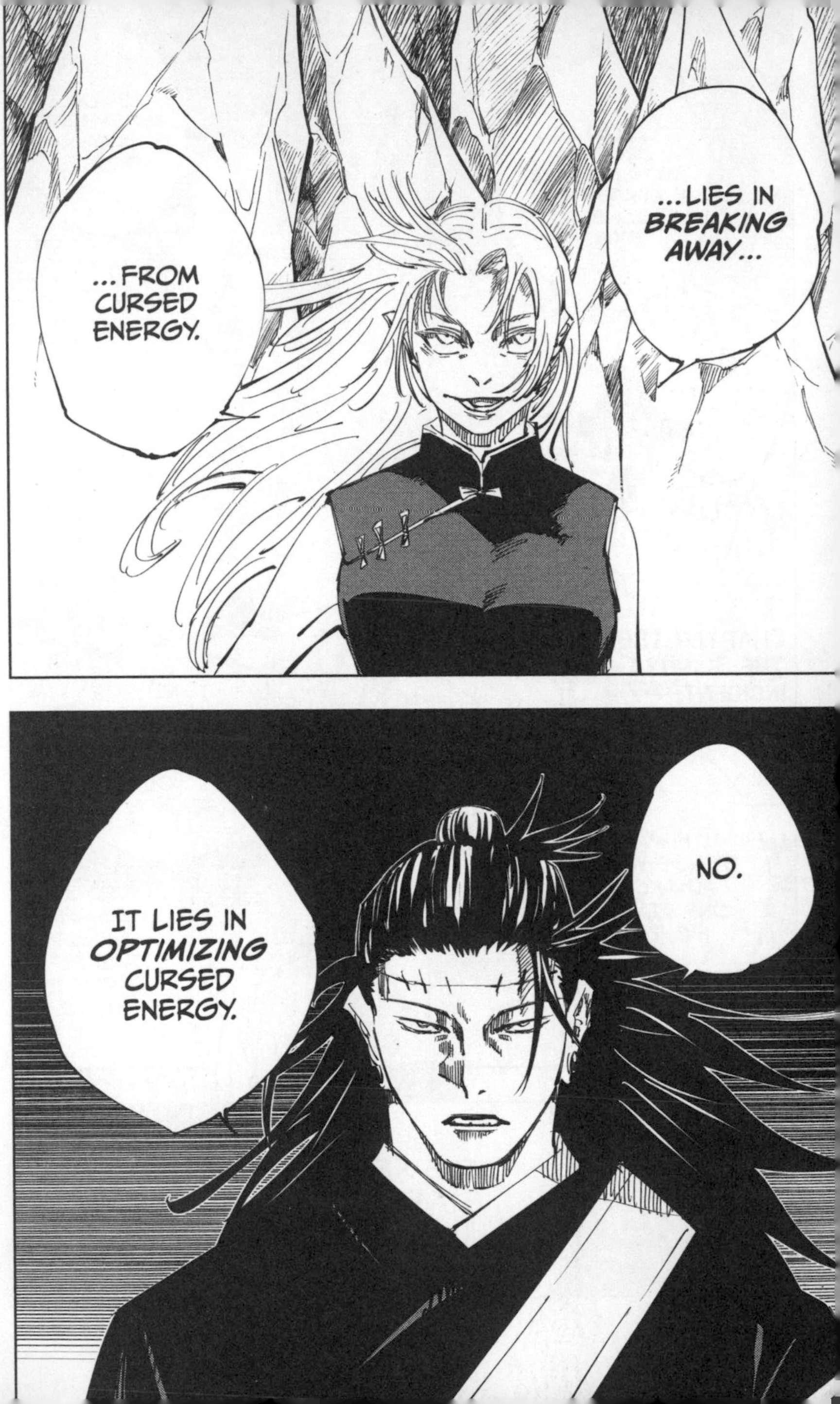
...LIES IN BREAKING AWAY...
...FROM CURSED ENERGY.
NO.
IT LIES IN OPTIMIZING CURSED ENERGY.

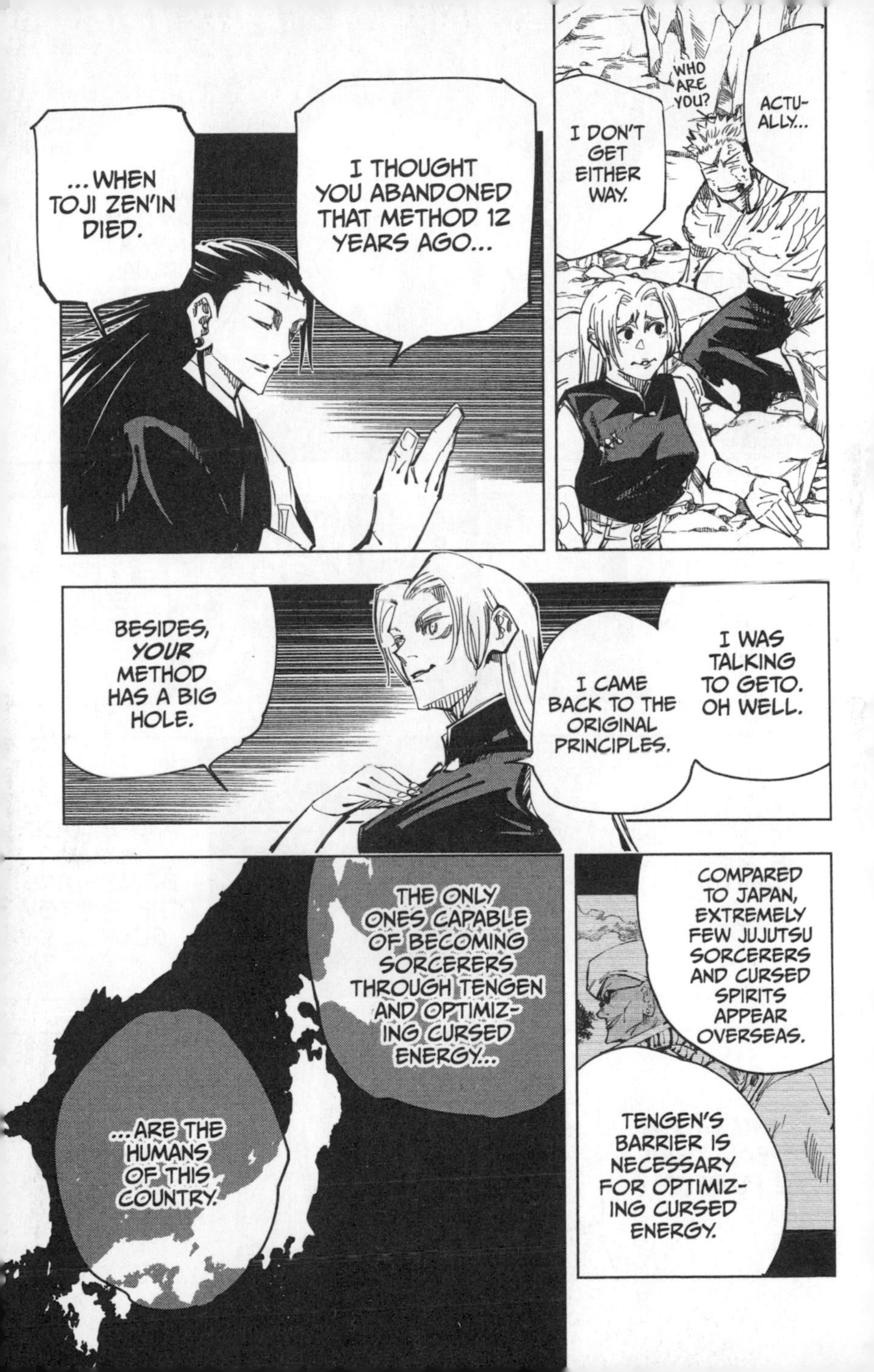
ACTU-
ALLY...
WHO ARE YOU?
I DON'T GET EITHER WAY.
I THOUGHT YOU ABANDONED THAT METHOD 12 YEARS AGO...
...WHEN TOJI ZEN'IN DIED.
I WAS TALKING TO GETO. OH WELL.
I CAME BACK TO THE ORIGINAL PRINCIPLES.
BESIDES, *YOUR* METHOD HAS A BIG HOLE.
COMPARED TO JAPAN, EXTREMELY FEW JUJUTSU SORCERERS AND CURSED SPIRITS APPEAR OVERSEAS.
TENGEN'S BARRIER IS NECESSARY FOR OPTIMIZ-
ING CURSED ENERGY.
THE ONLY ONES CAPABLE OF BECOMING SORCERERS THROUGH TENGEN AND OPTIMIZ-
ING CURSED ENERGY...
...ARE THE HUMANS OF THIS COUNTRY.

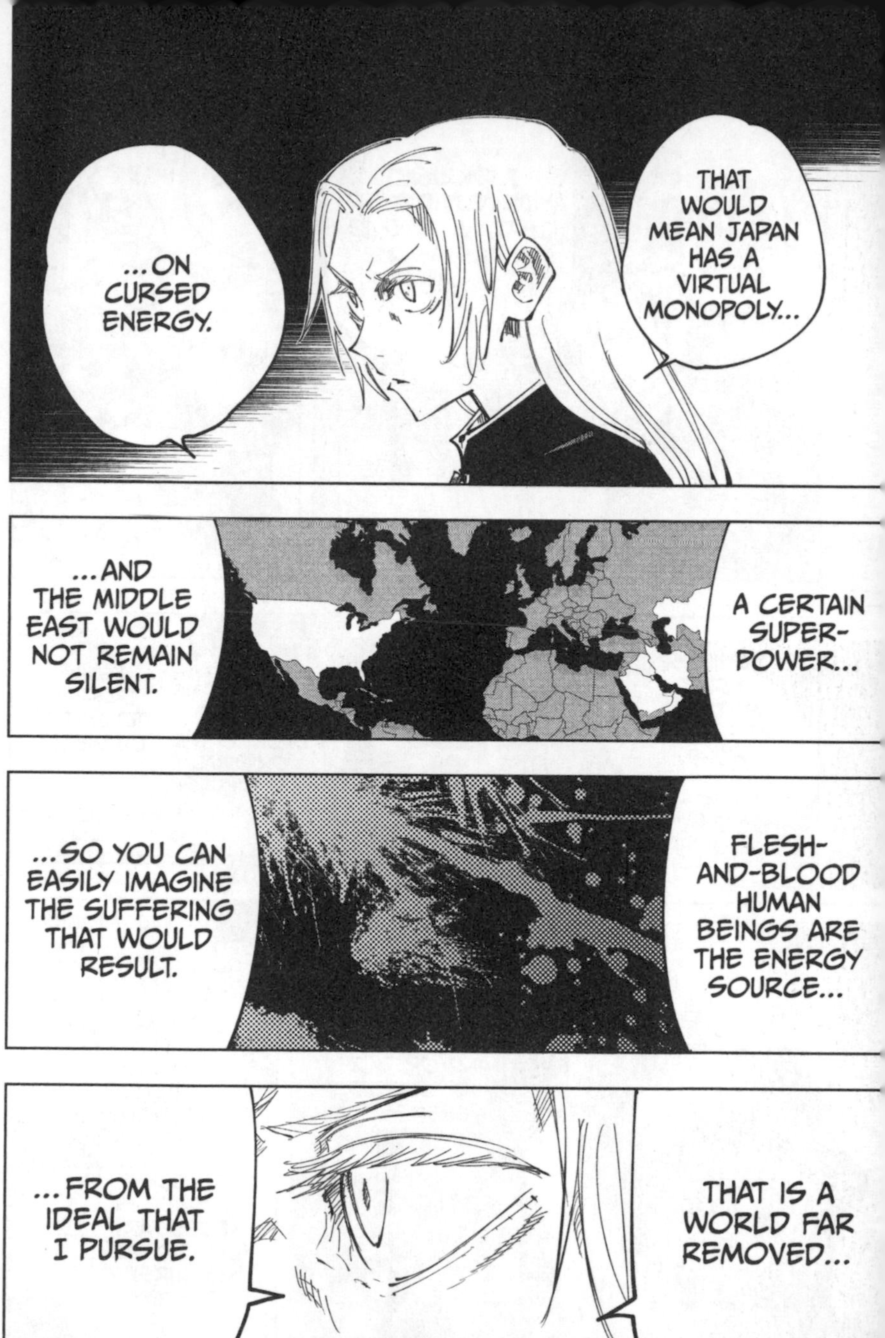
THAT WOULD MEAN JAPAN HAS A VIRTUAL MONOPOLY...
...ON CURSED ENERGY.
A CERTAIN SUPER-POWER...
...AND THE MIDDLE EAST WOULD NOT REMAIN SILENT.
FLESH-AND-BLOOD HUMAN BEINGS ARE THE ENERGY SOURCE...
...SO YOU CAN EASILY IMAGINE THE SUFFERING THAT WOULD RESULT.
THAT IS A WORLD FAR REMOVED...
...FROM THE IDEAL THAT I PURSUE.

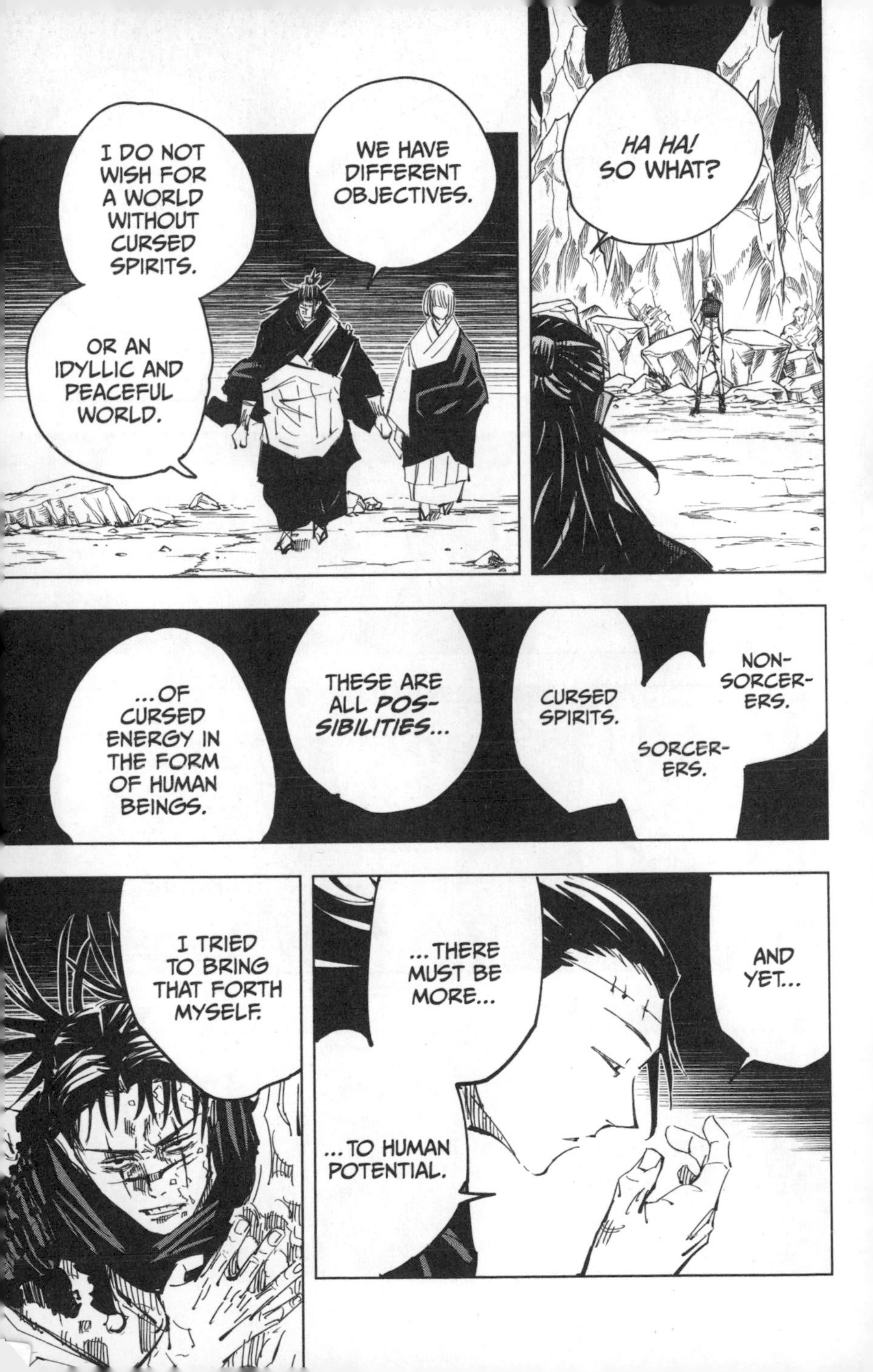
HA HA! SO WHAT?
WE HAVE DIFFERENT OBJECTIVES.
I DO NOT WISH FOR A WORLD WITHOUT CURSED SPIRITS.
OR AN IDYLLIC AND PEACEFUL WORLD.
NON-SORCERERS.
CURSED SPIRITS.
SORCERERS.
THESE ARE ALL *POSSIBILITIES*...
...OF CURSED ENERGY IN THE FORM OF HUMAN BEINGS.
AND YET...
...THERE MUST BE MORE...
...TO HUMAN POTENTIAL.
I TRIED TO BRING THAT FORTH MYSELF.

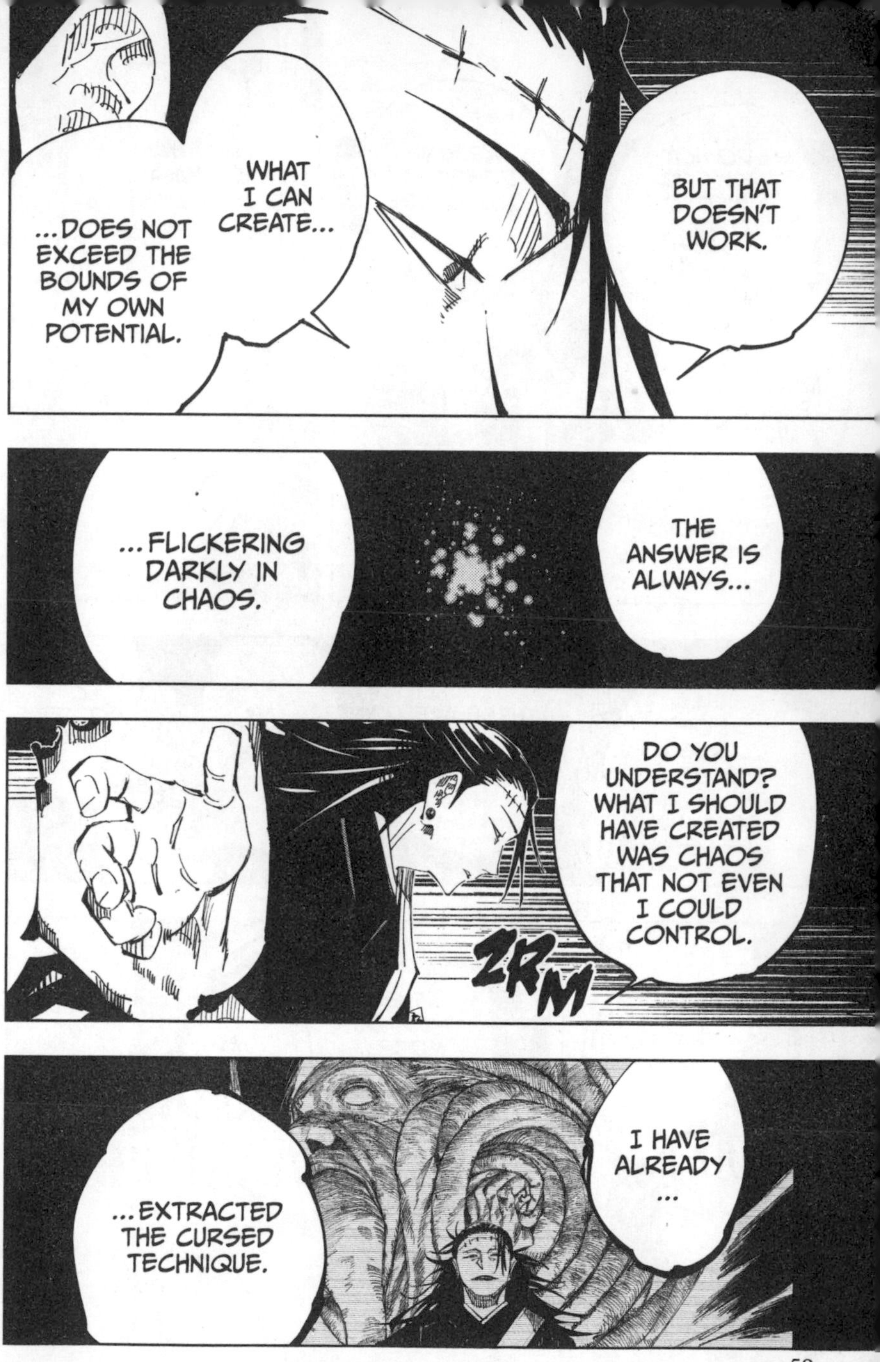
BUT THAT DOESN'T WORK.
WHAT I CAN CREATE...
...DOES NOT EXCEED THE BOUNDS OF MY OWN POTENTIAL.
THE ANSWER IS ALWAYS...
...FLICKERING DARKLY IN CHAOS.
DO YOU UNDERSTAND? WHAT I SHOULD HAVE CREATED WAS CHAOS THAT NOT EVEN I COULD CONTROL.
ZRM
I HAVE ALREADY ...
...EXTRACTED THE CURSED TECHNIQUE.

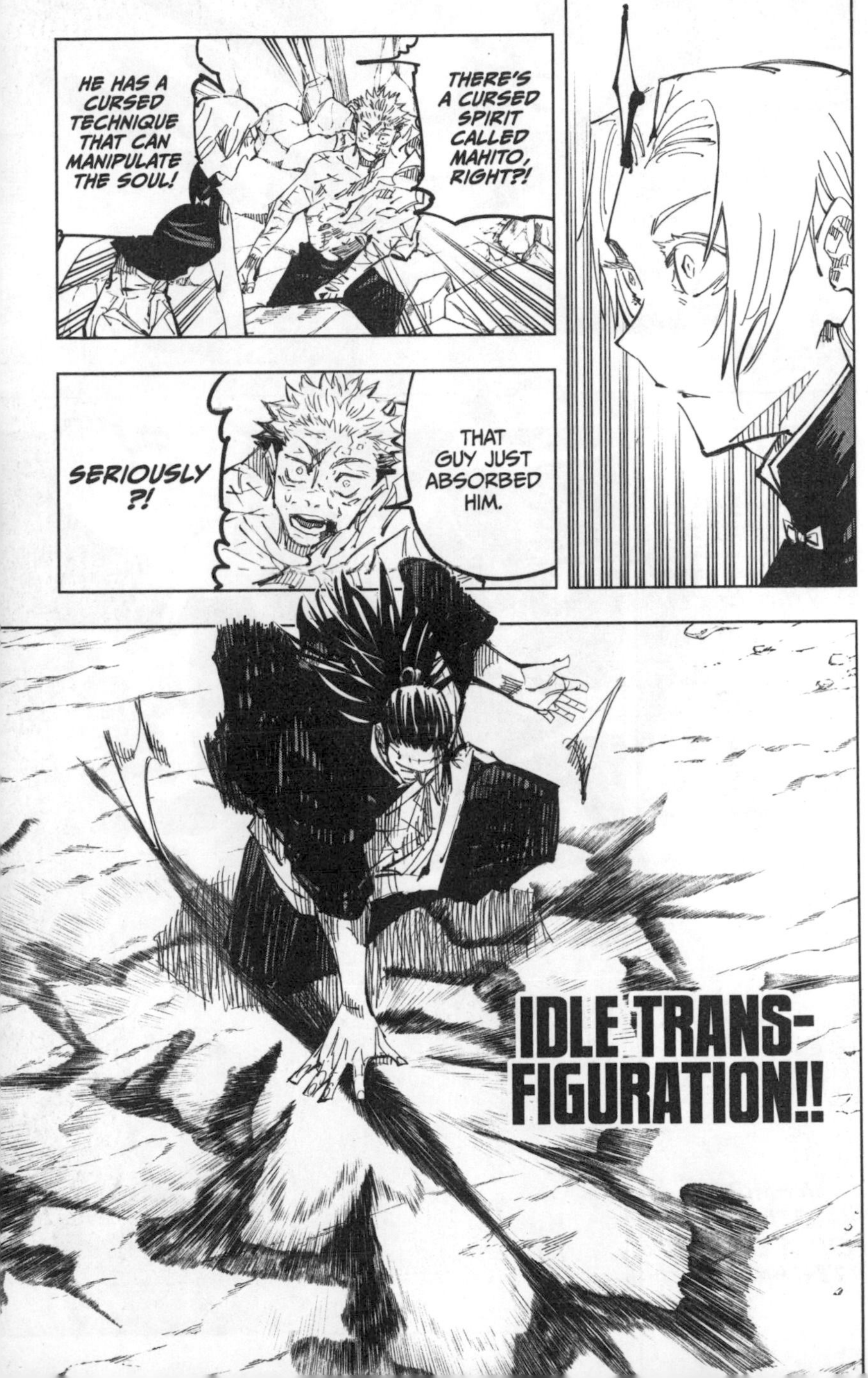
THERE'S A CURSED SPIRIT CALLED MAHITO, RIGHT?!
HE HAS A CURSED TECHNIQUE THAT CAN MANIPULATE THE SOUL!
THAT GUY JUST ABSORBED HIM.
SERIOUSLY?!
IDLE TRANS-FIGURATION!!

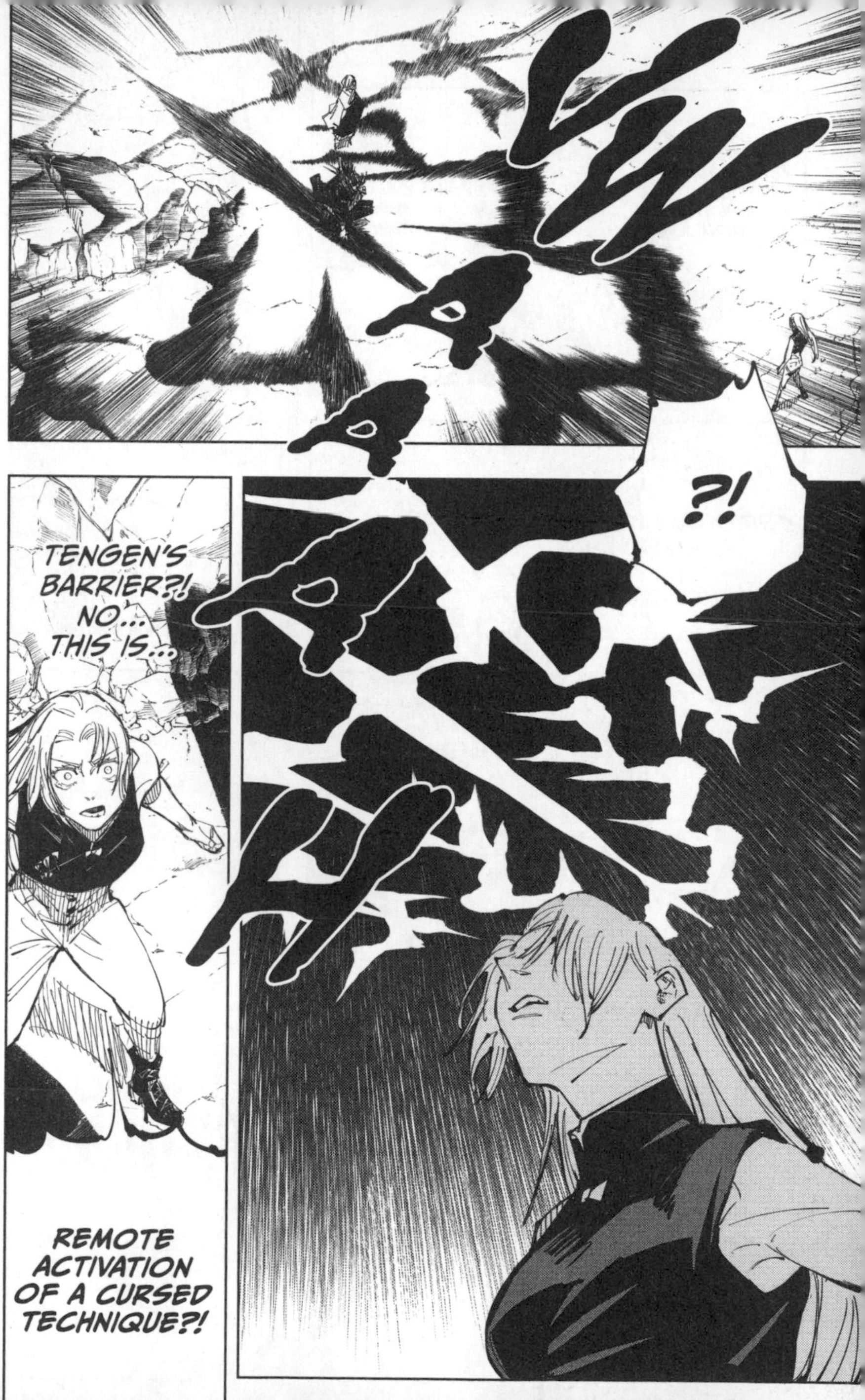
?!
TENGEN'S BARRIER?! NO... THIS IS...
REMOTE ACTIVATION OF A CURSED TECHNIQUE?!

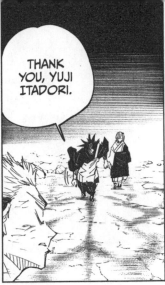

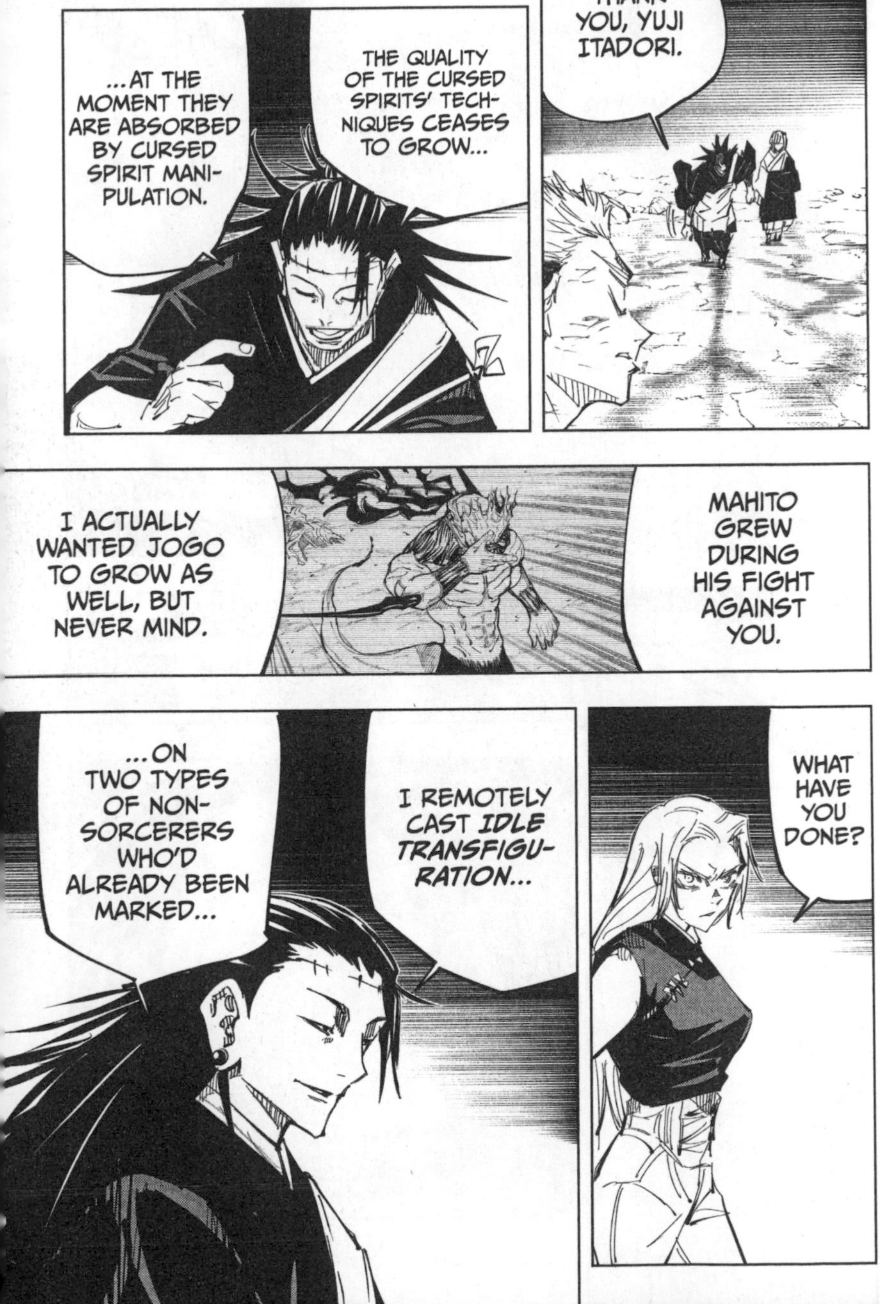
THANK YOU, YUJI ITADORI.
THE QUALITY OF THE CURSED SPIRITS' TECH-NIQUES CEASES TO GROW...
...AT THE MOMENT THEY ARE ABSORBED BY CURSED SPIRIT MANI-PULATION.
MAHITO GREW DURING HIS FIGHT AGAINST YOU.
I ACTUALLY WANTED JOGO TO GROW AS WELL, BUT NEVER MIND.
WHAT HAVE YOU DONE?
I REMOTELY CAST *IDLE TRANSFIGU-RATION*...
...ON TWO TYPES OF NON-SORCERERS WHO'D ALREADY BEEN MARKED...

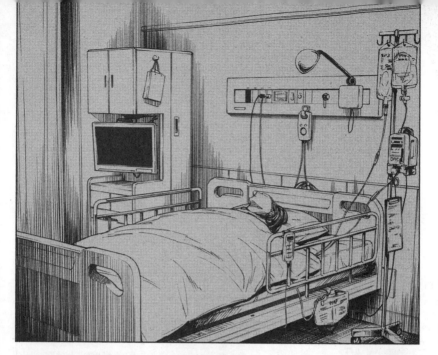

TSUMIKI FUSHIGURO

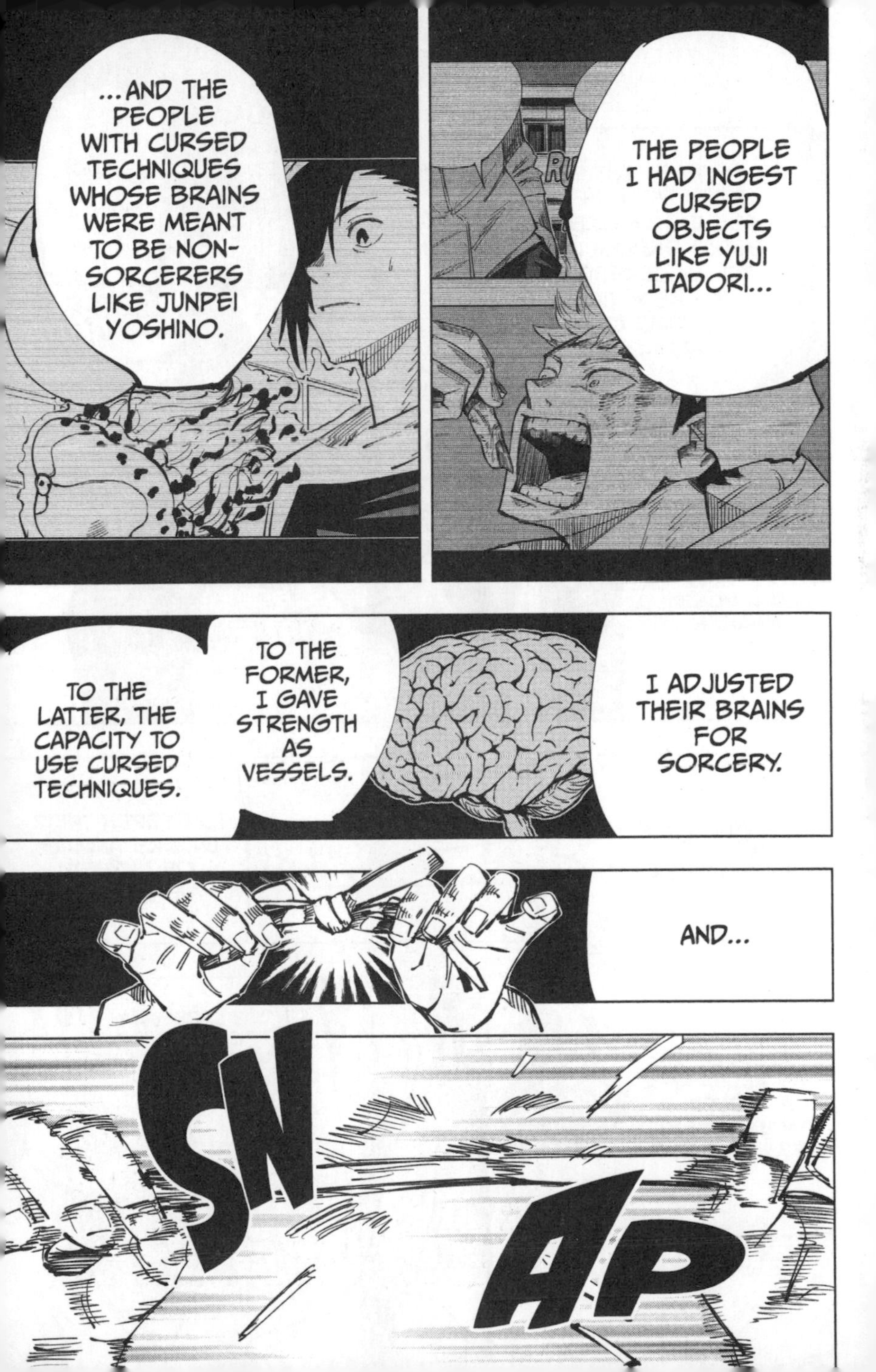
THE PEOPLE I HAD INGEST CURSED OBJECTS LIKE YUJI ITADORI...
...AND THE PEOPLE WITH CURSED TECHNIQUES WHOSE BRAINS WERE MEANT TO BE NON-SORCERERS LIKE JUNPEI YOSHINO.
I ADJUSTED THEIR BRAINS FOR SORCERY.
TO THE FORMER, I GAVE STRENGTH AS VESSELS.
TO THE LATTER, THE CAPACITY TO USE CURSED TECHNIQUES.
AND...
SNAP

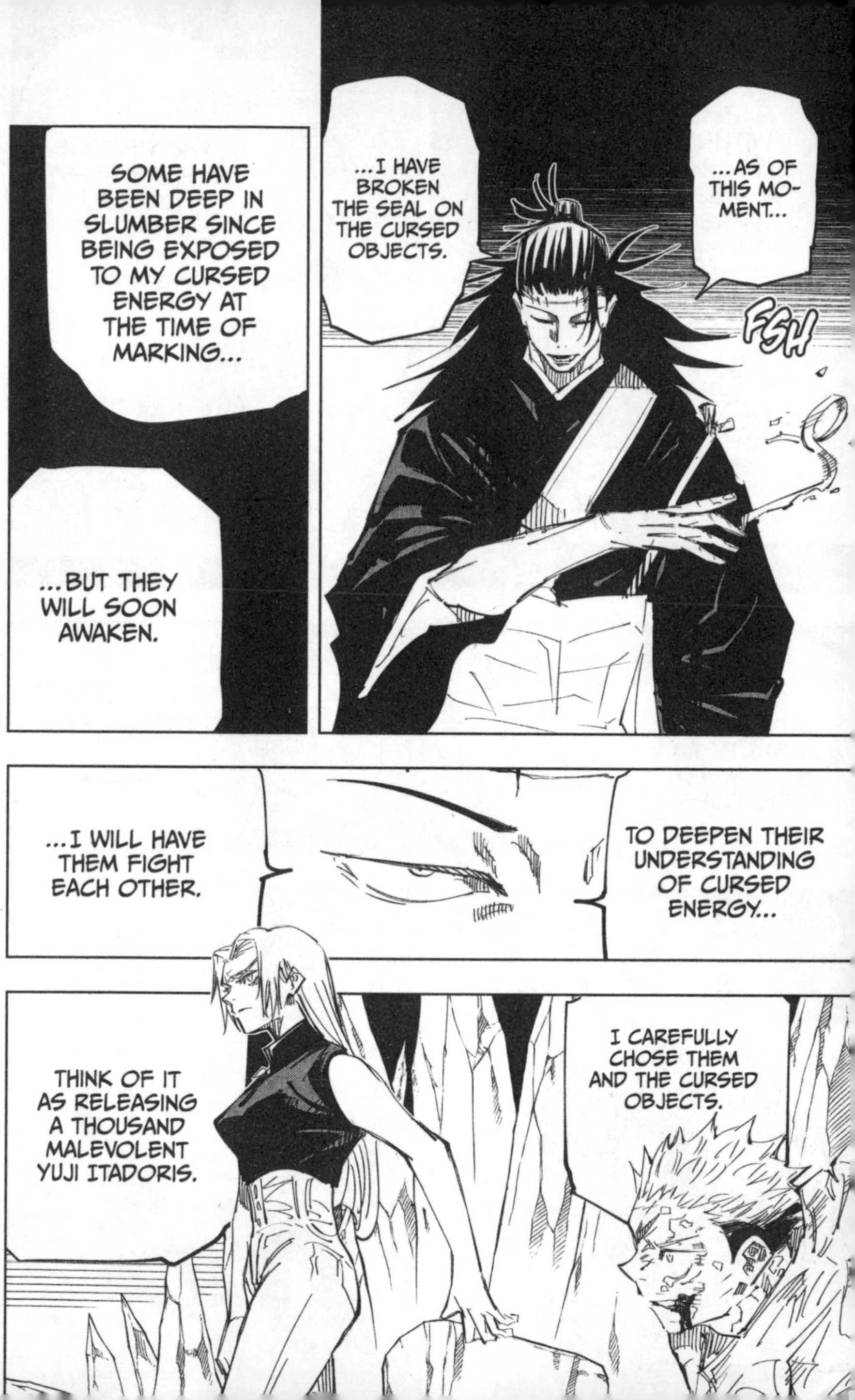
...AS OF THIS MOMENT...
...I HAVE BROKEN THE SEAL ON THE CURSED OBJECTS.
FSH
SOME HAVE BEEN DEEP IN SLUMBER SINCE BEING EXPOSED TO MY CURSED ENERGY AT THE TIME OF MARKING...
...BUT THEY WILL SOON AWAKEN.
TO DEEPEN THEIR UNDERSTANDING OF CURSED ENERGY...
...I WILL HAVE THEM FIGHT EACH OTHER.
I CAREFULLY CHOSE THEM AND THE CURSED OBJECTS.
THINK OF IT AS RELEASING A THOUSAND MALEVOLENT YUJI ITADORIS.

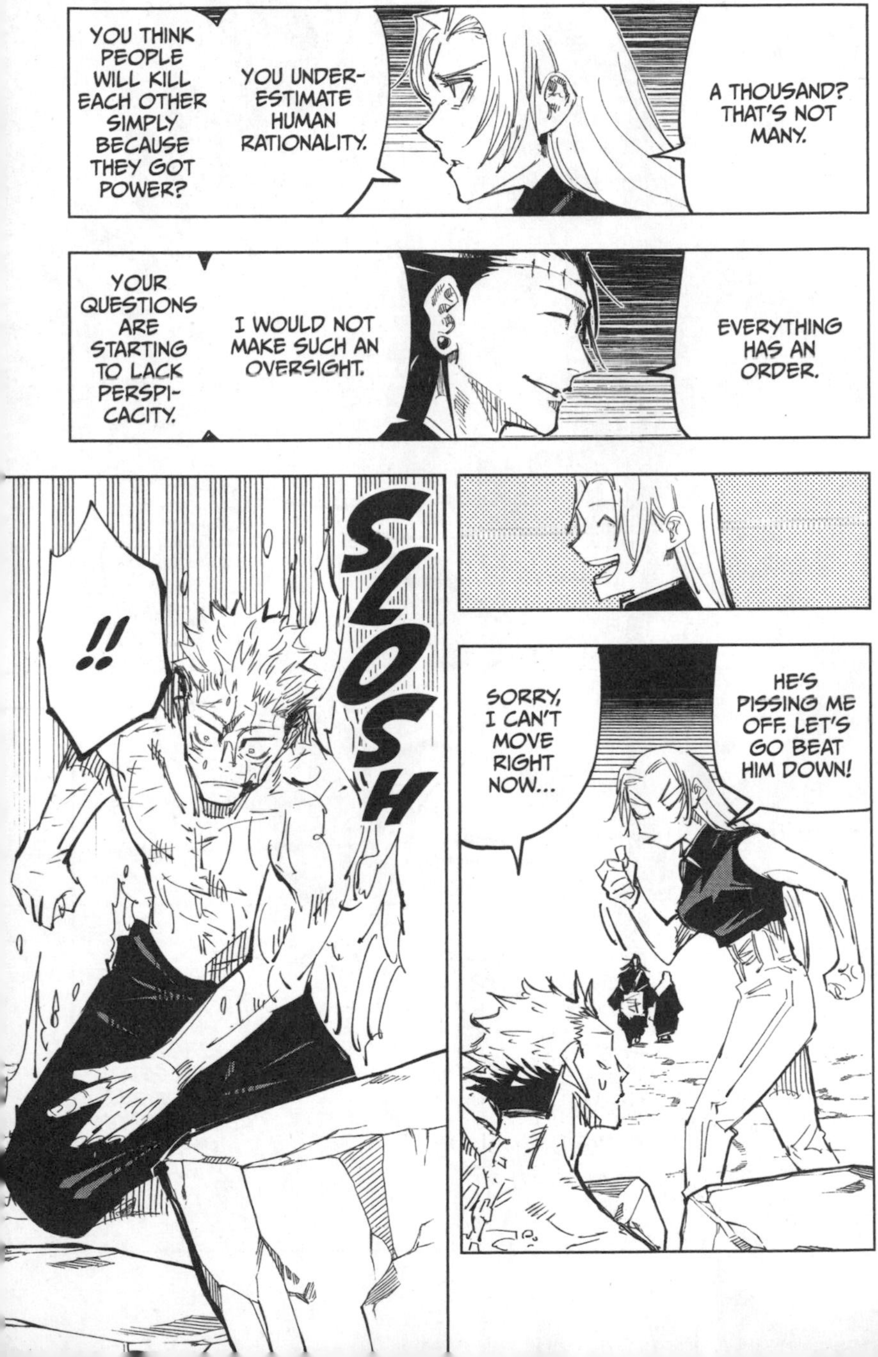
A THOUSAND? THAT'S NOT MANY.
YOU UNDER-ESTIMATE HUMAN RATIONALITY.
YOU THINK PEOPLE WILL KILL EACH OTHER SIMPLY BECAUSE THEY GOT POWER?
EVERYTHING HAS AN ORDER.
I WOULD NOT MAKE SUCH AN OVERSIGHT.
YOUR QUESTIONS ARE STARTING TO LACK PERSPI-CACITY.
HE'S PISSING ME OFF. LET'S GO BEAT HIM DOWN!
SORRY, I CAN'T MOVE RIGHT NOW...
SLOSH
!!

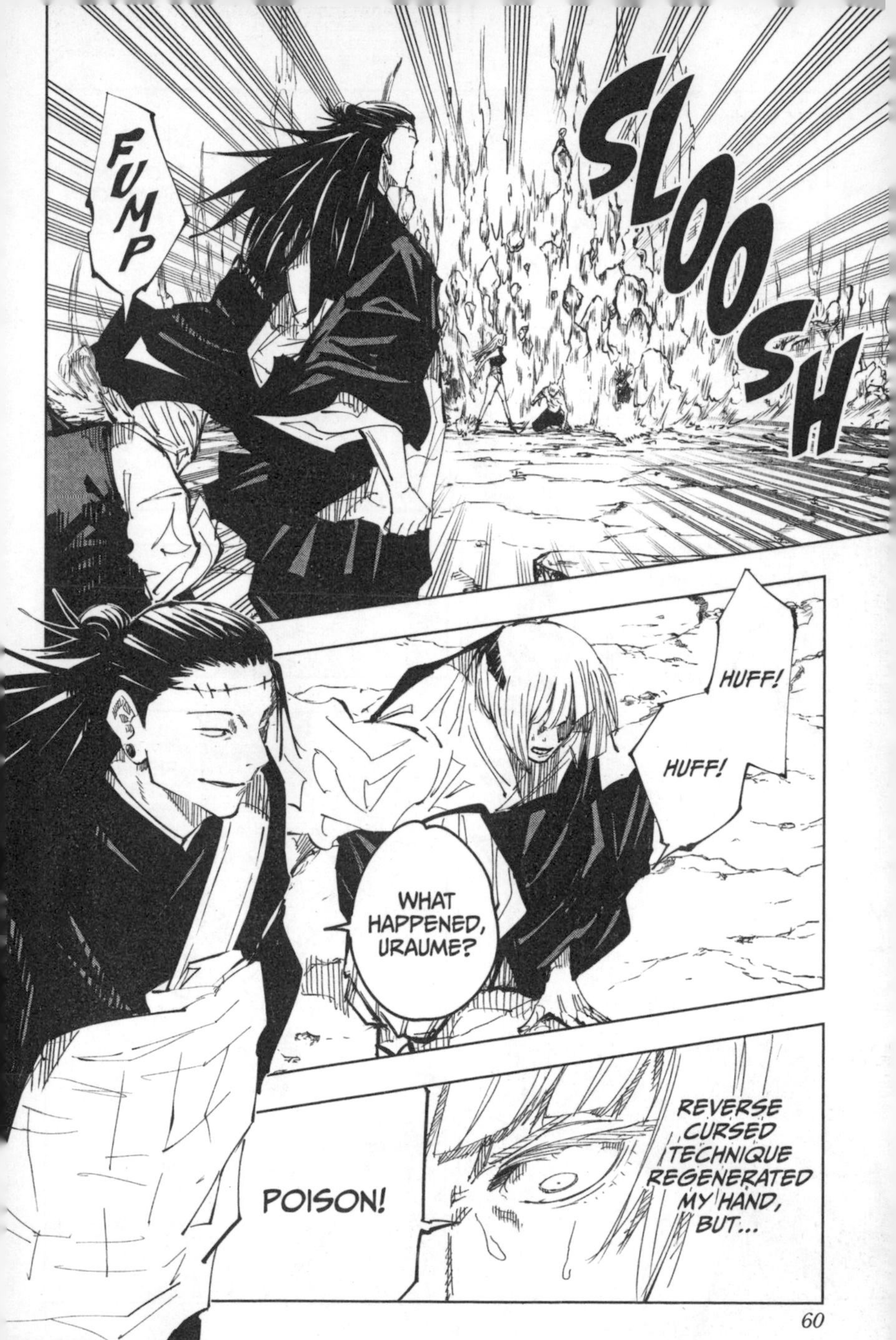
SLOOSH
FUMP
HUFF!
HUFF!
WHAT HAPPENED, URAUME?
REVERSE CURSED TECHNIQUE REGENERATED MY HAND, BUT...
POISON!

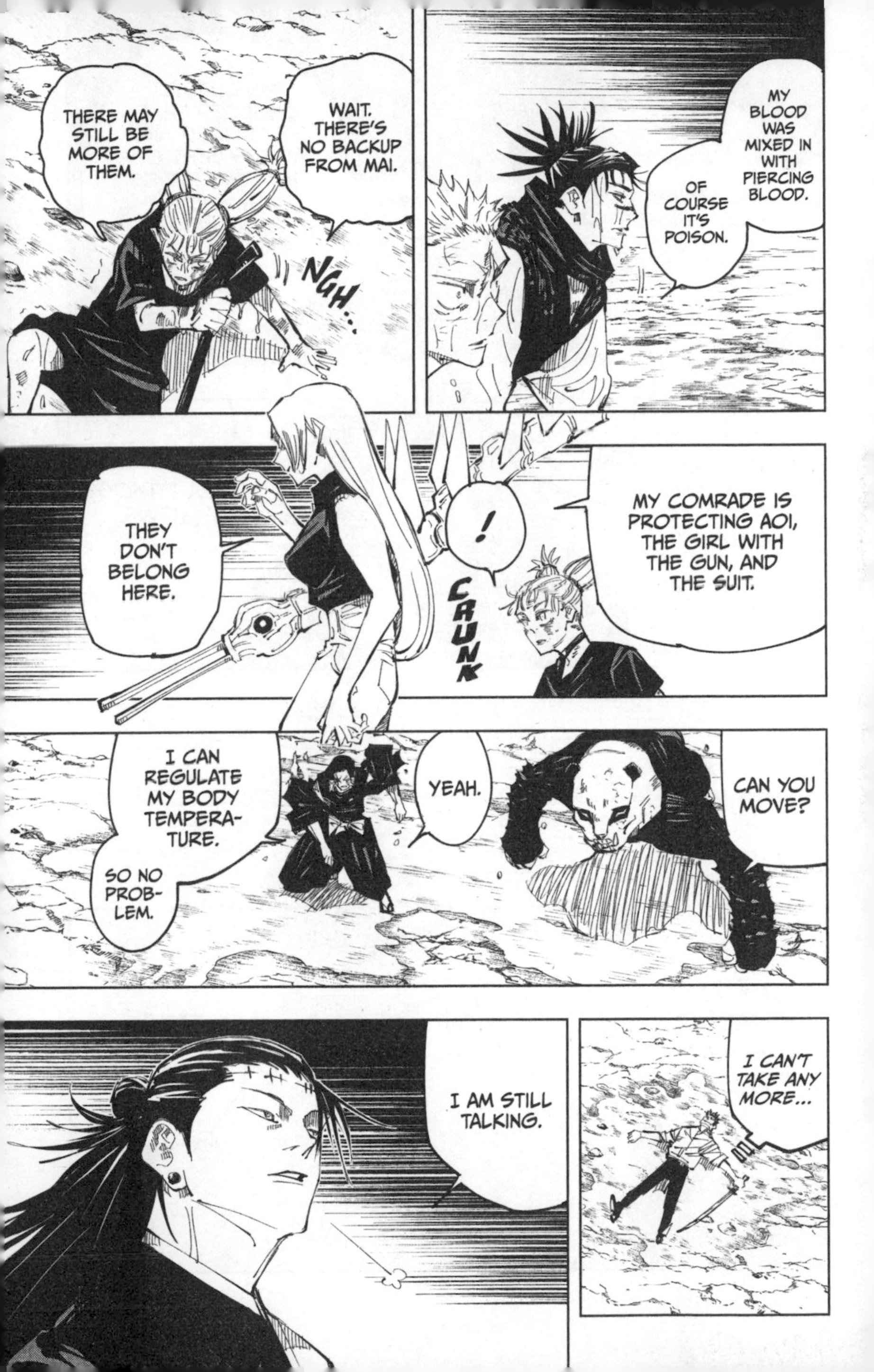
MY BLOOD WAS MIXED IN WITH PIERCING BLOOD.
OF COURSE IT'S POISON.
WAIT. THERE'S NO BACKUP FROM MAI.
NGH...
THERE MAY STILL BE MORE OF THEM.
MY COMRADE IS PROTECTING AOI, THE GIRL WITH THE GUN, AND THE SUIT.
!
CRUNK
THEY DON'T BELONG HERE.
CAN YOU MOVE?
YEAH.
I CAN REGULATE MY BODY TEMPERA-TURE.
SO NO PROB-LEM.
I CAN'T TAKE ANY MORE...
I AM STILL TALKING.

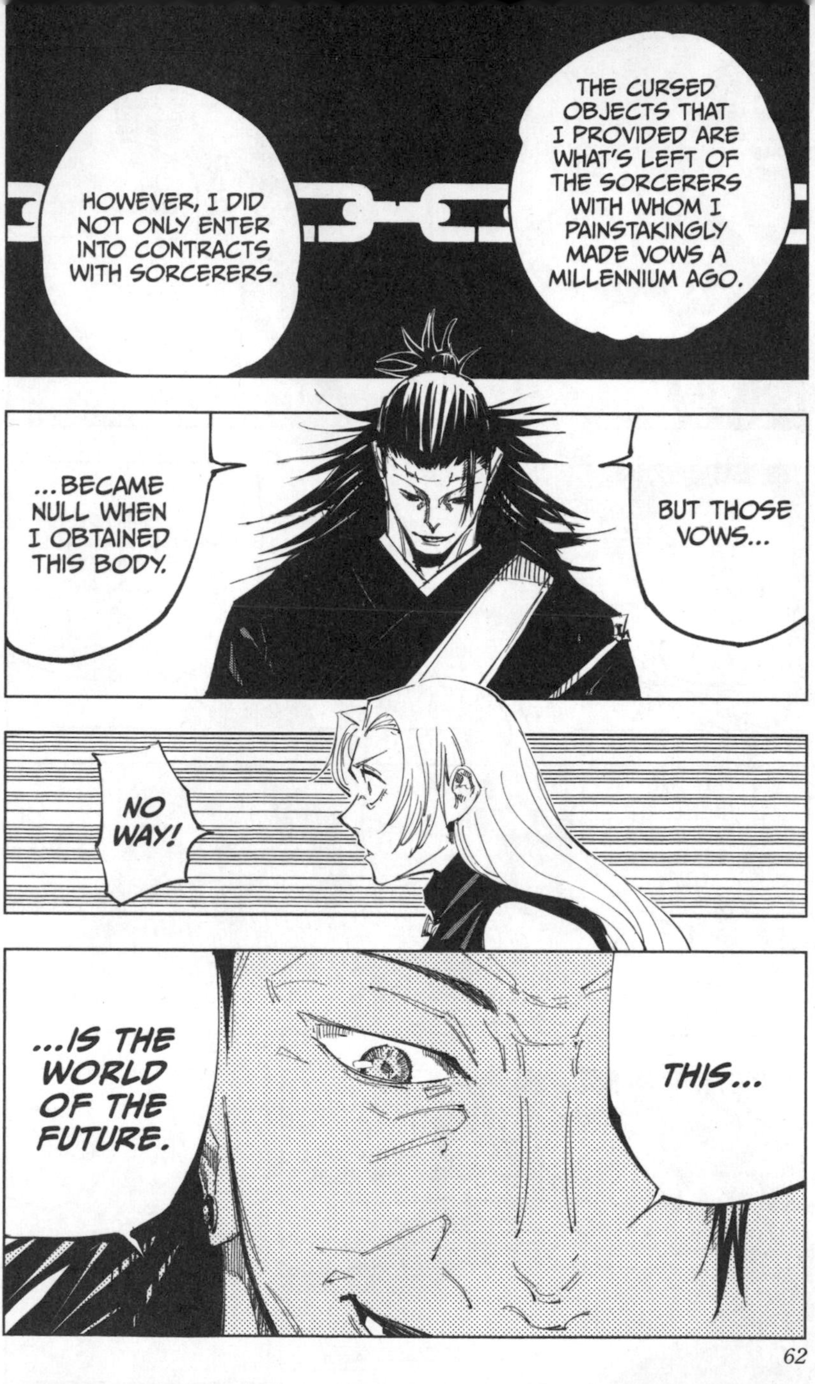
THE CURSED OBJECTS THAT I PROVIDED ARE WHAT'S LEFT OF THE SORCERERS WITH WHOM I PAINSTAKINGLY MADE VOWS A MILLENNIUM AGO.
HOWEVER, I DID NOT ONLY ENTER INTO CONTRACTS WITH SORCERERS.
BUT THOSE VOWS...
...BECAME NULL WHEN I OBTAINED THIS BODY.
NO WAY!
THIS...
...IS THE WORLD OF THE FUTURE.

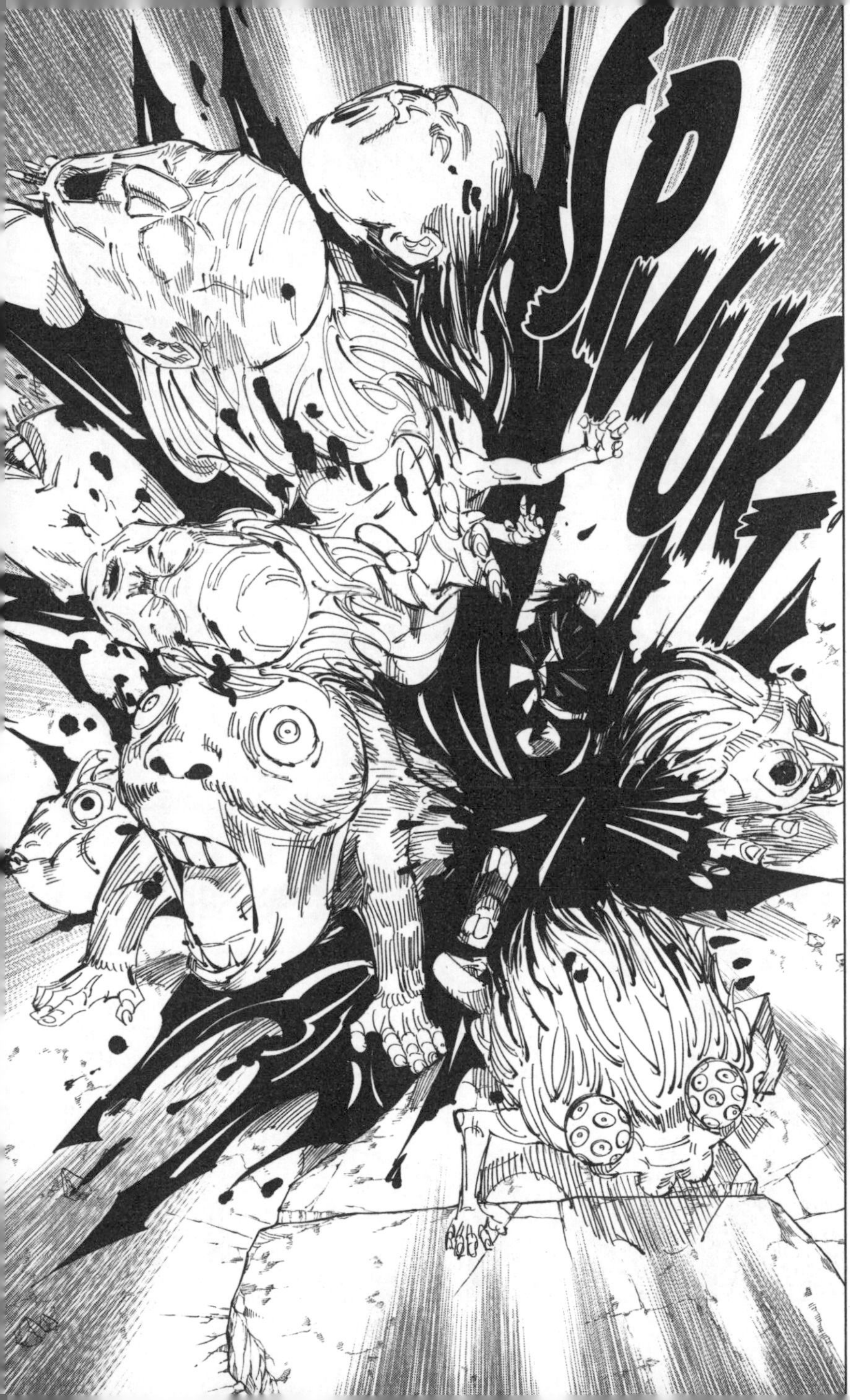

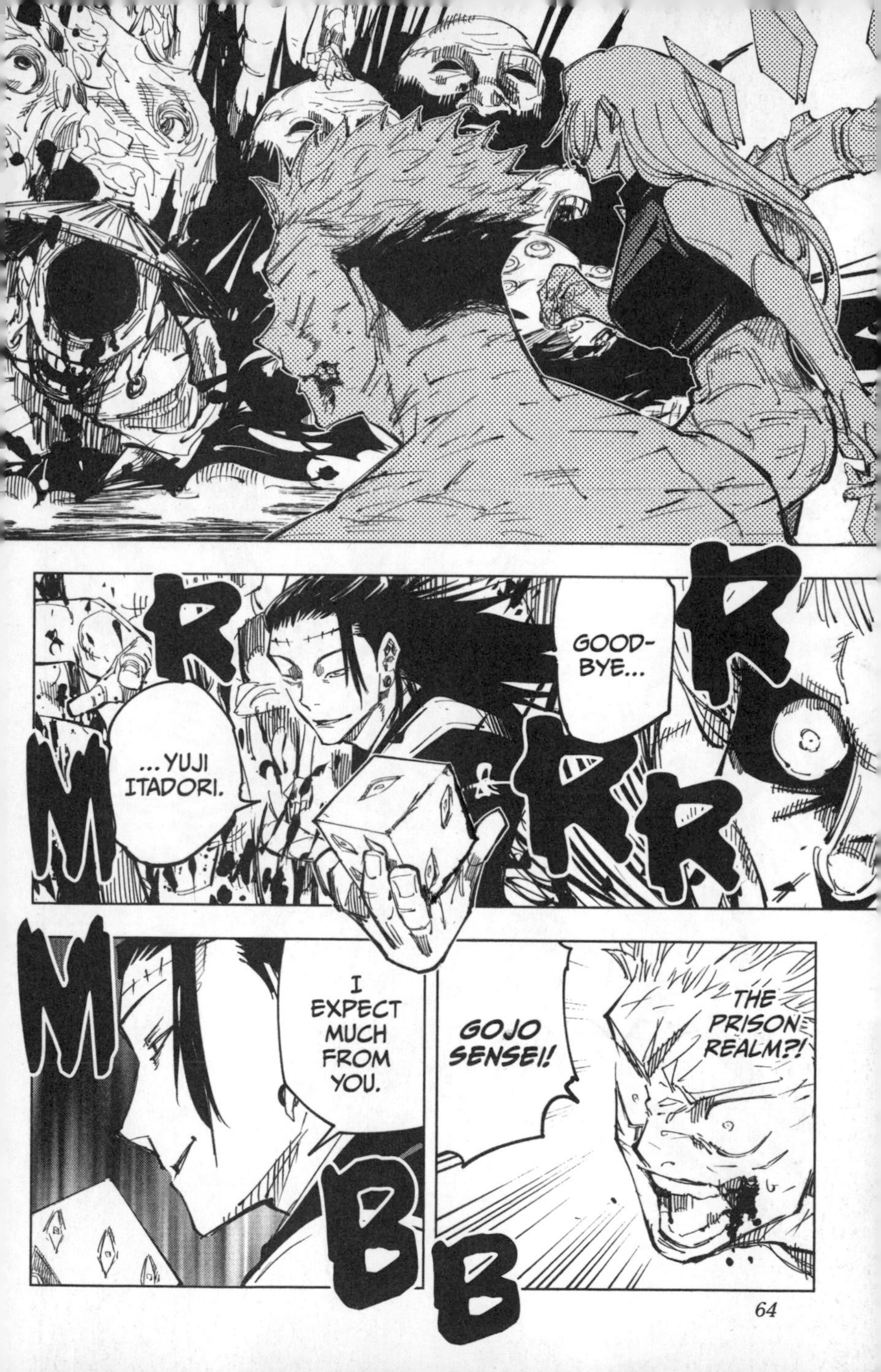

RRRR
GOOD-BYE...
...YUJI ITADORI.
MM
THE PRISON REALM?!
GOJO SENSEI!
I EXPECT MUCH FROM YOU.
BB

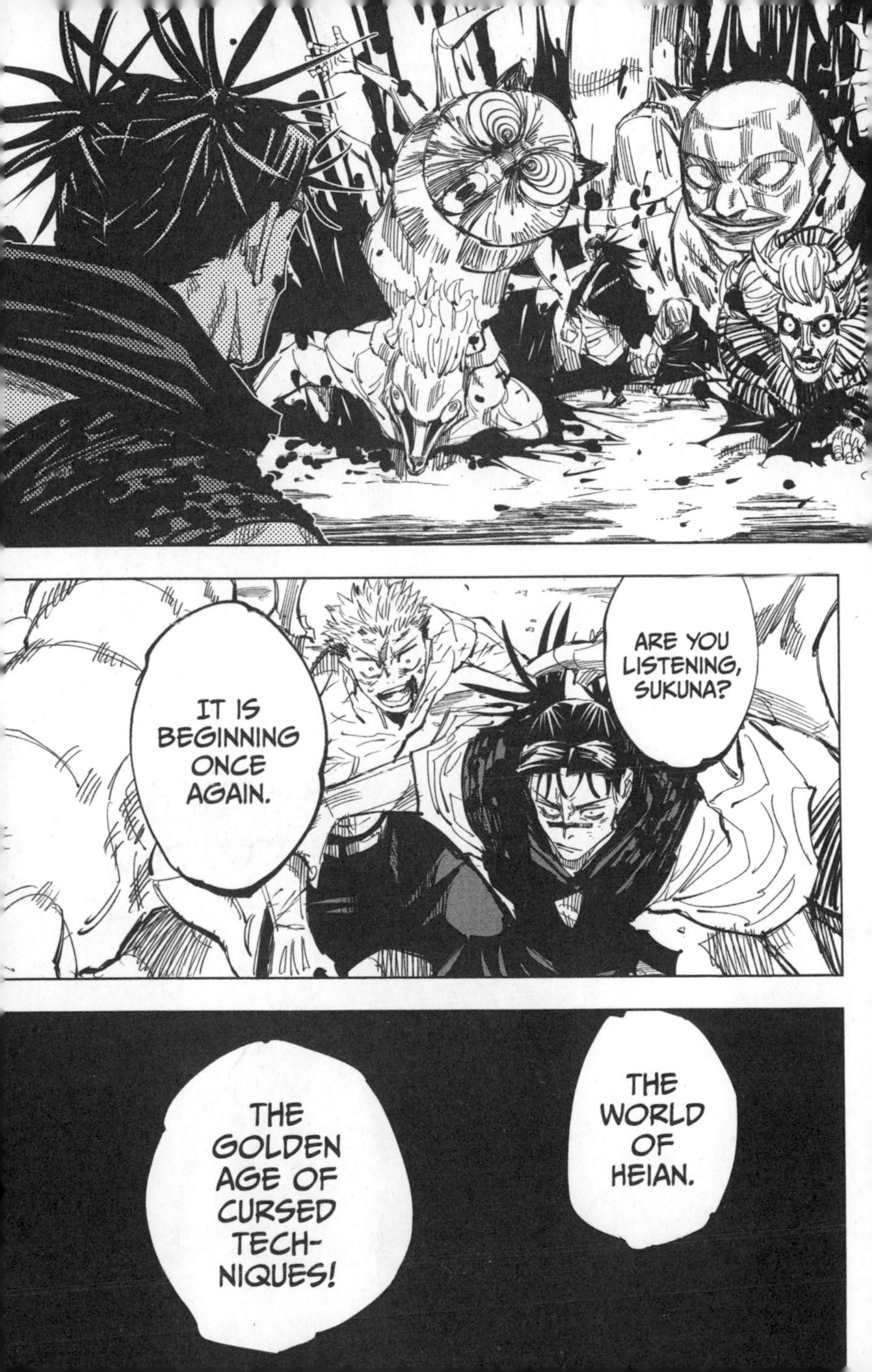
ARE YOU LISTENING, SUKUNA?
IT IS BEGINNING ONCE AGAIN.
THE WORLD OF HEIAN.
THE GOLDEN AGE OF CURSED TECH-NIQUES!

KENJAKU

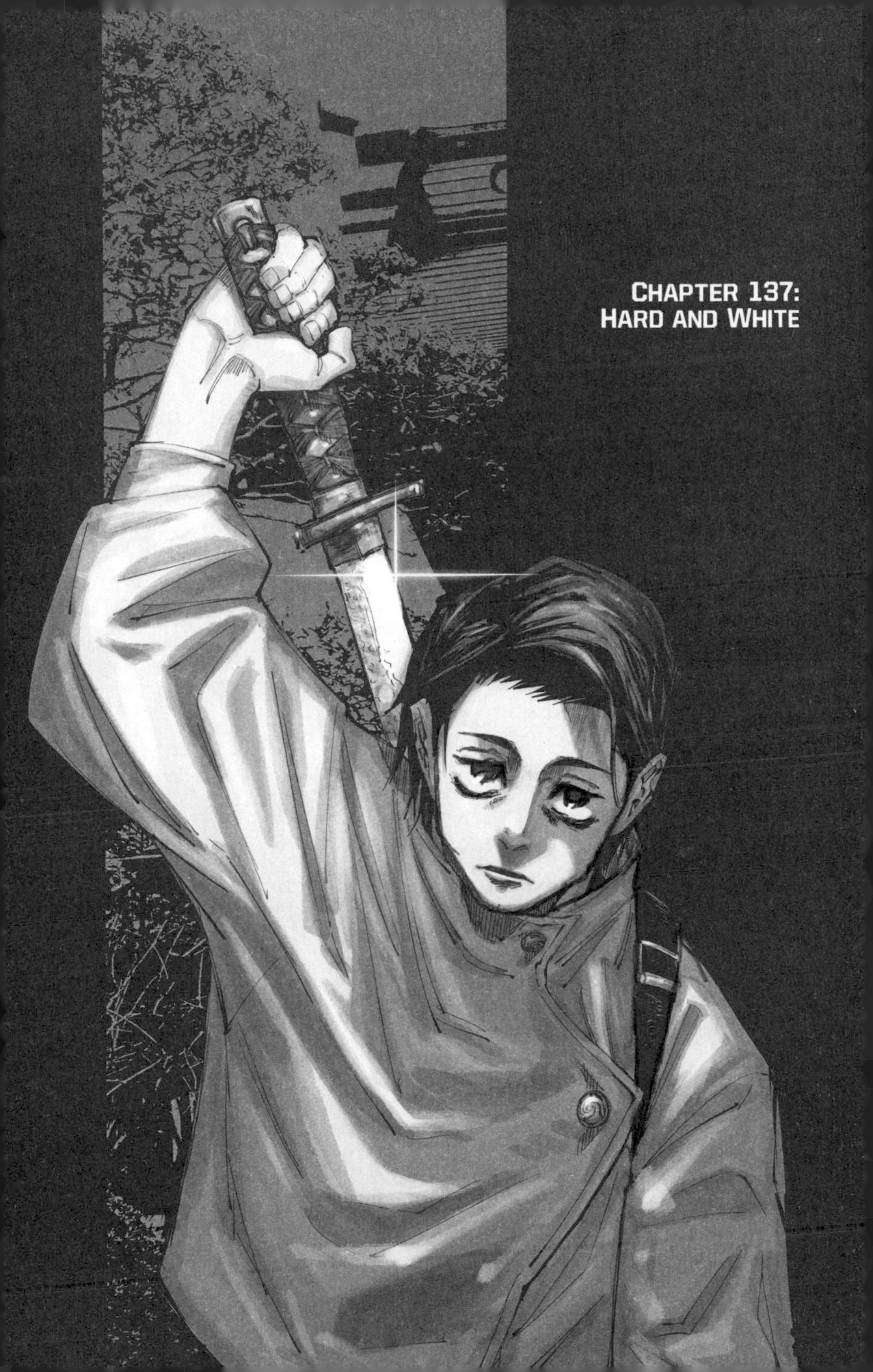
CHAPTER 137:
HARD AND WHITE

JUJUTSU KAISEN

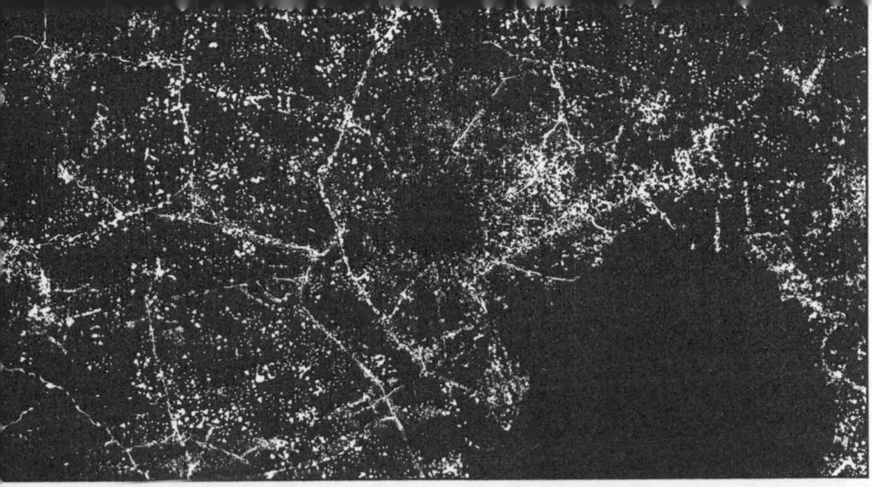
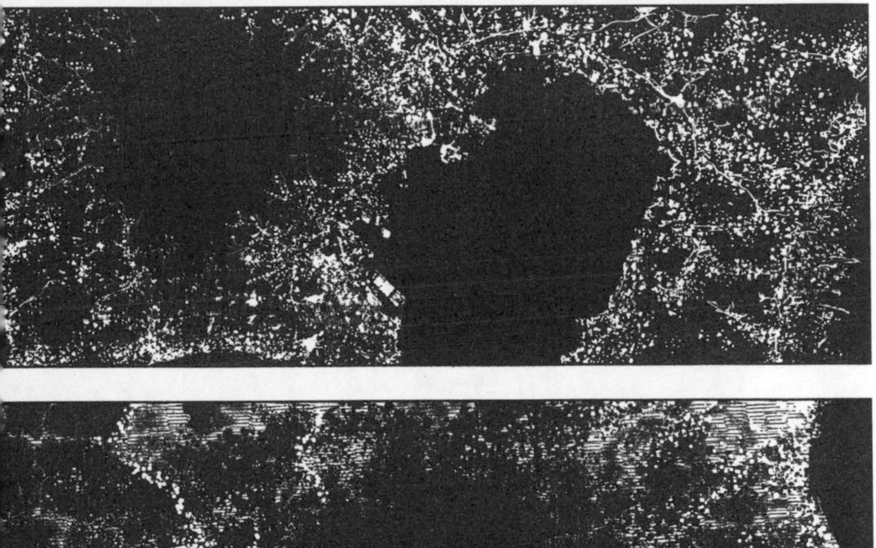
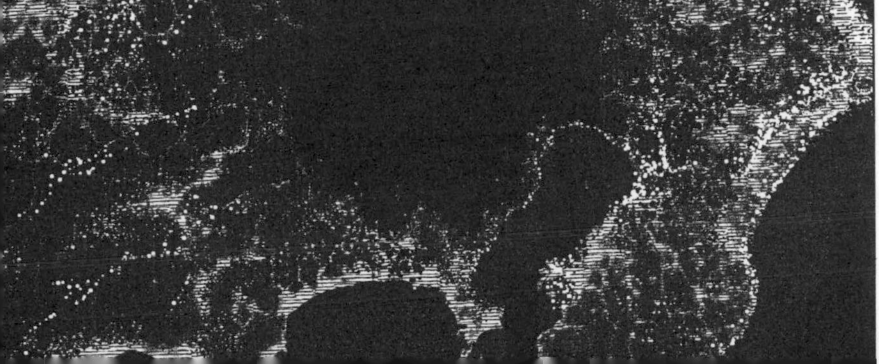

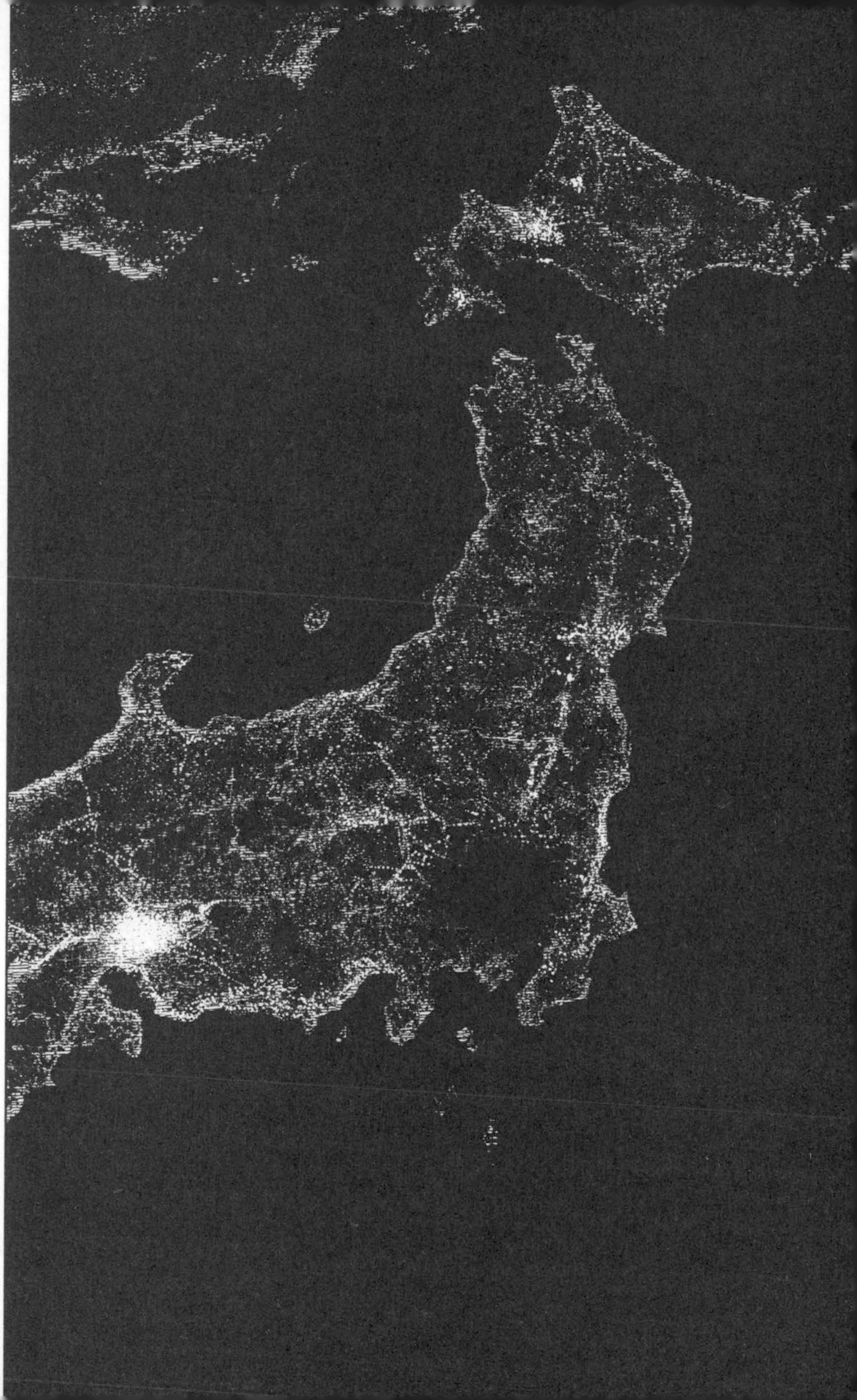

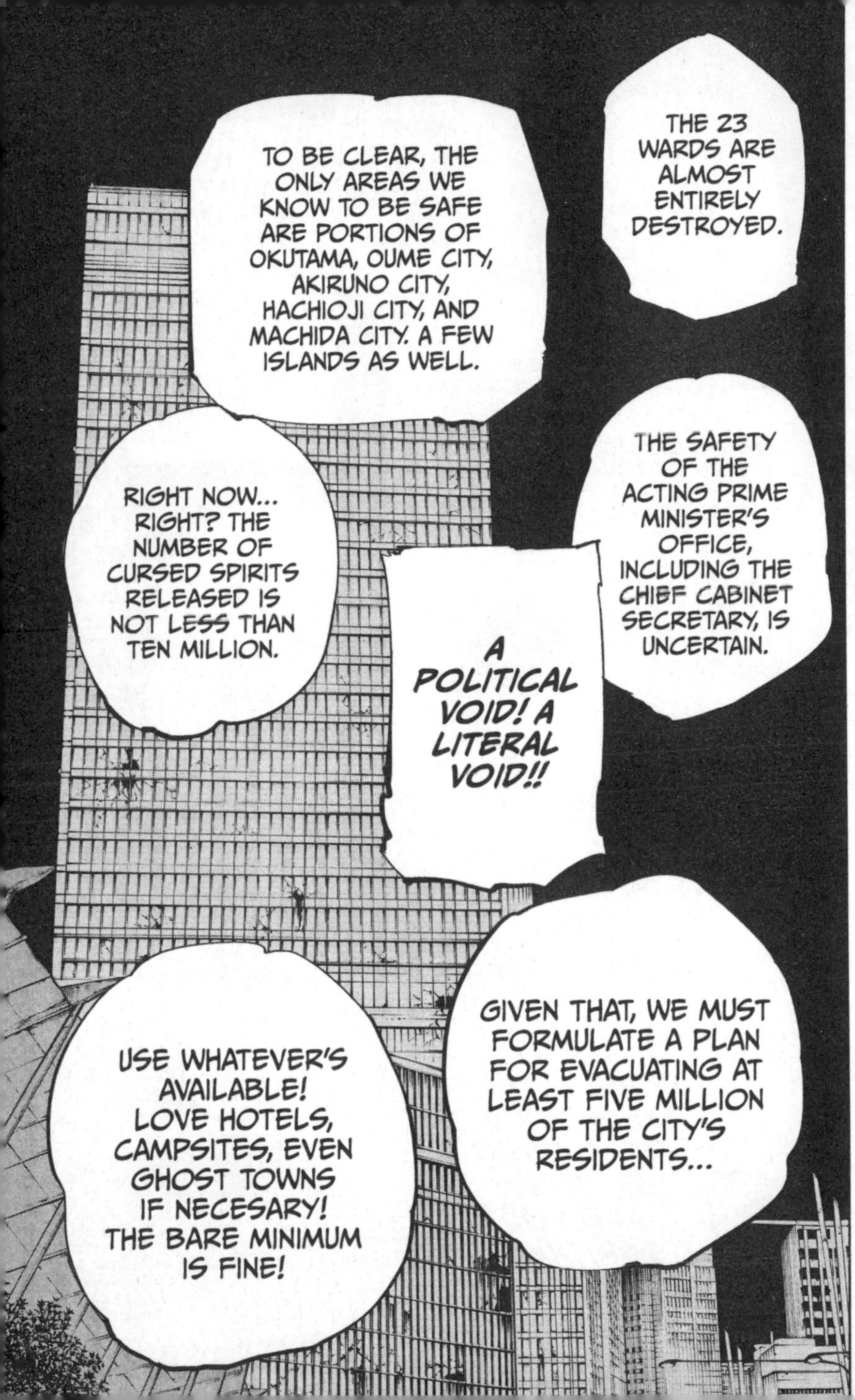
THE 23 WARDS ARE ALMOST ENTIRELY DESTROYED.
TO BE CLEAR, THE ONLY AREAS WE KNOW TO BE SAFE ARE PORTIONS OF OKUTAMA, OUME CITY, AKIRUNO CITY, HACHIOJI CITY, AND MACHIDA CITY. A FEW ISLANDS AS WELL.
THE SAFETY OF THE ACTING PRIME MINISTER'S OFFICE, INCLUDING THE CHIEF CABINET SECRETARY, IS UNCERTAIN.
A POLITICAL VOID! A LITERAL VOID!!
RIGHT NOW... RIGHT? THE NUMBER OF CURSED SPIRITS RELEASED IS NOT LESS THAN TEN MILLION.
GIVEN THAT, WE MUST FORMULATE A PLAN FOR EVACUATING AT LEAST FIVE MILLION OF THE CITY'S RESIDENTS...
USE WHATEVER'S AVAILABLE! LOVE HOTELS, CAMPSITES, EVEN GHOST TOWNS IF NECESARY! THE BARE MINIMUM IS FINE!

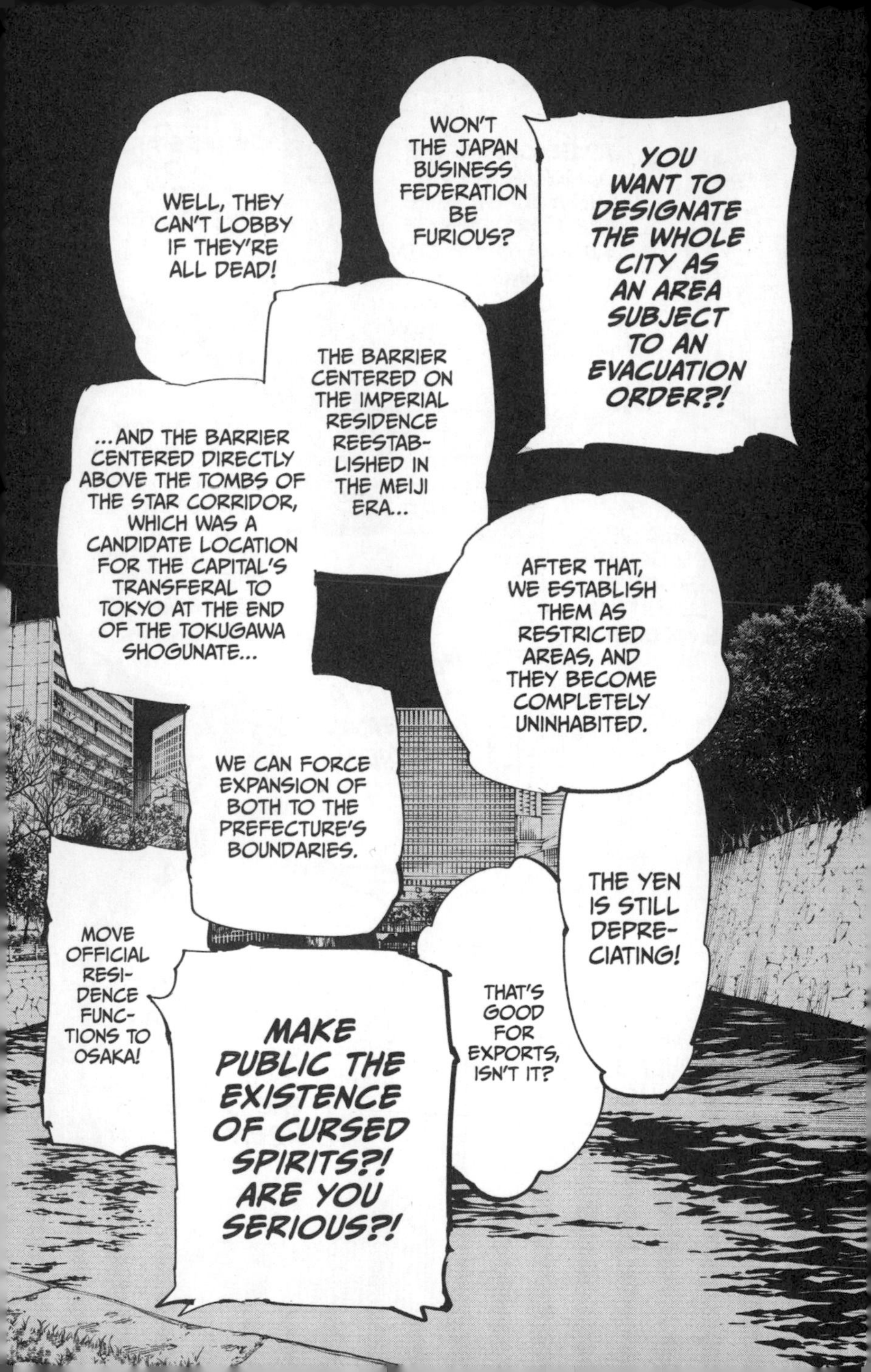
YOU WANT TO DESIGNATE THE WHOLE CITY AS AN AREA SUBJECT TO AN EVACUATION ORDER?!
WON'T THE JAPAN BUSINESS FEDERATION BE FURIOUS?
WELL, THEY CAN'T LOBBY IF THEY'RE ALL DEAD!
THE BARRIER CENTERED ON THE IMPERIAL RESIDENCE REESTAB-LISHED IN THE MEIJI ERA...
...AND THE BARRIER CENTERED DIRECTLY ABOVE THE TOMBS OF THE STAR CORRIDOR, WHICH WAS A CANDIDATE LOCATION FOR THE CAPITAL'S TRANSFERAL TO TOKYO AT THE END OF THE TOKUGAWA SHOGUNATE...
WE CAN FORCE EXPANSION OF BOTH TO THE PREFECTURE'S BOUNDARIES.
AFTER THAT, WE ESTABLISH THEM AS RESTRICTED AREAS, AND THEY BECOME COMPLETELY UNINHABITED.
THE YEN IS STILL DEPRE-CIATING!
THAT'S GOOD FOR EXPORTS, ISN'T IT?
MAKE PUBLIC THE EXISTENCE OF CURSED SPIRITS?! ARE YOU SERIOUS?!
MOVE OFFICIAL RESI-DENCE FUNC-TIONS TO OSAKA!

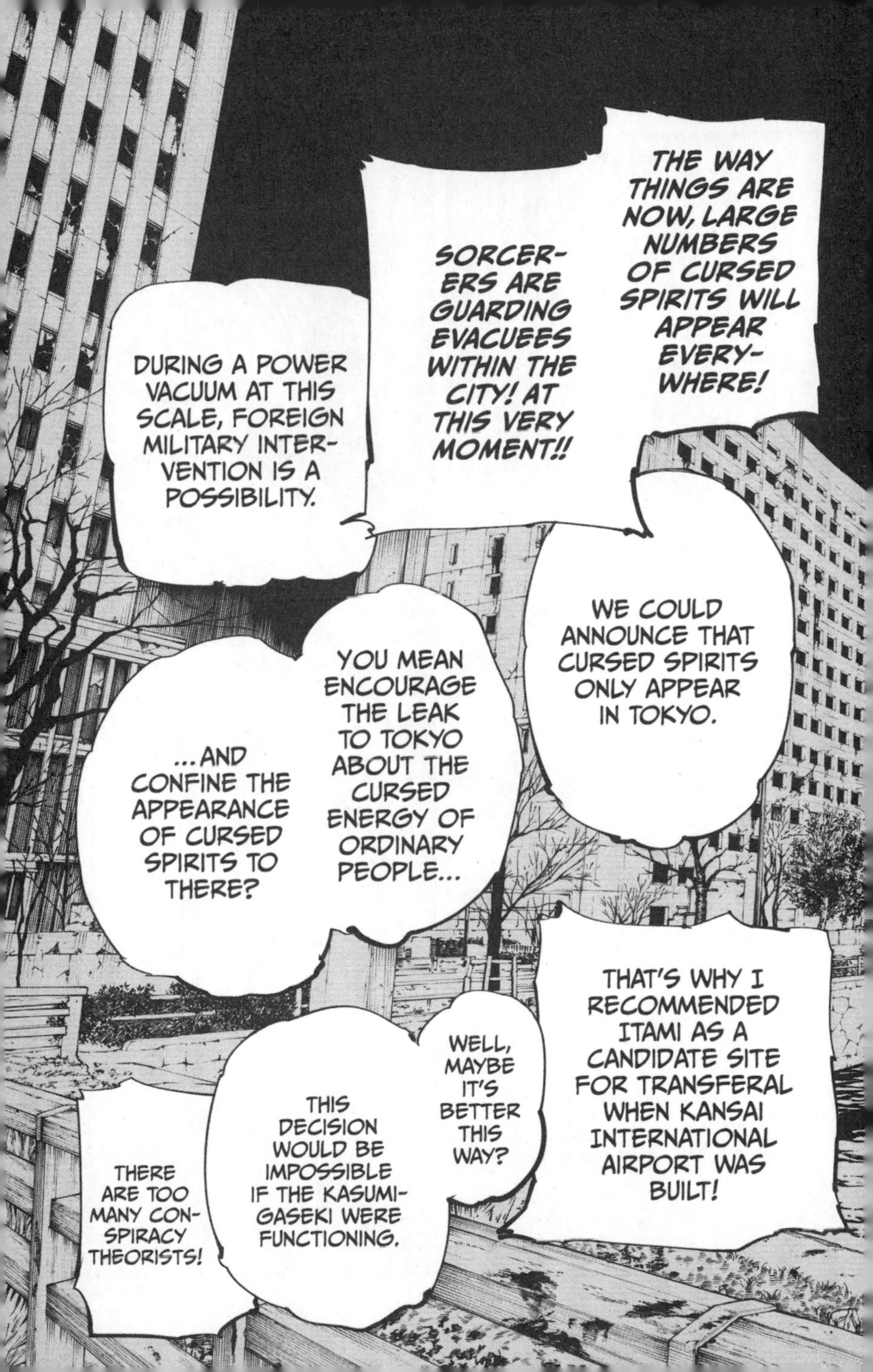
THE WAY THINGS ARE NOW, LARGE NUMBERS OF CURSED SPIRITS WILL APPEAR EVERY-WHERE!
SORCER-ERS ARE GUARDING EVACUEES WITHIN THE CITY! AT THIS VERY MOMENT!!
DURING A POWER VACUUM AT THIS SCALE, FOREIGN MILITARY INTER-VENTION IS A POSSIBILITY.
WE COULD ANNOUNCE THAT CURSED SPIRITS ONLY APPEAR IN TOKYO.
YOU MEAN ENCOURAGE THE LEAK TO TOKYO ABOUT THE CURSED ENERGY OF ORDINARY PEOPLE...
...AND CONFINE THE APPEARANCE OF CURSED SPIRITS TO THERE?
THAT'S WHY I RECOMMENDED ITAMI AS A CANDIDATE SITE FOR TRANSFERAL WHEN KANSAI INTERNATIONAL AIRPORT WAS BUILT!
WELL, MAYBE IT'S BETTER THIS WAY?
THIS DECISION WOULD BE IMPOSSIBLE IF THE KASUMI-GASEKI WERE FUNCTIONING.
THERE ARE TOO MANY CON-SPIRACY THEORISTS!

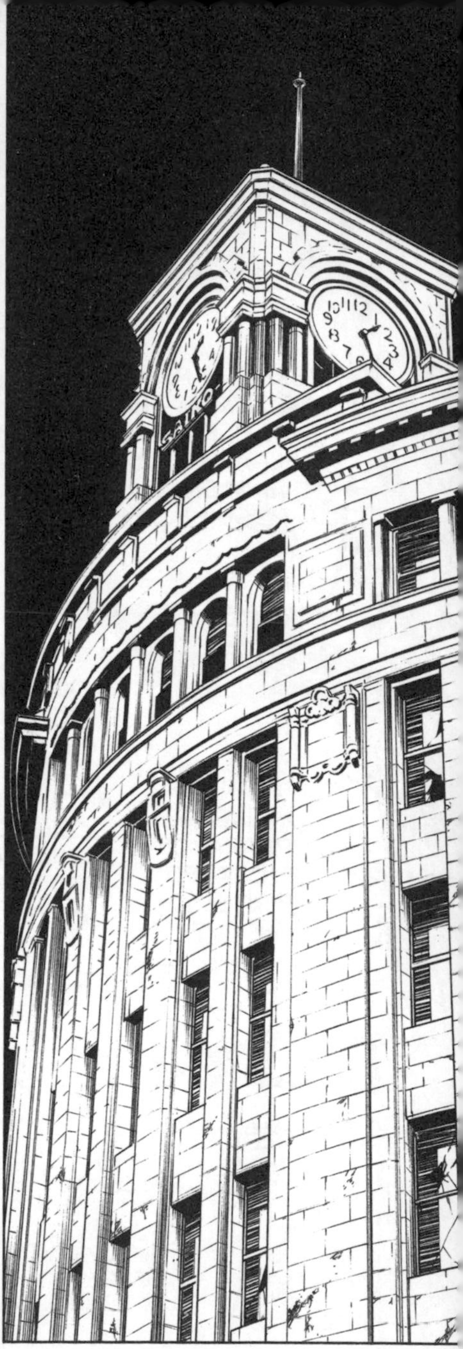
SAINO

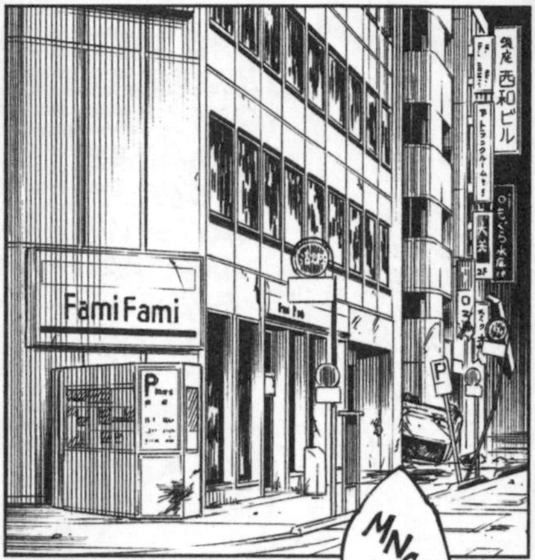
Fami Fami
西和ビル
MNCH MNCH

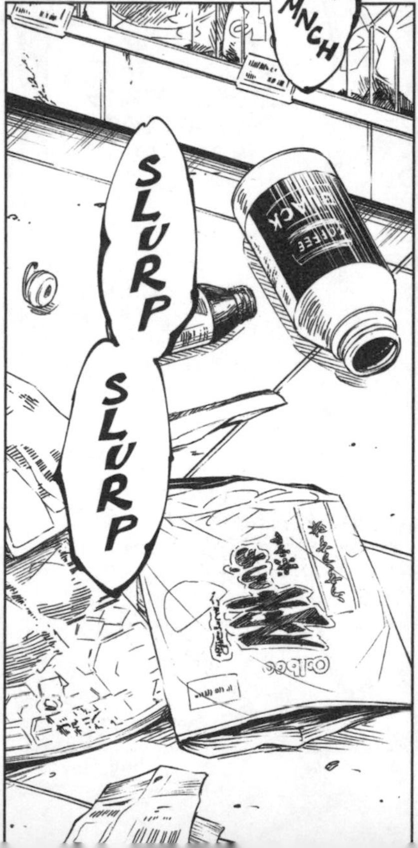
SLURP SLURP

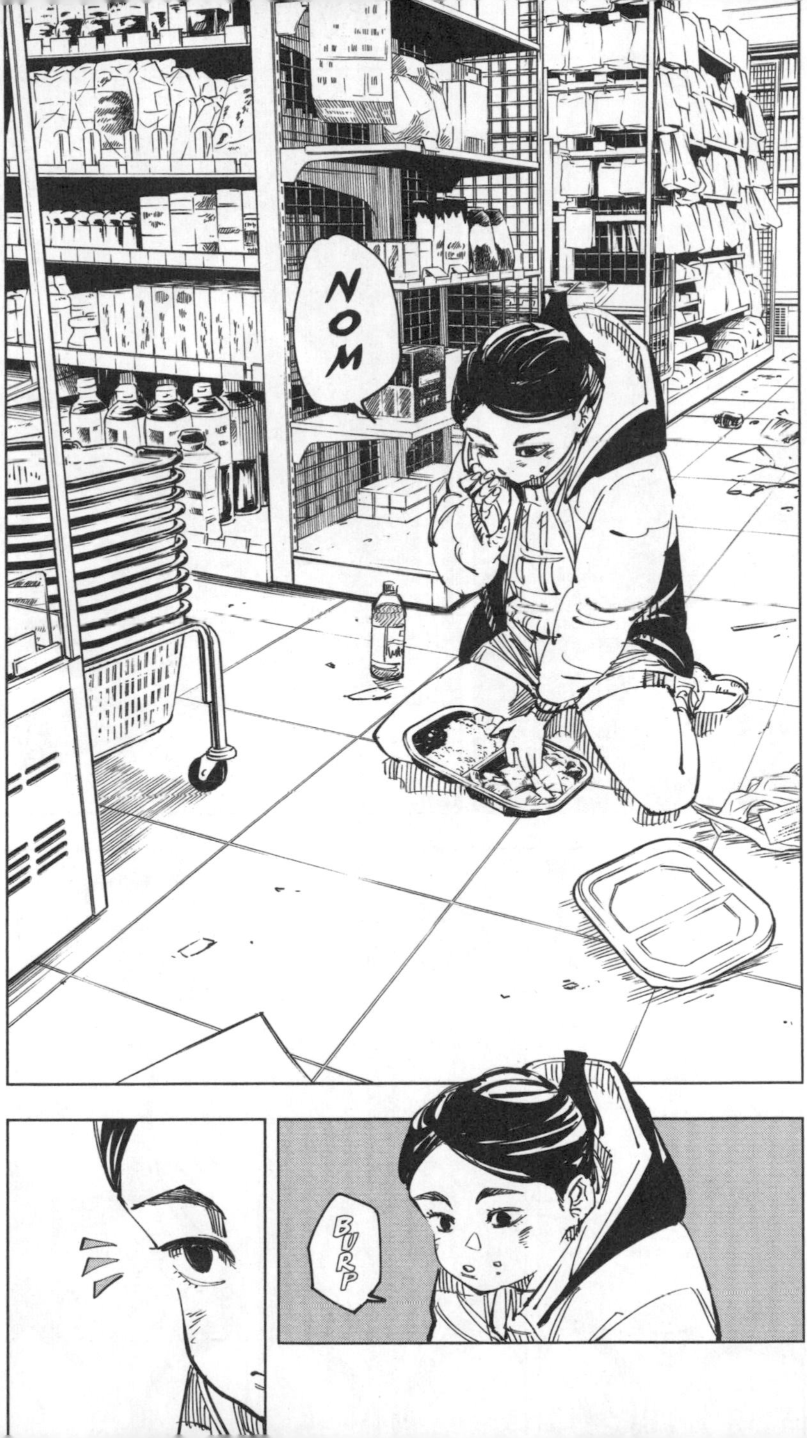
NOM
BURP

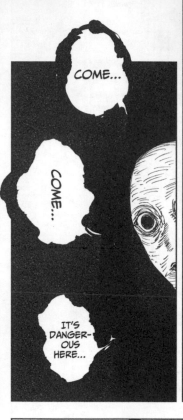

COME...

COME...

IT'S DANGEROUS HERE...

A HOT BA권...

WHERE'S MY MOM?

AND YOU CAN SING SONGS...

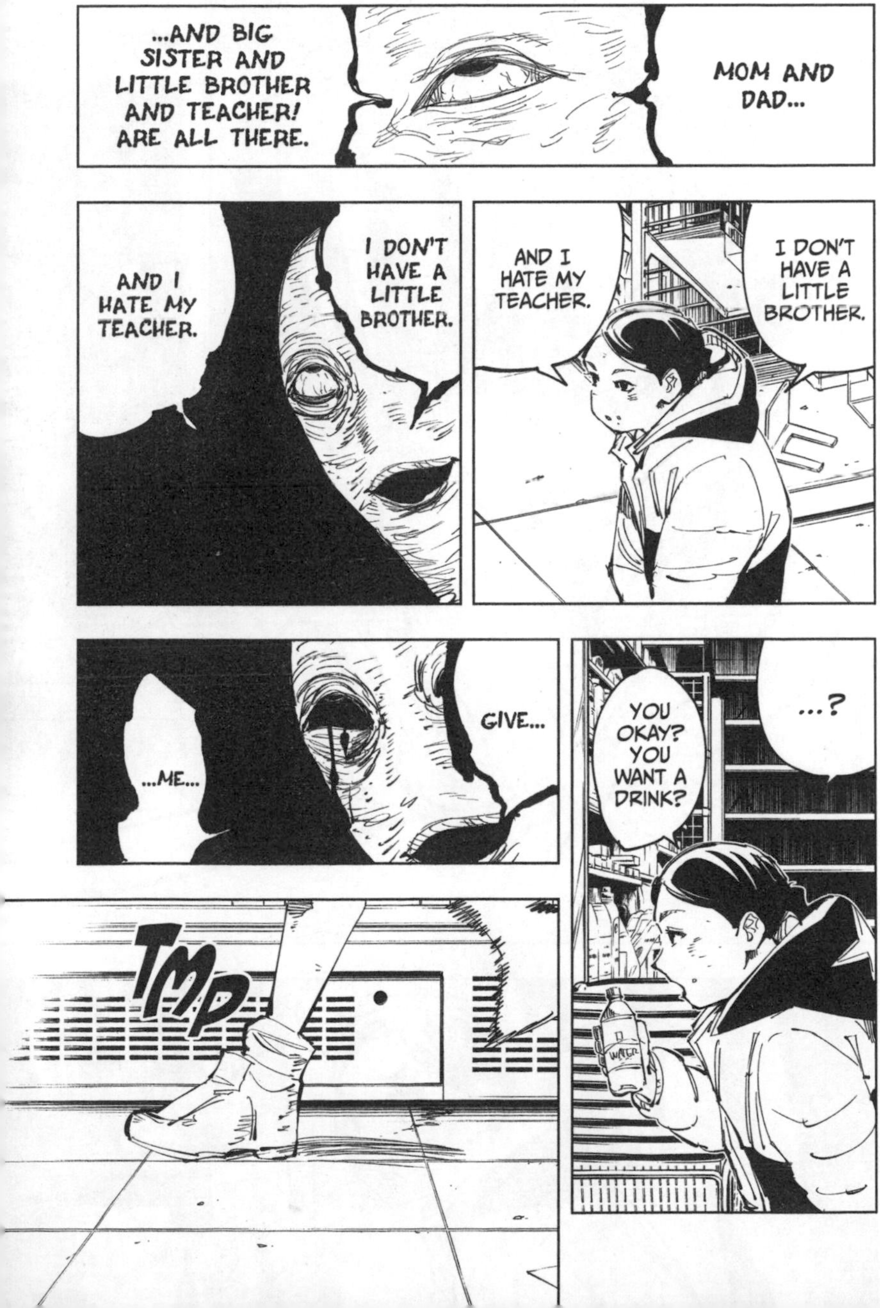
MOM AND DAD...
...AND BIG SISTER AND LITTLE BROTHER AND TEACHER! ARE ALL THERE.
I DON'T HAVE A LITTLE BROTHER.
AND I HATE MY TEACHER.
I DON'T HAVE A LITTLE BROTHER.
AND I HATE MY TEACHER.
...?
YOU OKAY? YOU WANT A DRINK?
GIVE...
...ME...
TMP

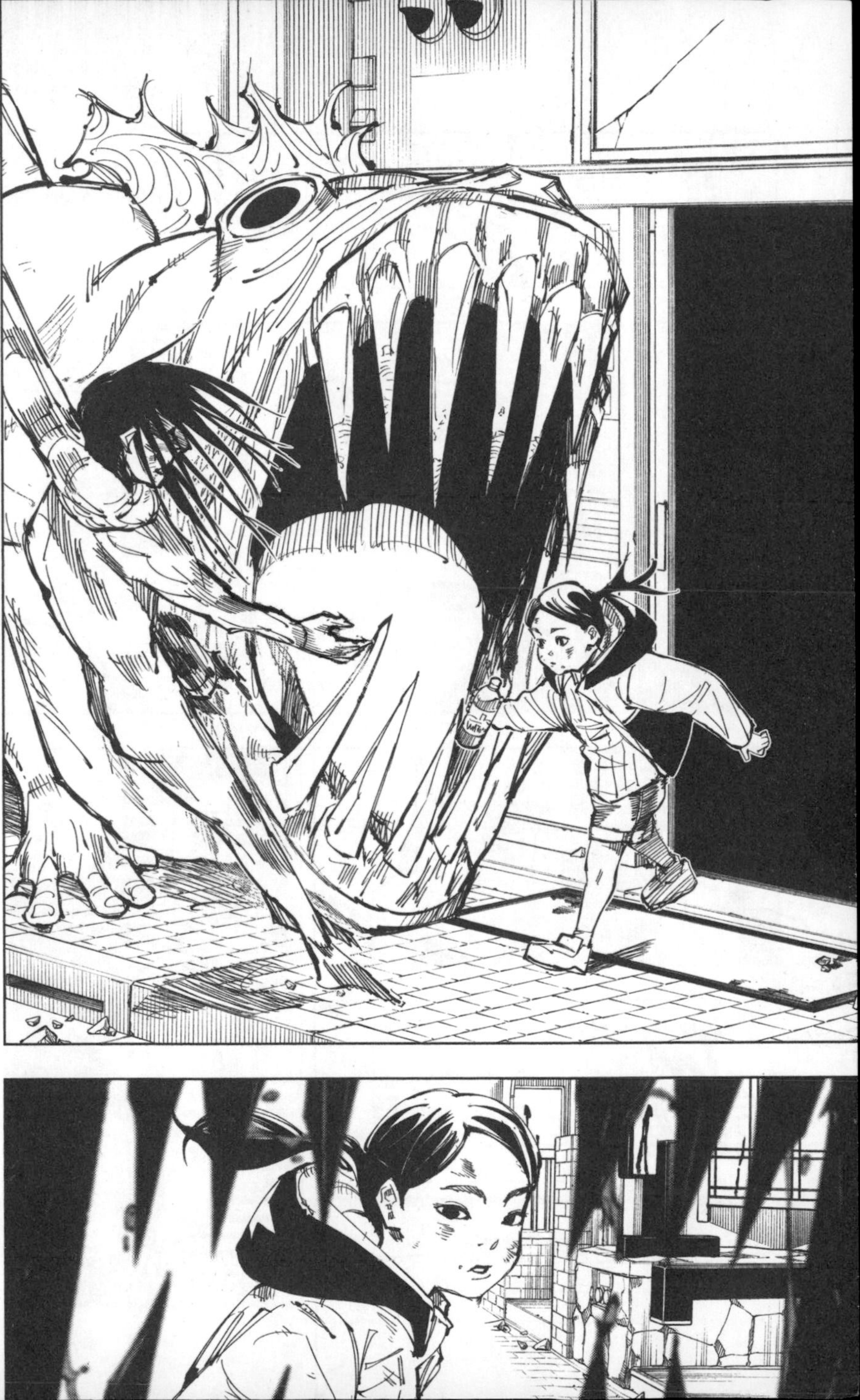

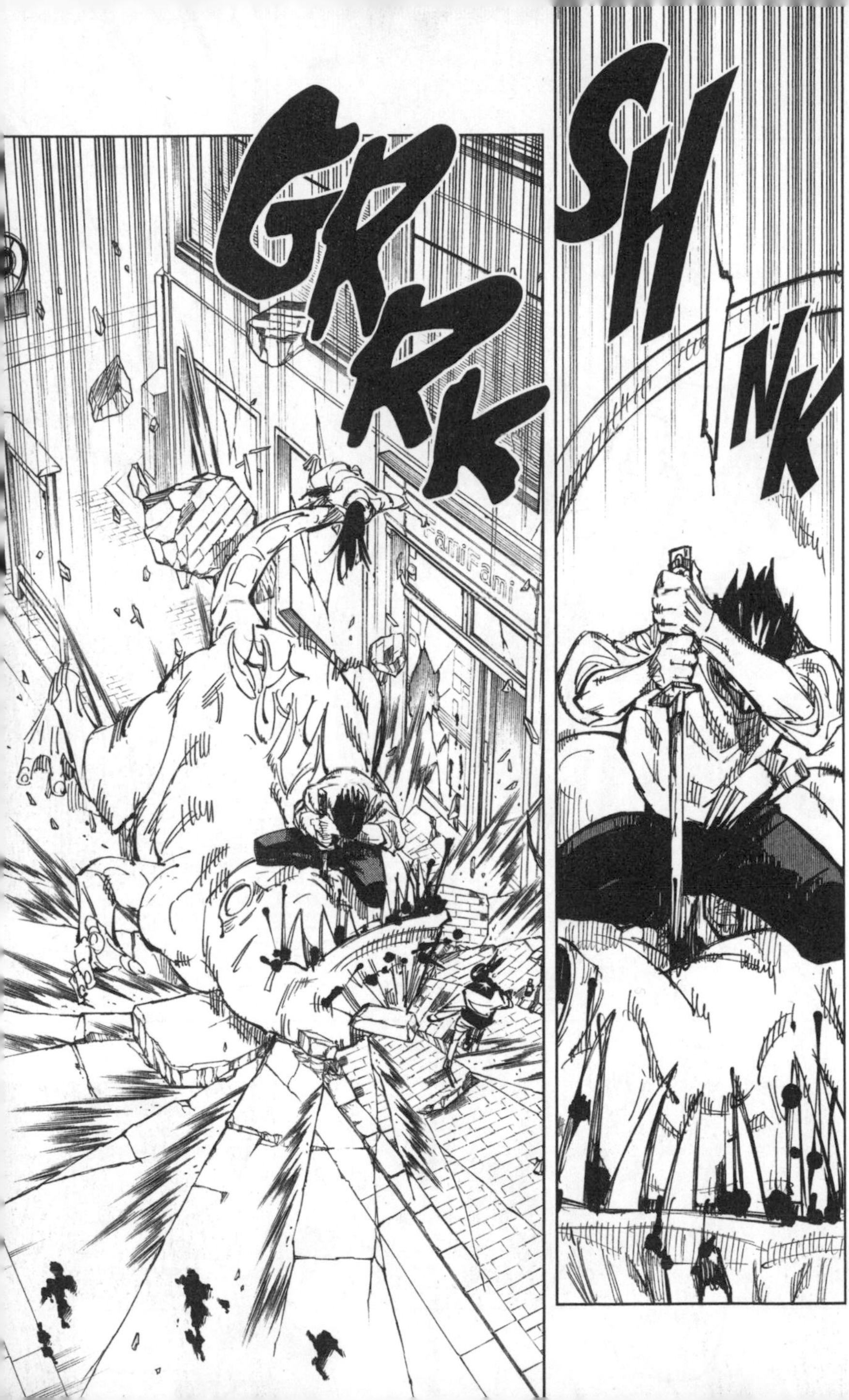
SHINK
GRRK
FamiFami

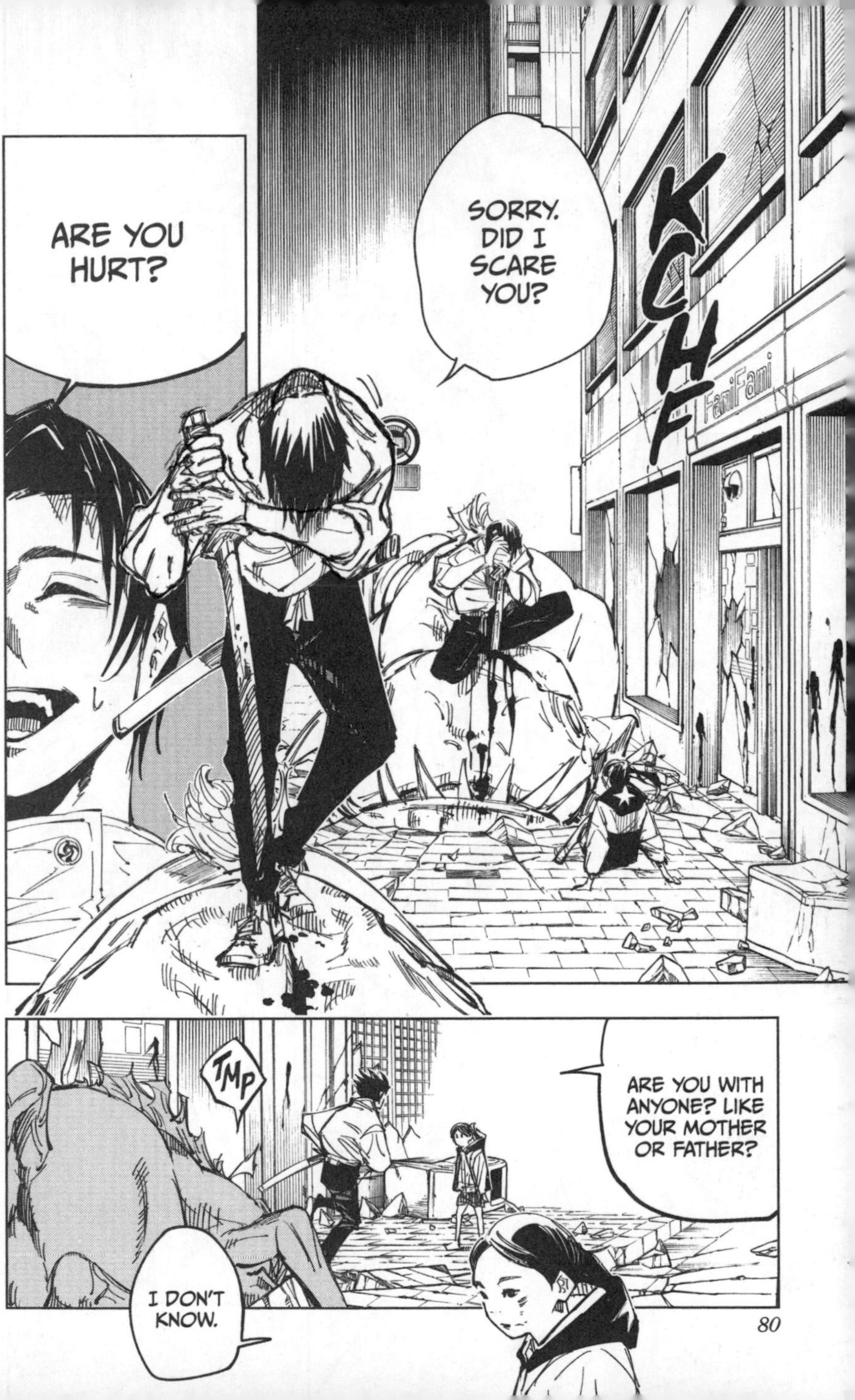
KCHF
FamiFami
SORRY. DID I SCARE YOU?
ARE YOU HURT?
ARE YOU WITH ANYONE? LIKE YOUR MOTHER OR FATHER?
TMP
I DON'T KNOW.

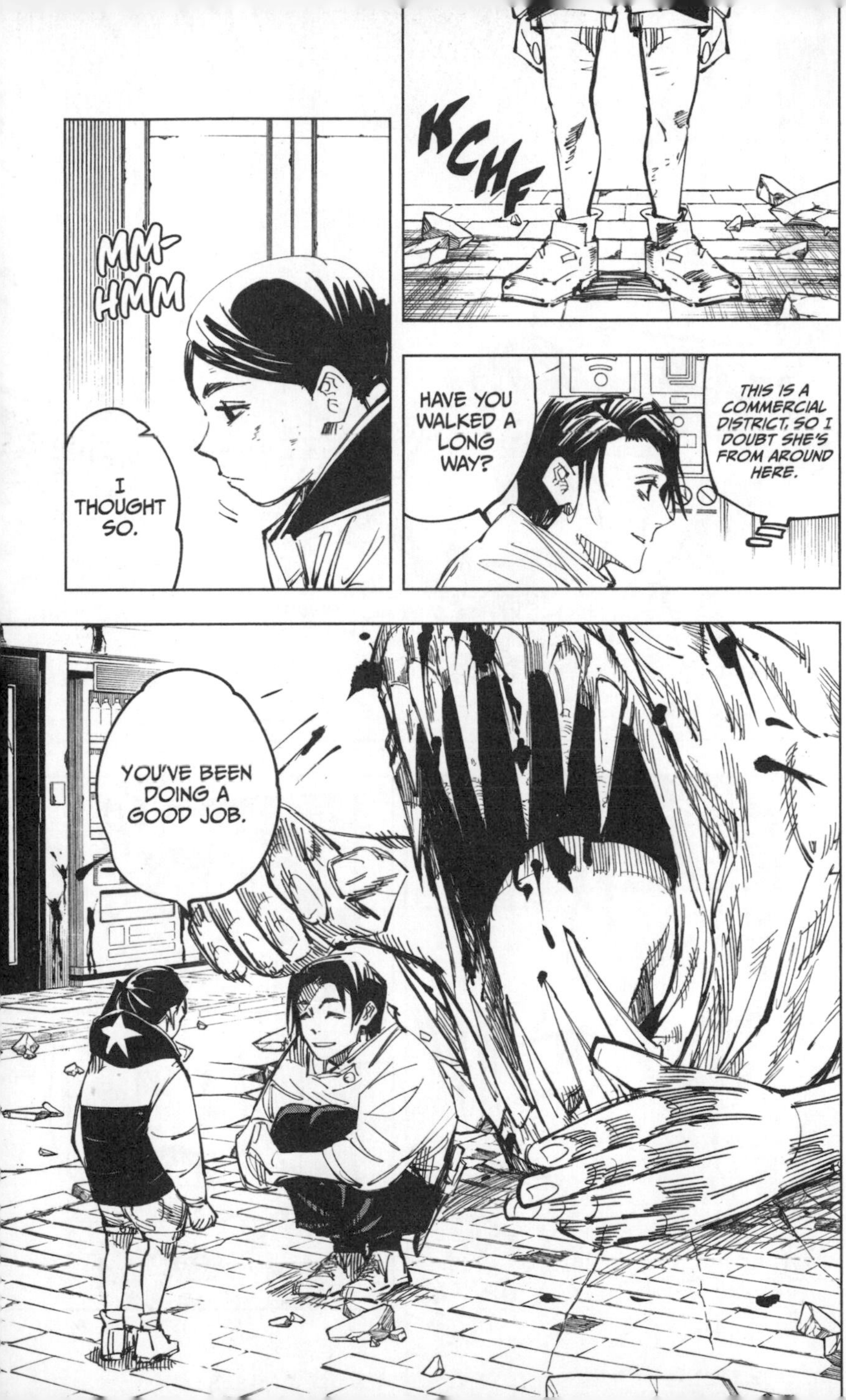
KCHF
THIS IS A COMMERCIAL DISTRICT, SO I DOUBT SHE'S FROM AROUND HERE.
HAVE YOU WALKED A LONG WAY?
MM-HMM
I THOUGHT SO.
YOU'VE BEEN DOING A GOOD JOB.

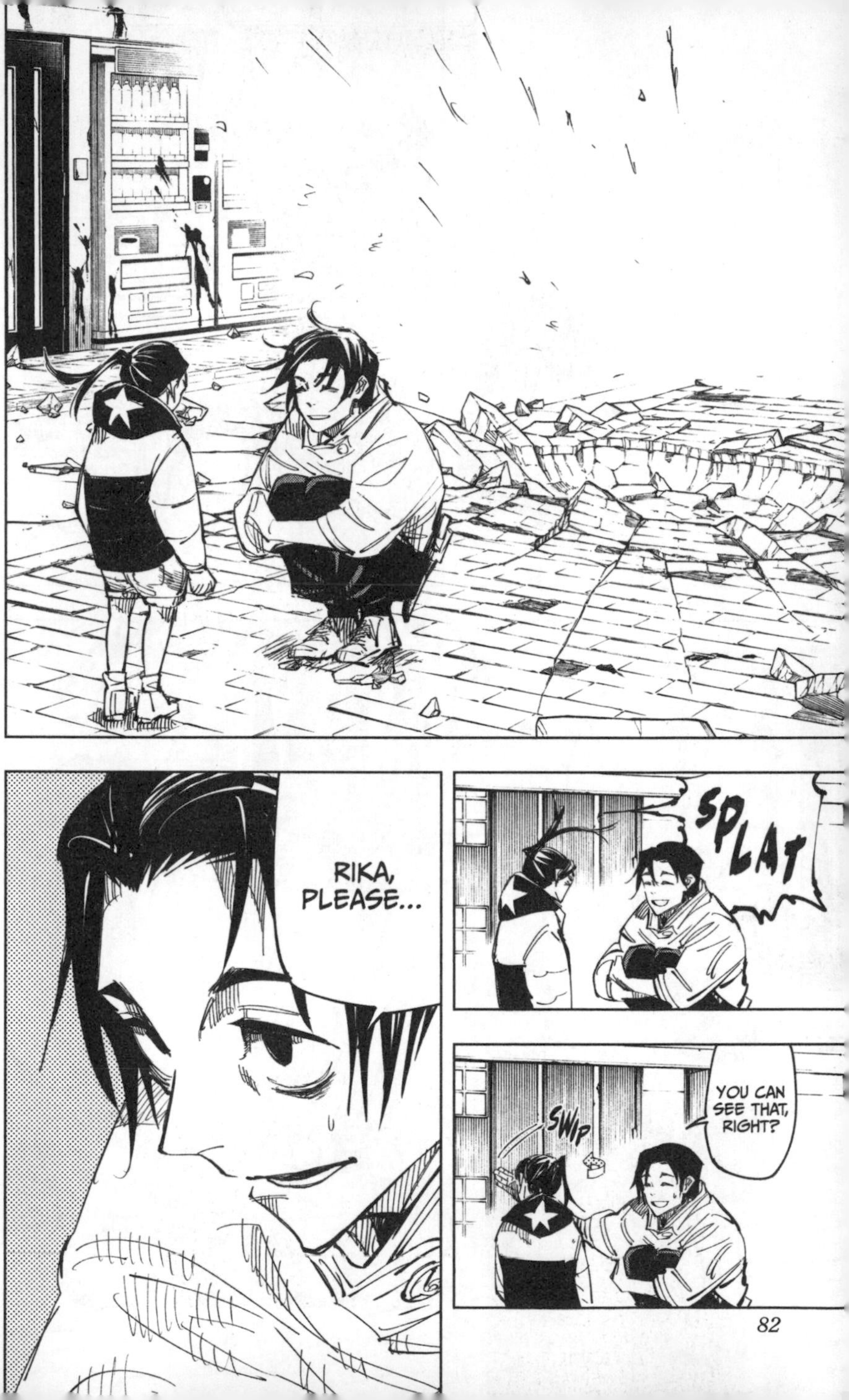
SPLAT
YOU CAN SEE THAT, RIGHT?
SWIP
RIKA, PLEASE...

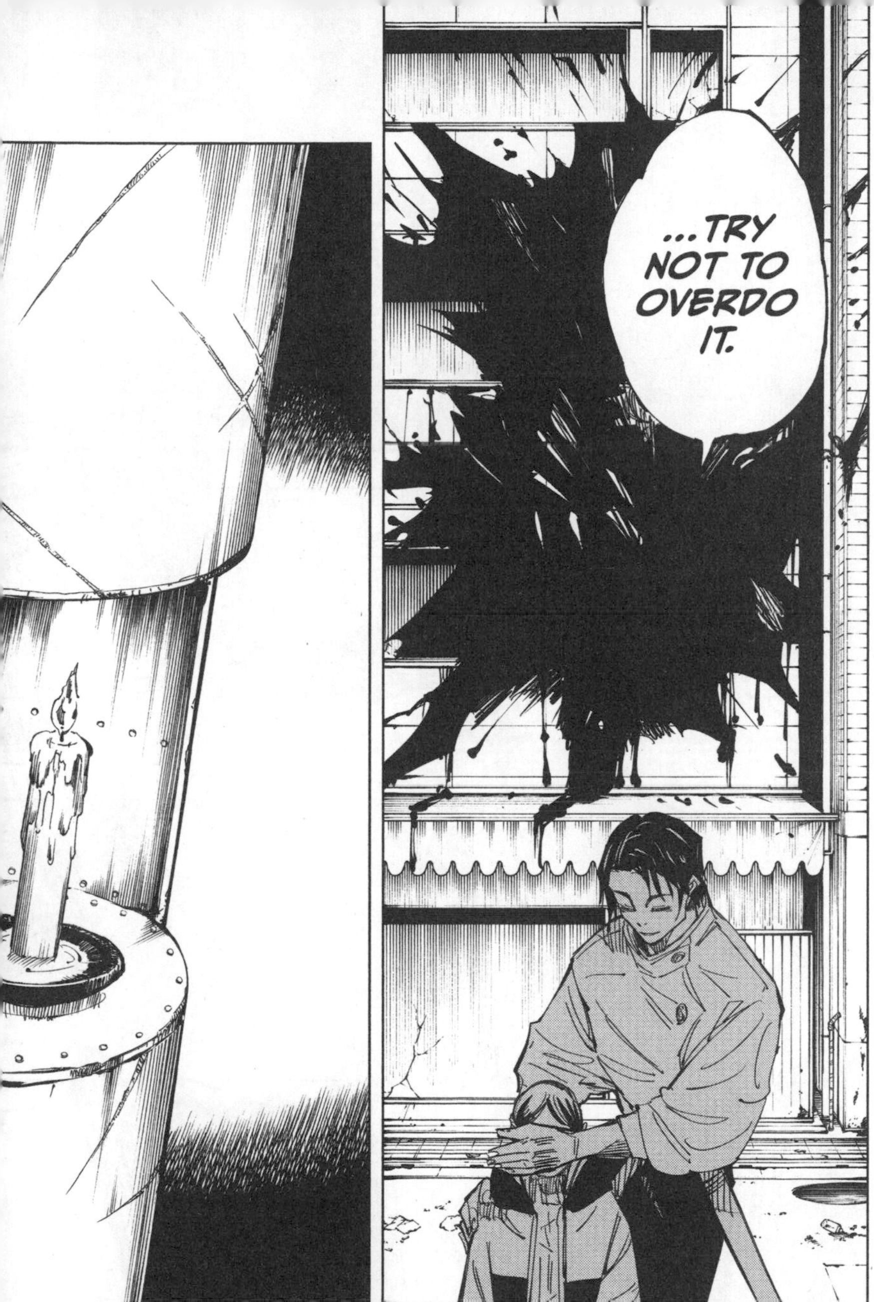
...TRY NOT TO OVERDO IT.

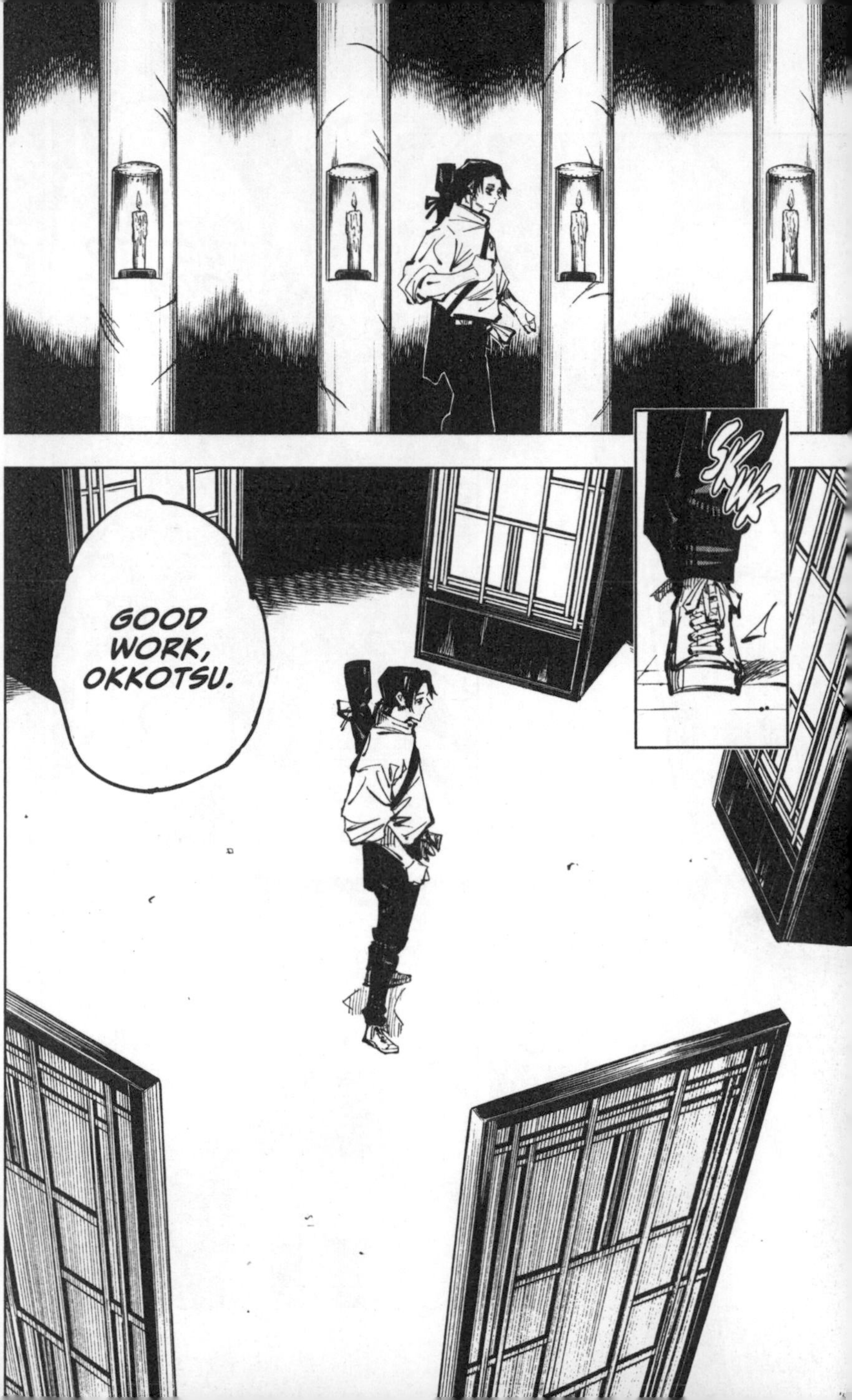
SKWK
GOOD WORK, OKKOTSU.

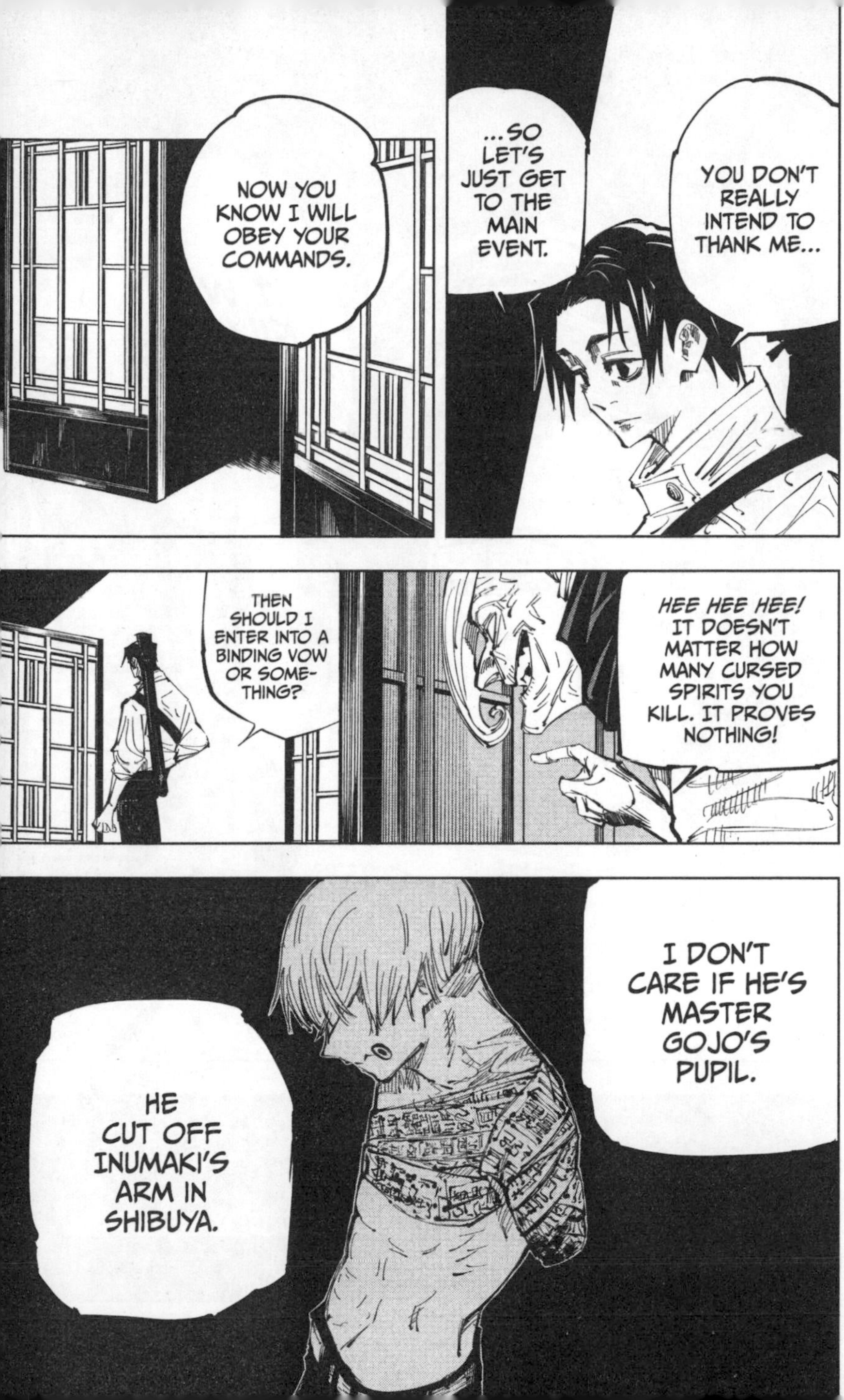
YOU DON'T REALLY INTEND TO THANK ME...
...SO LET'S JUST GET TO THE MAIN EVENT.
NOW YOU KNOW I WILL OBEY YOUR COMMANDS.
HEE HEE HEE! IT DOESN'T MATTER HOW MANY CURSED SPIRITS YOU KILL. IT PROVES NOTHING!
THEN SHOULD I ENTER INTO A BINDING VOW OR SOME-THING?
I DON'T CARE IF HE'S MASTER GOJO'S PUPIL.
HE CUT OFF INUMAKI'S ARM IN SHIBUYA.

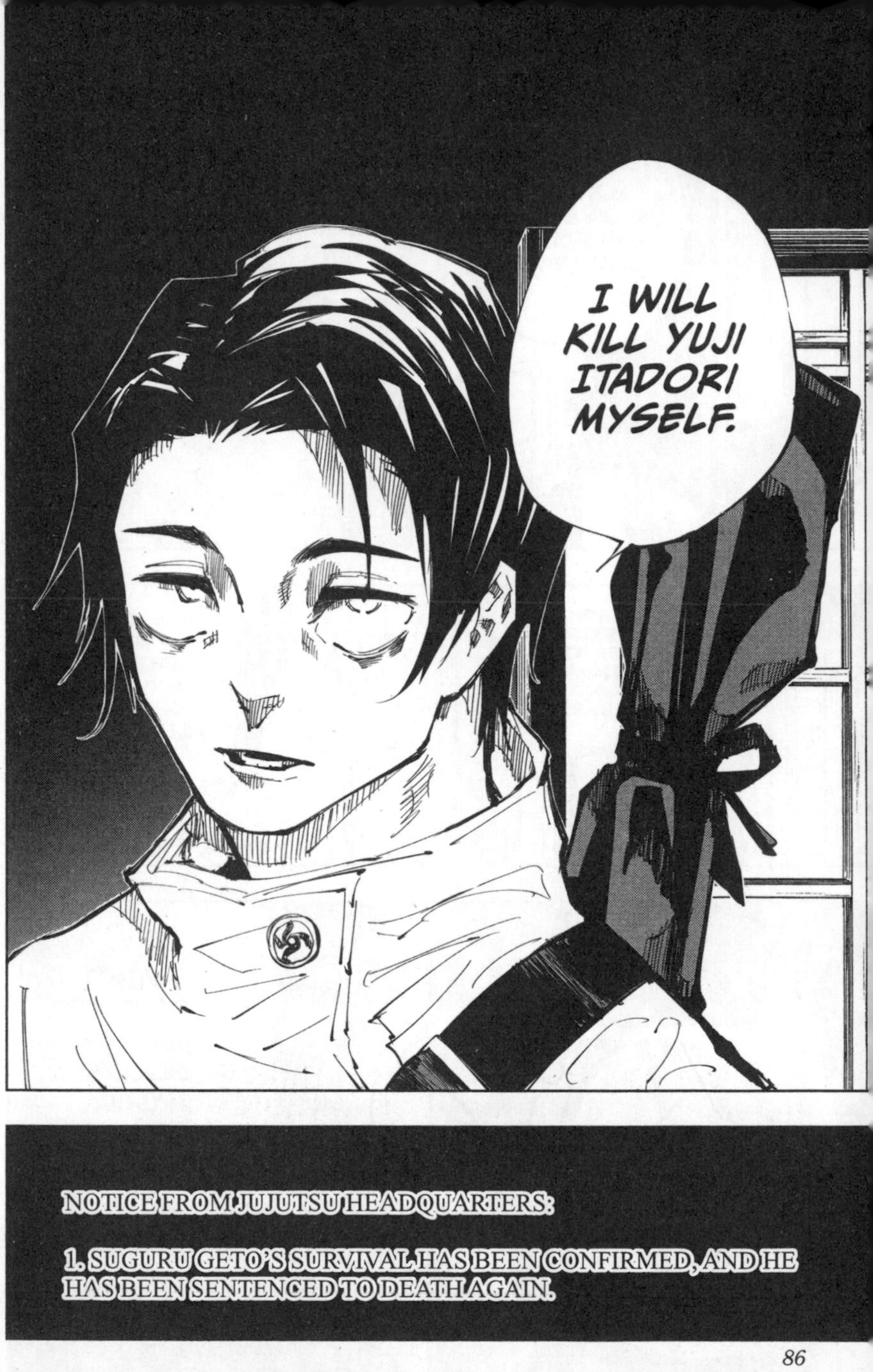
I WILL KILL YUJI ITADORI MYSELF.

NOTICE FROM JUJUTSU HEADQUARTERS:

1. SUGURU GETO'S SURVIVAL HAS BEEN CONFIRMED, AND HE HAS BEEN SENTENCED TO DEATH AGAIN.

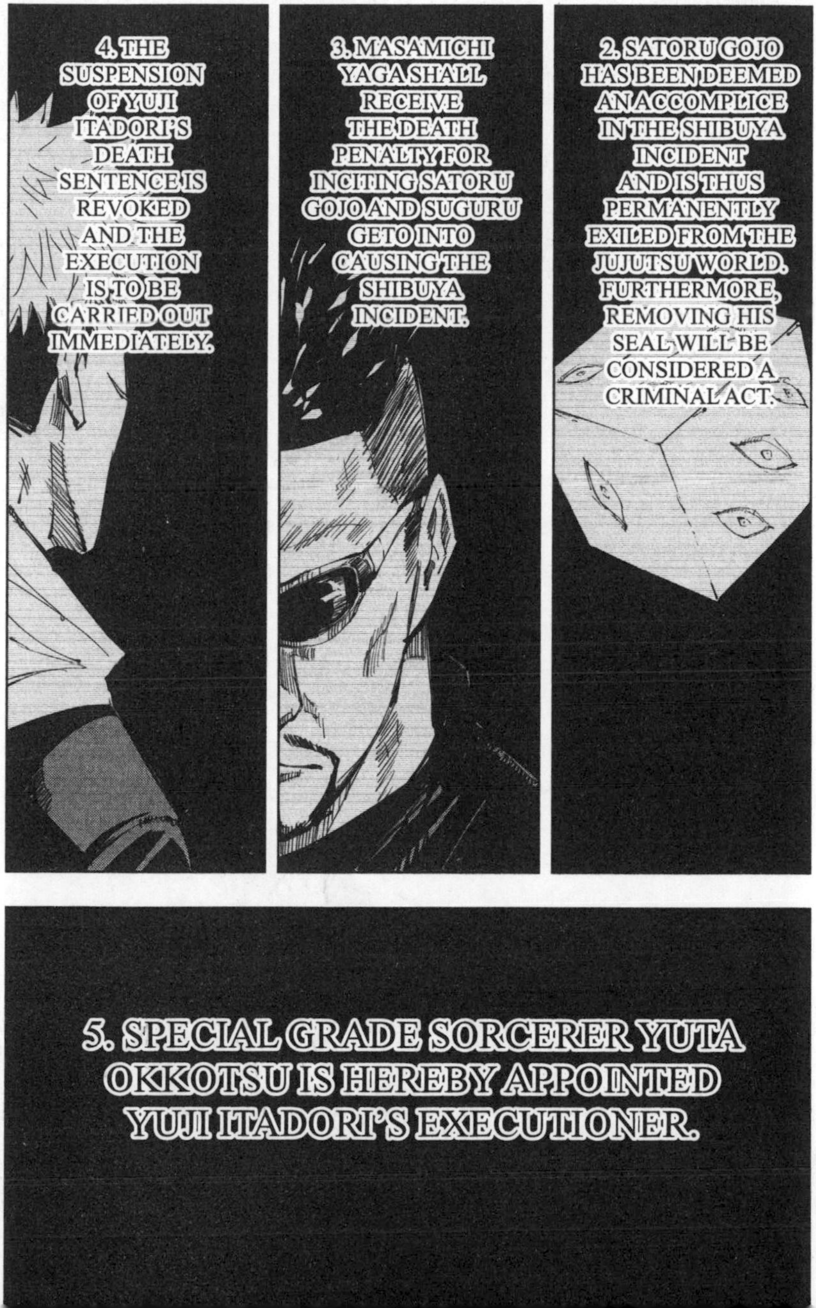
2. SATORU GOJO HAS BEEN DEEMED AN ACCOMPLICE IN THE SHIBUYA INCIDENT AND IS THUS PERMANENTLY EXILED FROM THE JUJUTSU WORLD. FURTHERMORE, REMOVING HIS SEAL WILL BE CONSIDERED A CRIMINAL ACT.
3. MASAMICHI YAGA SHALL RECEIVE THE DEATH PENALTY FOR INCITING SATORU GOJO AND SUGURU GETO INTO CAUSING THE SHIBUYA INCIDENT.
4. THE SUSPENSION OF YUJI ITADORI'S DEATH SENTENCE IS REVOKED AND THE EXECUTION IS TO BE CARRIED OUT IMMEDIATELY.
5. SPECIAL GRADE SORCERER YUTA OKKOTSU IS HEREBY APPOINTED YUJI ITADORI'S EXECUTIONER.

TSUKUMO

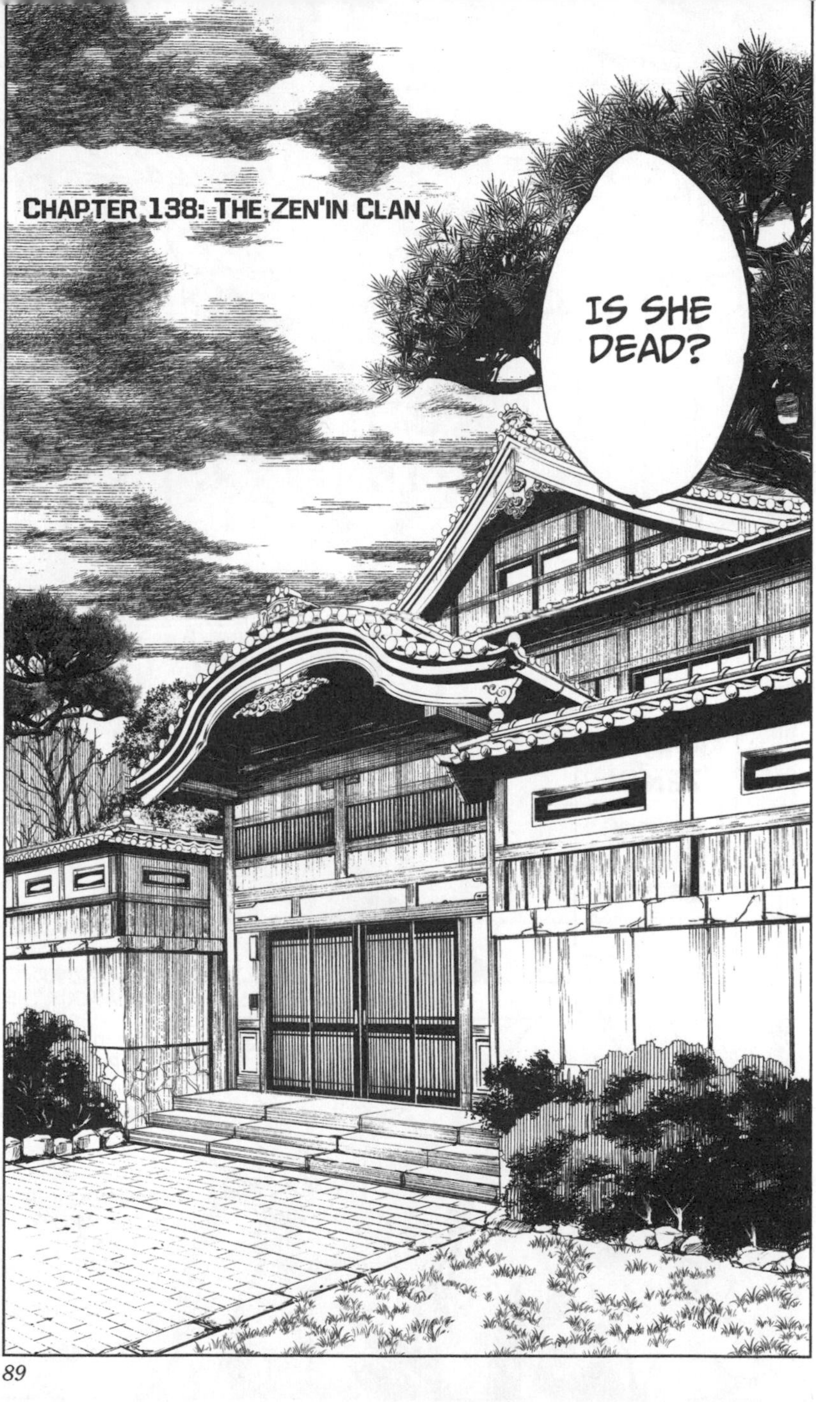
CHAPTER 138: THE ZEN'IN CLAN
IS SHE DEAD?

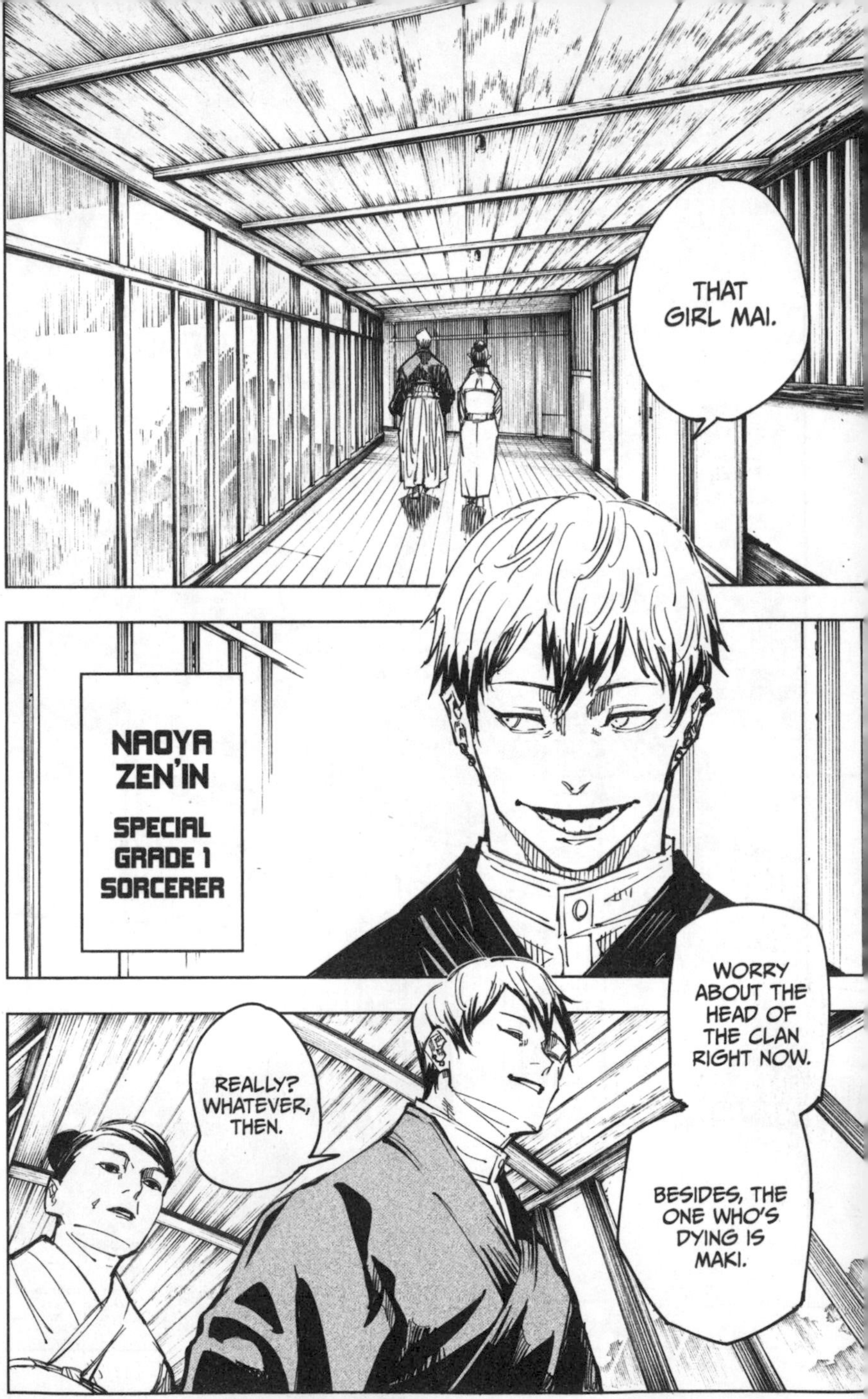
THAT GIRL MAI.
NAOYA ZEN'IN
SPECIAL GRADE 1 SORCERER
WORRY ABOUT THE HEAD OF THE CLAN RIGHT NOW.
REALLY? WHATEVER, THEN.
BESIDES, THE ONE WHO'S DYING IS MAKI.

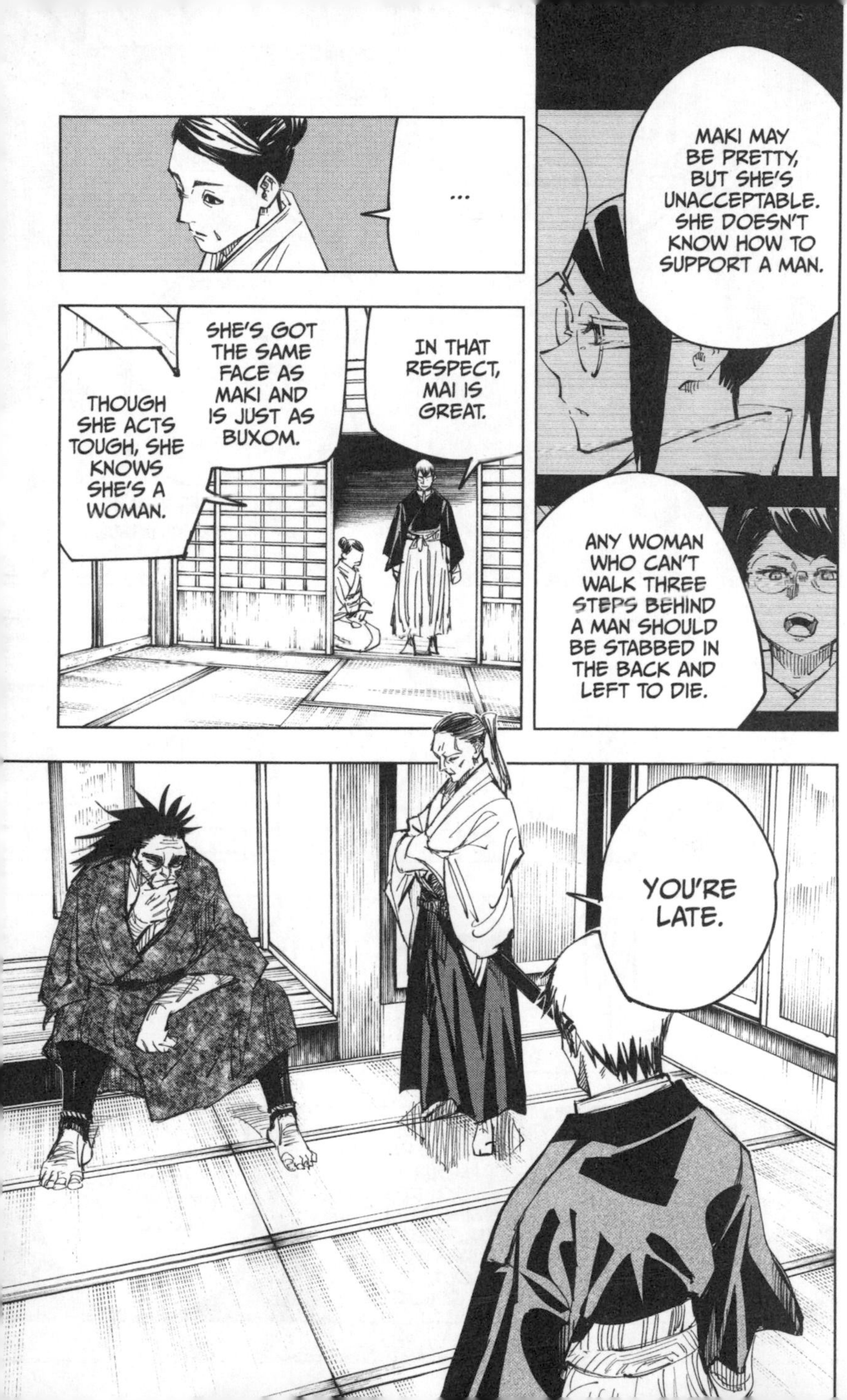
MAKI MAY BE PRETTY, BUT SHE'S UNACCEPTABLE. SHE DOESN'T KNOW HOW TO SUPPORT A MAN.
ANY WOMAN WHO CAN'T WALK THREE STEPS BEHIND A MAN SHOULD BE STABBED IN THE BACK AND LEFT TO DIE.
...
IN THAT RESPECT, MAI IS GREAT.
SHE'S GOT THE SAME FACE AS MAKI AND IS JUST AS BUXOM.
THOUGH SHE ACTS TOUGH, SHE KNOWS SHE'S A WOMAN.
YOU'RE LATE.

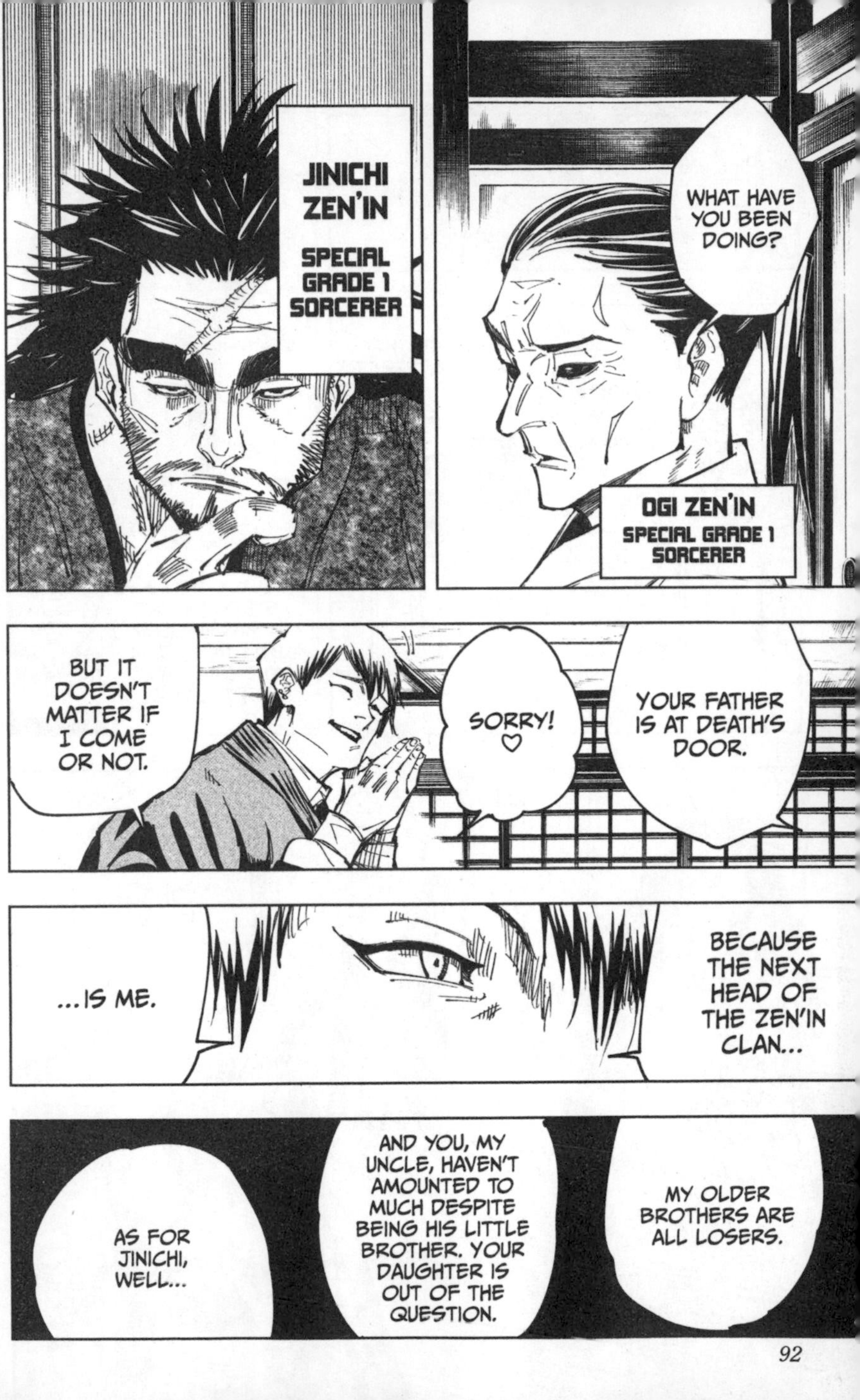
WHAT HAVE YOU BEEN DOING?
OGI ZEN'IN SPECIAL GRADE 1 SORCERER
JINICHI ZEN'IN SPECIAL GRADE 1 SORCERER
YOUR FATHER IS AT DEATH'S DOOR.
SORRY! ♡
BUT IT DOESN'T MATTER IF I COME OR NOT.
BECAUSE THE NEXT HEAD OF THE ZEN'IN CLAN...
...IS ME.
MY OLDER BROTHERS ARE ALL LOSERS.
AND YOU, MY UNCLE, HAVEN'T AMOUNTED TO MUCH DESPITE BEING HIS LITTLE BROTHER. YOUR DAUGHTER IS OUT OF THE QUESTION.
AS FOR JINICHI, WELL...

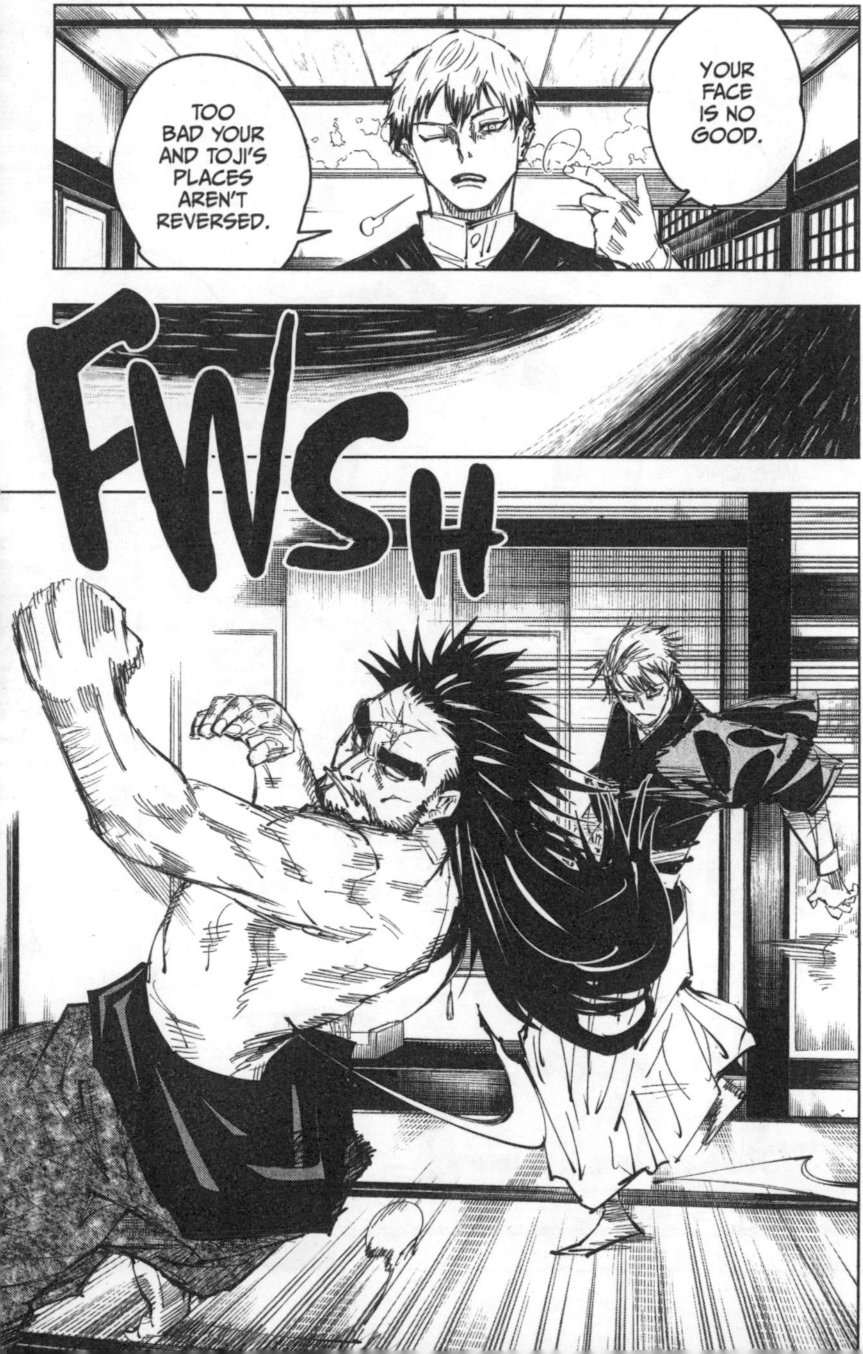
YOUR FACE IS NO GOOD.
TOO BAD YOUR AND TOJI'S PLACES AREN'T REVERSED.
FWSH

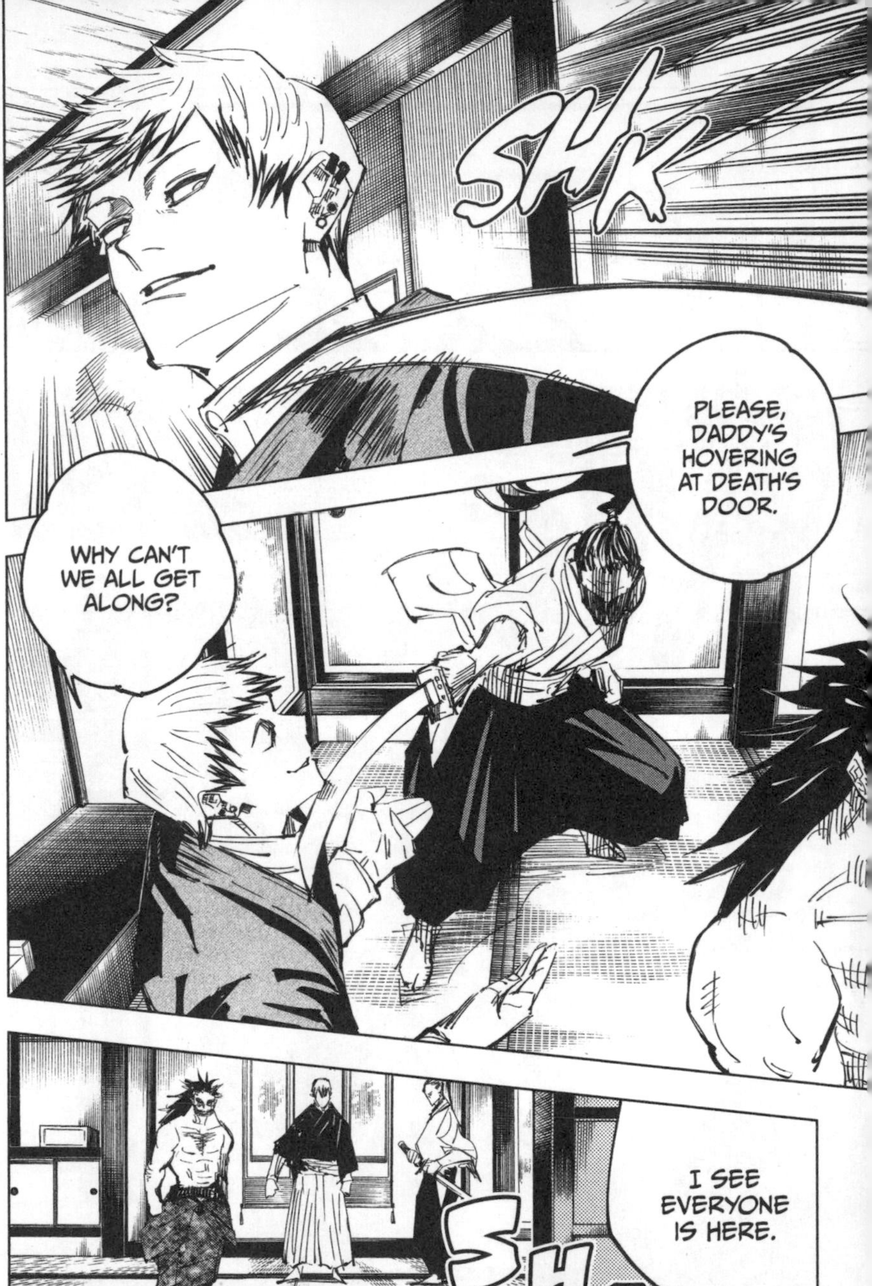
SHK
PLEASE, DADDY'S HOVERING AT DEATH'S DOOR.
WHY CAN'T WE ALL GET ALONG?
I SEE EVERYONE IS HERE.
SHF..

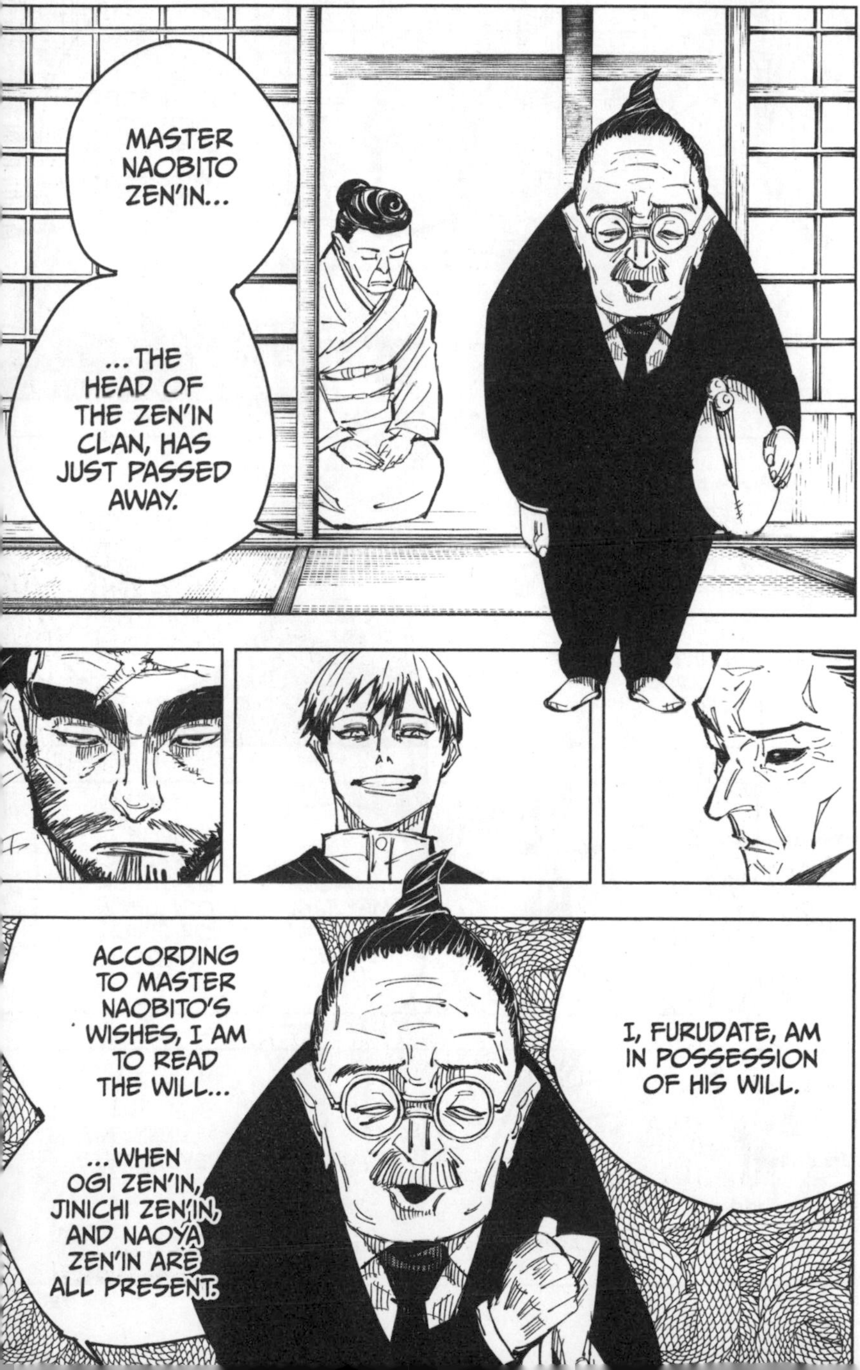
MASTER NAOBITO ZEN'IN... ...THE HEAD OF THE ZEN'IN CLAN, HAS JUST PASSED AWAY.
I, FURUDATE, AM IN POSSESSION OF HIS WILL.
ACCORDING TO MASTER NAOBITO'S WISHES, I AM TO READ THE WILL...
...WHEN OGI ZEN'IN, JINICHI ZEN'IN, AND NAOYA ZEN'IN ARE ALL PRESENT.

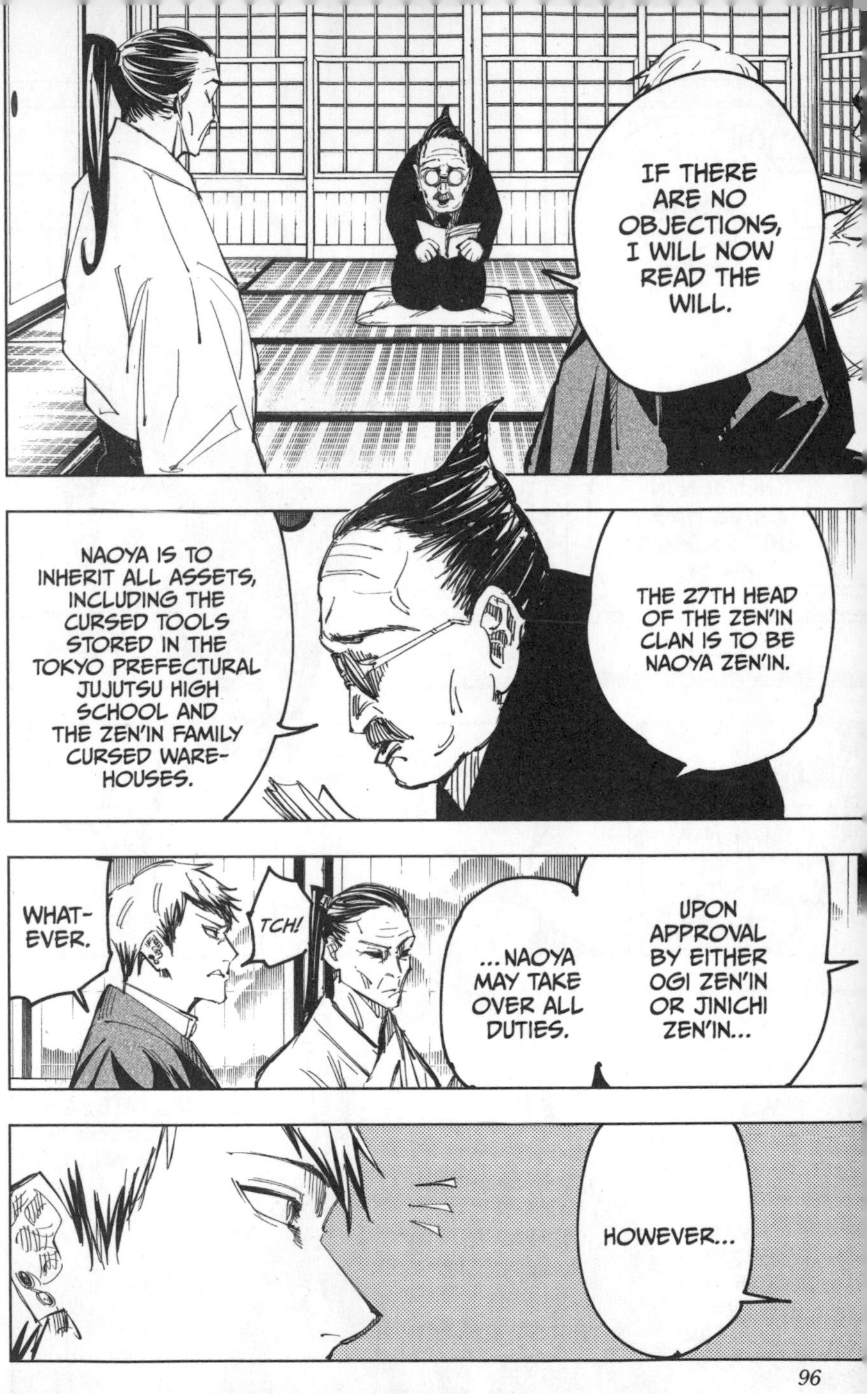
IF THERE ARE NO OBJECTIONS, I WILL NOW READ THE WILL.
THE 27TH HEAD OF THE ZEN'IN CLAN IS TO BE NAOYA ZEN'IN.
NAOYA IS TO INHERIT ALL ASSETS, INCLUDING THE CURSED TOOLS STORED IN THE TOKYO PREFECTURAL JUJUTSU HIGH SCHOOL AND THE ZEN'IN FAMILY CURSED WARE-HOUSES.
UPON APPROVAL BY EITHER OGI ZEN'IN OR JINICHI ZEN'IN...
...NAOYA MAY TAKE OVER ALL DUTIES.
TCH!
WHAT-EVER.
HOWEVER...

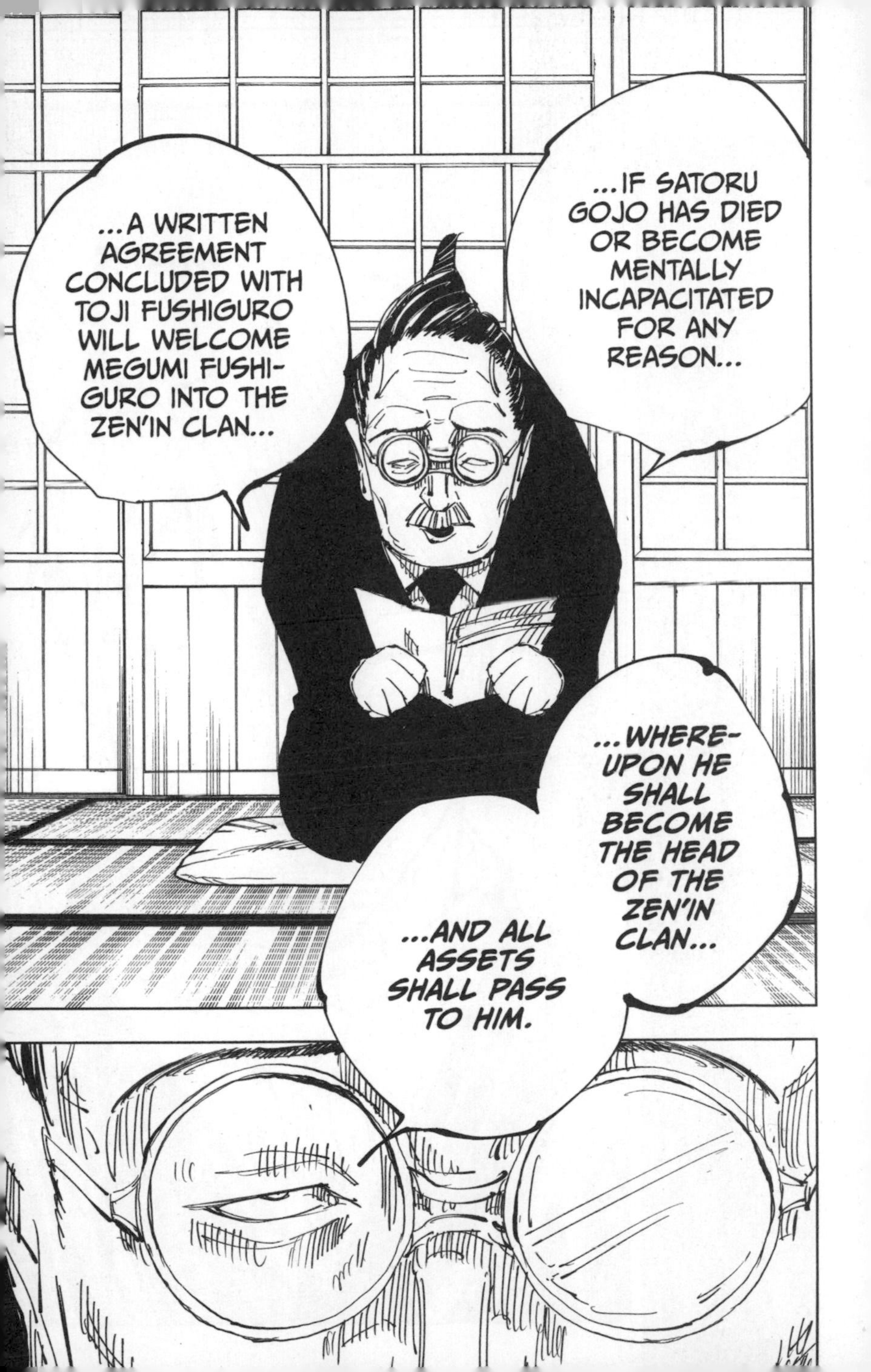
...IF SATORU GOJO HAS DIED OR BECOME MENTALLY INCAPACITATED FOR ANY REASON...
...A WRITTEN AGREEMENT CONCLUDED WITH TOJI FUSHIGURO WILL WELCOME MEGUMI FUSHI-GURO INTO THE ZEN'IN CLAN...
...WHERE-UPON HE SHALL BECOME THE HEAD OF THE ZEN'IN CLAN...
...AND ALL ASSETS SHALL PASS TO HIM.

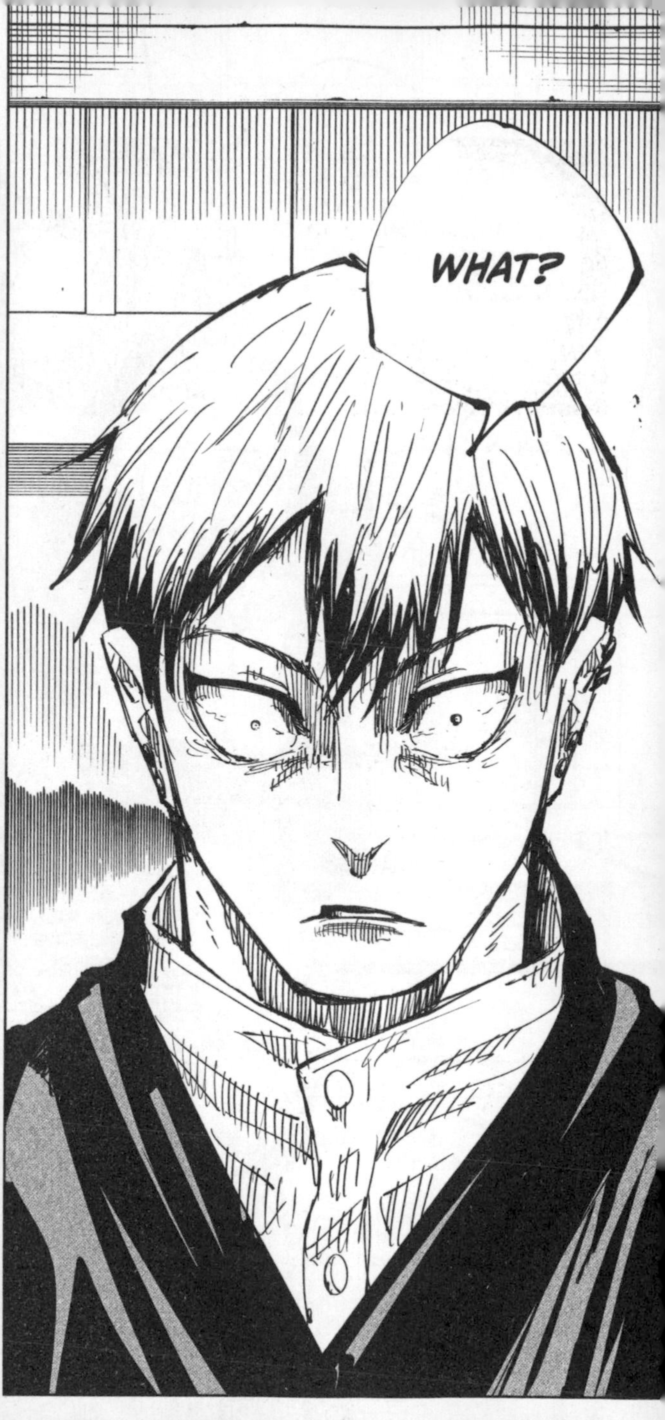
WHAT?

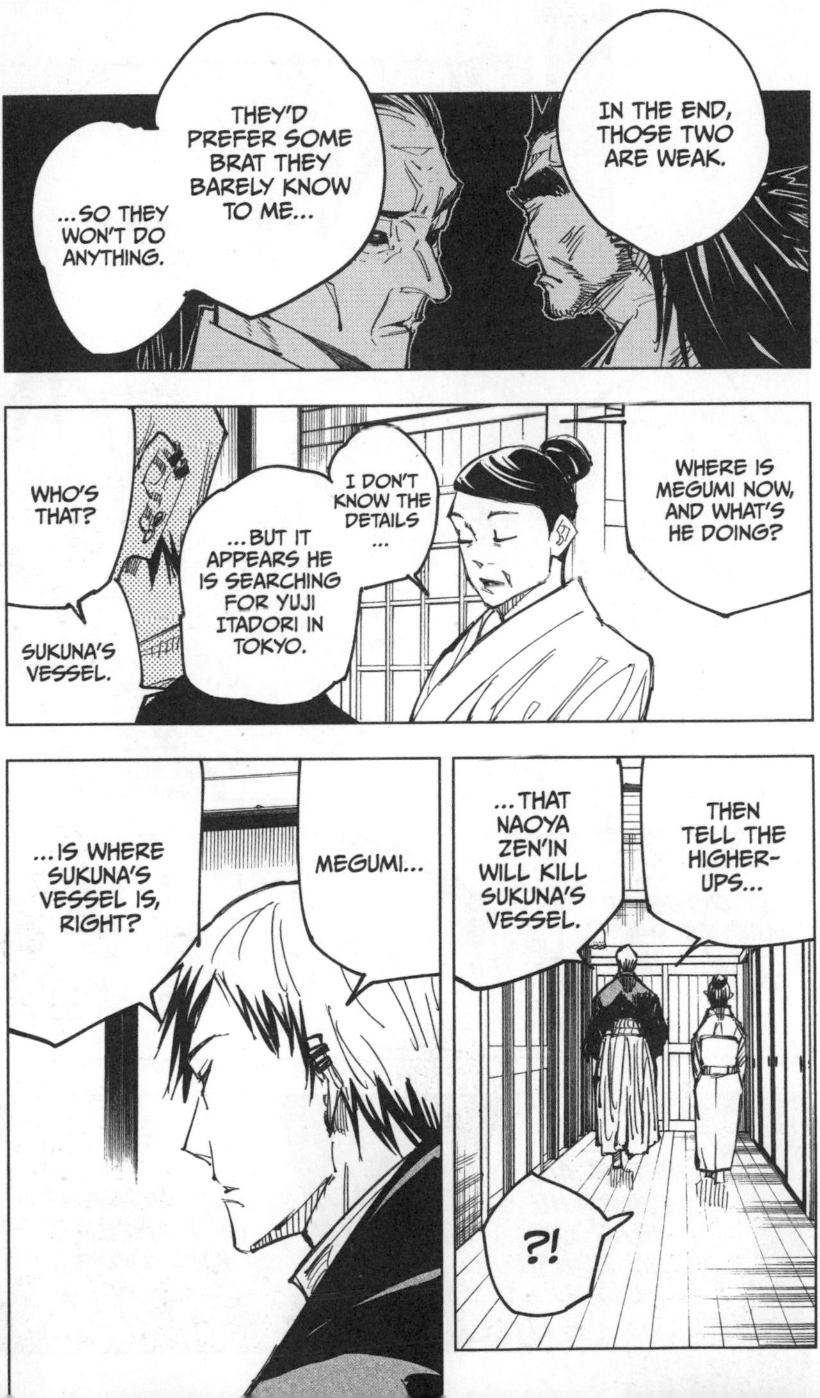
IN THE END, THOSE TWO ARE WEAK.
THEY'D PREFER SOME BRAT THEY BARELY KNOW TO ME...
...SO THEY WON'T DO ANYTHING.
WHERE IS MEGUMI NOW, AND WHAT'S HE DOING?
I DON'T KNOW THE DETAILS...
...BUT IT APPEARS HE IS SEARCHING FOR YUJI ITADORI IN TOKYO.
WHO'S THAT?
SUKUNA'S VESSEL.
THEN TELL THE HIGHER-UPS...
...THAT NAOYA ZEN'IN WILL KILL SUKUNA'S VESSEL.
?!
MEGUMI...
...IS WHERE SUKUNA'S VESSEL IS, RIGHT?

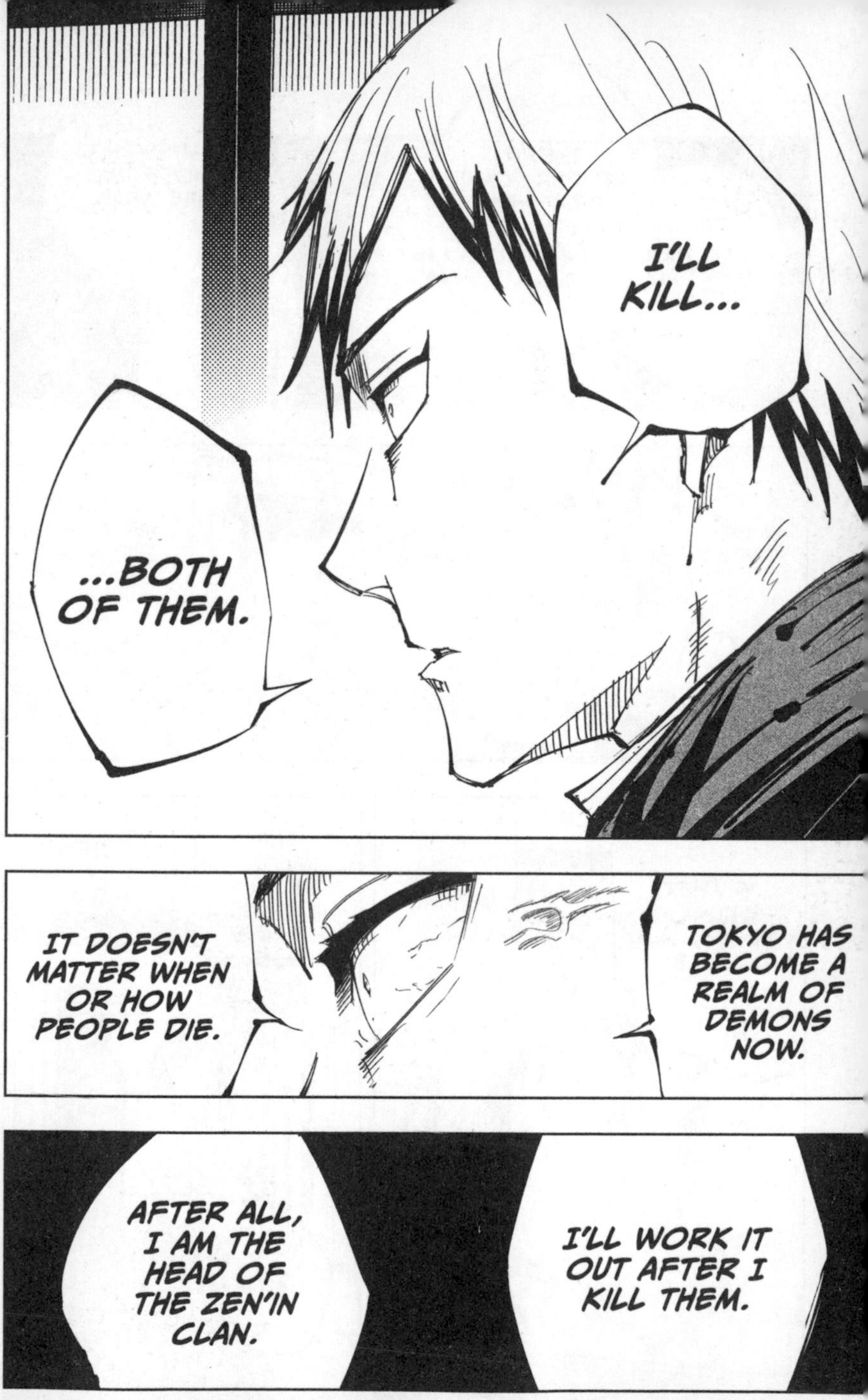
I'LL KILL...
...BOTH OF THEM.
TOKYO HAS BECOME A REALM OF DEMONS NOW.
IT DOESN'T MATTER WHEN OR HOW PEOPLE DIE.
I'LL WORK IT OUT AFTER I KILL THEM.
AFTER ALL, I AM THE HEAD OF THE ZEN'IN CLAN.

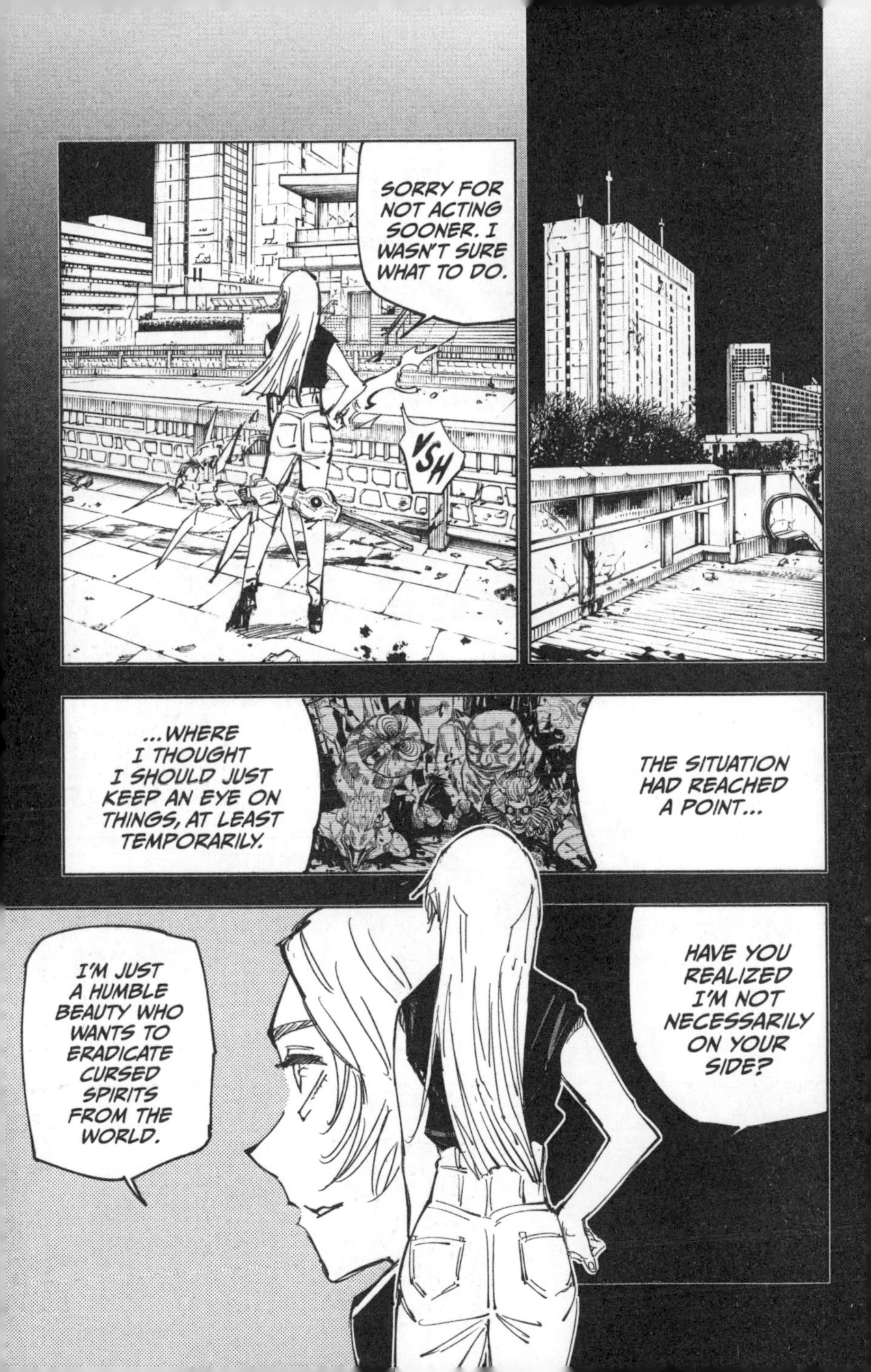
SORRY FOR NOT ACTING SOONER. I WASN'T SURE WHAT TO DO.
VSH
THE SITUATION HAD REACHED A POINT...
...WHERE I THOUGHT I SHOULD JUST KEEP AN EYE ON THINGS, AT LEAST TEMPORARILY.
HAVE YOU REALIZED I'M NOT NECESSARILY ON YOUR SIDE?
I'M JUST A HUMBLE BEAUTY WHO WANTS TO ERADICATE CURSED SPIRITS FROM THE WORLD.

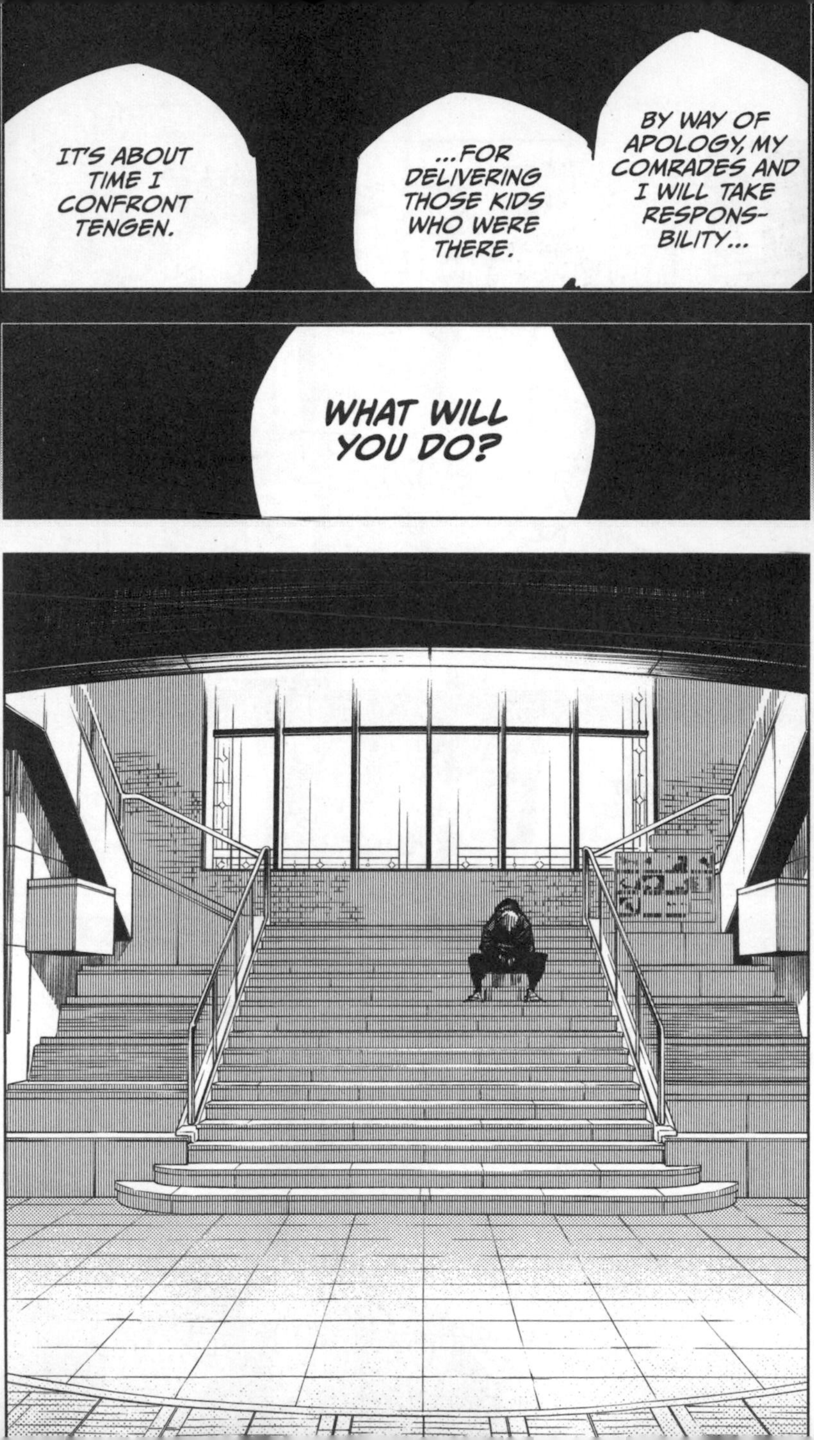
BY WAY OF APOLOGY, MY COMRADES AND I WILL TAKE RESPONSIBILITY...
...FOR DELIVERING THOSE KIDS WHO WERE THERE.
IT'S ABOUT TIME I CONFRONT TENGEN.
WHAT WILL YOU DO?

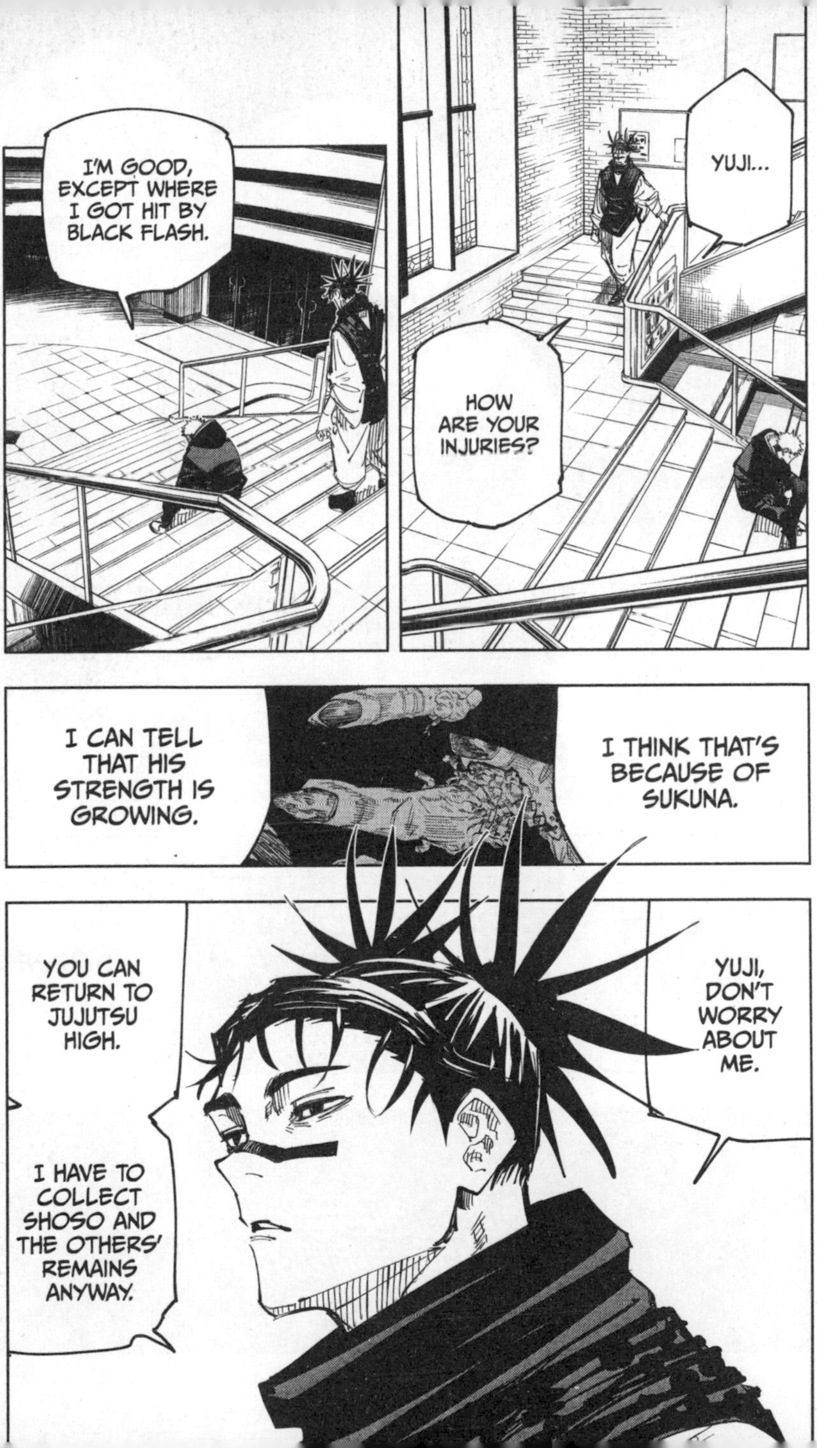
YUJI...
HOW ARE YOUR INJURIES?
I'M GOOD, EXCEPT WHERE I GOT HIT BY BLACK FLASH.
I THINK THAT'S BECAUSE OF SUKUNA.
I CAN TELL THAT HIS STRENGTH IS GROWING.
YUJI, DON'T WORRY ABOUT ME.
YOU CAN RETURN TO JUJUTSU HIGH.
I HAVE TO COLLECT SHOSO AND THE OTHERS' REMAINS ANYWAY.

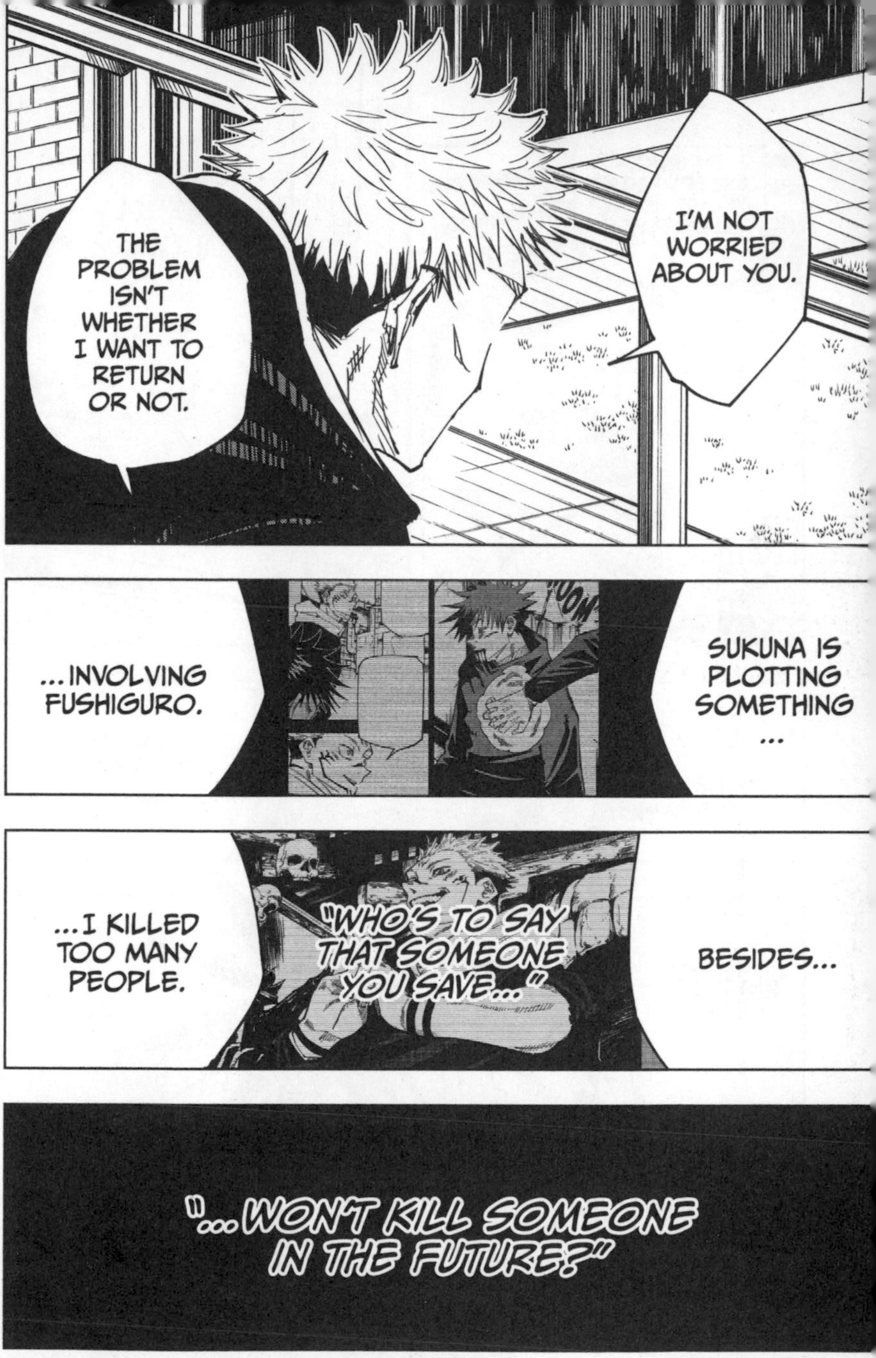
I'M NOT WORRIED ABOUT YOU.
THE PROBLEM ISN'T WHETHER I WANT TO RETURN OR NOT.
SUKUNA IS PLOTTING SOMETHING ...
...INVOLVING FUSHIGURO.
BESIDES...
"WHO'S TO SAY THAT SOMEONE YOU SAVE..."
...I KILLED TOO MANY PEOPLE.
"...WON'T KILL SOMEONE IN THE FUTURE?"

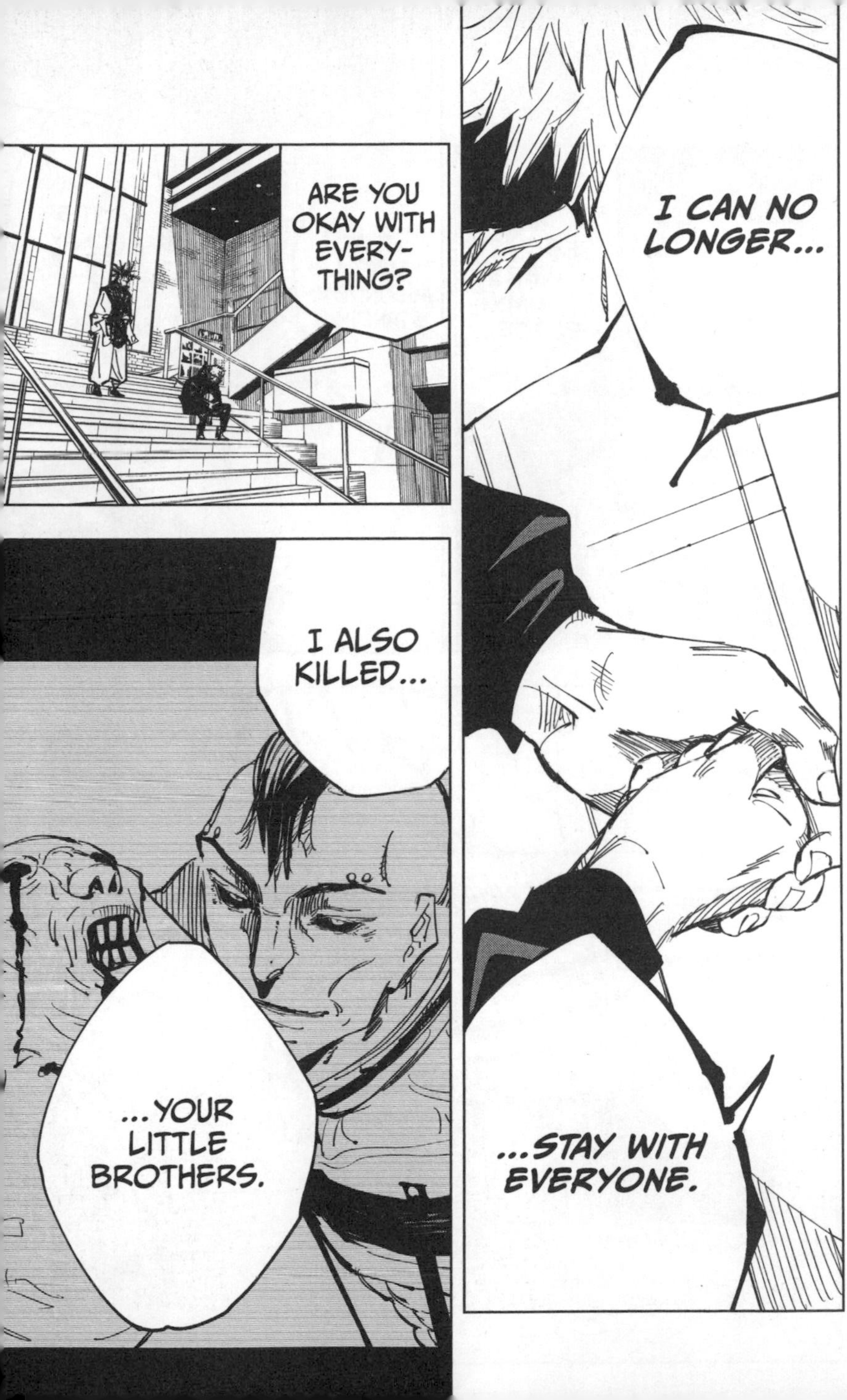
I CAN NO LONGER...
...STAY WITH EVERYONE.
ARE YOU OKAY WITH EVERY-THING?
I ALSO KILLED...
...YOUR LITTLE BROTHERS.

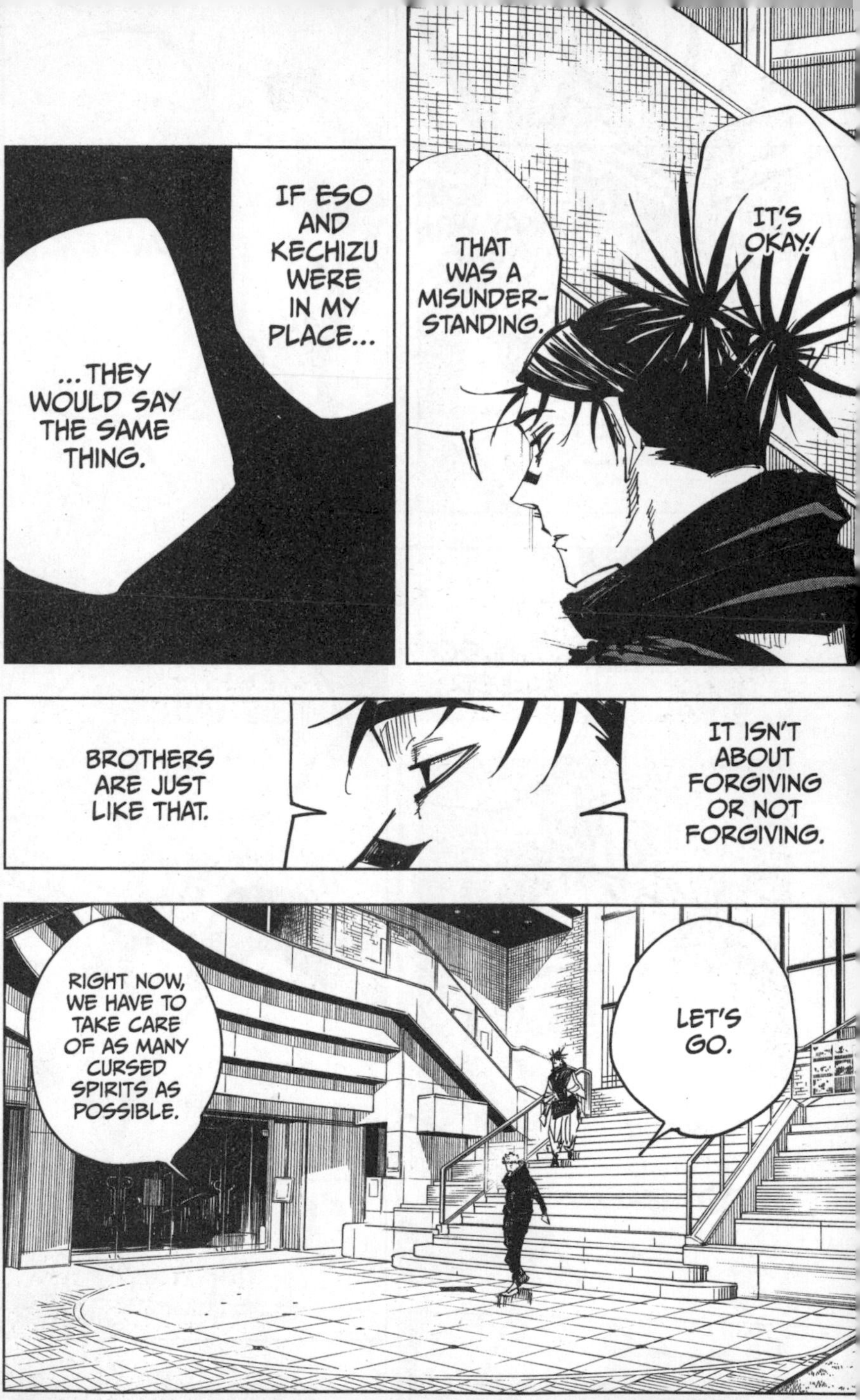
IT'S OKAY!
THAT WAS A MISUNDERSTANDING.
IF ESO AND KECHIZU WERE IN MY PLACE...
...THEY WOULD SAY THE SAME THING.
IT ISN'T ABOUT FORGIVING OR NOT FORGIVING.
BROTHERS ARE JUST LIKE THAT.
LET'S GO.
RIGHT NOW, WE HAVE TO TAKE CARE OF AS MANY CURSED SPIRITS AS POSSIBLE.

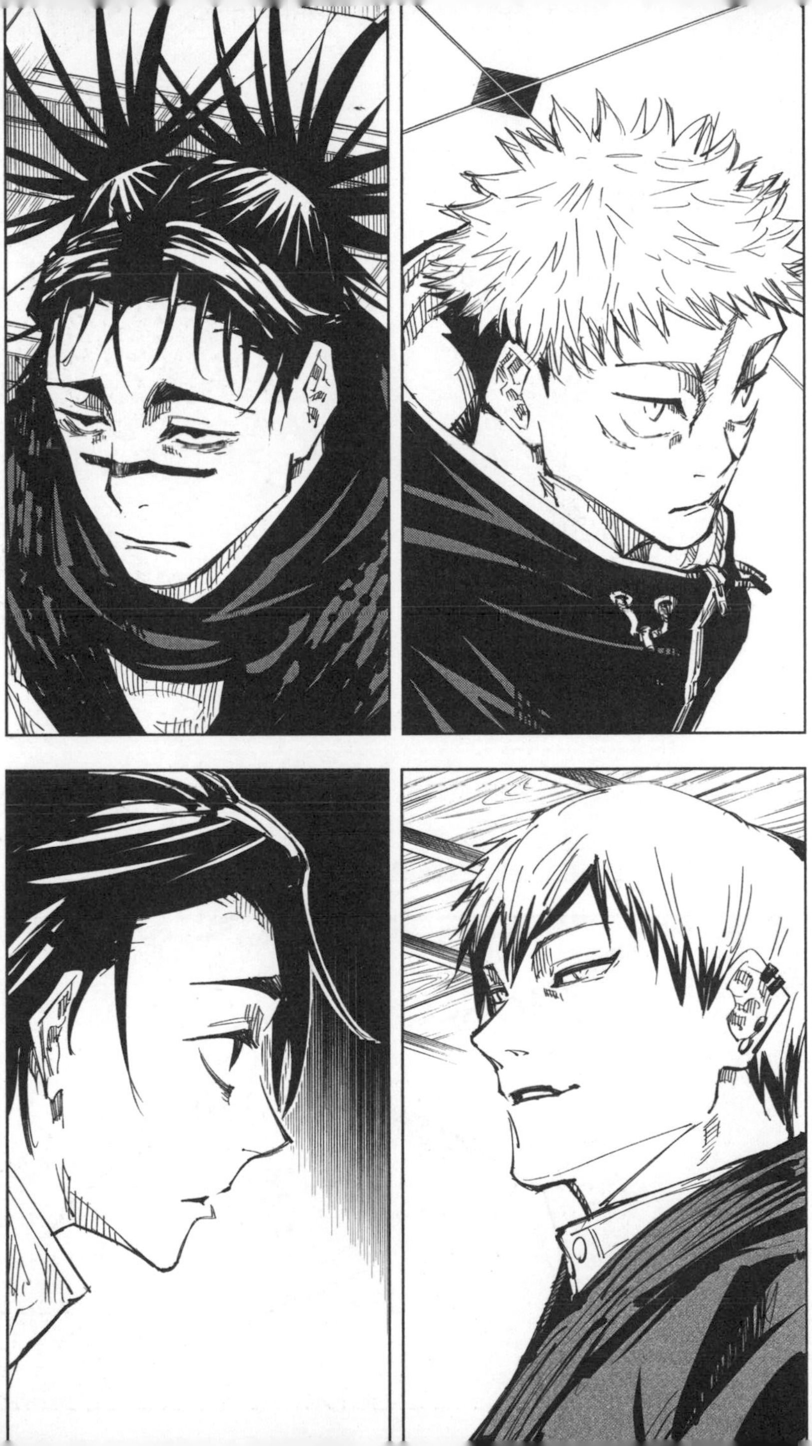

CHOSO

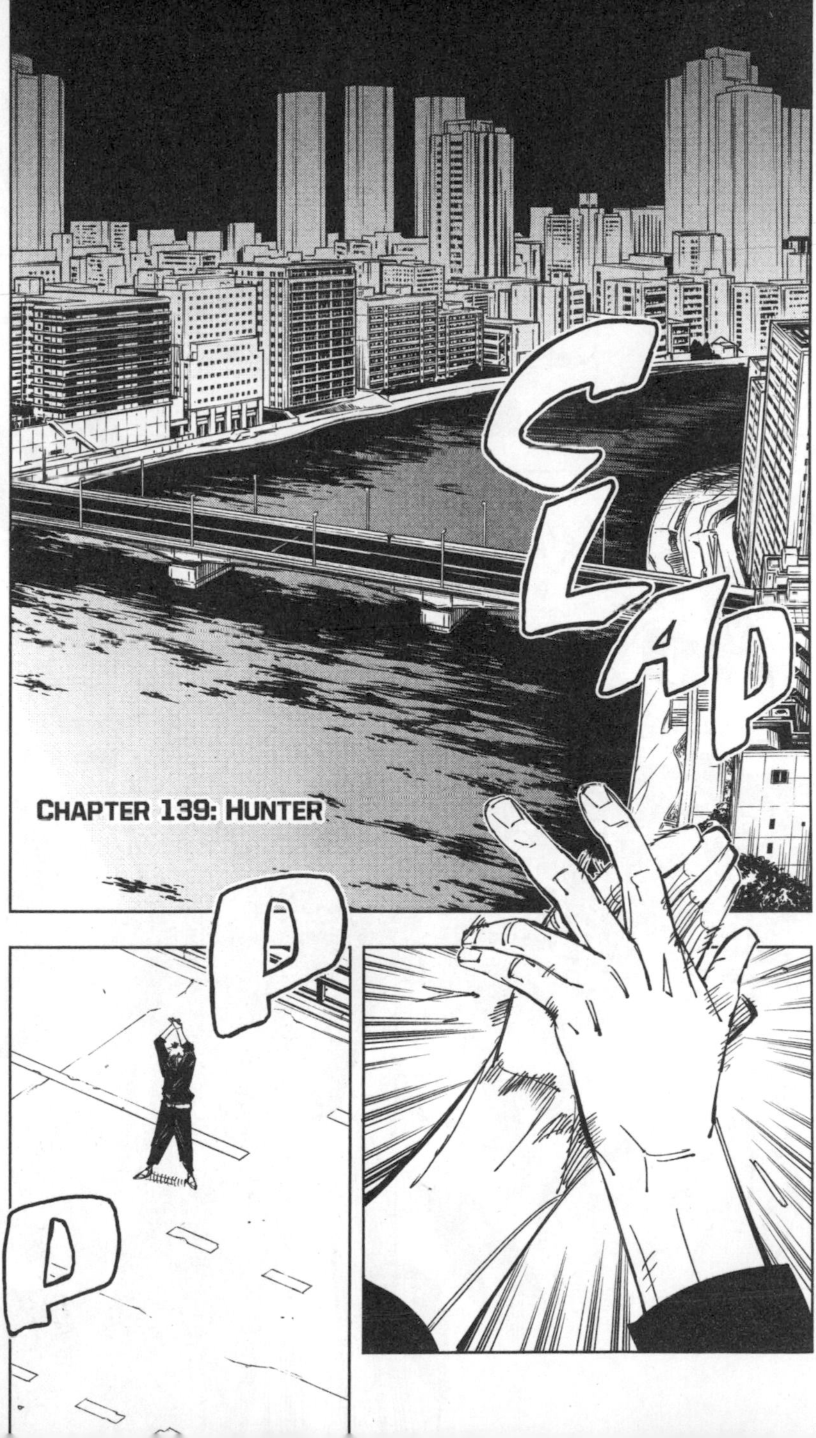
CLAP
CHAPTER 139: HUNTER
P
P

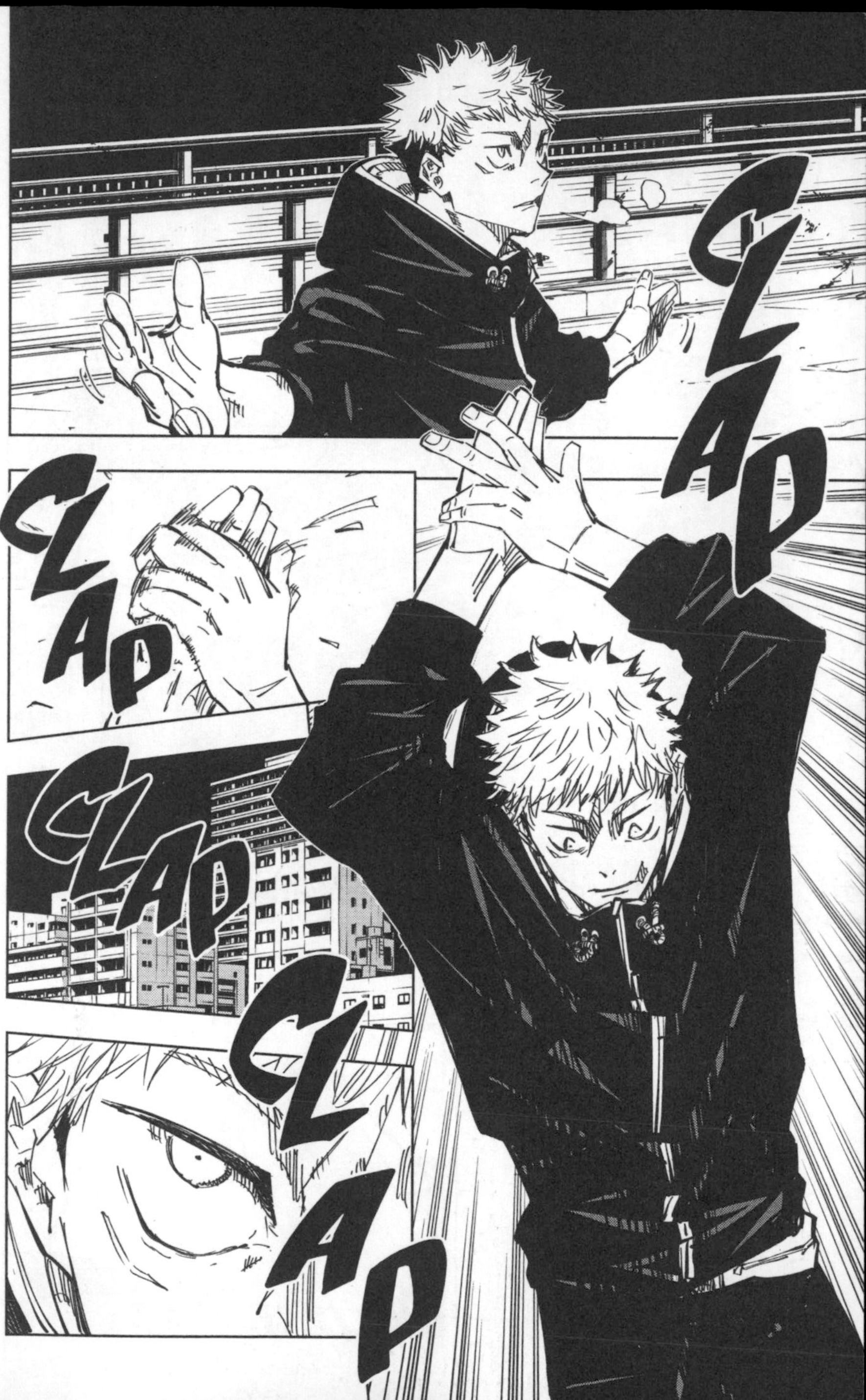
CLAP
CLAP
CLAP
CLAP

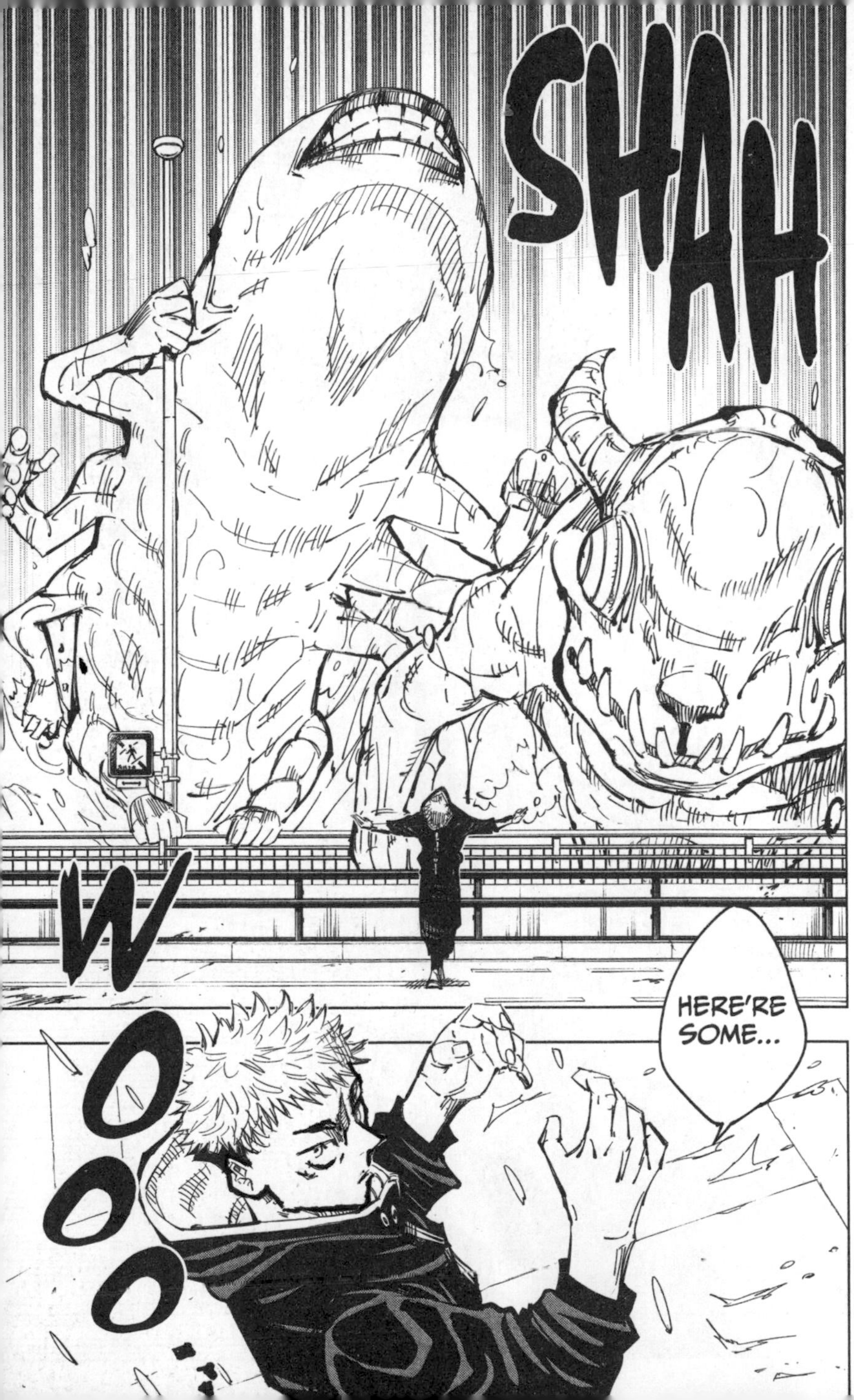
SHAH
HERE'RE SOME...
WOOO

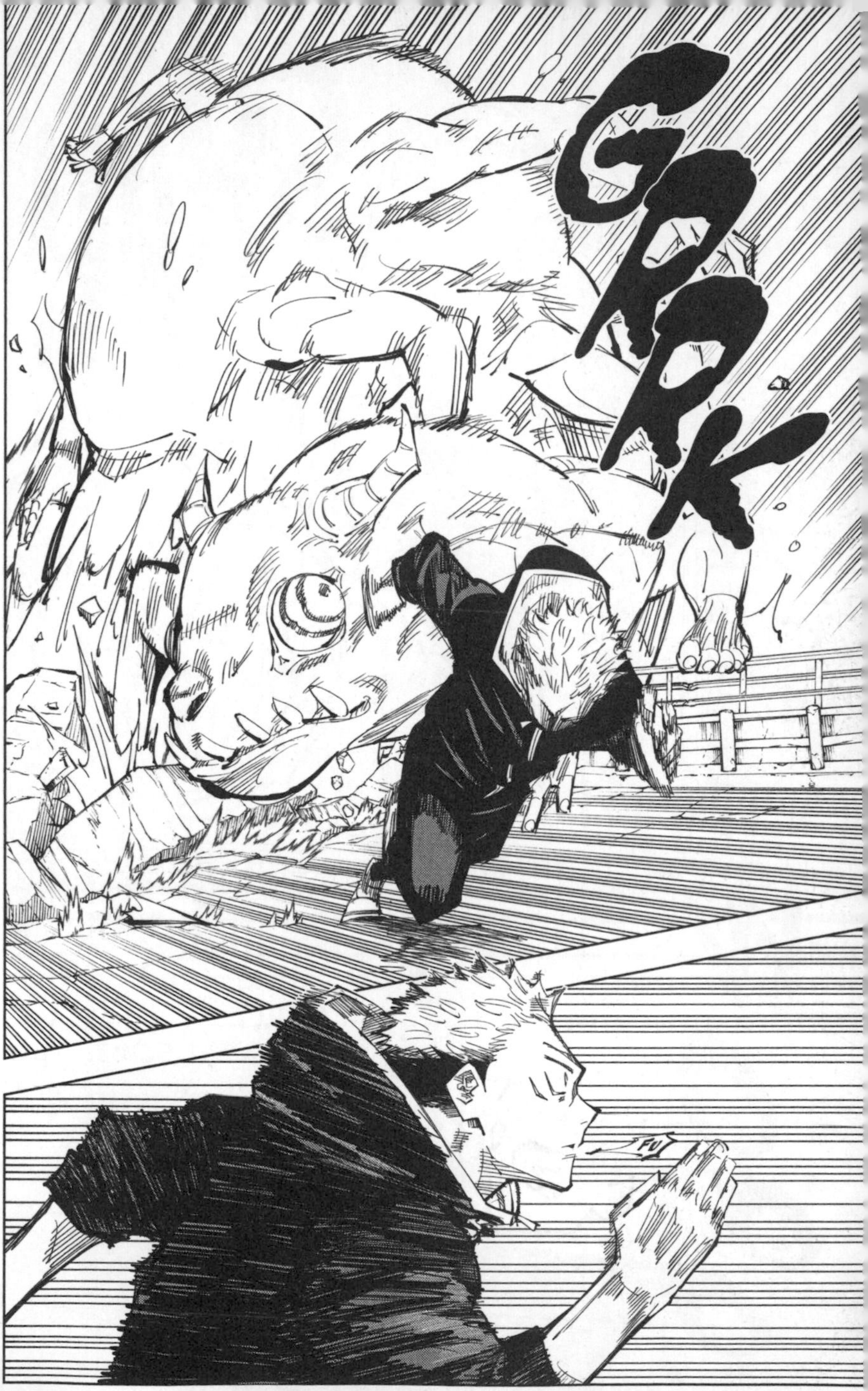
GRRK
FU

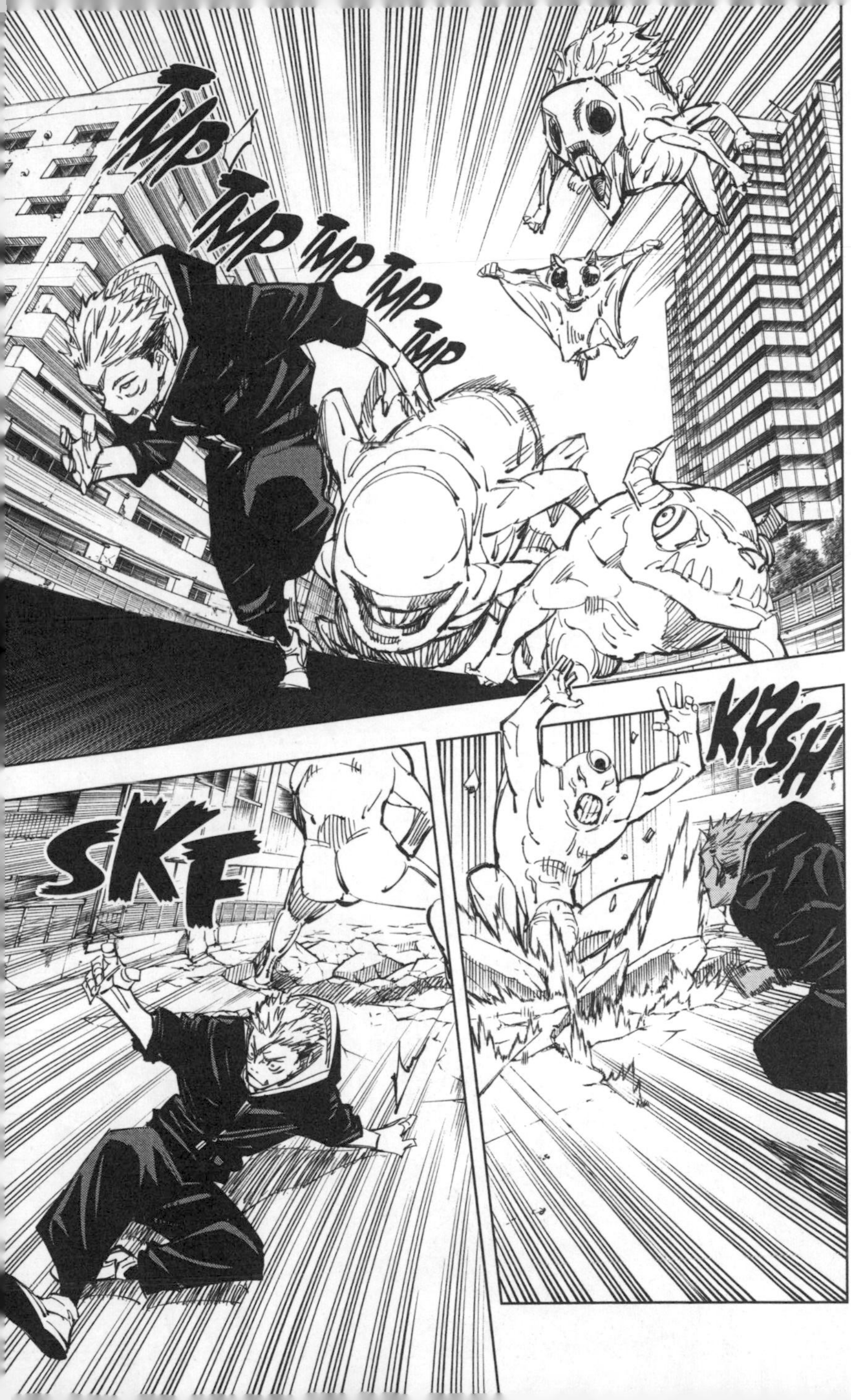
TMP TMP TMP TMP TMP TMP
KRSH
SKF

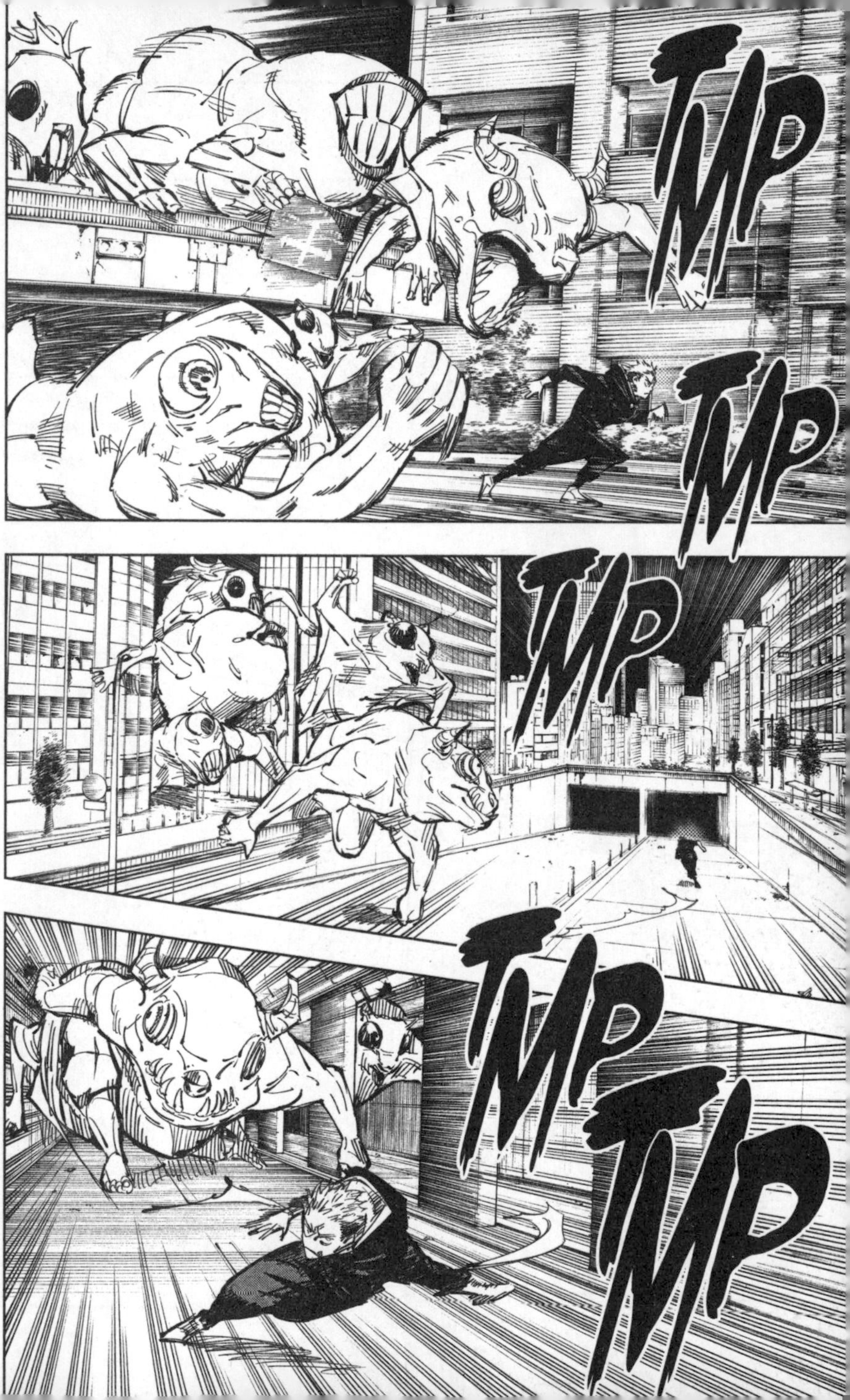
TMP
TMP
TMP
TMP
TMP

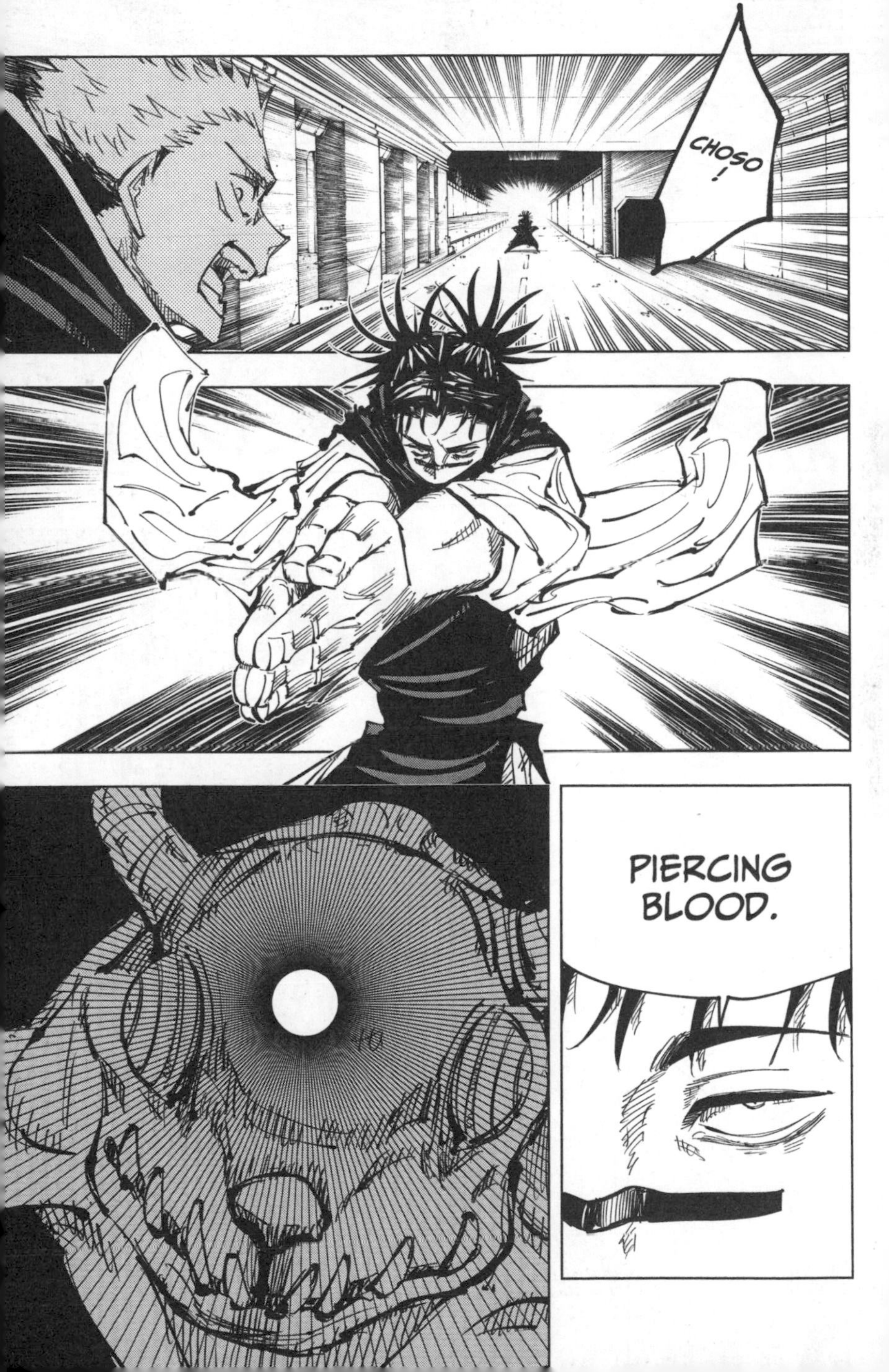
CHOSO!
PIERCING BLOOD.

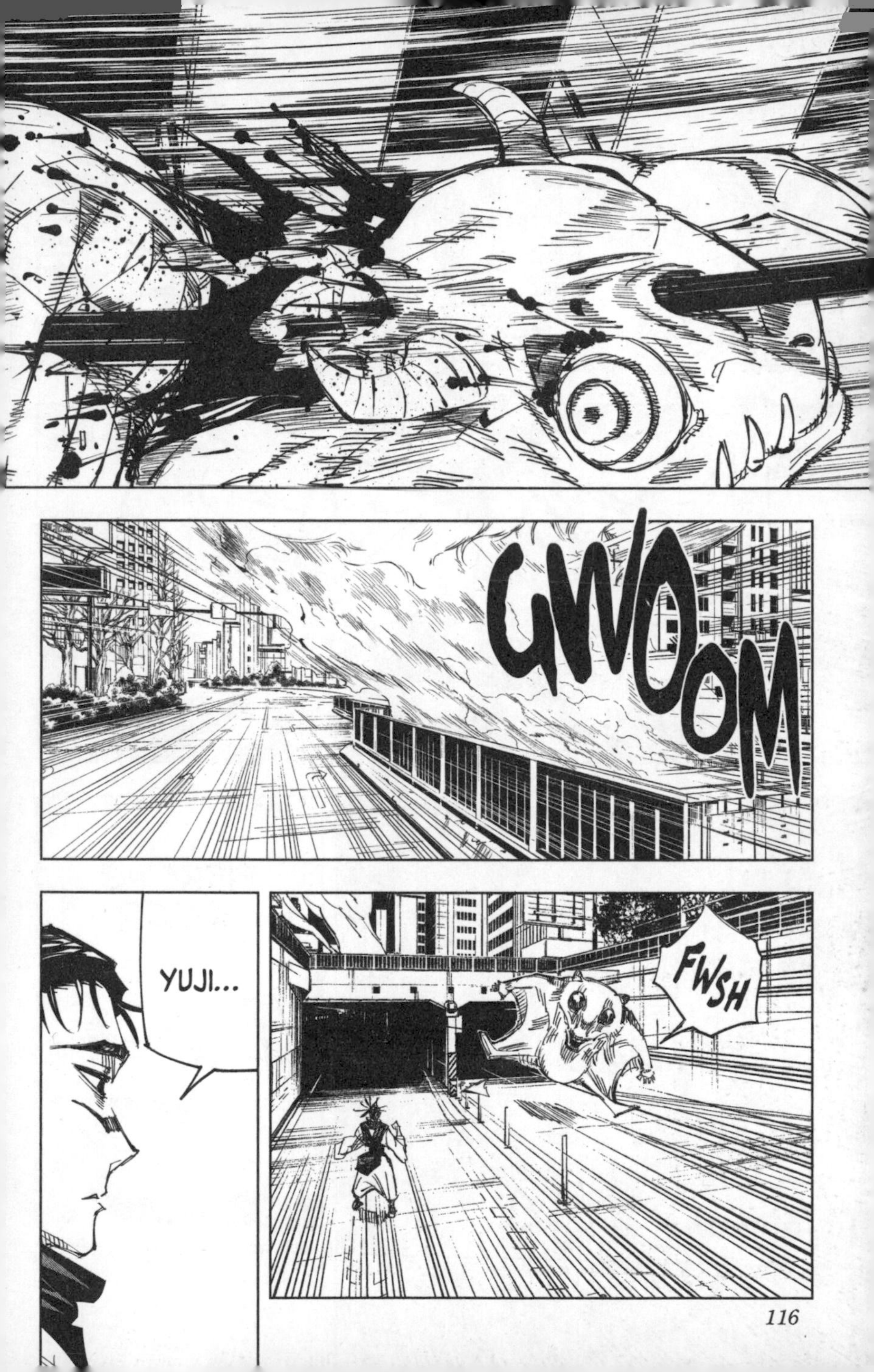
GWOOM
FWSH
YUJI...

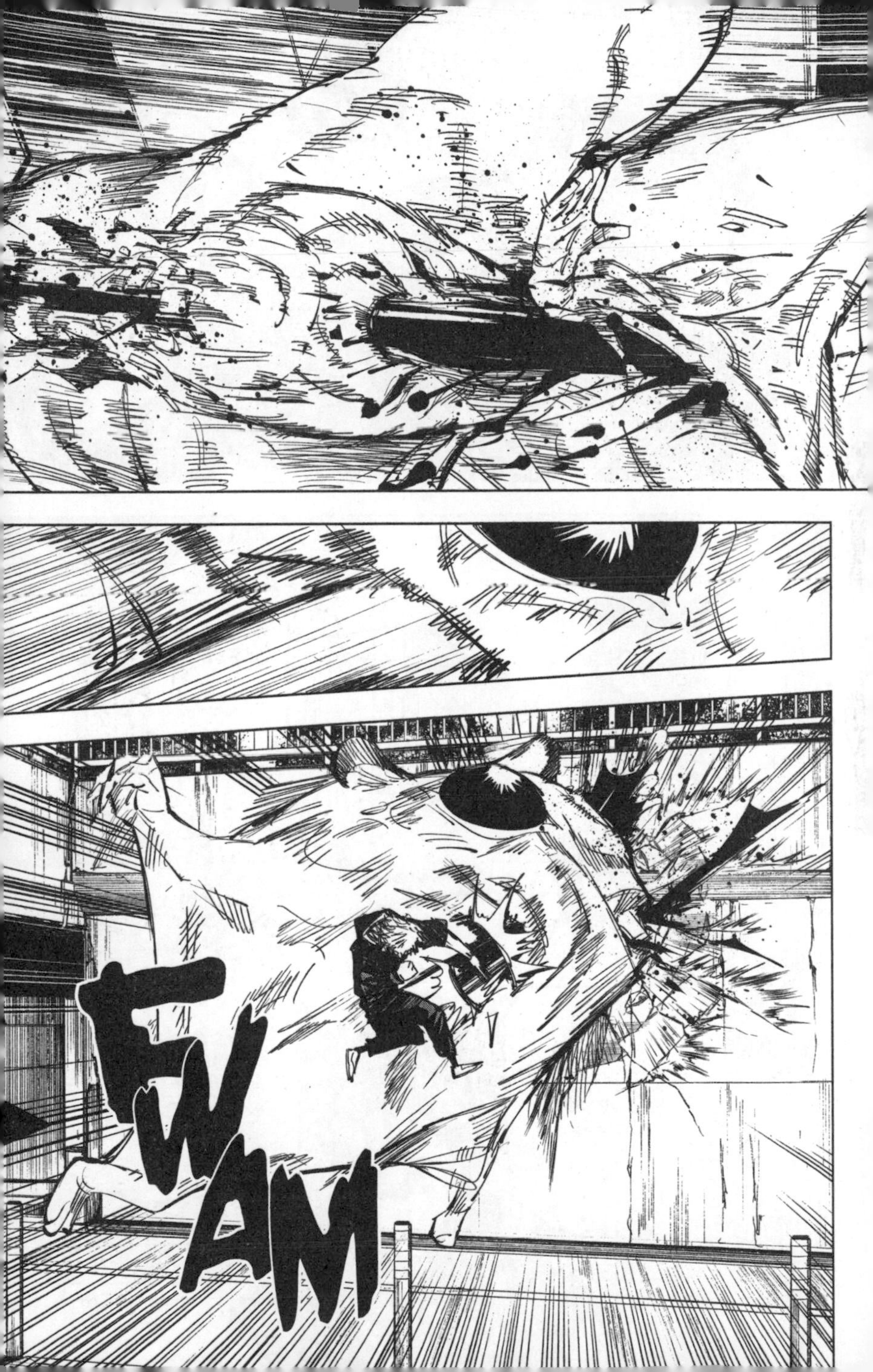
FWAM

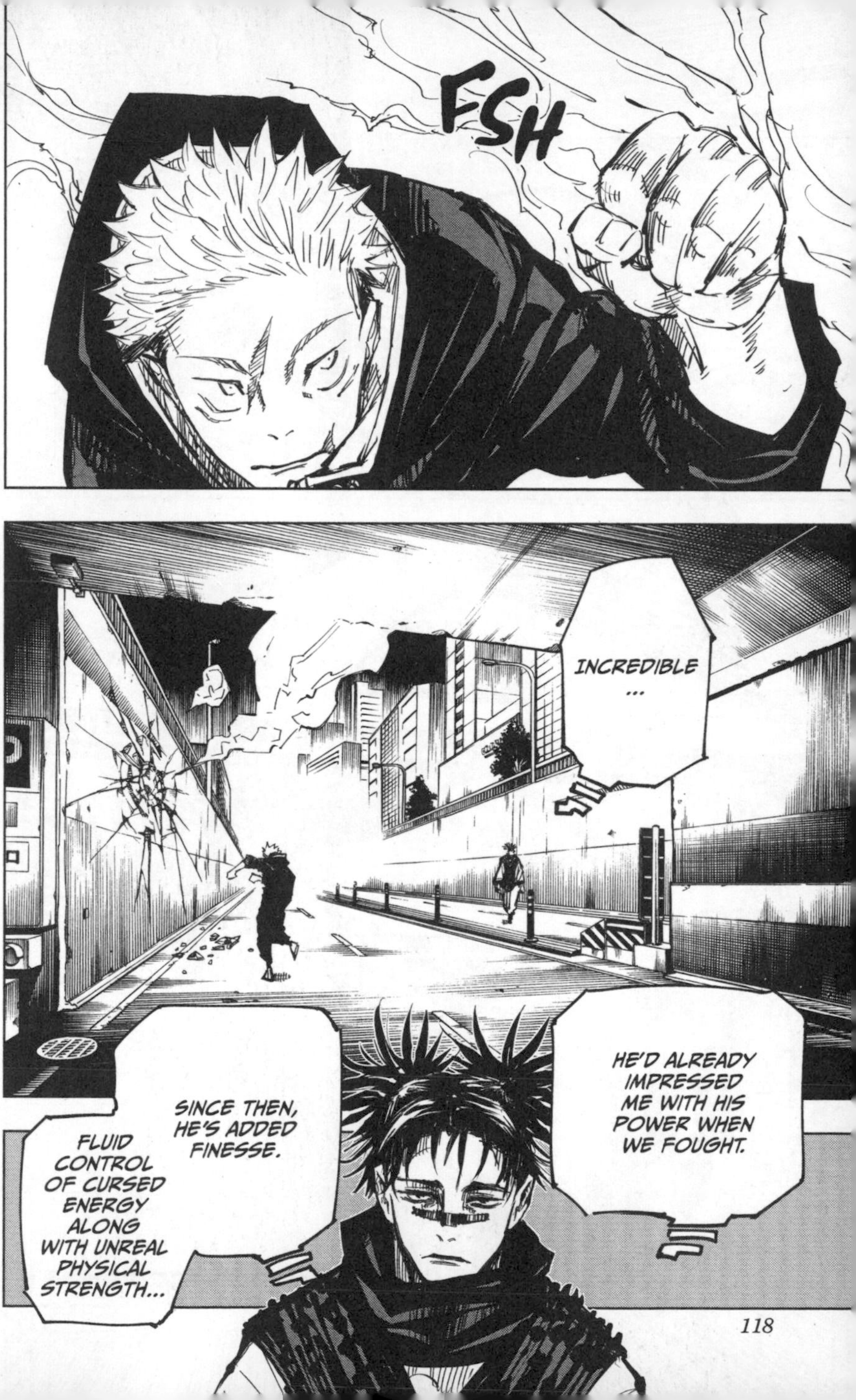
FSH
INCREDIBLE ...
HE'D ALREADY IMPRESSED ME WITH HIS POWER WHEN WE FOUGHT.
SINCE THEN, HE'S ADDED FINESSE.
FLUID CONTROL OF CURSED ENERGY ALONG WITH UNREAL PHYSICAL STRENGTH...

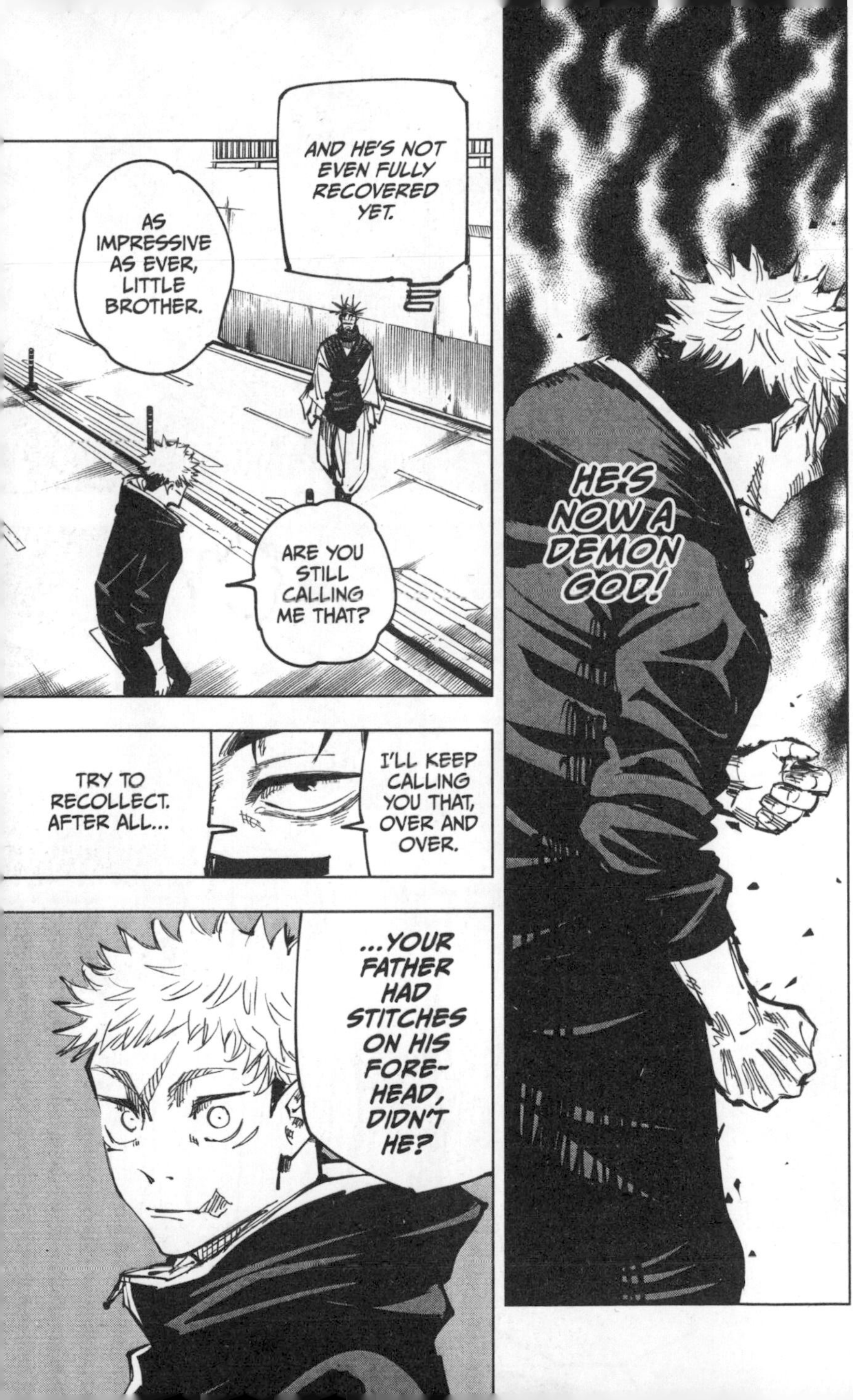
HE'S NOW A DEMON GOD!
AND HE'S NOT EVEN FULLY RECOVERED YET.
AS IMPRESSIVE AS EVER, LITTLE BROTHER.
ARE YOU STILL CALLING ME THAT?
I'LL KEEP CALLING YOU THAT, OVER AND OVER.
TRY TO RECOLLECT. AFTER ALL...
...YOUR FATHER HAD STITCHES ON HIS FORE-HEAD, DIDN'T HE?

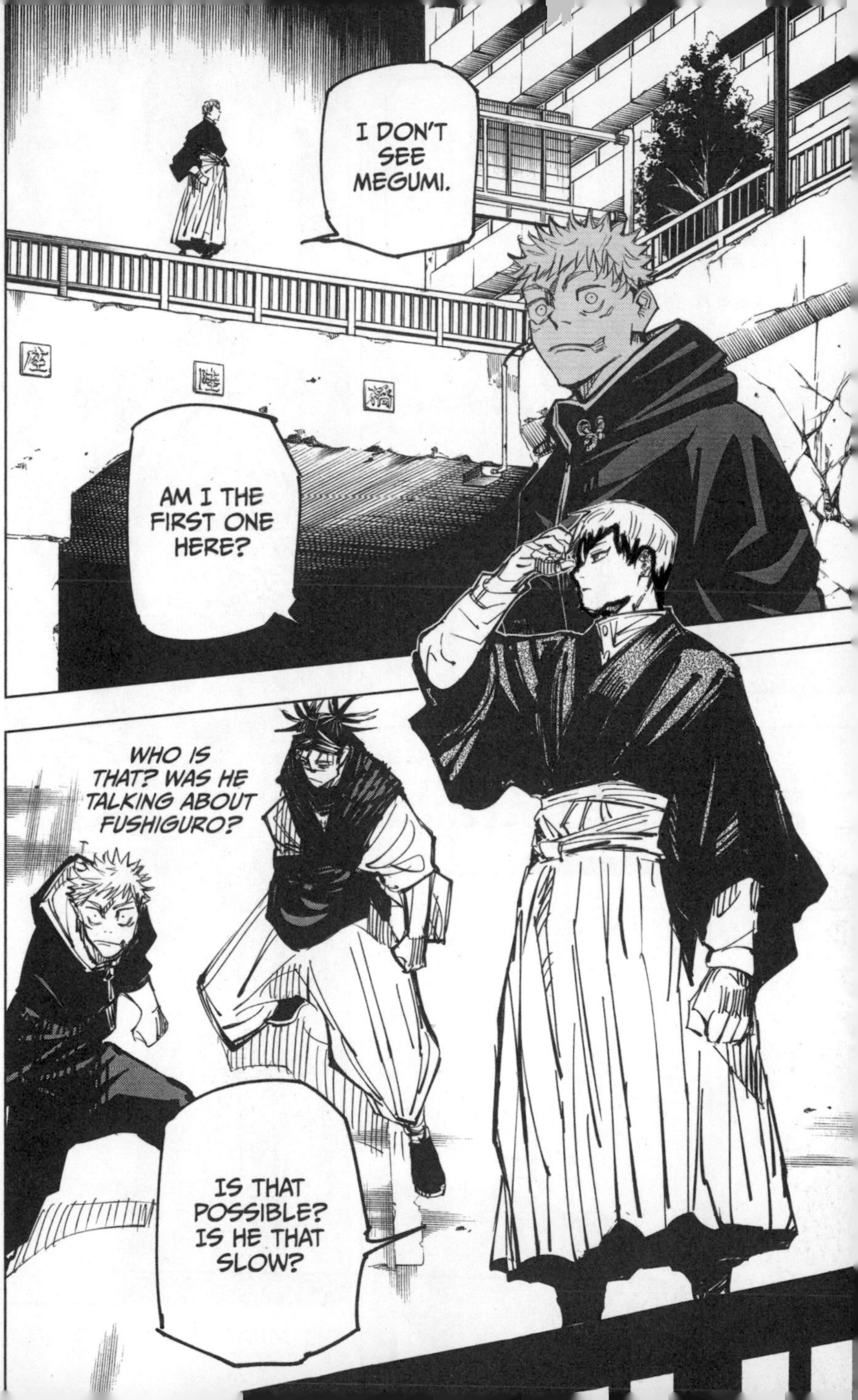
I DON'T SEE MEGUMI.
AM I THE FIRST ONE HERE?
WHO IS THAT? WAS HE TALKING ABOUT FUSHIGURO?
IS THAT POSSIBLE? IS HE THAT SLOW?

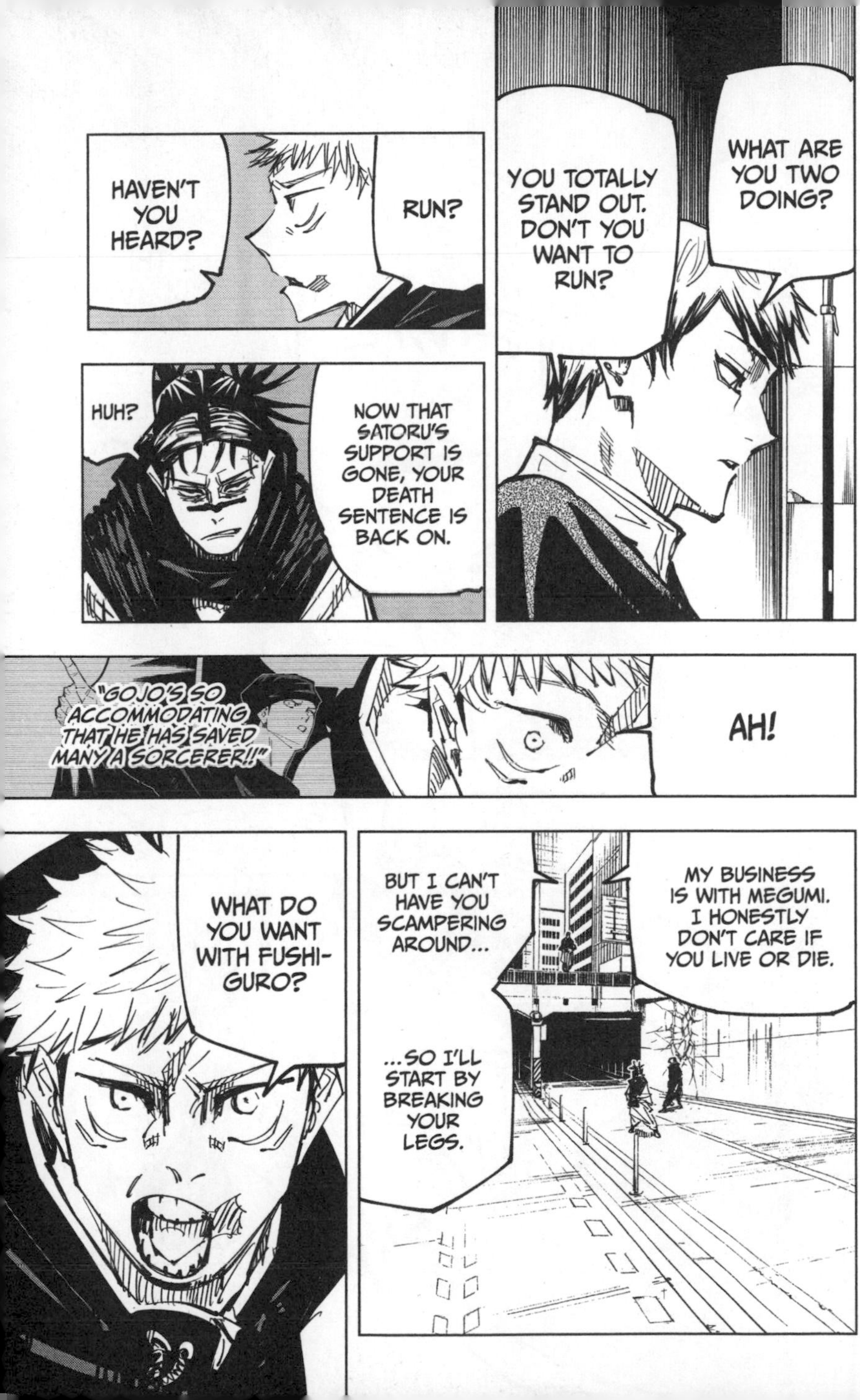
WHAT ARE YOU TWO DOING?
YOU TOTALLY STAND OUT. DON'T YOU WANT TO RUN?
RUN?
HAVEN'T YOU HEARD?
NOW THAT SATORU'S SUPPORT IS GONE, YOUR DEATH SENTENCE IS BACK ON.
HUH?
AH!
"GOJO'S SO ACCOMMODATING THAT HE HAS SAVED MANY A SORCERER!!"
MY BUSINESS IS WITH MEGUMI. I HONESTLY DON'T CARE IF YOU LIVE OR DIE.
BUT I CAN'T HAVE YOU SCAMPERING AROUND...
...SO I'LL START BY BREAKING YOUR LEGS.
WHAT DO YOU WANT WITH FUSHI-GURO?

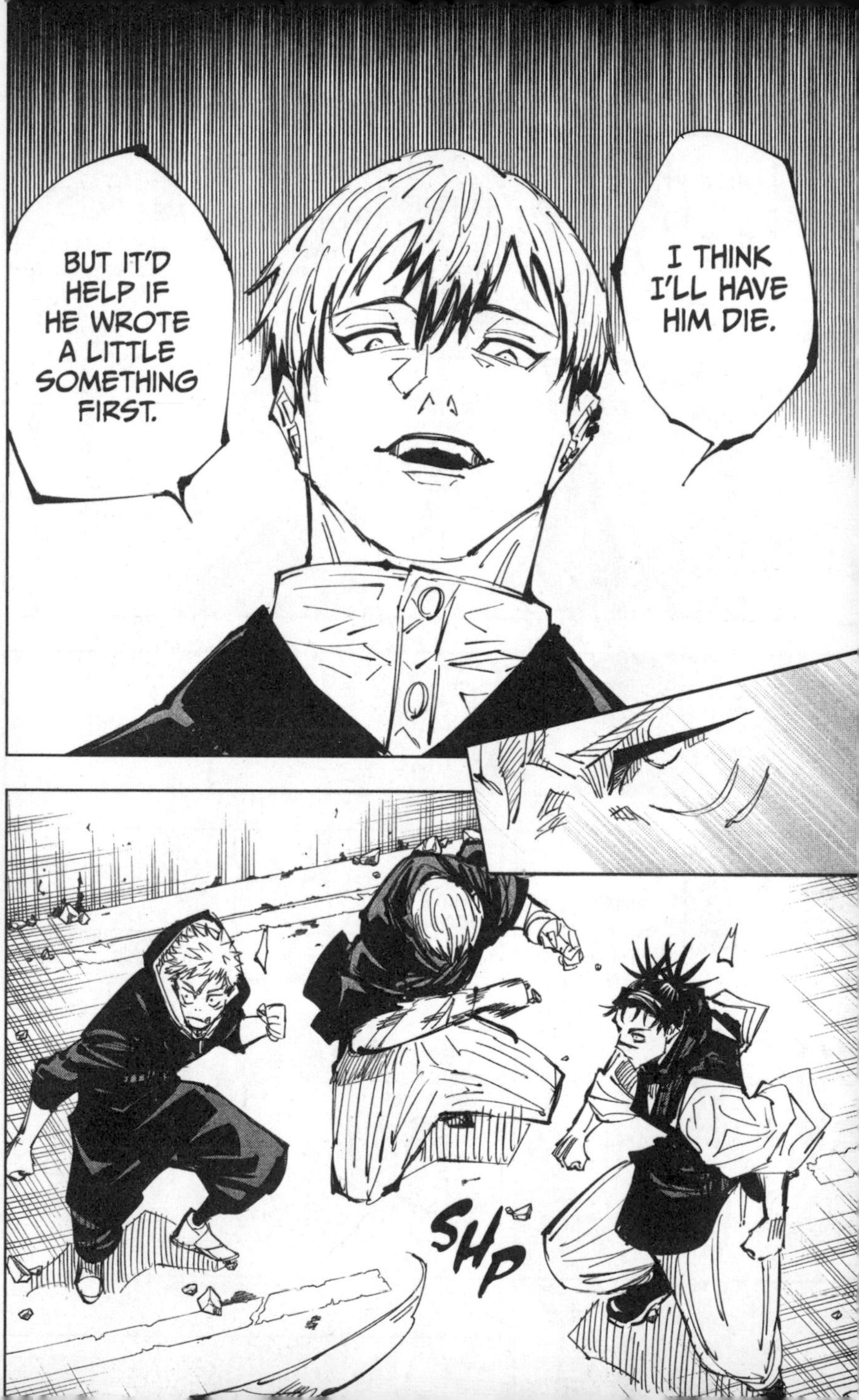
I THINK I'LL HAVE HIM DIE.
BUT IT'D HELP IF HE WROTE A LITTLE SOMETHING FIRST.
SHP

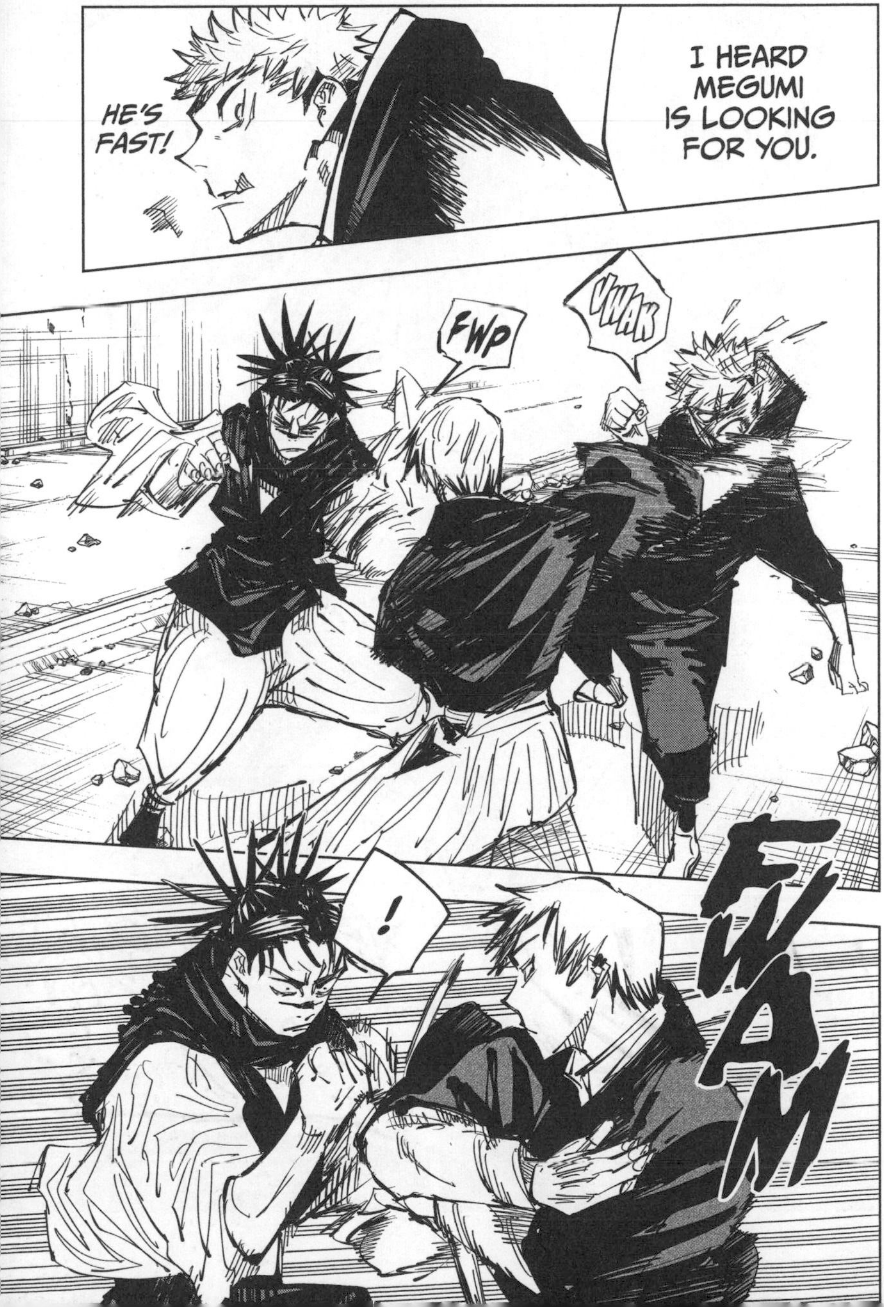
I HEARD MEGUMI IS LOOKING FOR YOU.
HE'S FAST!
WHAK
FWP
FWAM
!

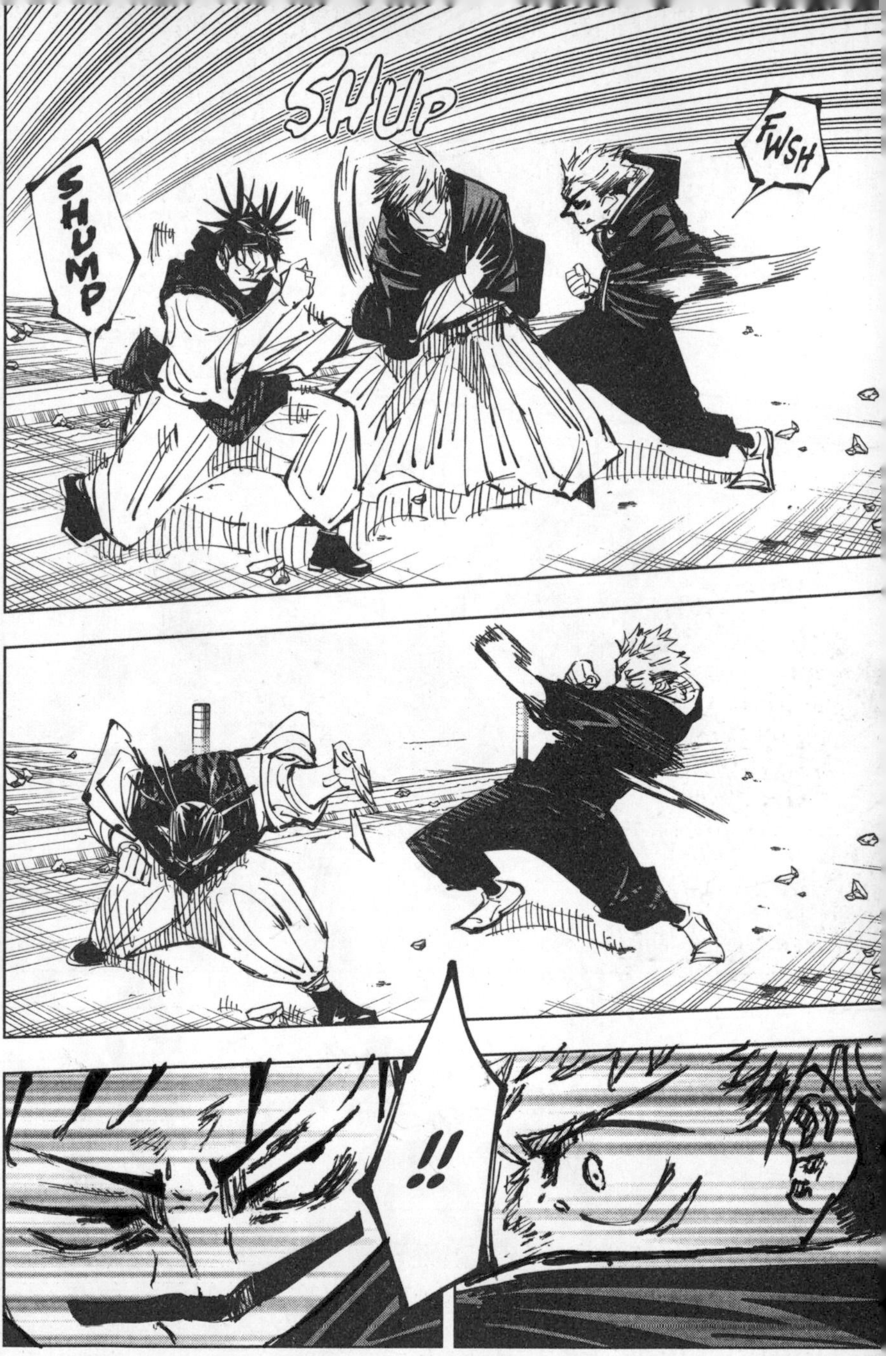
FWSH
SHUP
SHUMP
!!

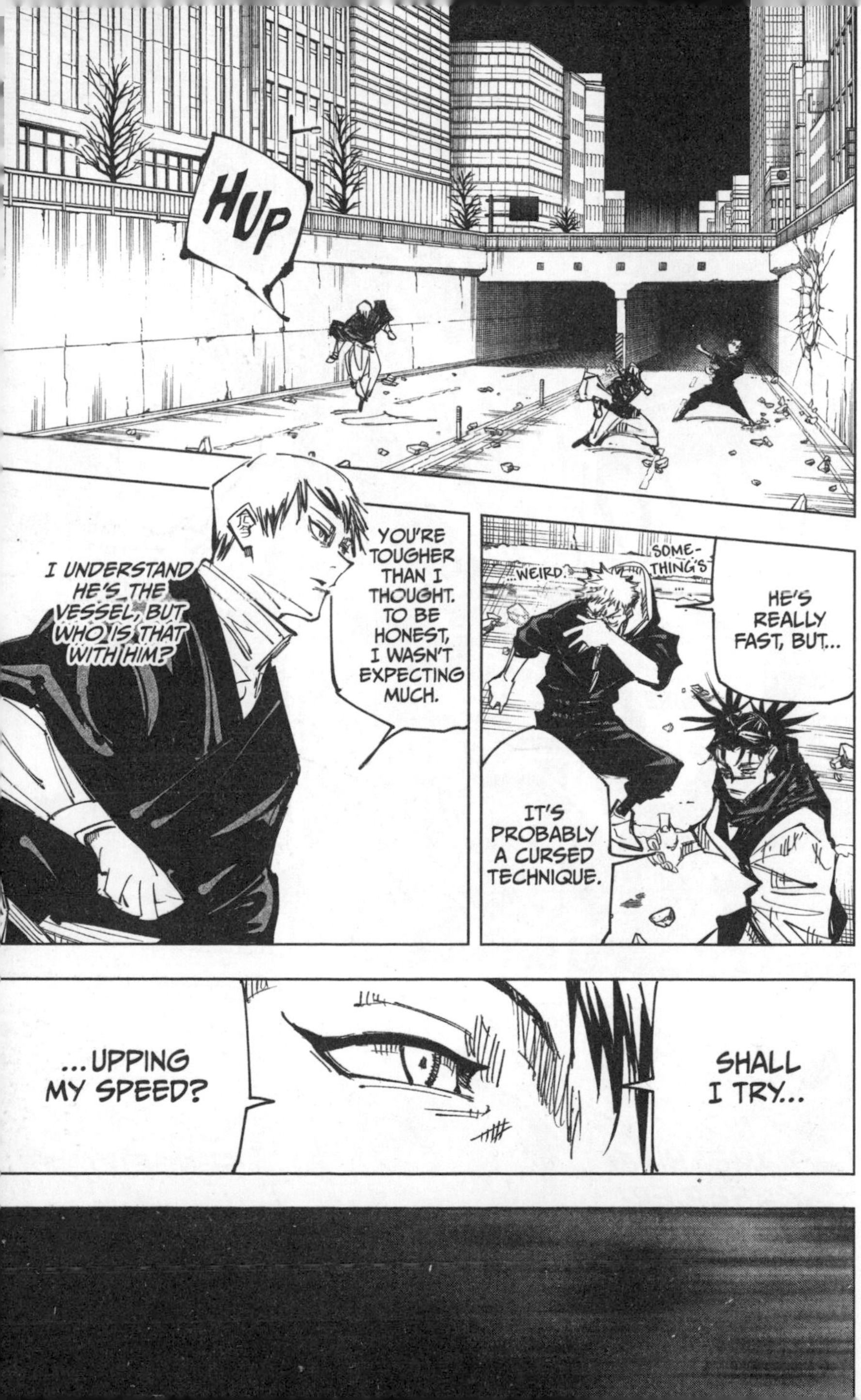
HUP
HE'S REALLY FAST, BUT...
SOME-THING'S ... WEIRD.
IT'S PROBABLY A CURSED TECHNIQUE.
YOU'RE TOUGHER THAN I THOUGHT. TO BE HONEST, I WASN'T EXPECTING MUCH.
I UNDERSTAND HE'S THE VESSEL, BUT WHO IS THAT WITH HIM?
SHALL I TRY...
...UPPING MY SPEED?

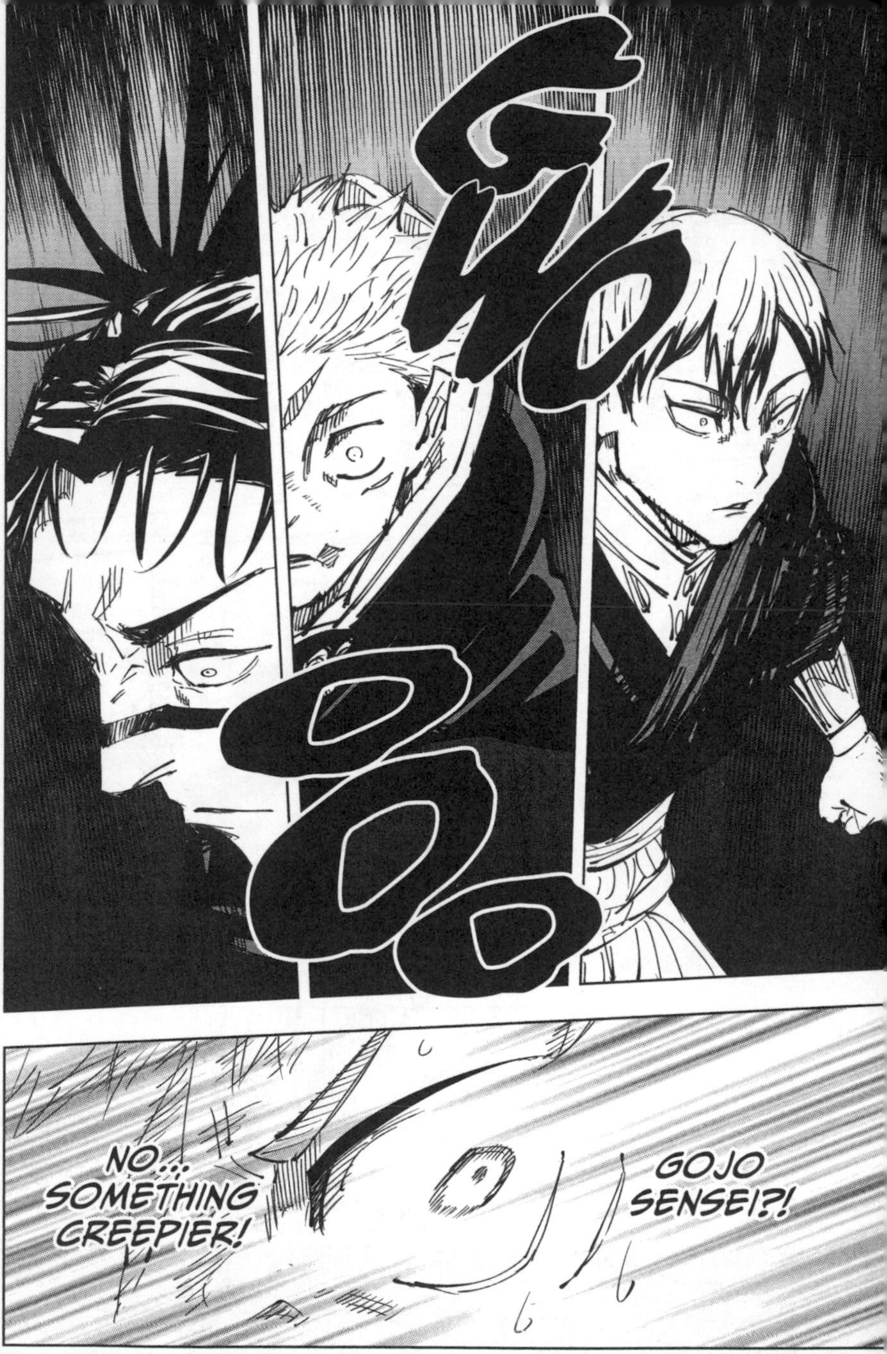
GOJO SENSEI?!
NO... SOMETHING CREEPIER!

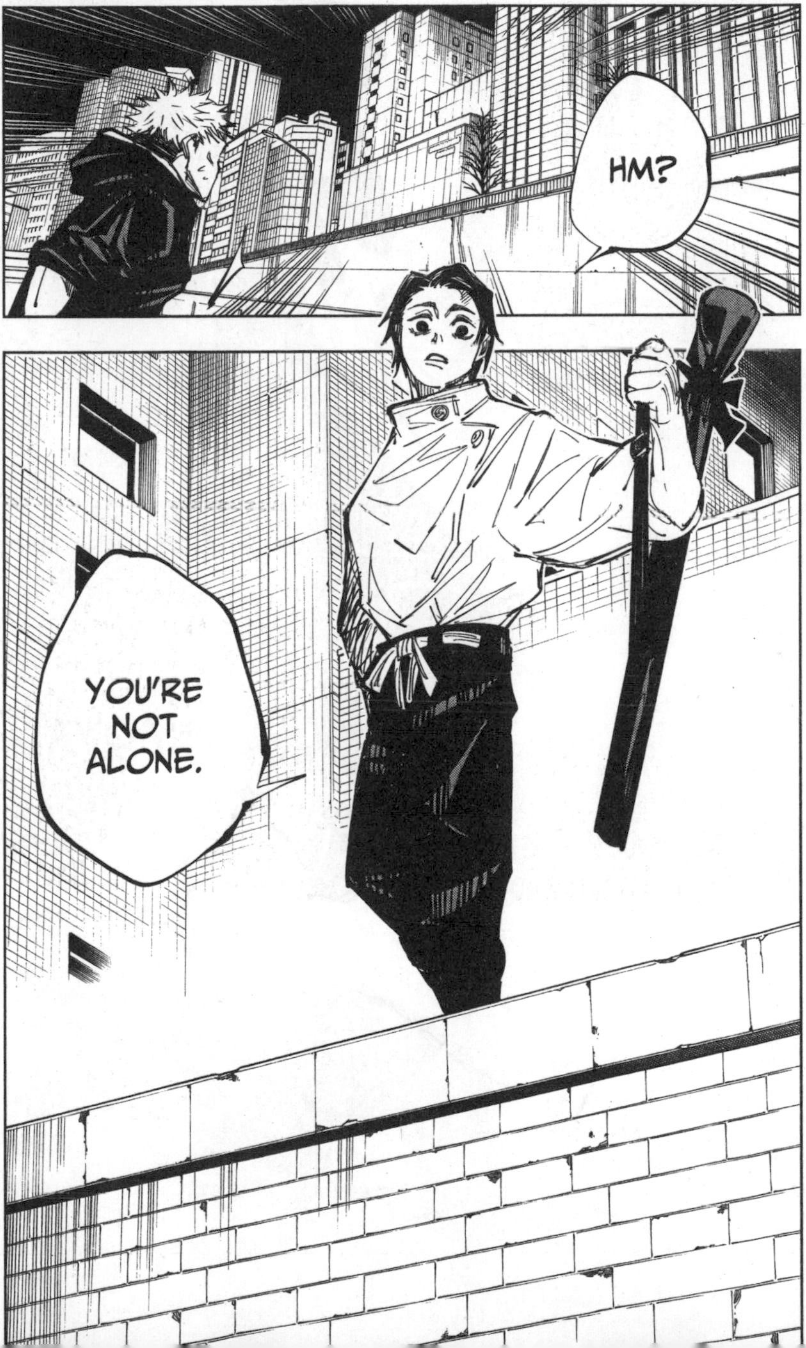
HM?
YOU'RE NOT ALONE.

NAOYA

ONE YEAR YOUNGER
THAN GOJO AND A
COMPLETE JERK.

CHAPTER 140: EXECUTION

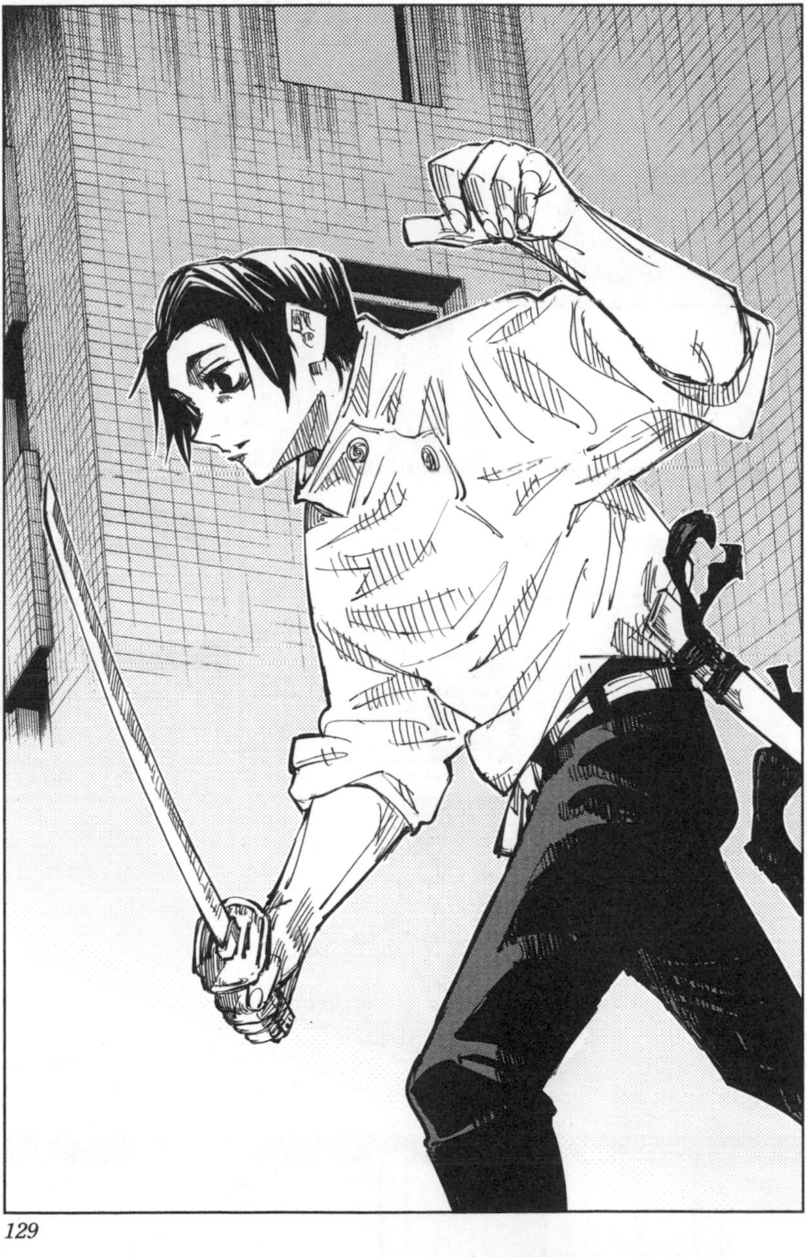

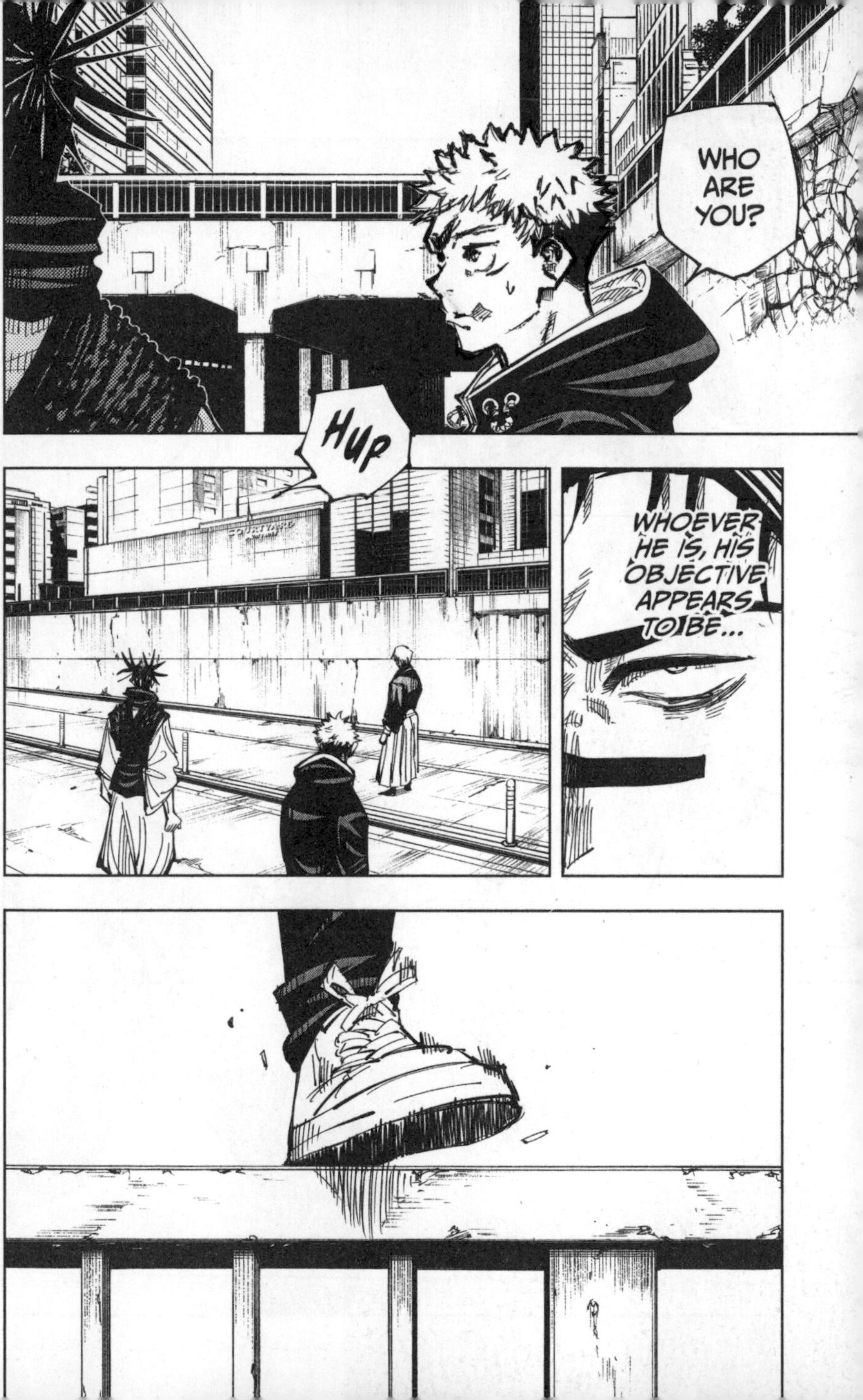
WHO ARE YOU?
HUP
WHOEVER HE IS, HIS OBJECTIVE APPEARS TO BE...

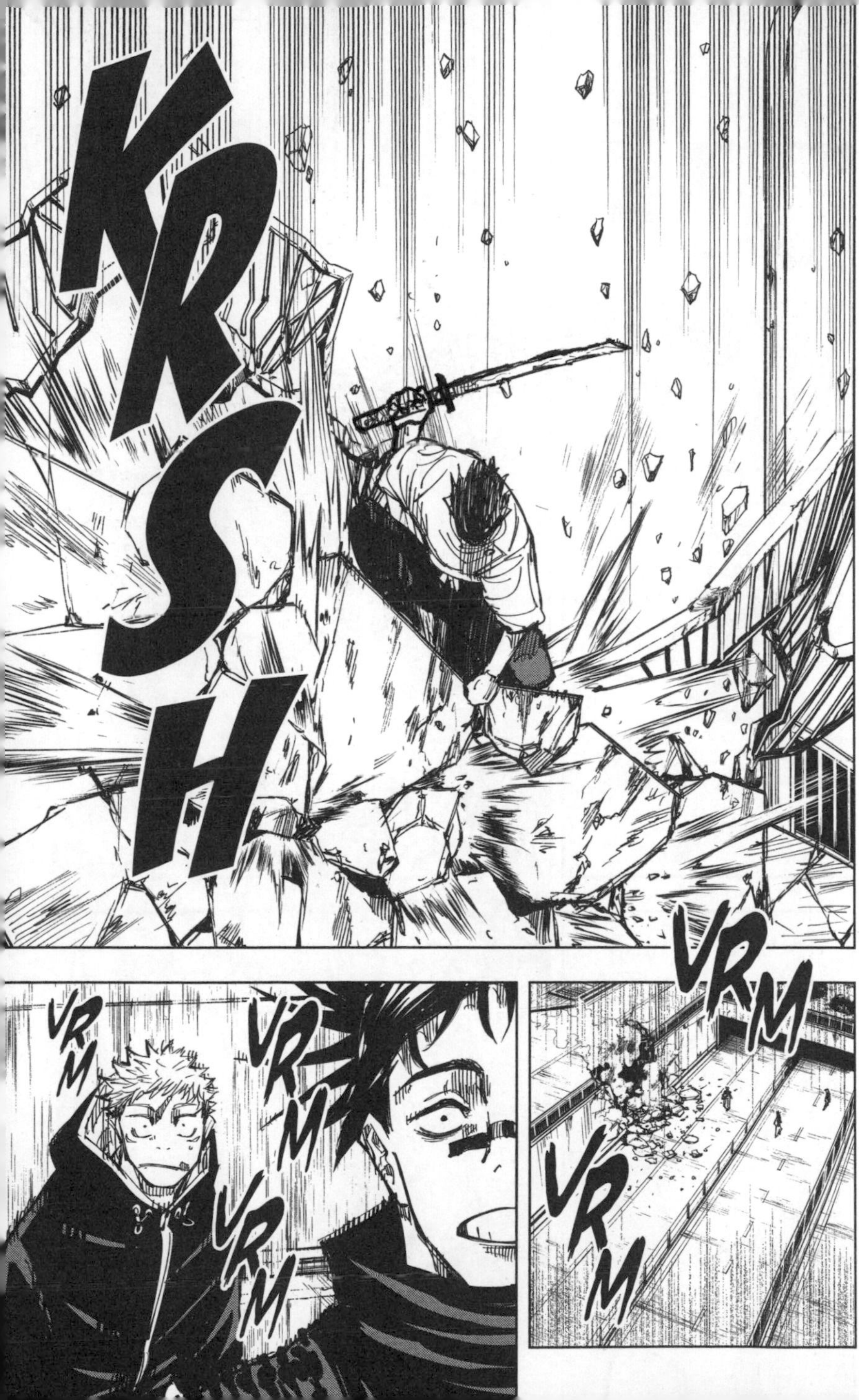
KRSH!
VRM
VRM
VRM
VRM
VRM
VRM

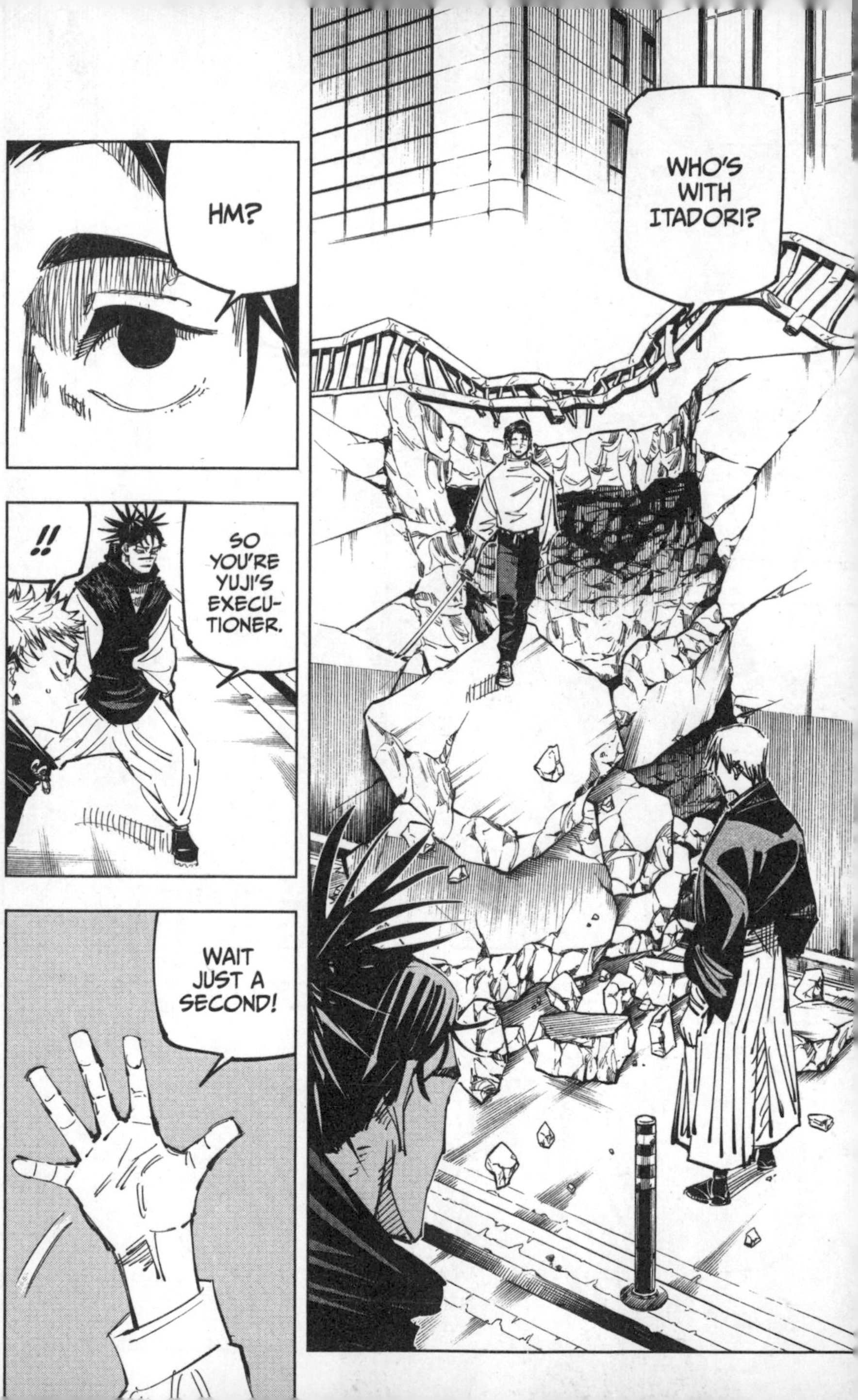
WHO'S WITH ITADORI?
HM?
SO YOU'RE YUJI'S EXECUTIONER.
!!
WAIT JUST A SECOND!

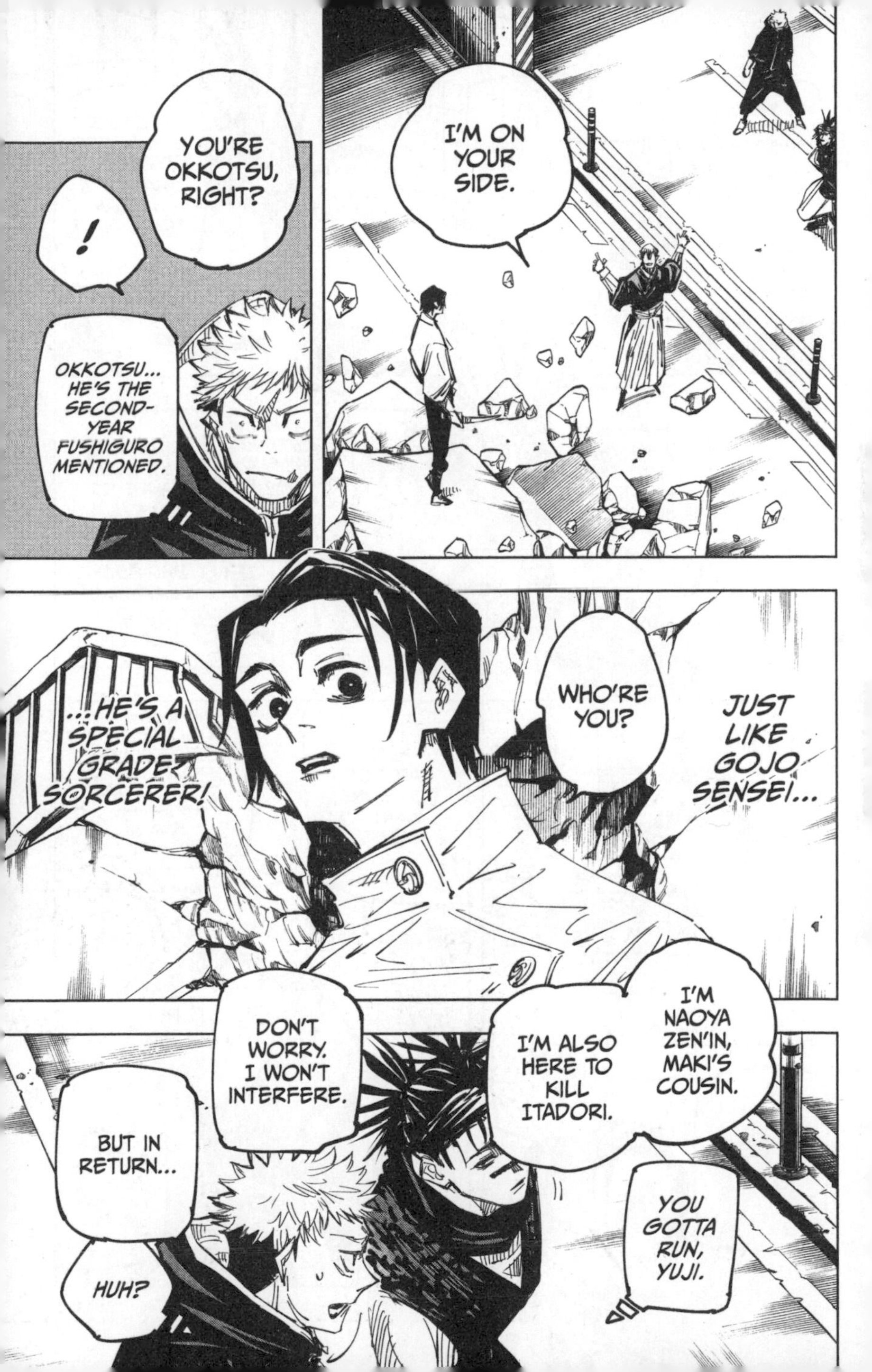
I'M ON YOUR SIDE.
YOU'RE OKKOTSU, RIGHT?
!
OKKOTSU... HE'S THE SECOND-YEAR FUSHIGURO MENTIONED.
JUST LIKE GOJO SENSEI...
WHO'RE YOU?
...HE'S A SPECIAL GRADE SORCERER!
I'M NAOYA ZEN'IN, MAKI'S COUSIN.
I'M ALSO HERE TO KILL ITADORI.
DON'T WORRY. I WON'T INTERFERE.
BUT IN RETURN...
YOU GOTTA RUN, YUJI.
HUH?

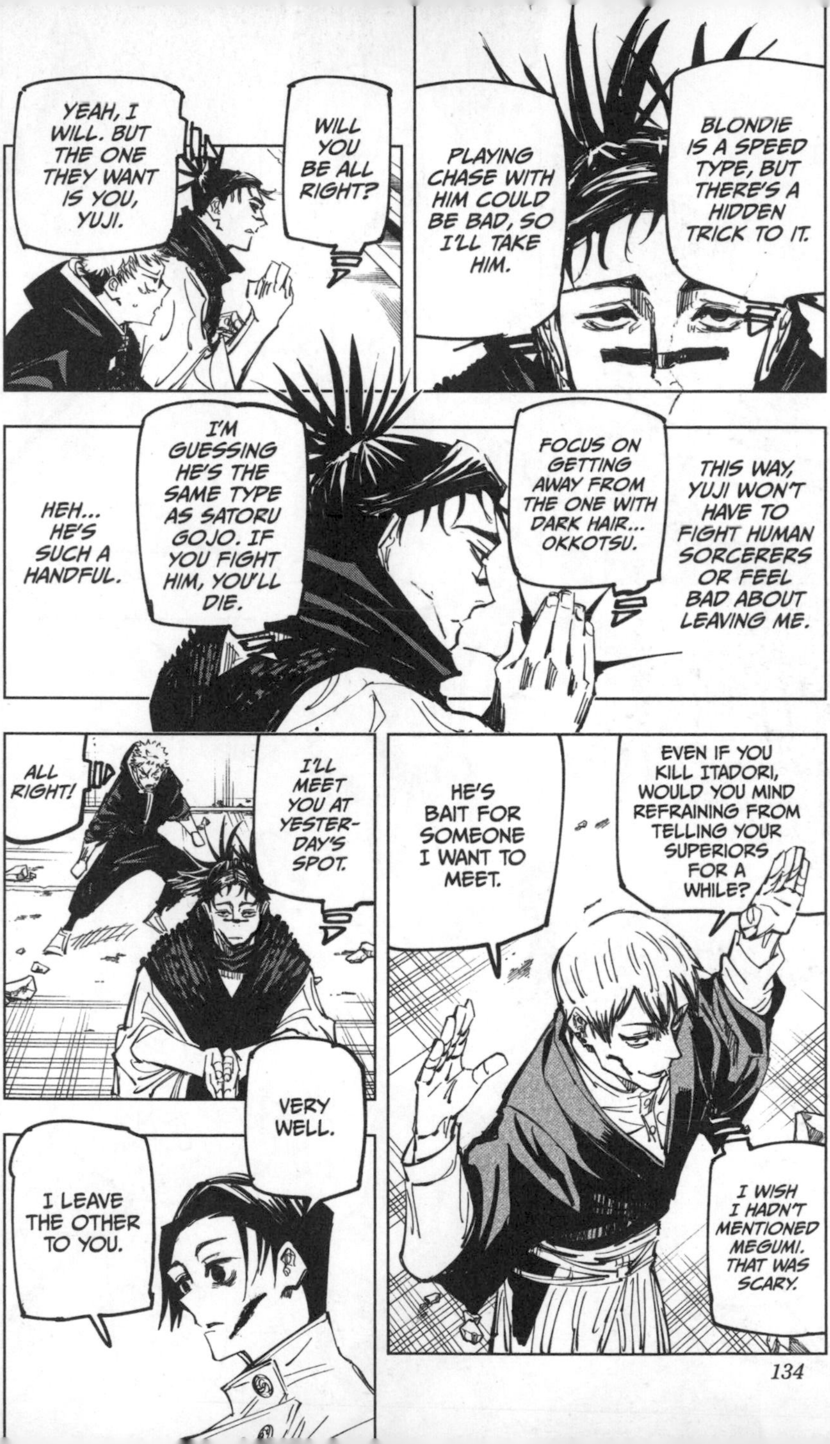
BLONDIE IS A SPEED TYPE, BUT THERE'S A HIDDEN TRICK TO IT.
PLAYING CHASE WITH HIM COULD BE BAD, SO I'LL TAKE HIM.
WILL YOU BE ALL RIGHT?
YEAH, I WILL. BUT THE ONE THEY WANT IS YOU, YUJI.
THIS WAY, YUJI WON'T HAVE TO FIGHT HUMAN SORCERERS OR FEEL BAD ABOUT LEAVING ME.
FOCUS ON GETTING AWAY FROM THE ONE WITH DARK HAIR... OKKOTSU.
I'M GUESSING HE'S THE SAME TYPE AS SATORU GOJO. IF YOU FIGHT HIM, YOU'LL DIE.
HEH... HE'S SUCH A HANDFUL.
EVEN IF YOU KILL ITADORI, WOULD YOU MIND REFRAINING FROM TELLING YOUR SUPERIORS FOR A WHILE?
HE'S BAIT FOR SOMEONE I WANT TO MEET.
I WISH I HADN'T MENTIONED MEGUMI. THAT WAS SCARY.
I'LL MEET YOU AT YESTER-DAY'S SPOT.
ALL RIGHT!
VERY WELL.
I LEAVE THE OTHER TO YOU.

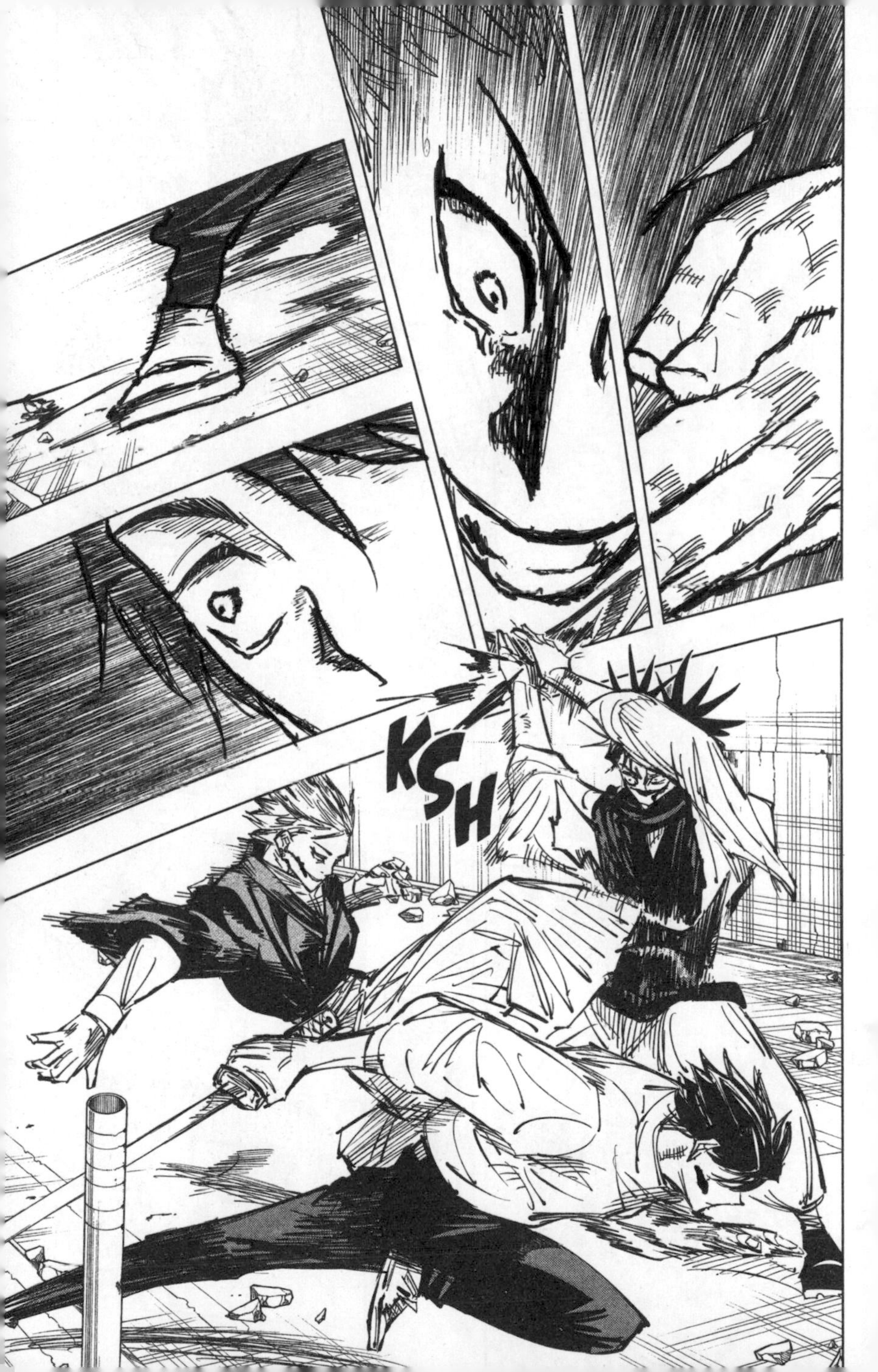
KSH

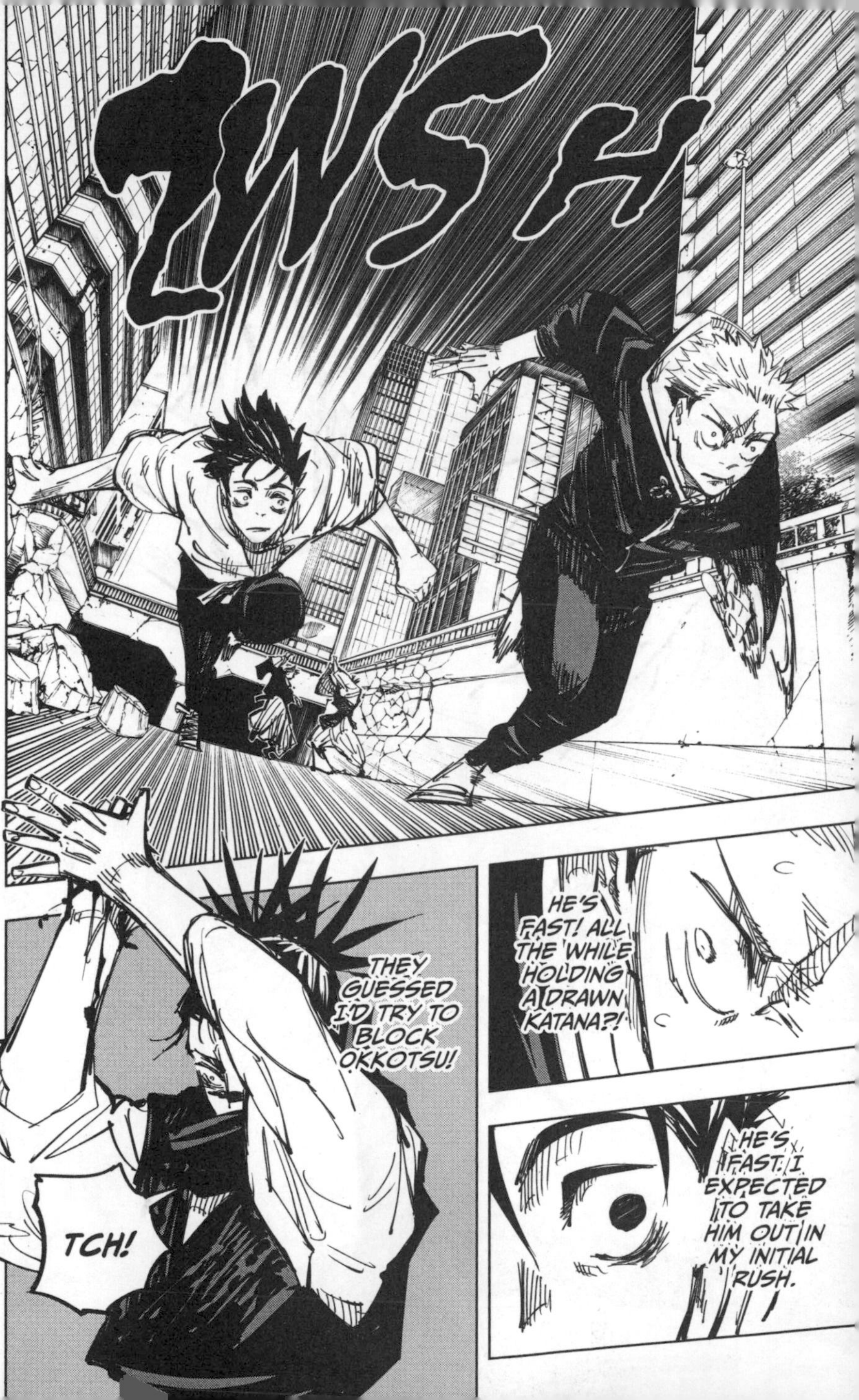
ZWSH
HE'S FAST! ALL THE WHILE HOLDING A DRAWN KATANA?!
HE'S FAST. I EXPECTED TO TAKE HIM OUT IN MY INITIAL RUSH.
THEY GUESSED I'D TRY TO BLOCK OKKOTSU!
TCH!

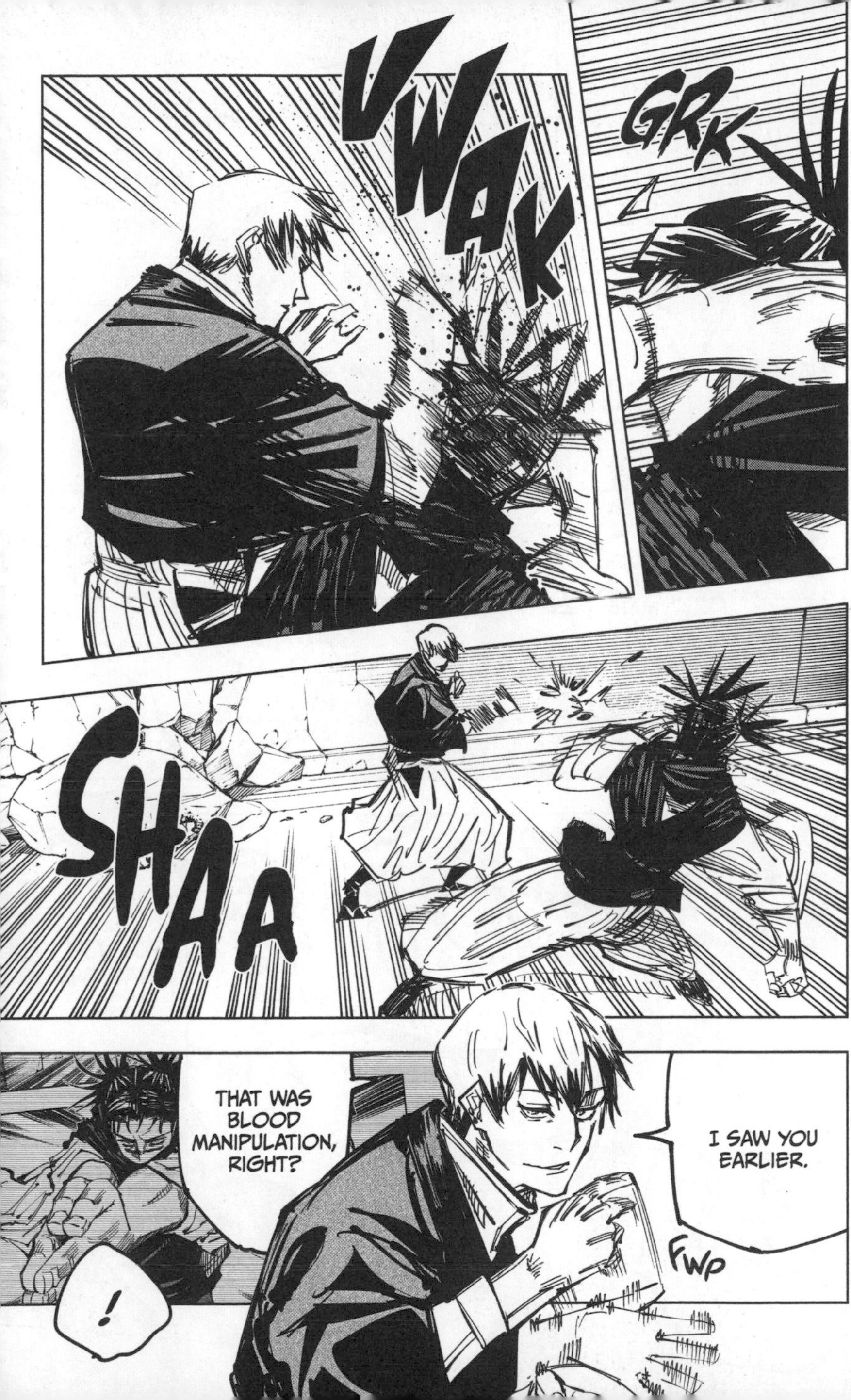
GRK
VWAK
SHAA
I SAW YOU EARLIER.
FWP
THAT WAS BLOOD MANIPULATION, RIGHT?
!

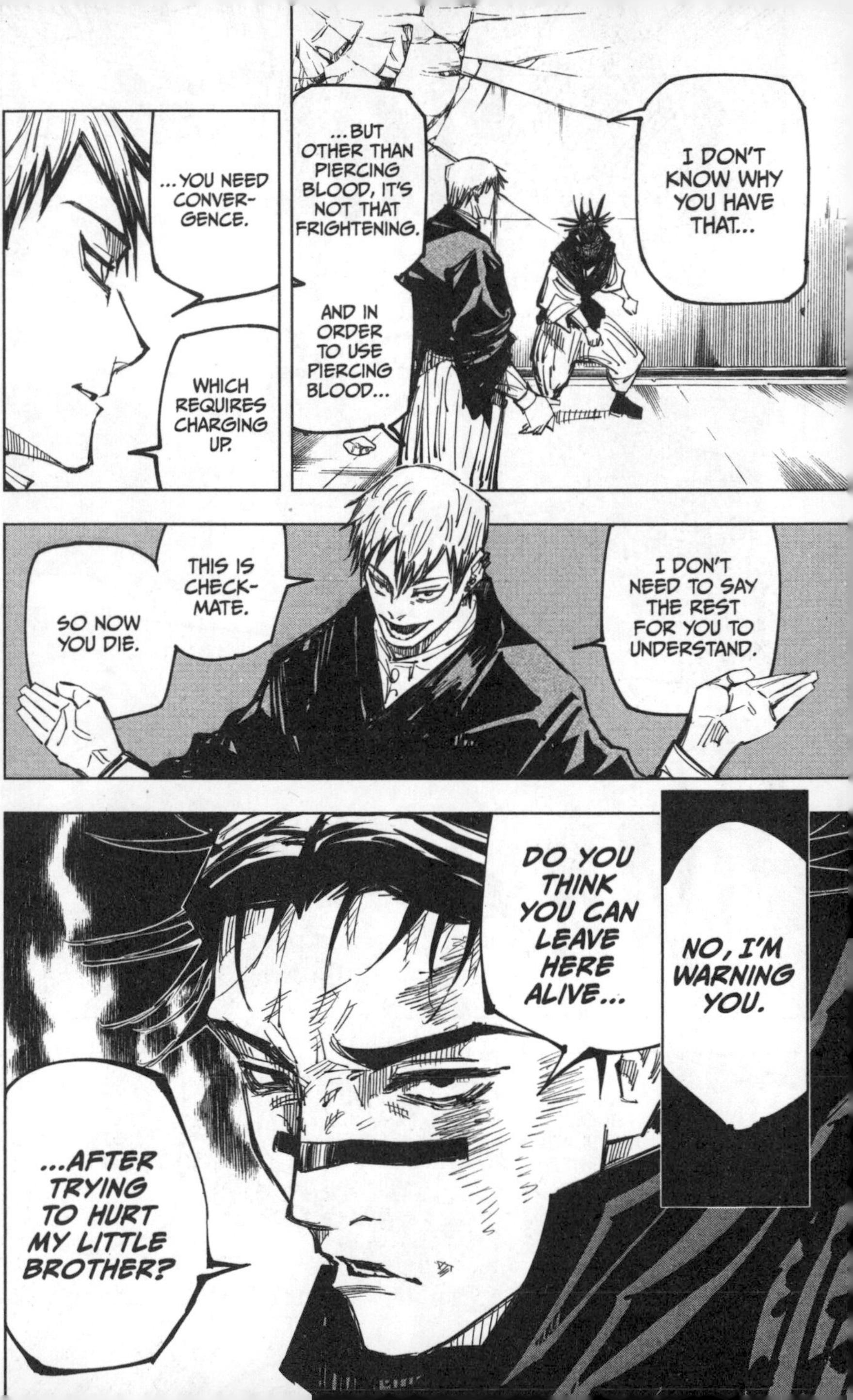
I DON'T KNOW WHY YOU HAVE THAT...
...BUT OTHER THAN PIERCING BLOOD, IT'S NOT THAT FRIGHTENING.
AND IN ORDER TO USE PIERCING BLOOD...
...YOU NEED CONVERGENCE.
WHICH REQUIRES CHARGING UP.
I DON'T NEED TO SAY THE REST FOR YOU TO UNDERSTAND.
THIS IS CHECKMATE.
SO NOW YOU DIE.
NO, I'M WARNING YOU.
DO YOU THINK YOU CAN LEAVE HERE ALIVE...
...AFTER TRYING TO HURT MY LITTLE BROTHER?

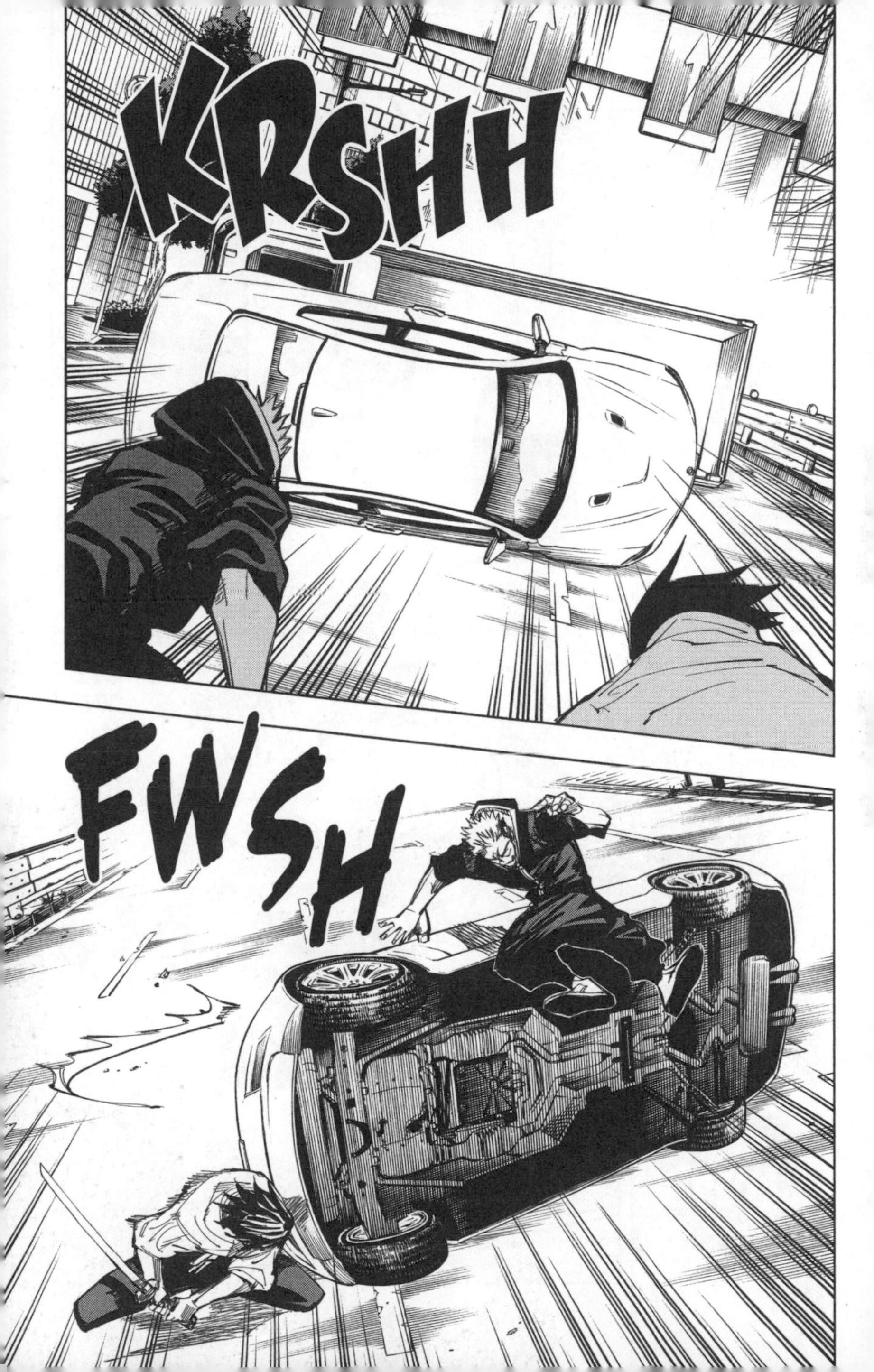
KRSHH
FWSH

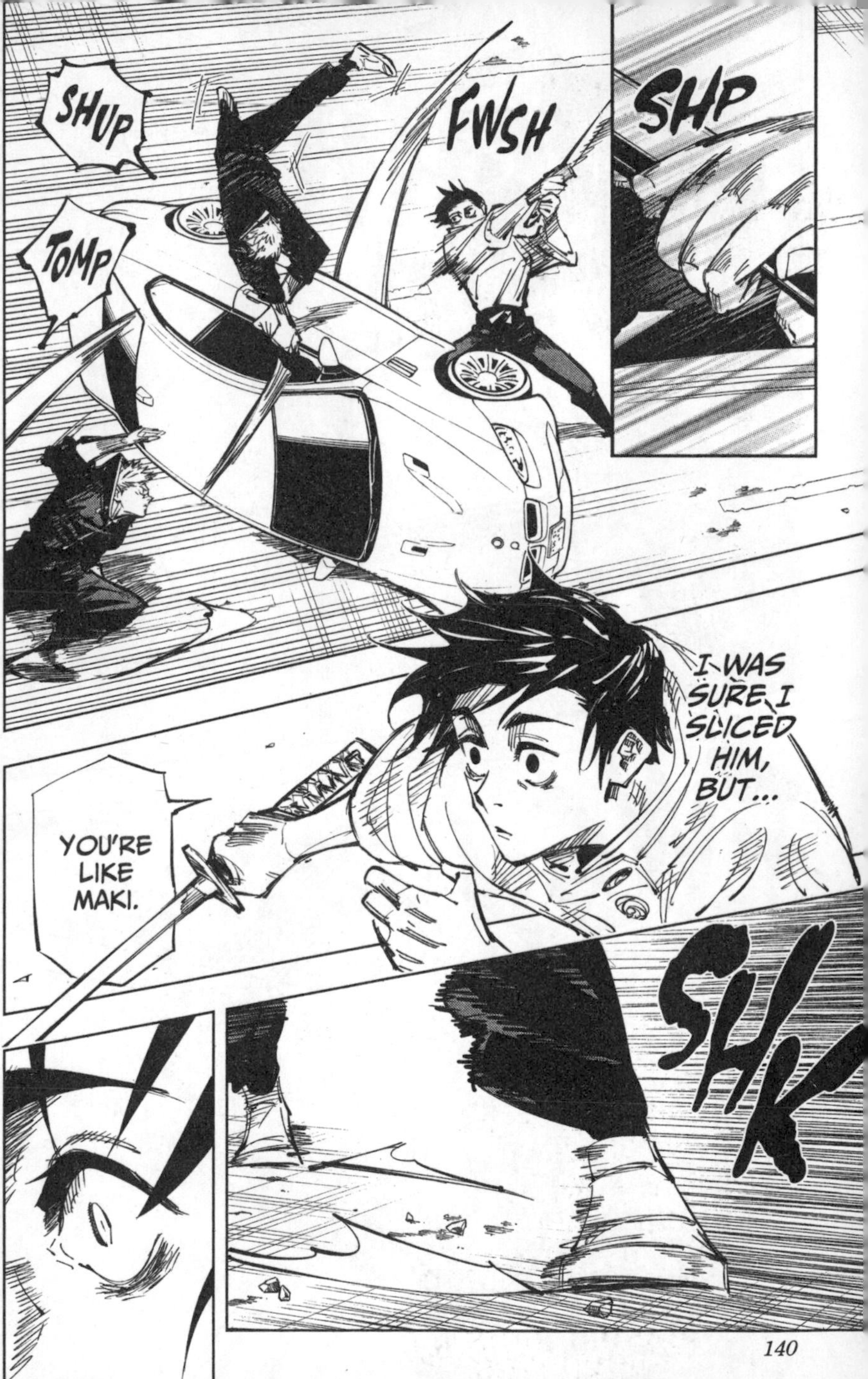
SHP
FWSH
SHUP
TOMP
I WAS SURE I SLICED HIM, BUT...
YOU'RE LIKE MAKI.
SHK

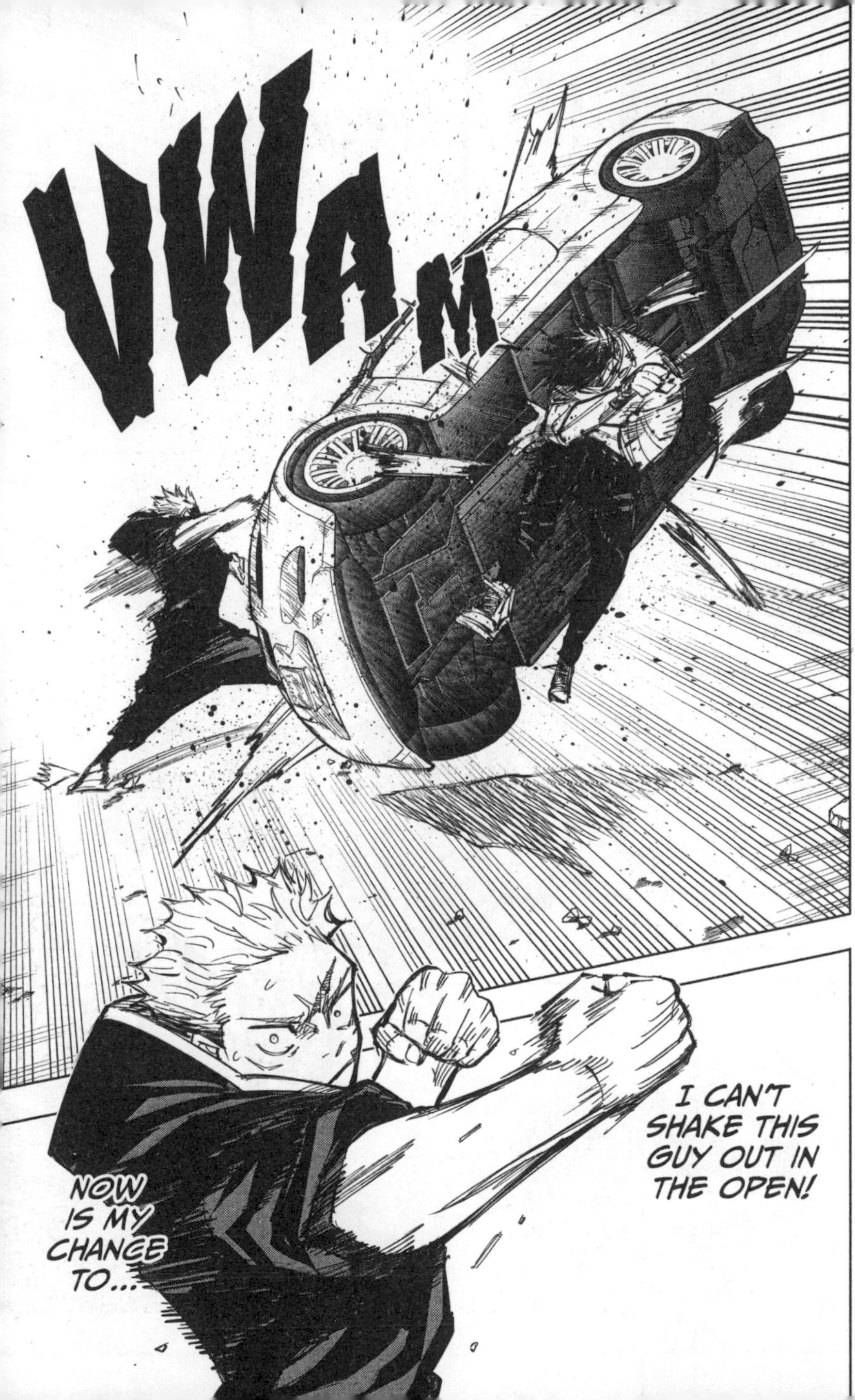
VWAM
I CAN'T SHAKE THIS GUY OUT IN THE OPEN!
NOW IS MY CHANCE TO...

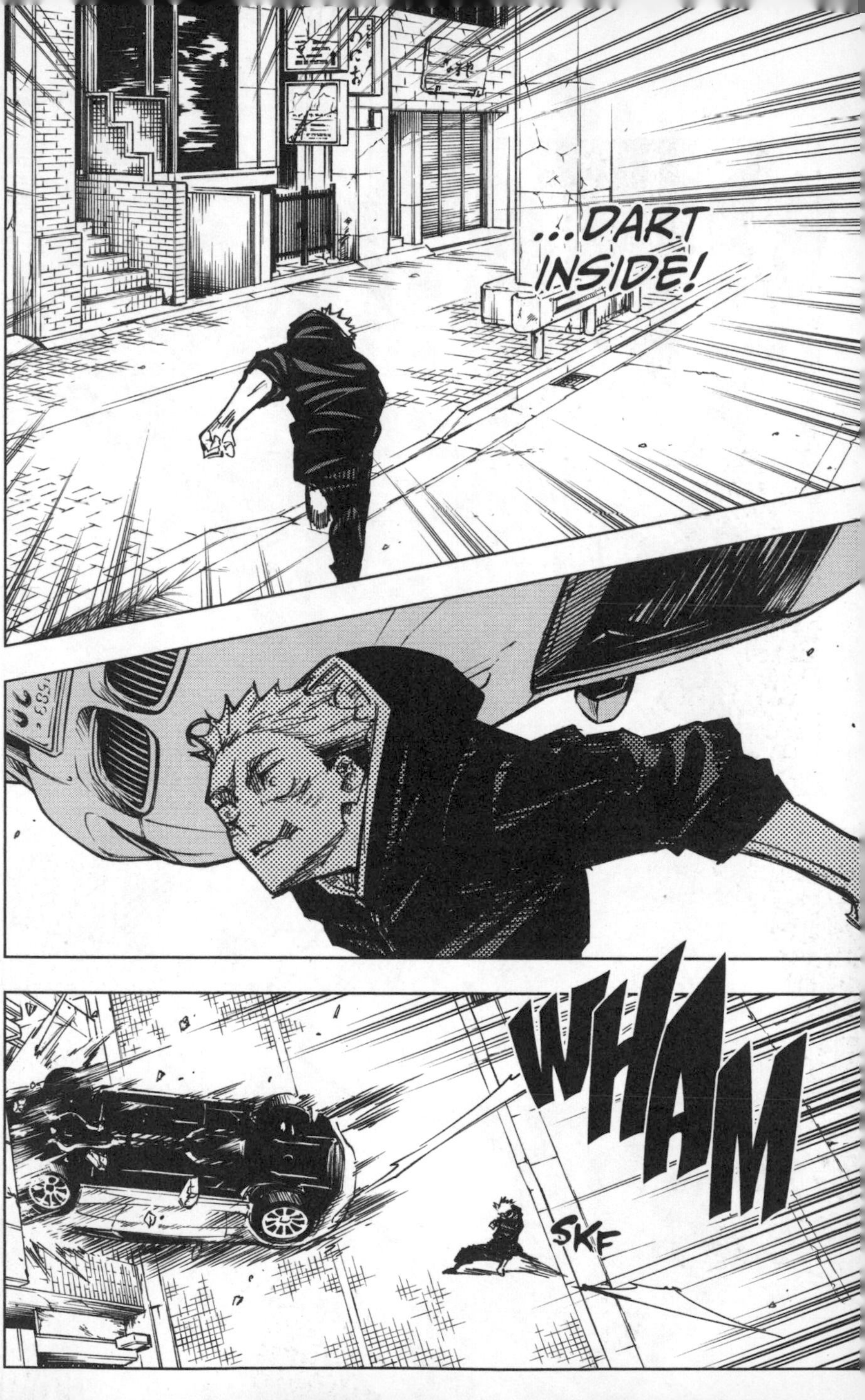
...DART INSIDE!
WHAM
SKF

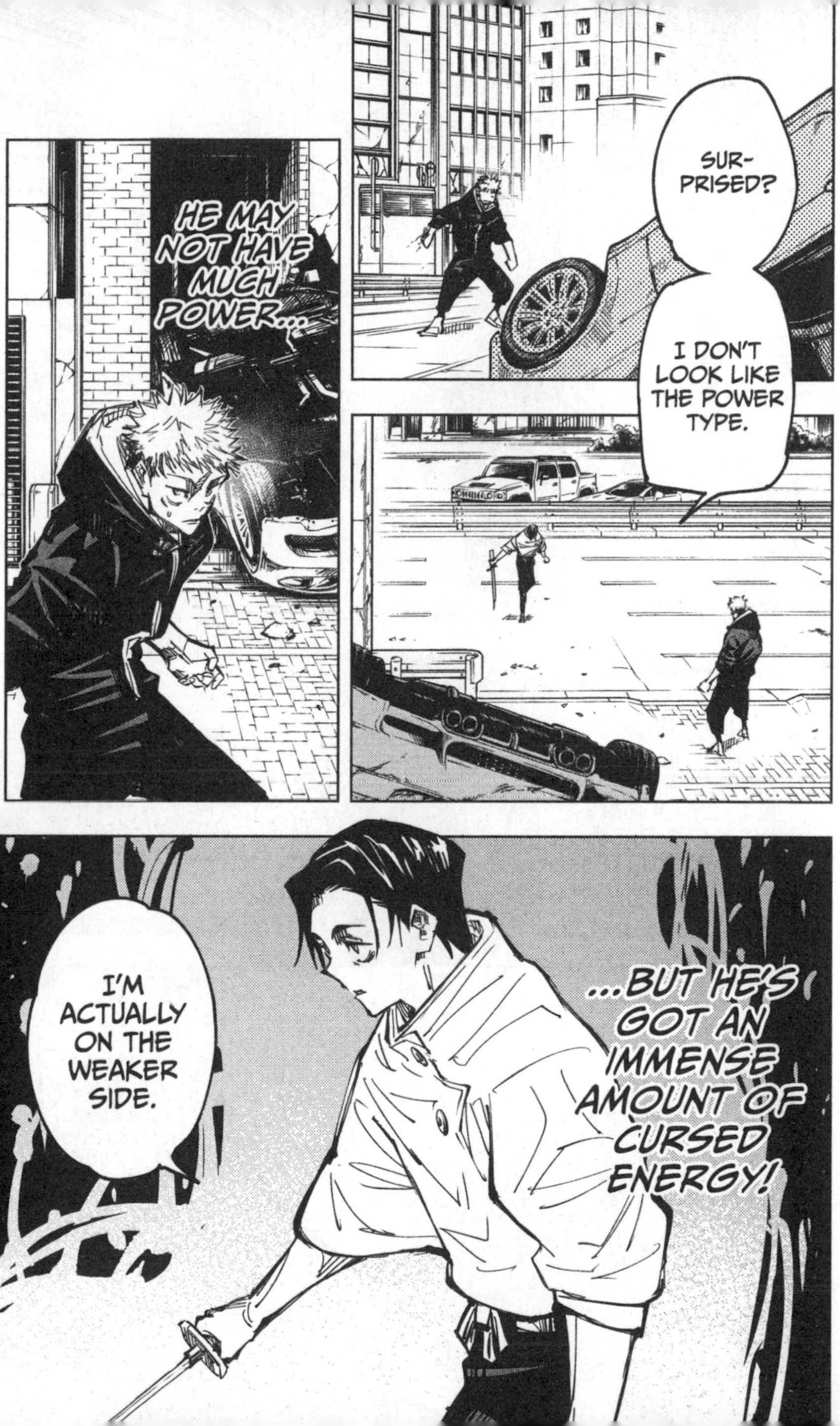
SUR-PRISED?
I DON'T LOOK LIKE THE POWER TYPE.
HE MAY NOT HAVE MUCH POWER...
...BUT HE'S GOT AN IMMENSE AMOUNT OF CURSED ENERGY!
I'M ACTUALLY ON THE WEAKER SIDE.

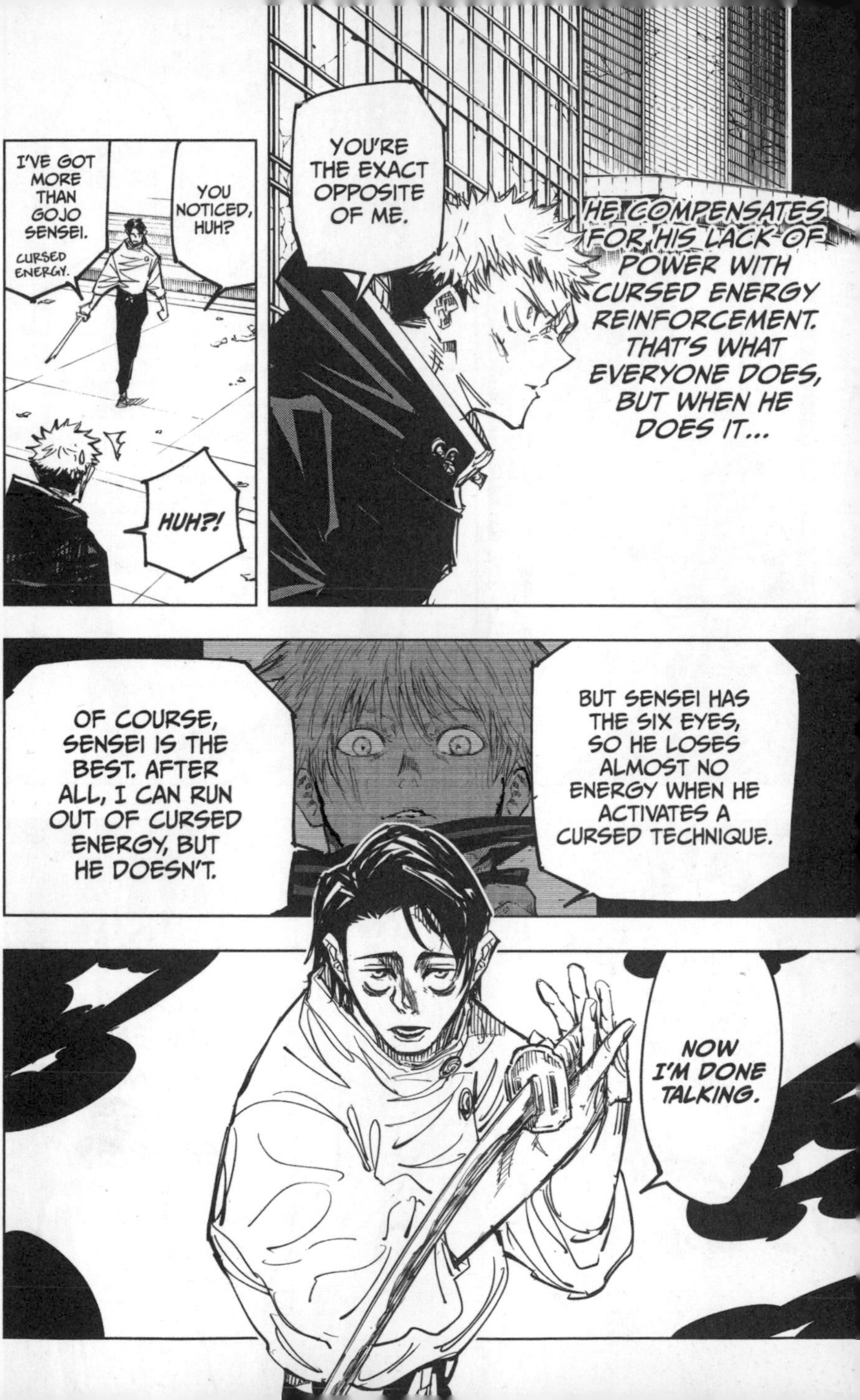
YOU'RE THE EXACT OPPOSITE OF ME.
HE COMPENSATES FOR HIS LACK OF POWER WITH CURSED ENERGY REINFORCEMENT. THAT'S WHAT EVERYONE DOES, BUT WHEN HE DOES IT...
YOU NOTICED, HUH?
I'VE GOT MORE THAN GOJO SENSEI.
CURSED ENERGY.
HUH?!
BUT SENSEI HAS THE SIX EYES, SO HE LOSES ALMOST NO ENERGY WHEN HE ACTIVATES A CURSED TECHNIQUE.
OF COURSE, SENSEI IS THE BEST. AFTER ALL, I CAN RUN OUT OF CURSED ENERGY, BUT HE DOESN'T.
NOW I'M DONE TALKING.

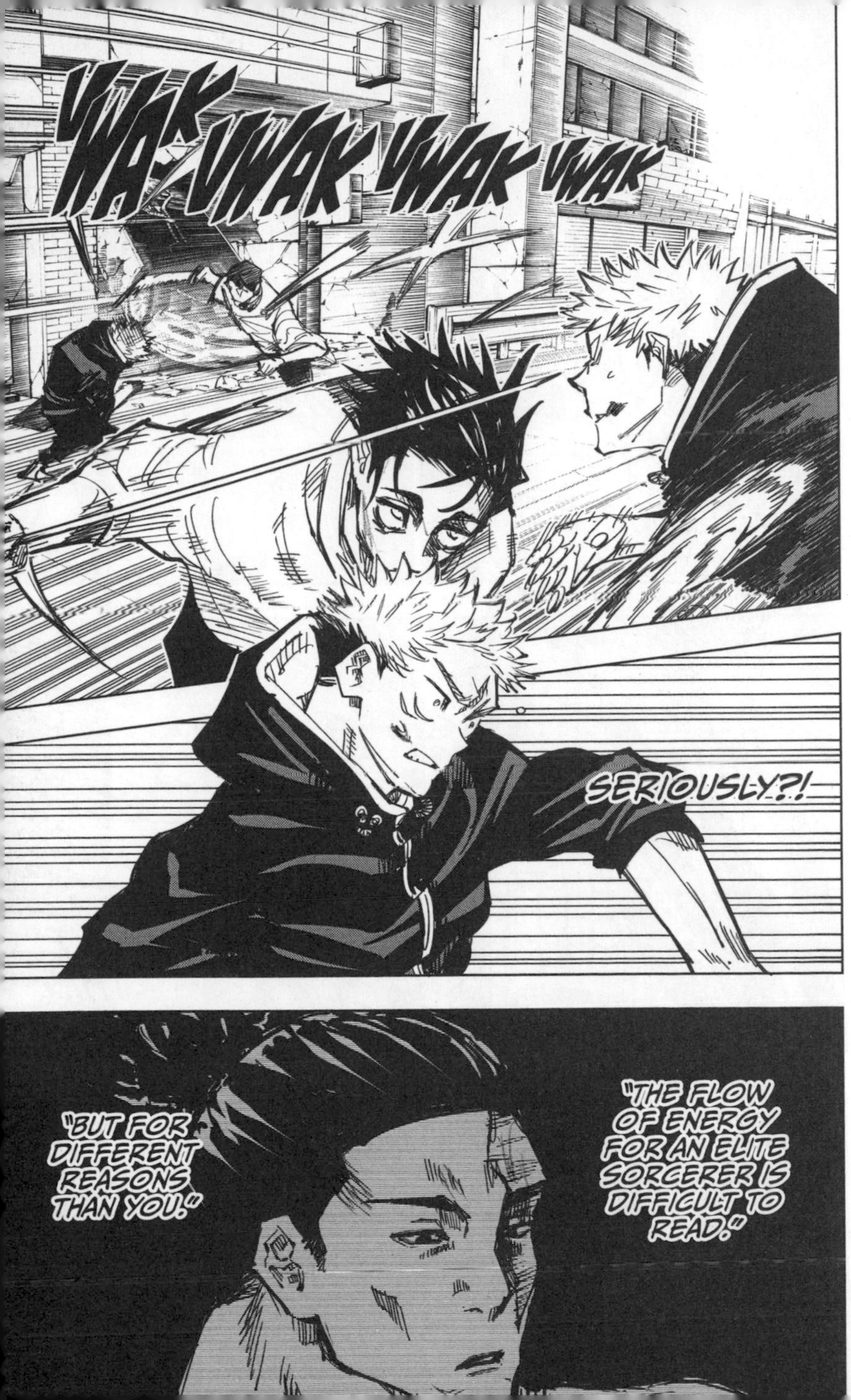
VWAK VWAK VWAK VWAK
SERIOUSLY?!
"THE FLOW OF ENERGY FOR AN ELITE SORCERER IS DIFFICULT TO READ."
"BUT FOR DIFFERENT REASONS THAN YOU."

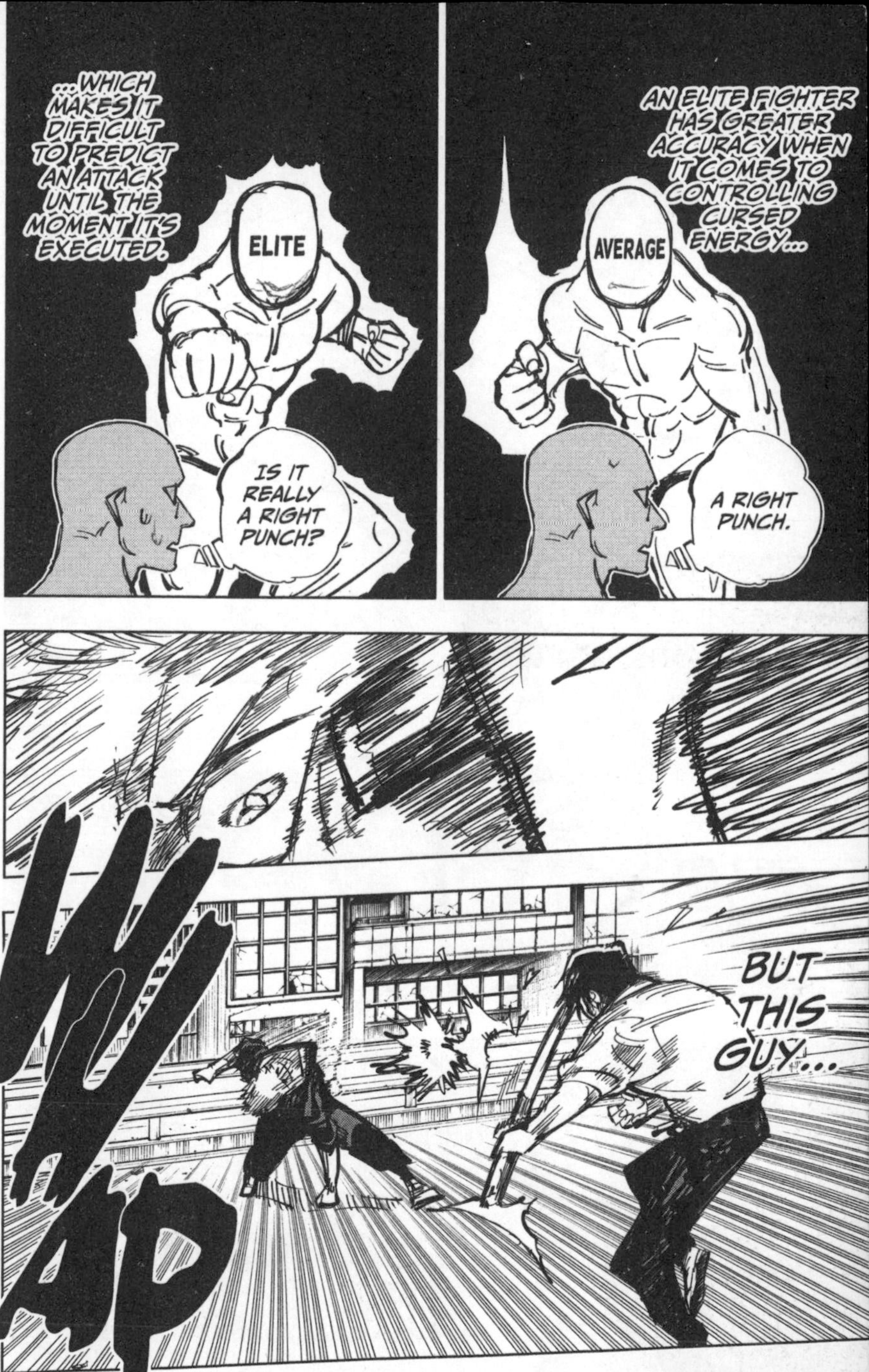
AN ELITE FIGHTER HAS GREATER ACCURACY WHEN IT COMES TO CONTROLLING CURSED ENERGY...
AVERAGE
A RIGHT PUNCH.
...WHICH MAKES IT DIFFICULT TO PREDICT AN ATTACK UNTIL THE MOMENT IT'S EXECUTED.
ELITE
IS IT REALLY A RIGHT PUNCH?
BUT THIS GUY...
WHAP

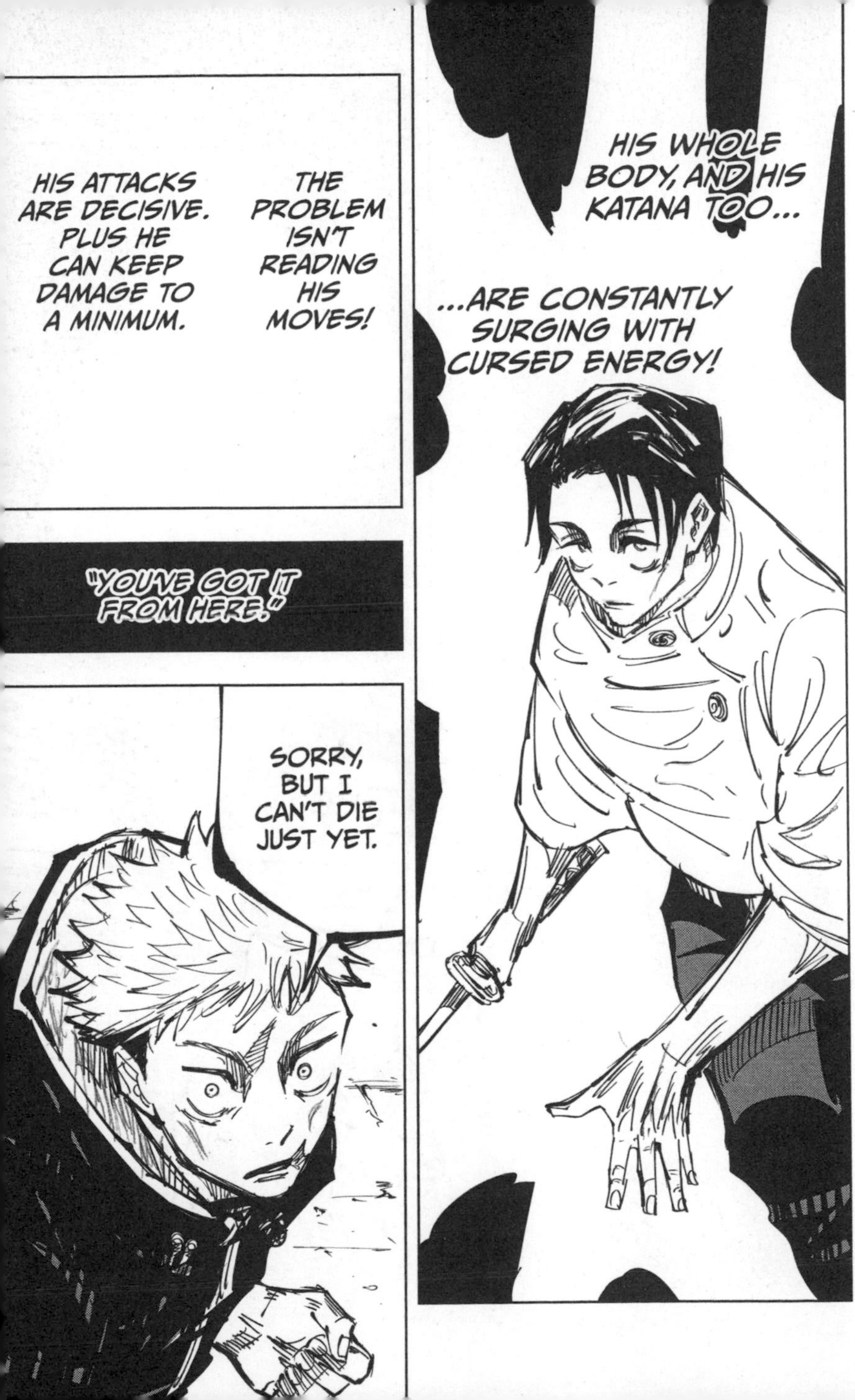
HIS WHOLE BODY, AND HIS KATANA TOO...
...ARE CONSTANTLY SURGING WITH CURSED ENERGY!
THE PROBLEM ISN'T READING HIS MOVES!
HIS ATTACKS ARE DECISIVE. PLUS HE CAN KEEP DAMAGE TO A MINIMUM.
"YOU'VE GOT IT FROM HERE."
SORRY, BUT I CAN'T DIE JUST YET.

OKKOTSU

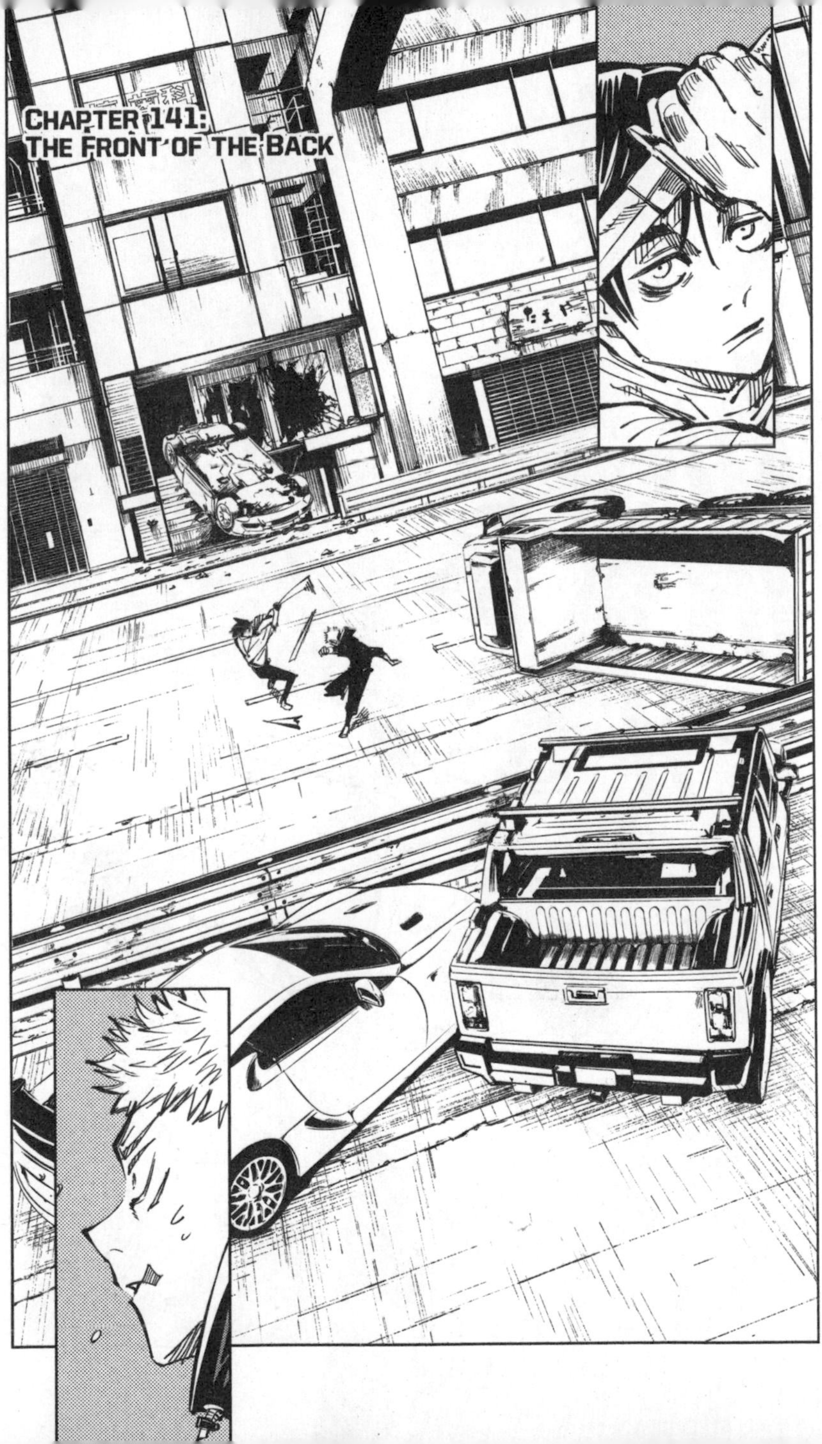
CHAPTER 141:
THE FRONT OF THE BACK

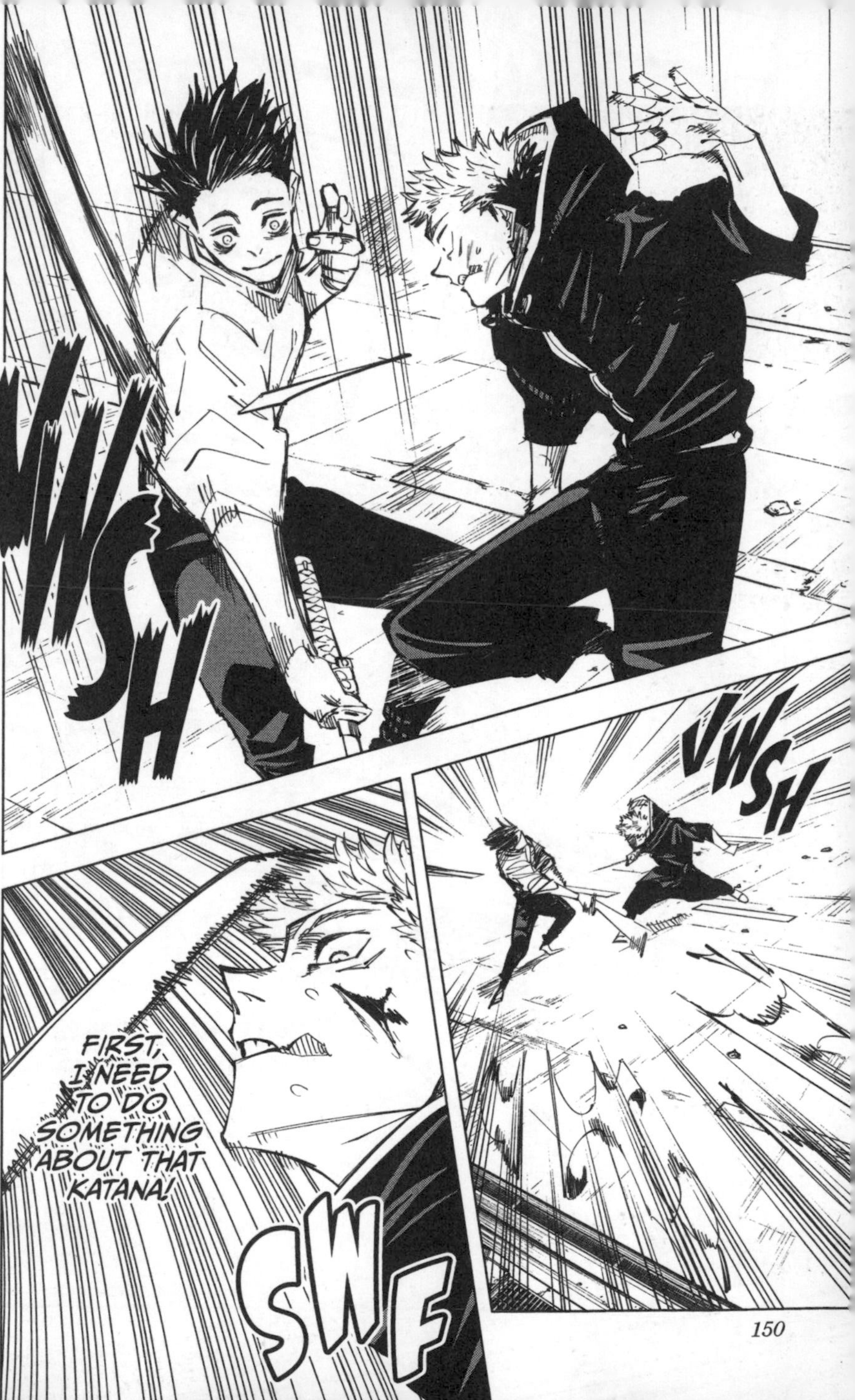
VWSH
VWSH
FIRST, I NEED TO DO SOMETHING ABOUT THAT KATANA!
SWF

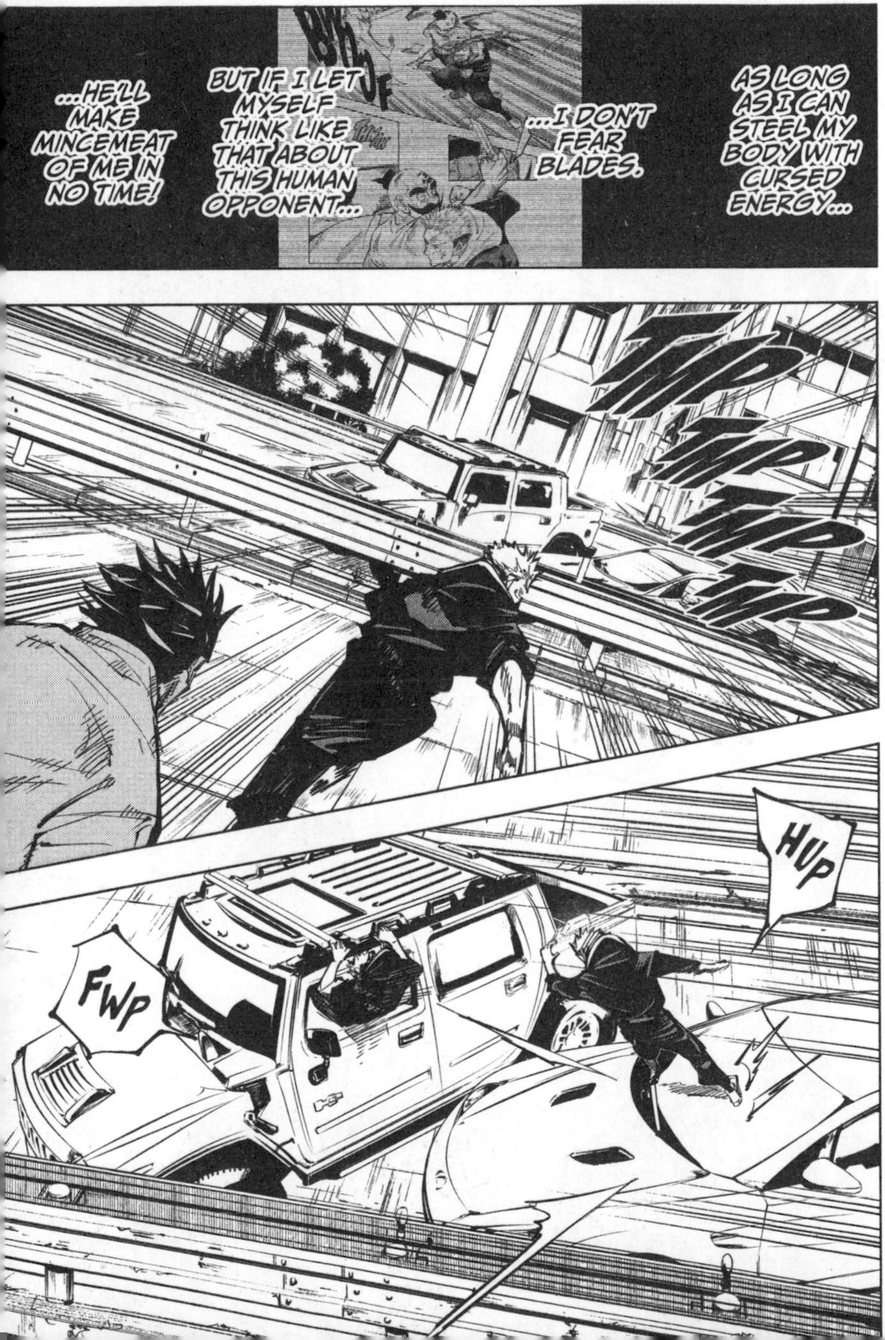
AS LONG AS I CAN STEEL MY BODY WITH CURSED ENERGY...
...I DON'T FEAR BLADES.
BUT IF I LET MYSELF THINK LIKE THAT ABOUT THIS HUMAN OPPONENT...
...HE'LL MAKE MINCEMEAT OF ME IN NO TIME!
TMP TMP TMP TMP
HUP
FWP

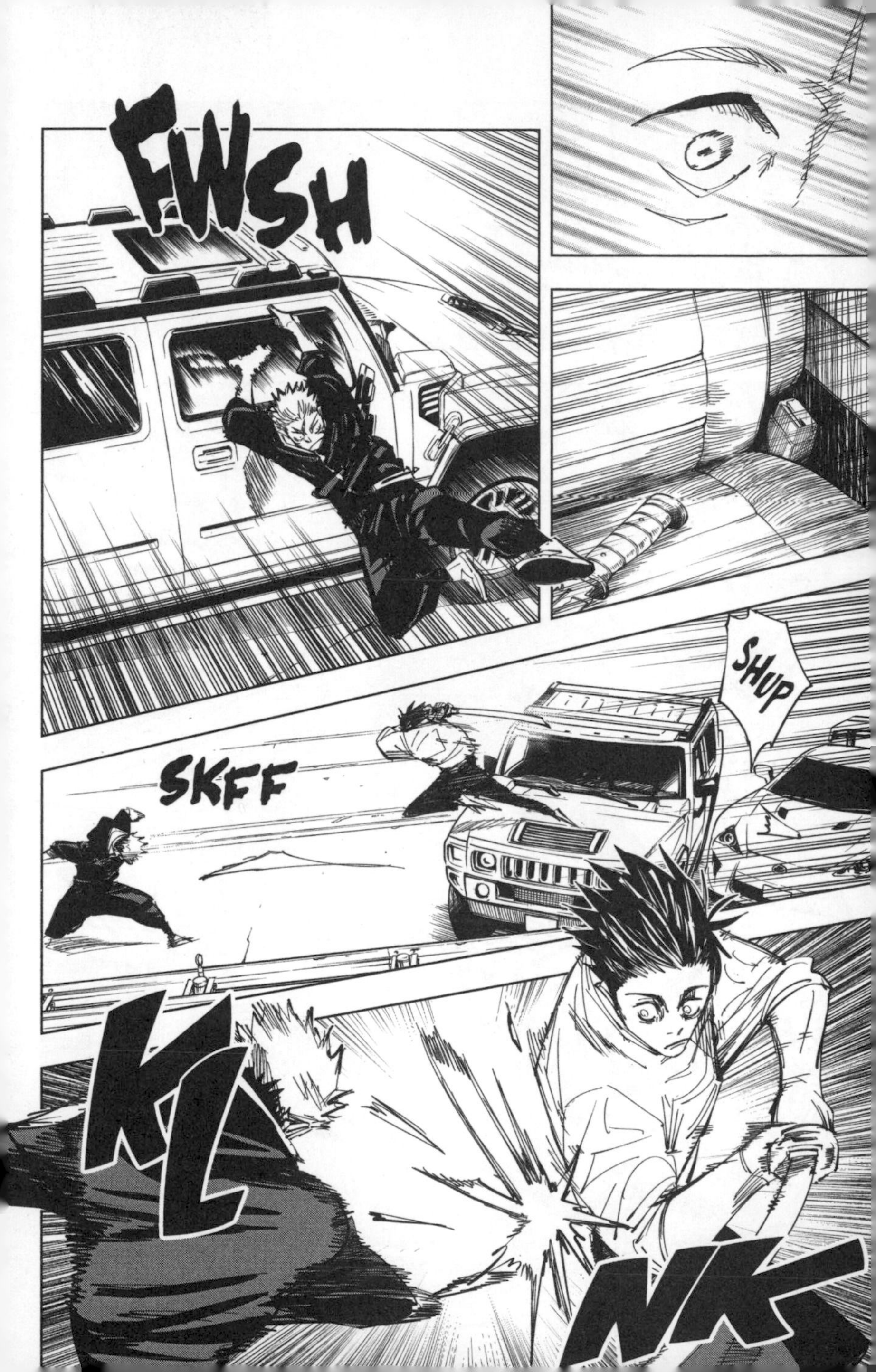
FWSH
SHUP
SKFF
KL
NK

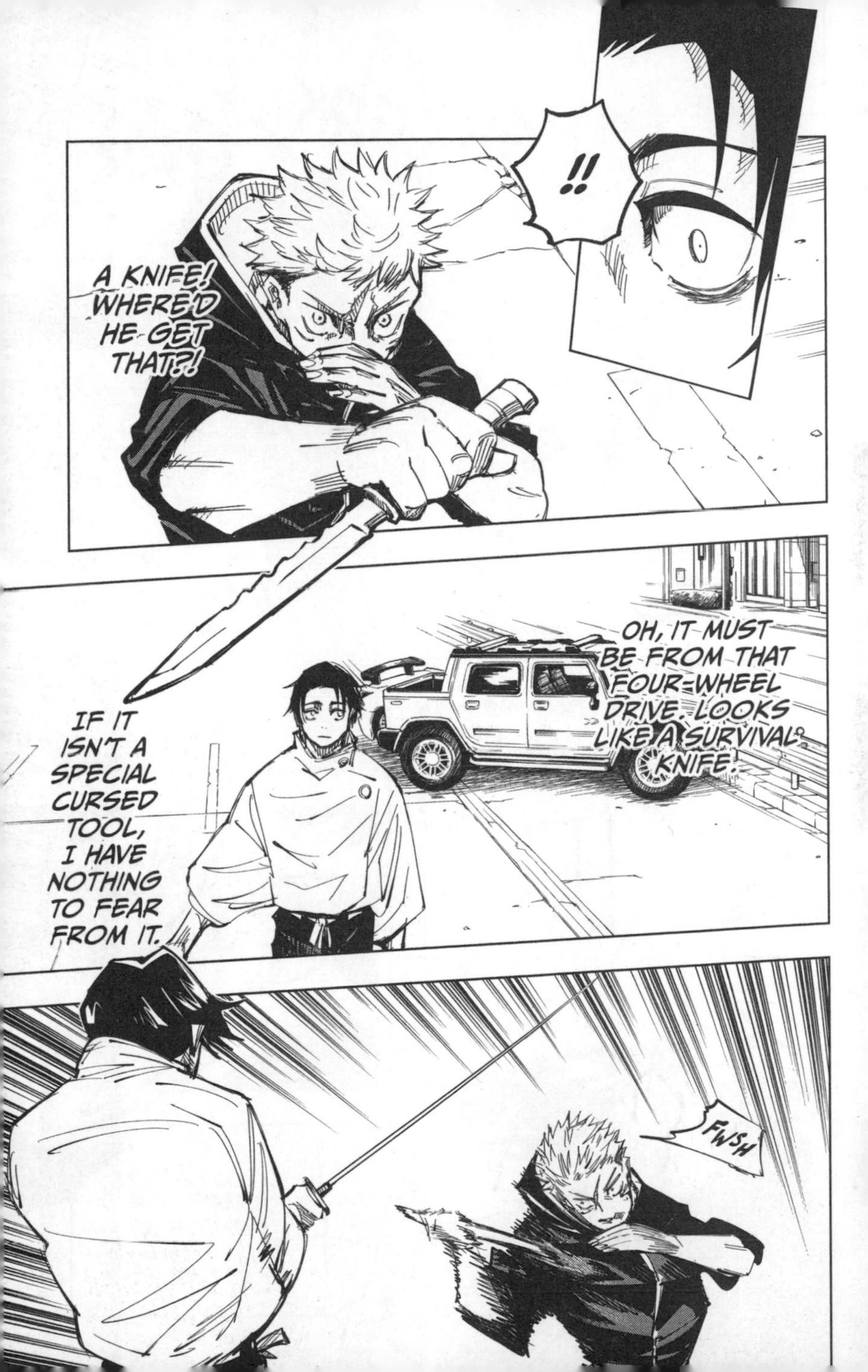
!!
A KNIFE! WHERE'D HE GET THAT?!
OH, IT MUST BE FROM THAT FOUR-WHEEL DRIVE. LOOKS LIKE A SURVIVAL KNIFE.
IF IT ISN'T A SPECIAL CURSED TOOL, I HAVE NOTHING TO FEAR FROM IT.
FWSH

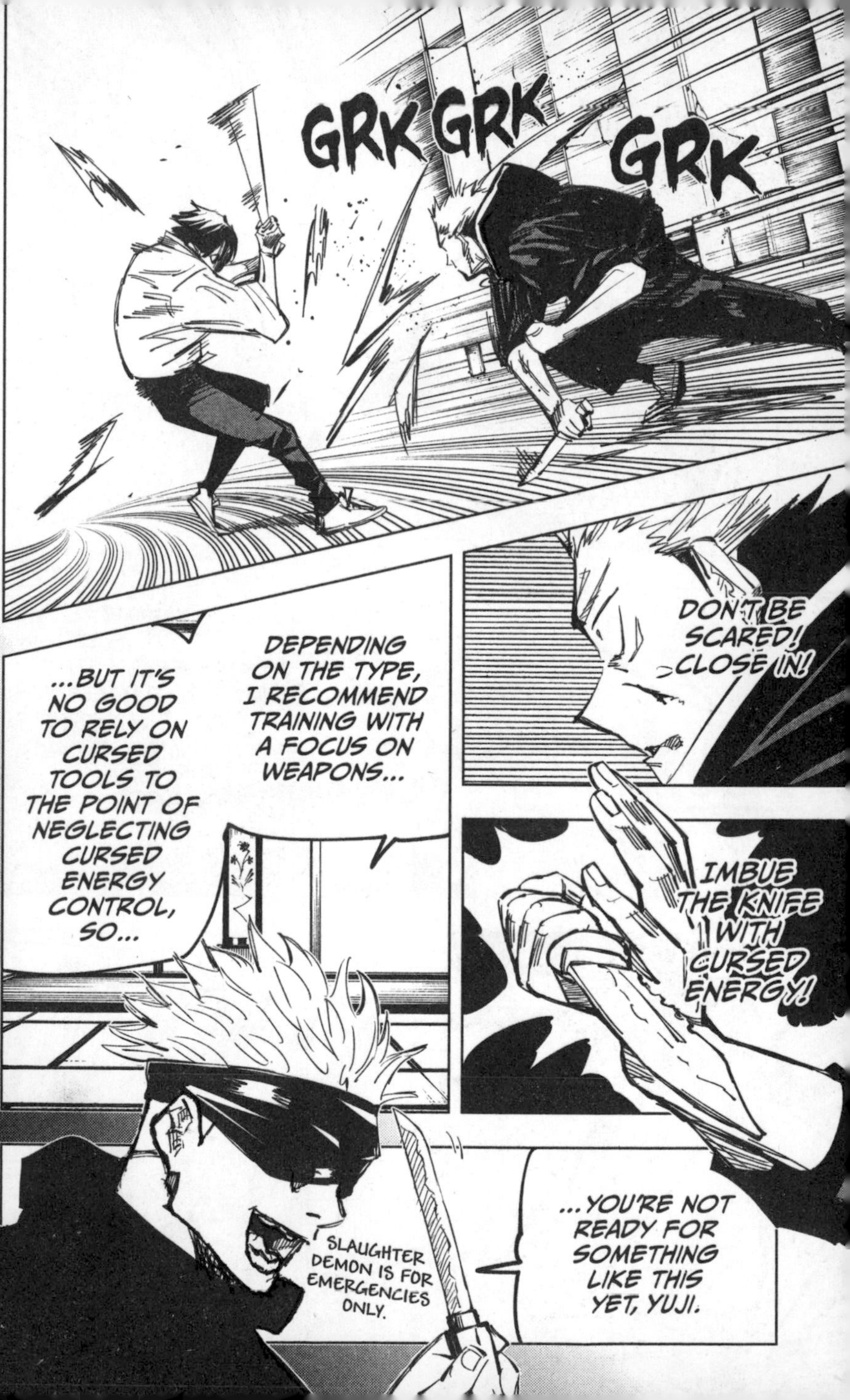
GRK GRK GRK
DON'T BE SCARED! CLOSE IN!
IMBUE THE KNIFE WITH CURSED ENERGY!
DEPENDING ON THE TYPE, I RECOMMEND TRAINING WITH A FOCUS ON WEAPONS...
...BUT IT'S NO GOOD TO RELY ON CURSED TOOLS TO THE POINT OF NEGLECTING CURSED ENERGY CONTROL, SO...
...YOU'RE NOT READY FOR SOMETHING LIKE THIS YET, YUJI.
SLAUGHTER DEMON IS FOR EMERGENCIES ONLY.

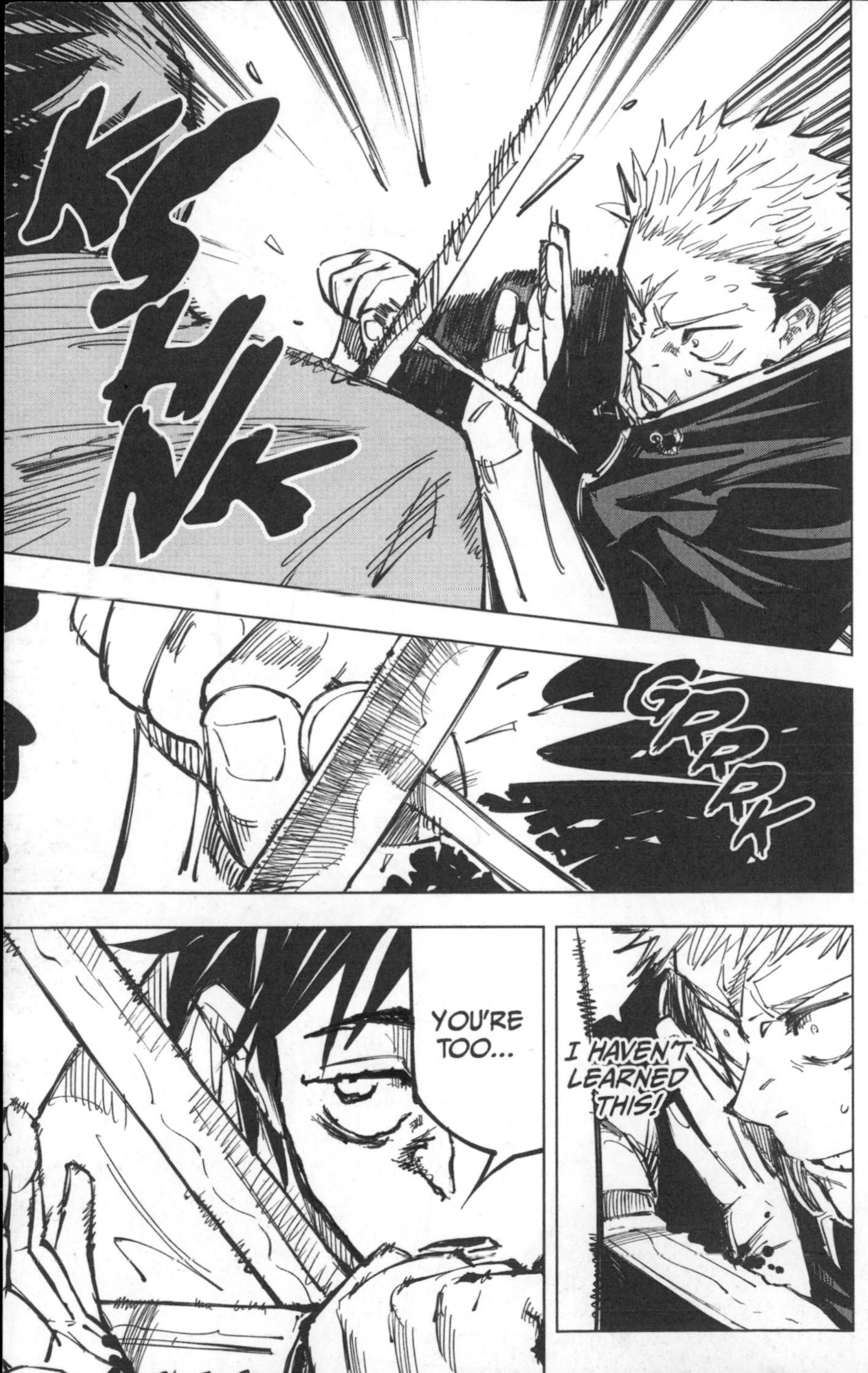
KSHNK
GRRRK
I HAVEN'T LEARNED THIS!
YOU'RE TOO...

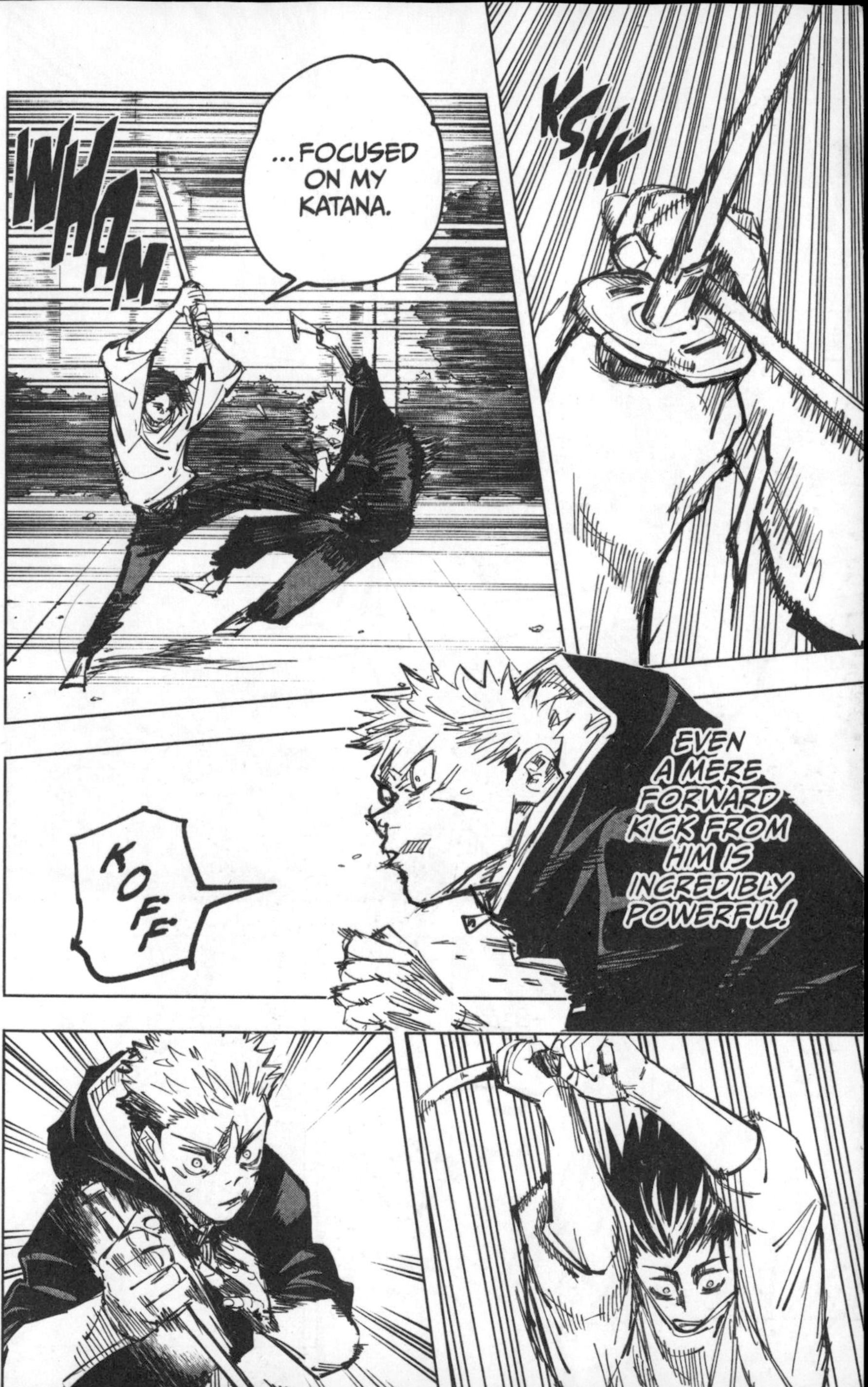
KSHK
...FOCUSED ON MY KATANA.
WHAM
EVEN A MERE FORWARD KICK FROM HIM IS INCREDIBLY POWERFUL!
KOFF

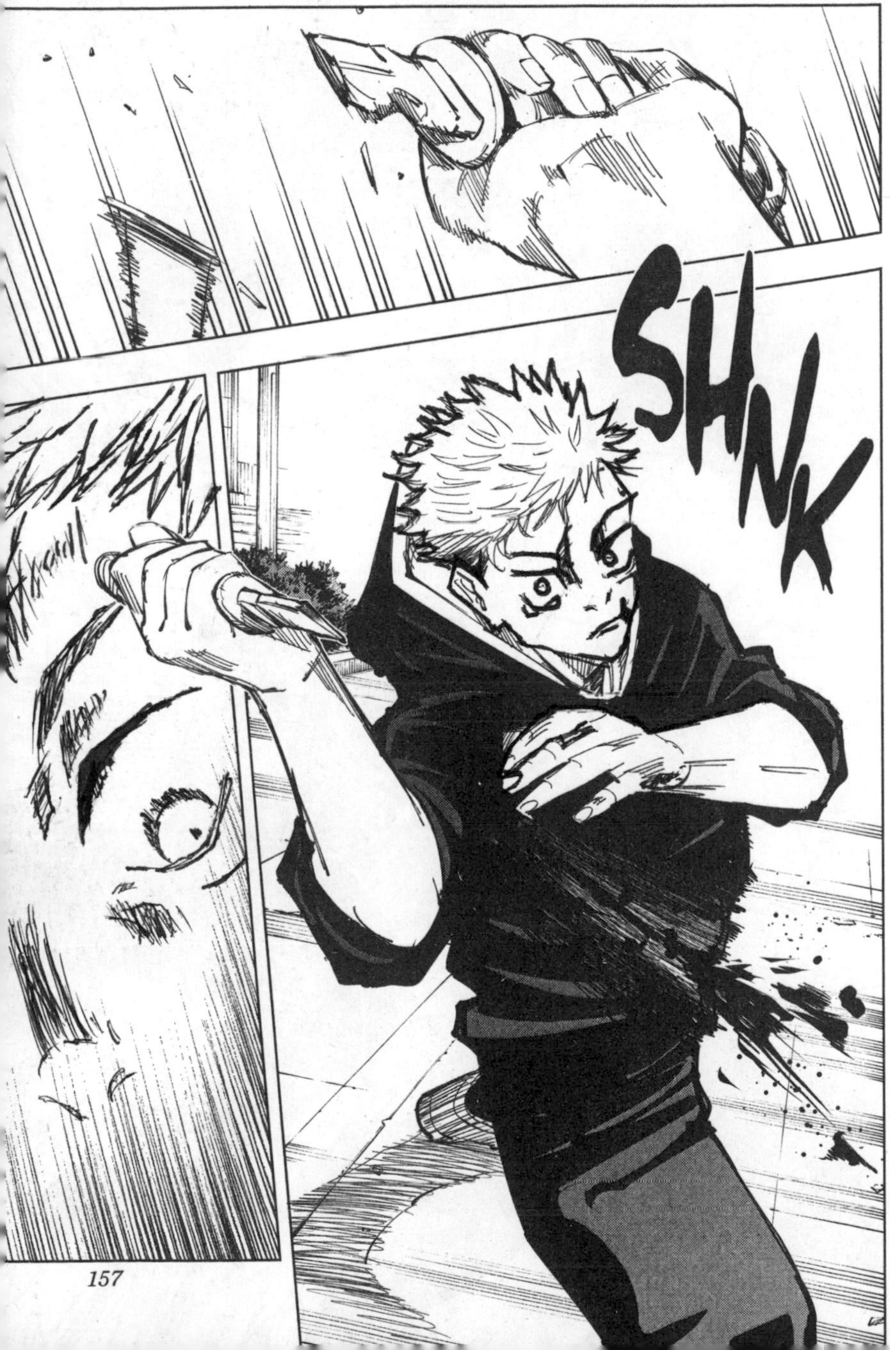
SHINK

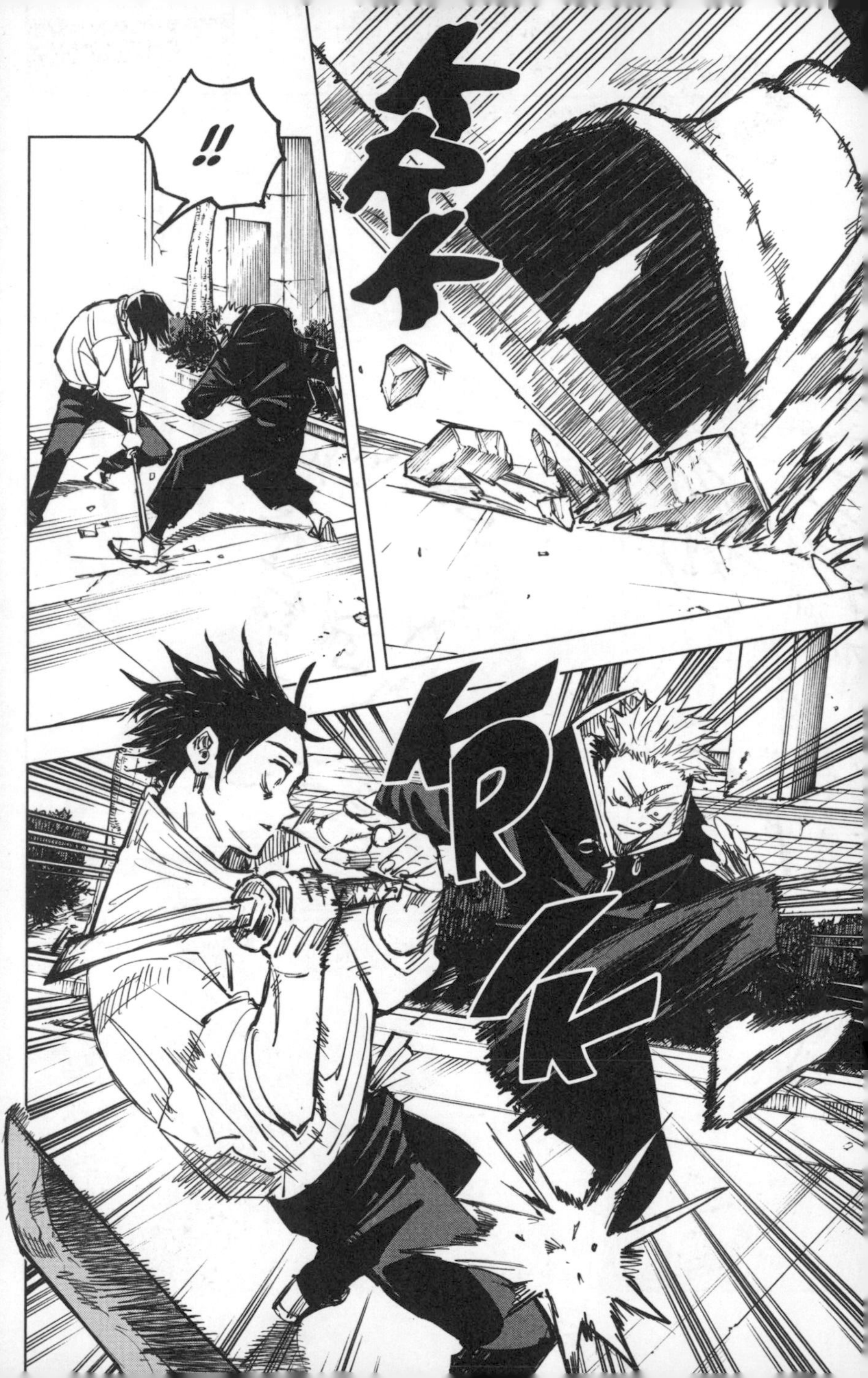
!!
KRIK

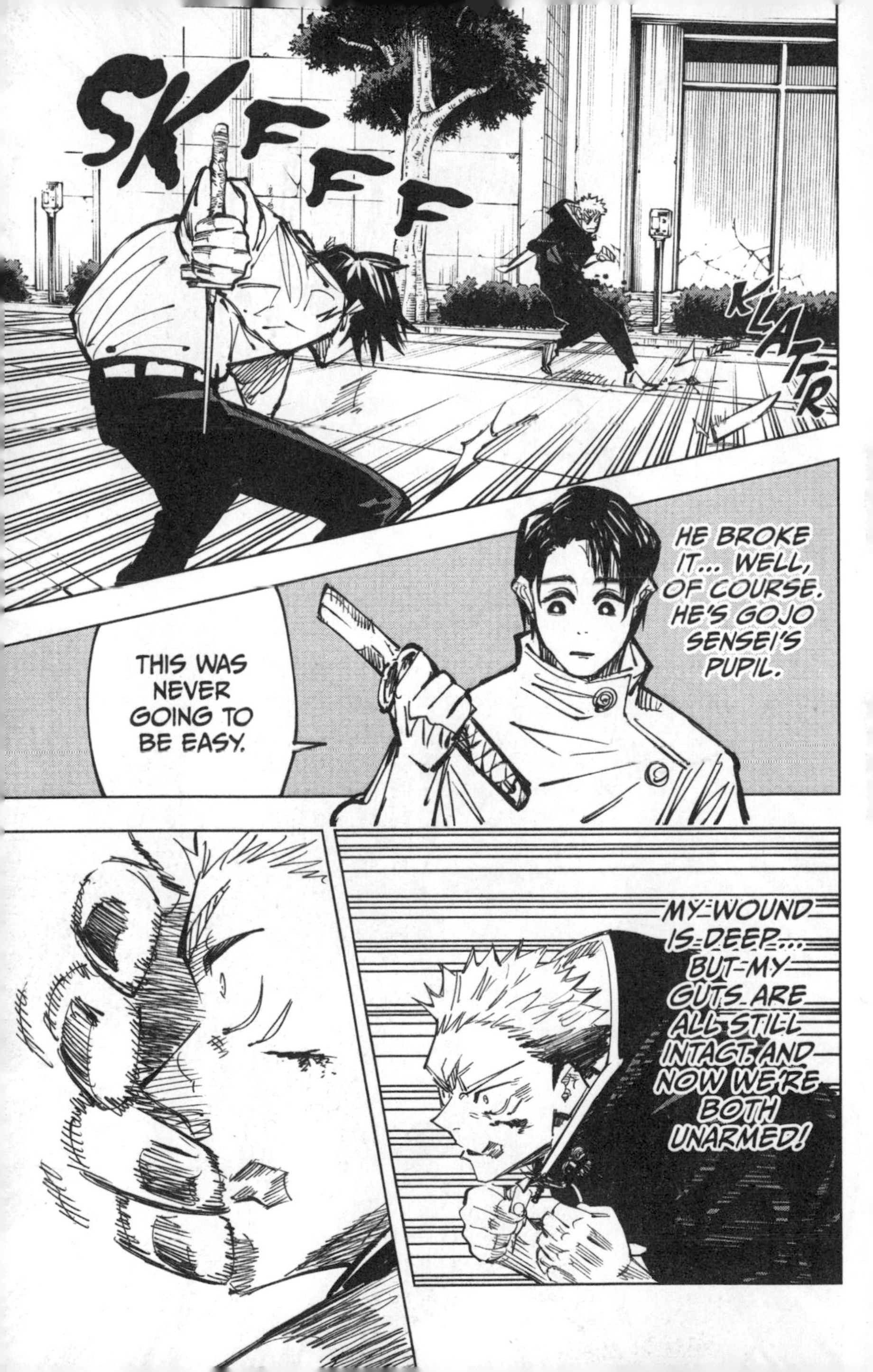
KLATTR
SKFFF
HE BROKE IT... WELL, OF COURSE. HE'S GOJO SENSEI'S PUPIL.
THIS WAS NEVER GOING TO BE EASY.
MY WOUND IS DEEP... BUT MY GUTS ARE ALL STILL INTACT AND NOW WE'RE BOTH UNARMED!

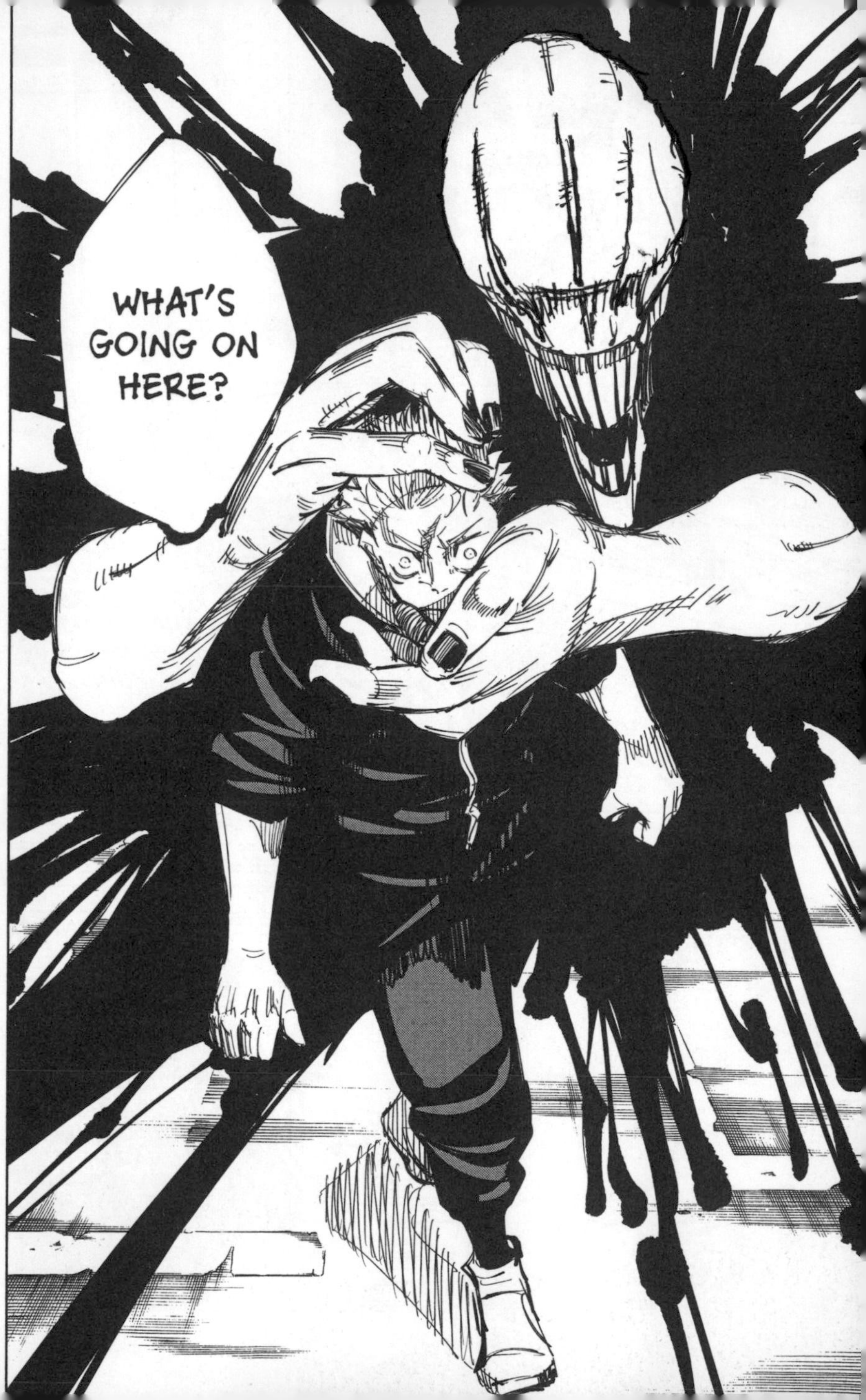
WHAT'S GOING ON HERE?

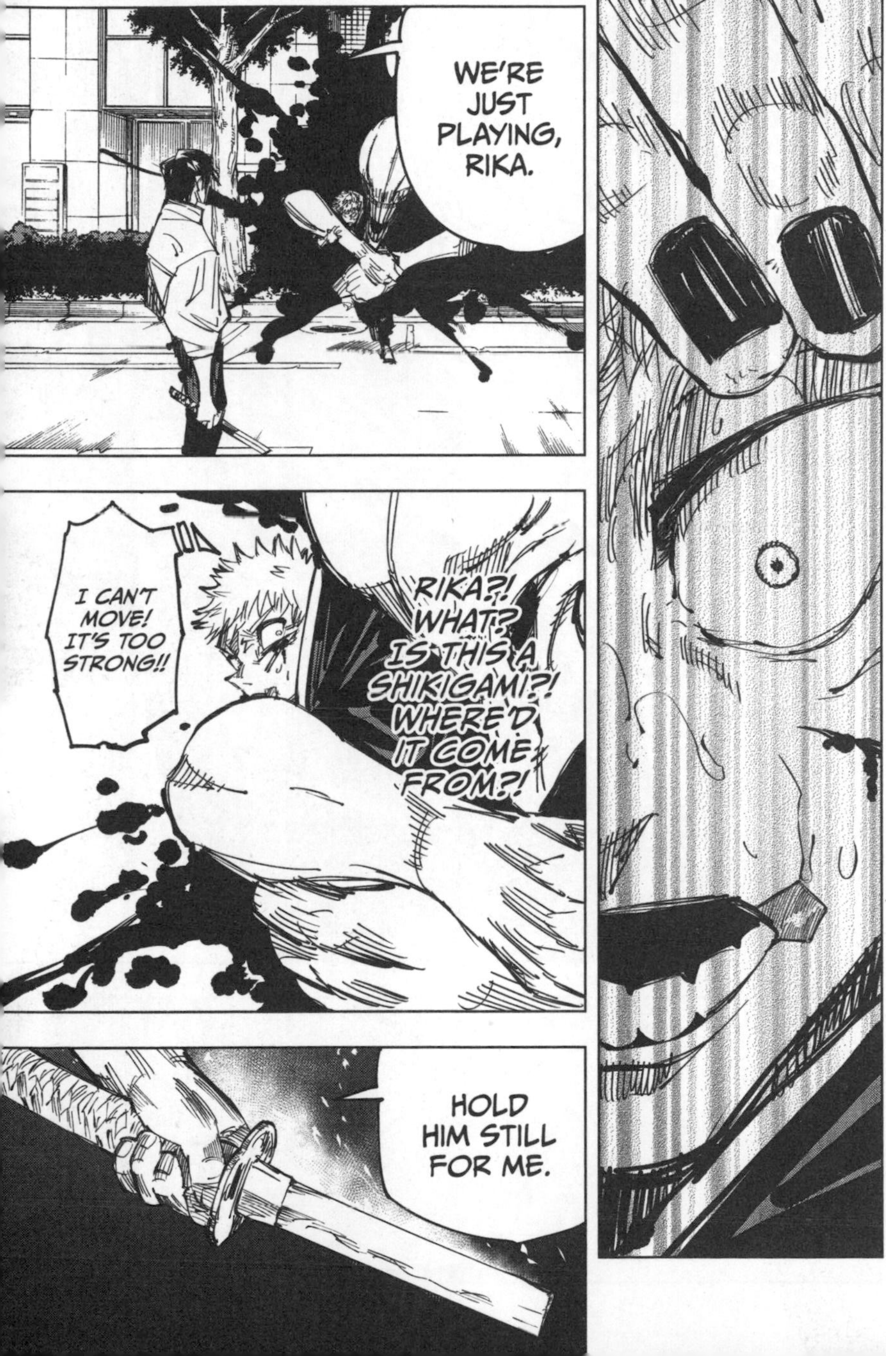
WE'RE JUST PLAYING, RIKA.
RIKA?! WHAT? IS THIS A SHIKIGAMI?! WHERE'D IT COME FROM?!
I CAN'T MOVE! IT'S TOO STRONG!!
HOLD HIM STILL FOR ME.

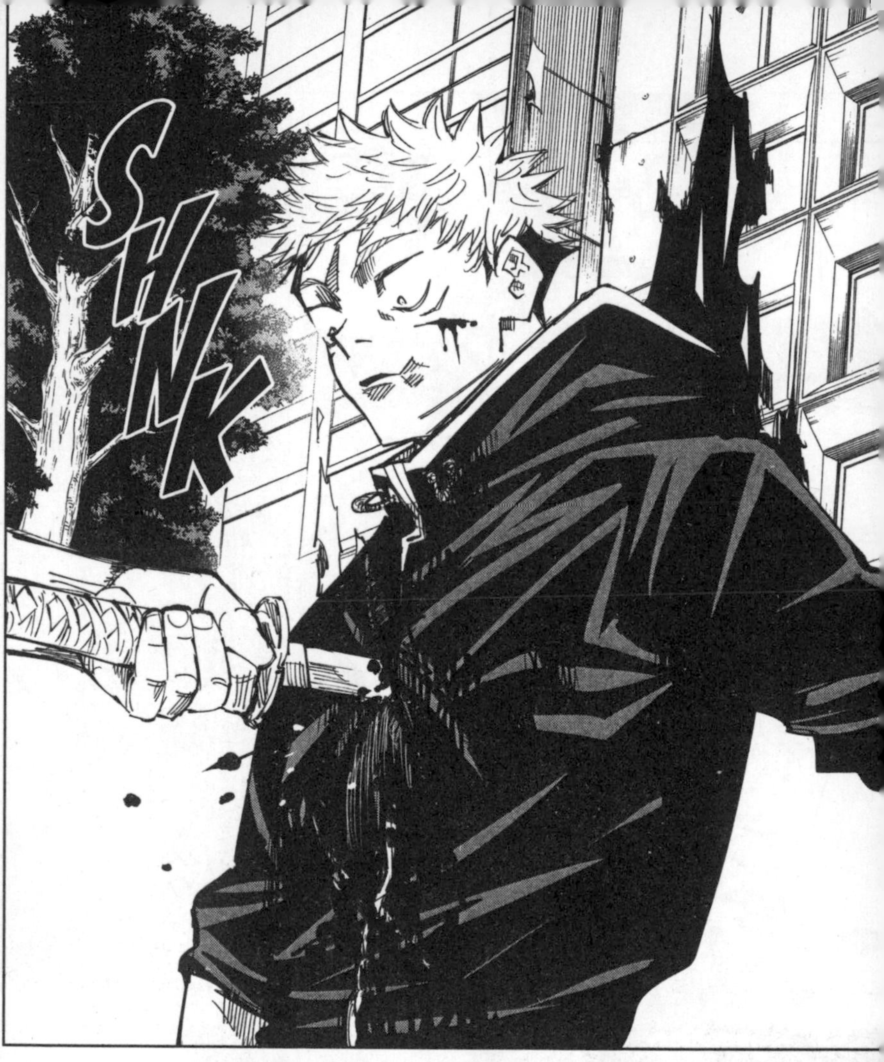
SHINK
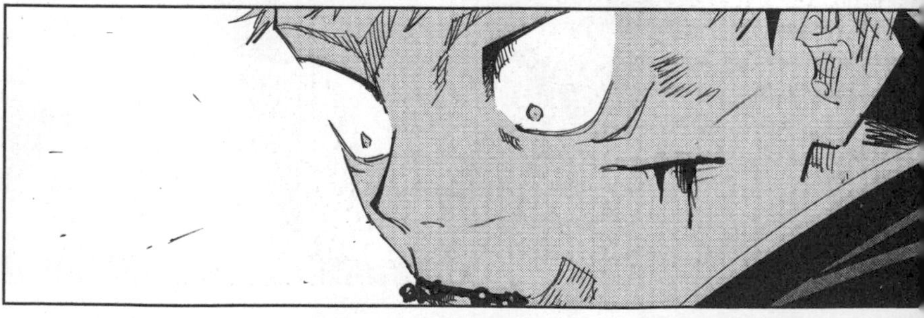

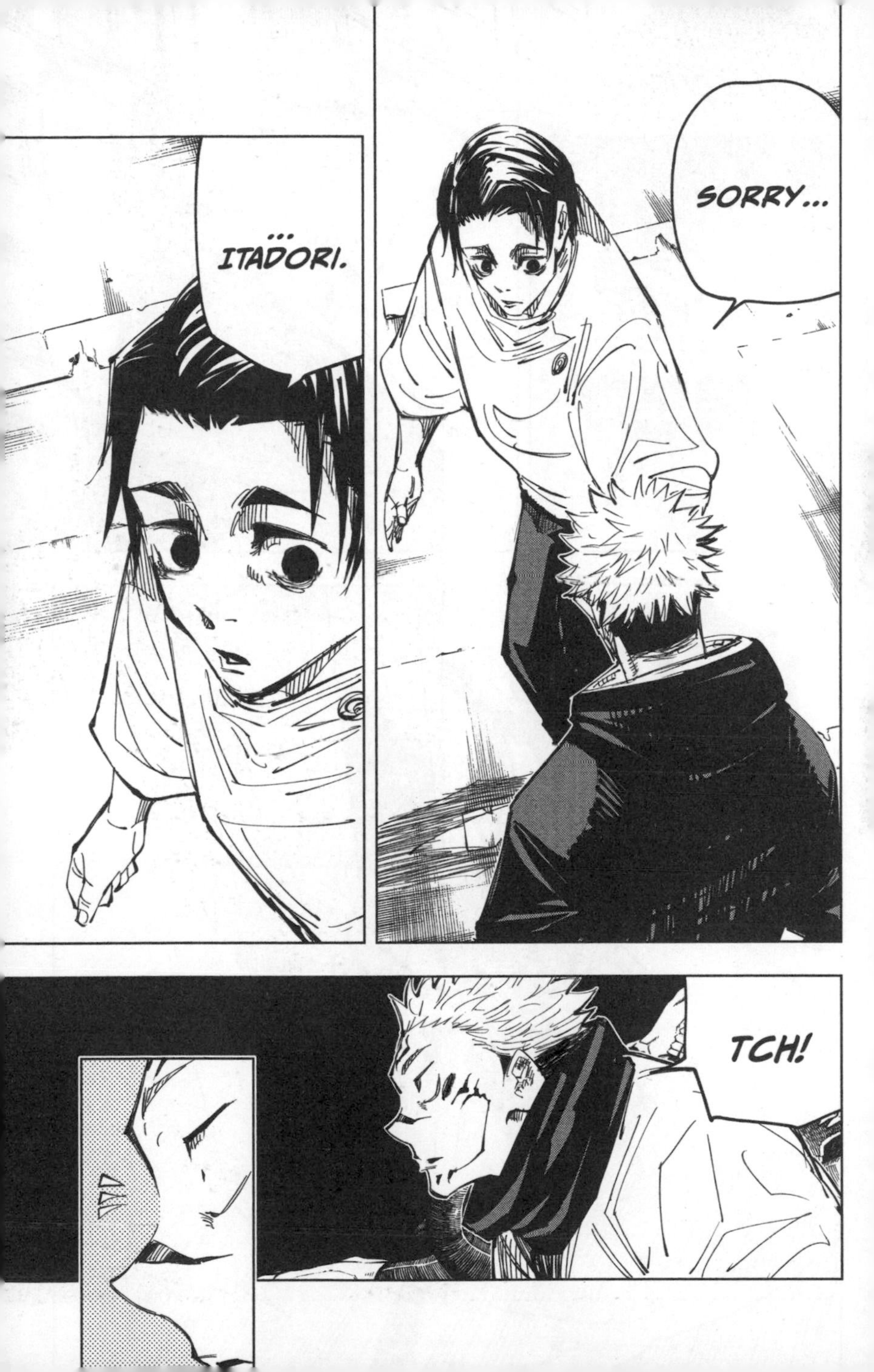
SORRY...
... ITADORI.
TCH!

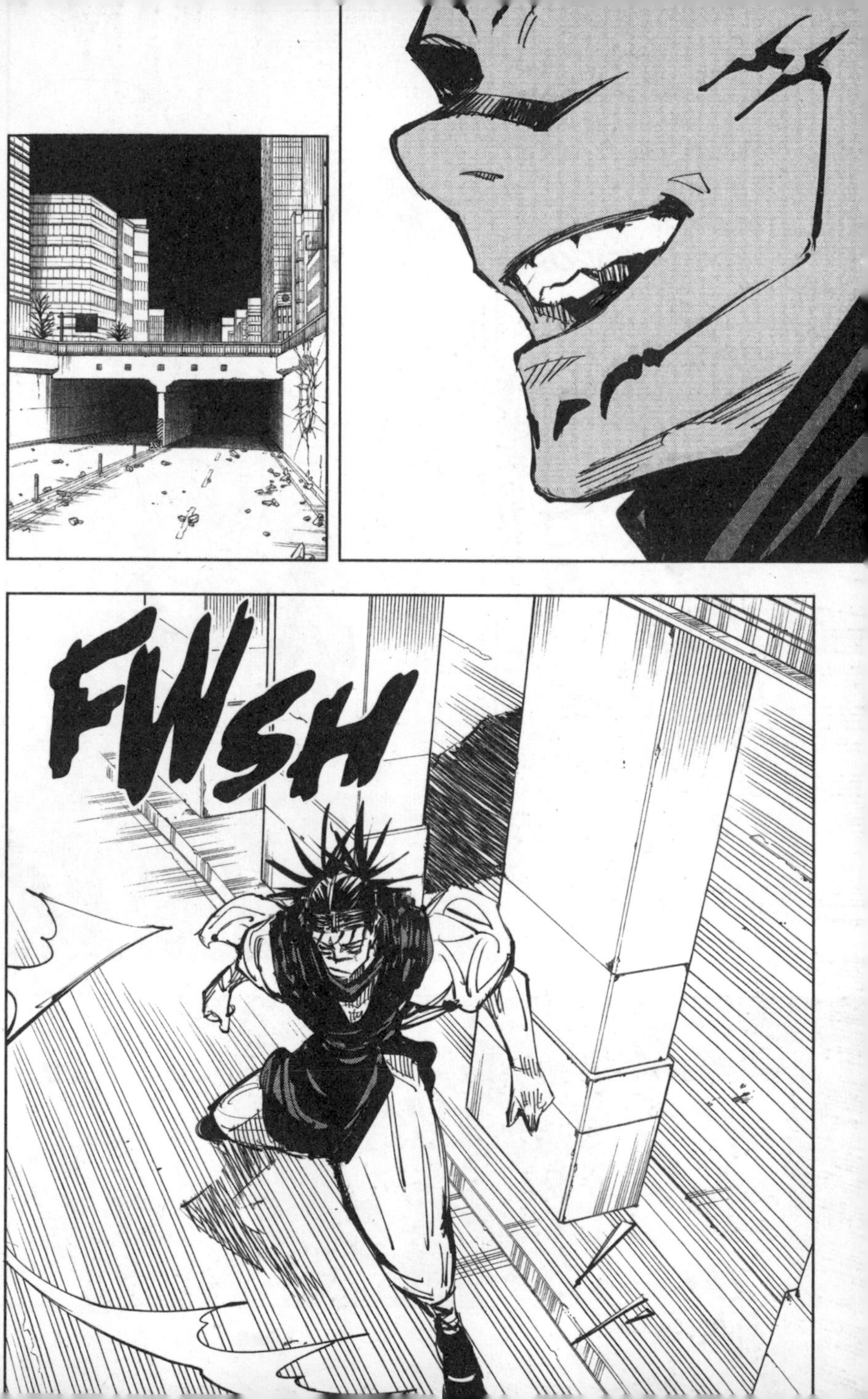
FWSH

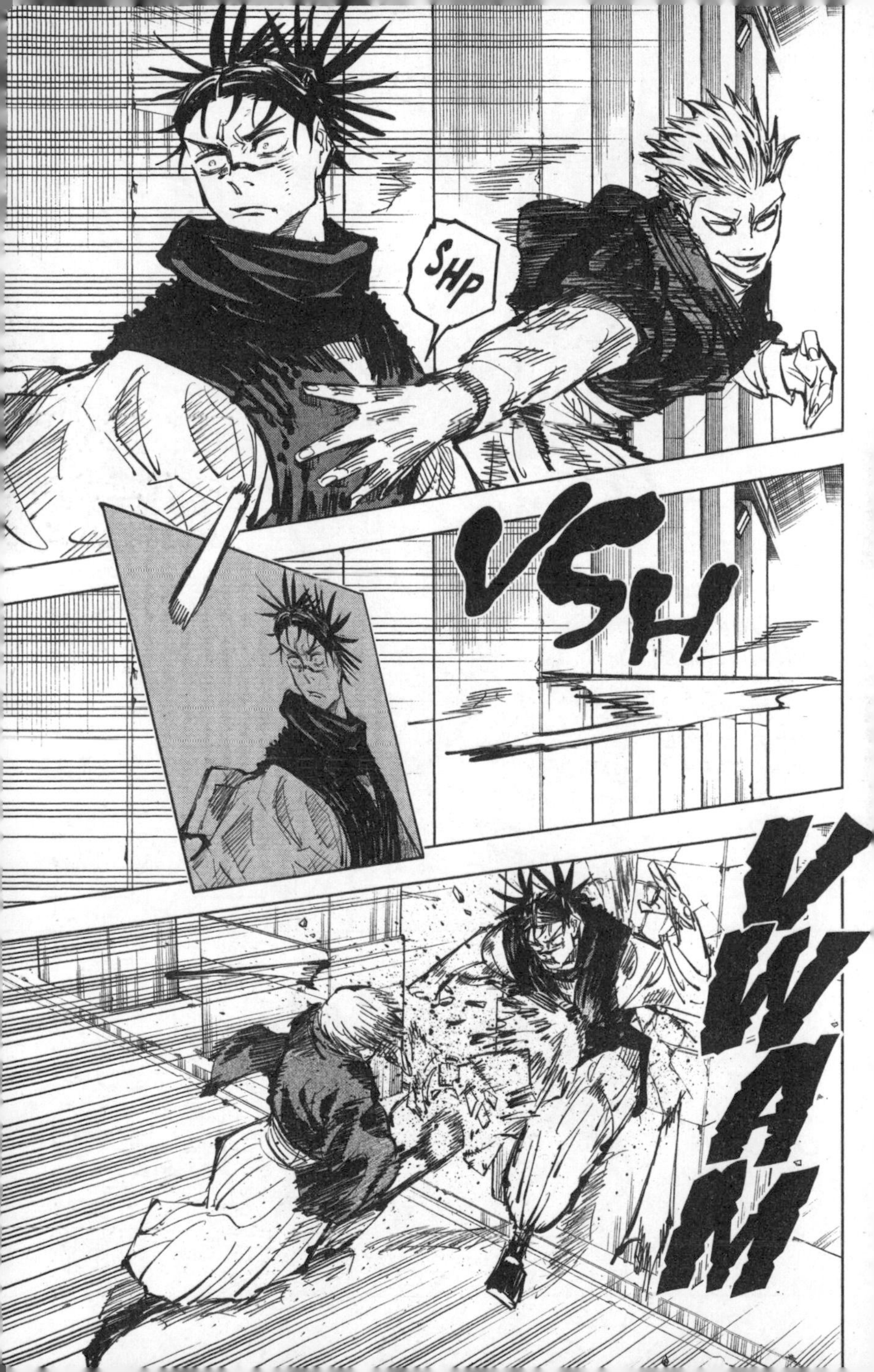
SHP
VSH
WHAM

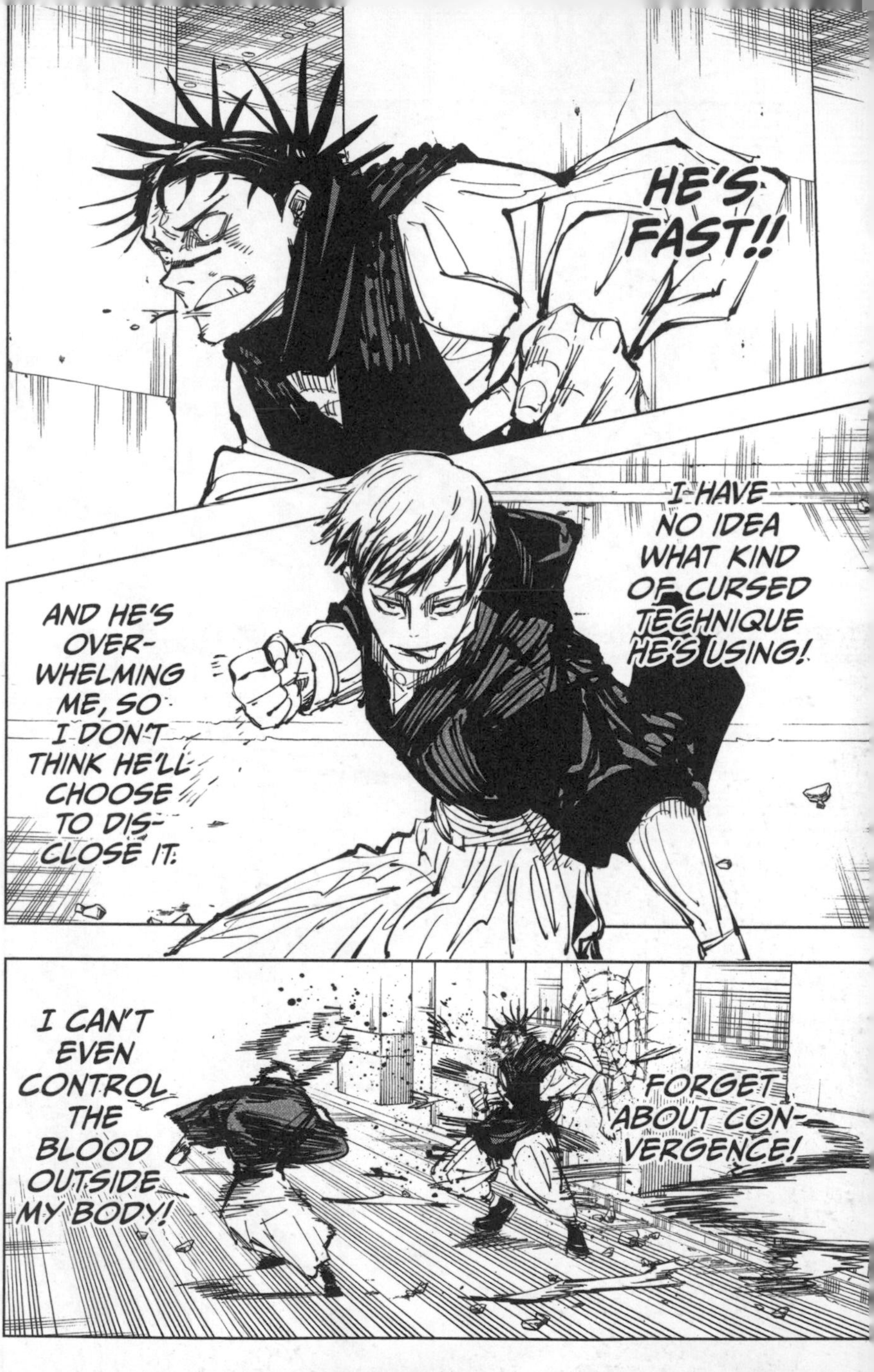
HE'S FAST!!
I HAVE NO IDEA WHAT KIND OF CURSED TECHNIQUE HE'S USING!
AND HE'S OVER-WHELMING ME, SO I DON'T THINK HE'LL CHOOSE TO DIS-CLOSE IT.
FORGET ABOUT CON-VERGENCE!
I CAN'T EVEN CONTROL THE BLOOD OUTSIDE MY BODY!

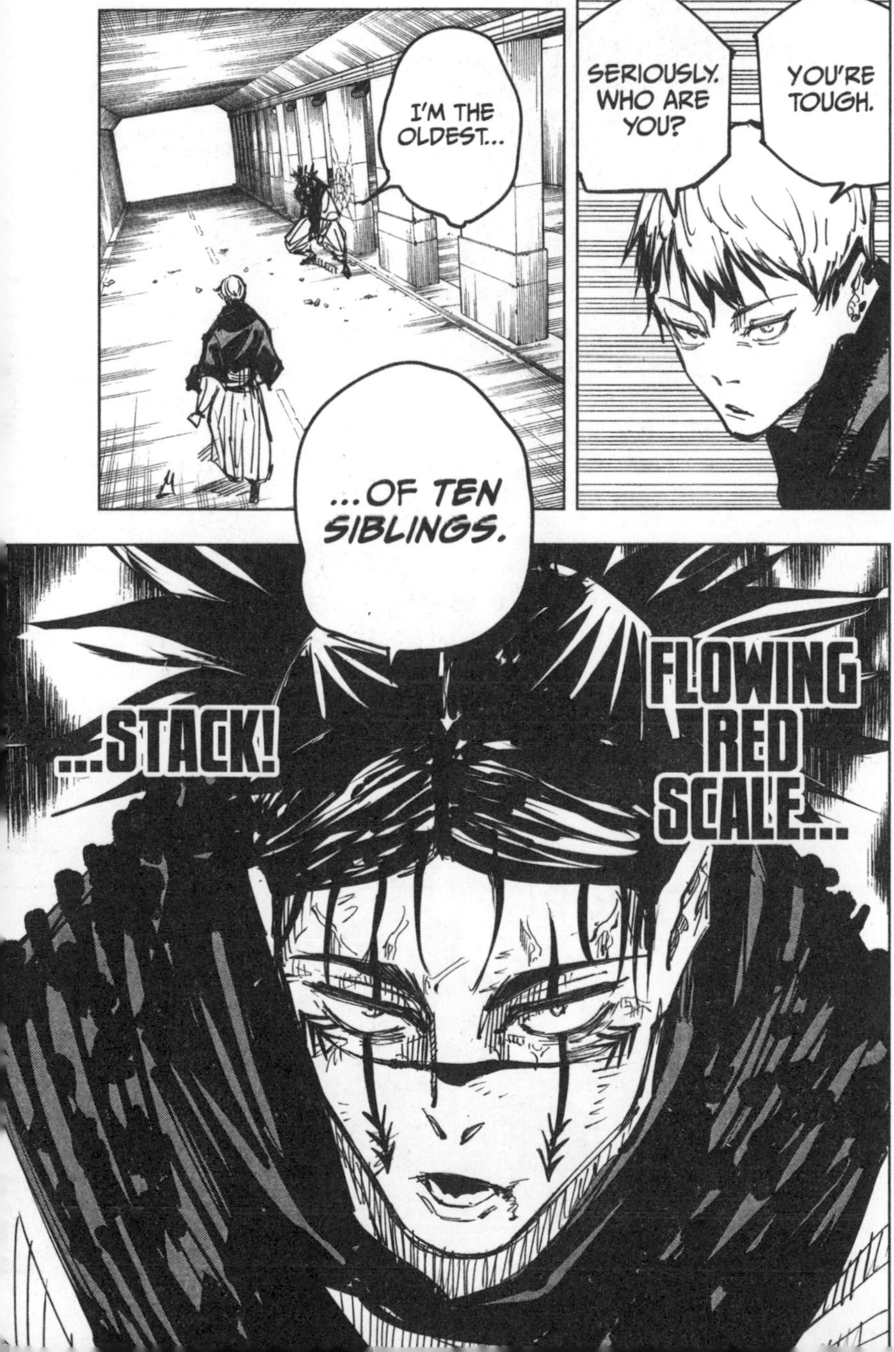
YOU'RE TOUGH.
SERIOUSLY. WHO ARE YOU?
I'M THE OLDEST...
...OF TEN SIBLINGS.
FLOWING RED SCALE...
...STACK!

ITADORI

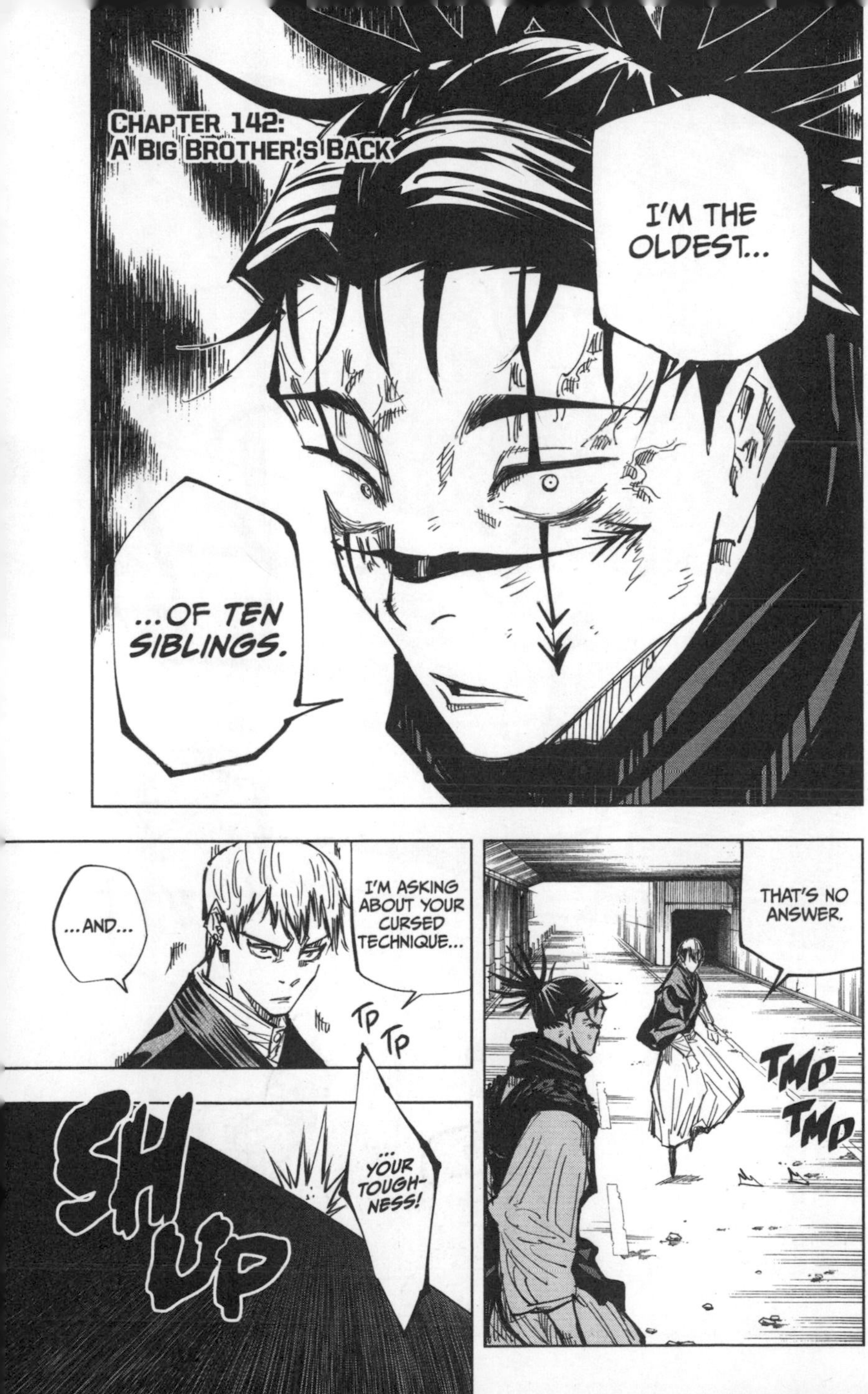
CHAPTER 142:
A BIG BROTHER'S BACK
I'M THE OLDEST...
...OF TEN SIBLINGS.
THAT'S NO ANSWER.
TMP TMP
I'M ASKING ABOUT YOUR CURSED TECHNIQUE...
...AND...
TP TP
...YOUR TOUGHNESS!
SHUP

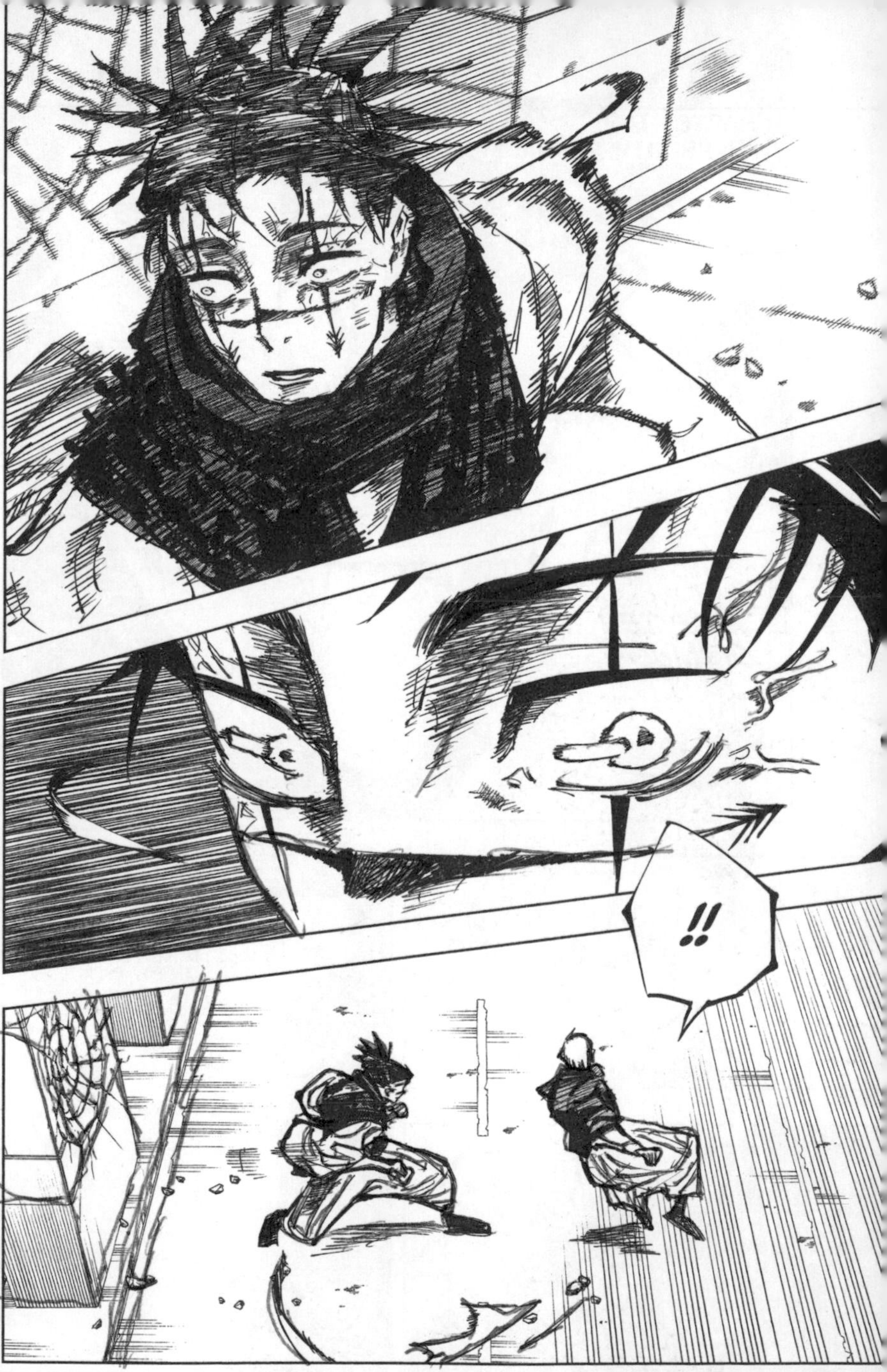
!!

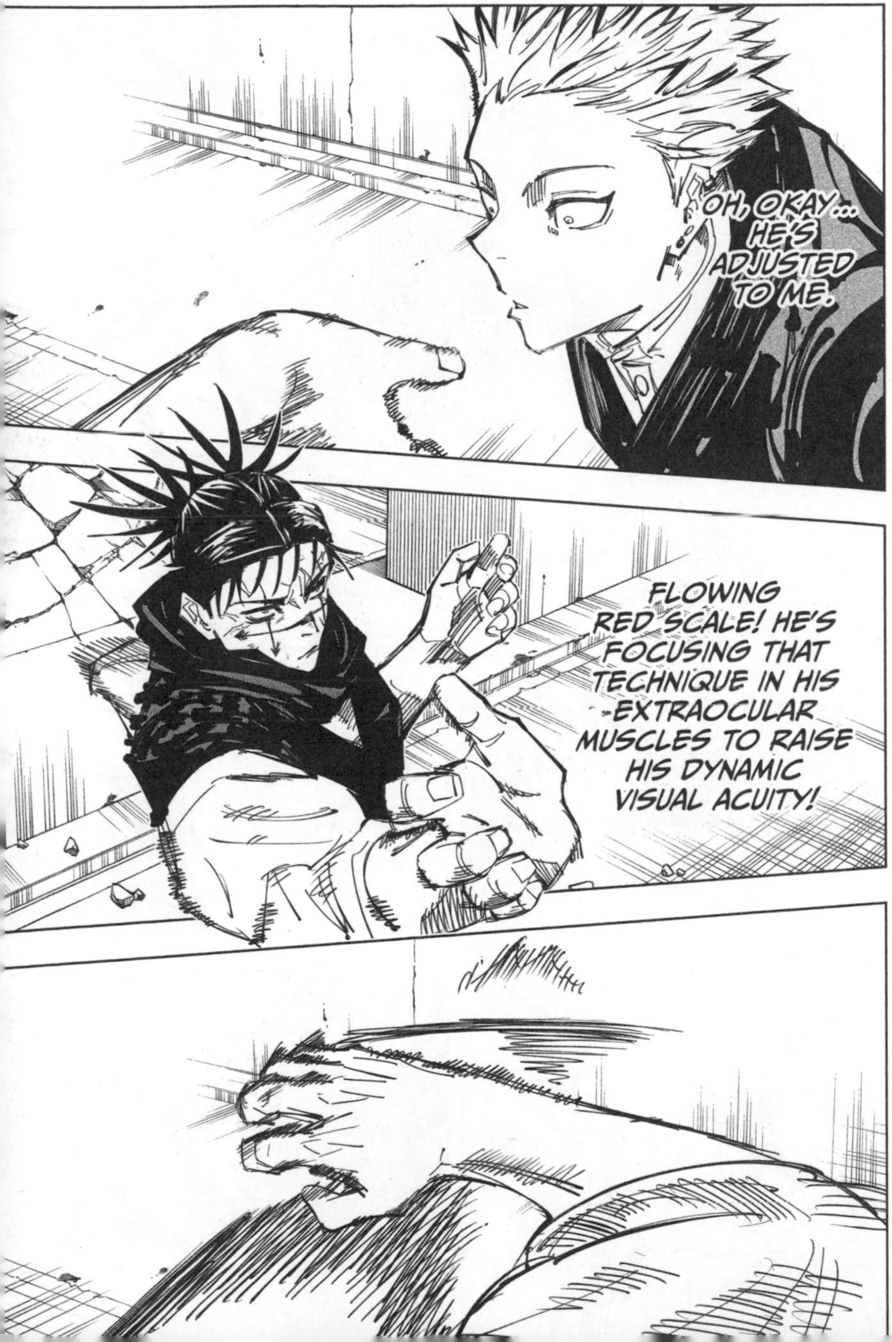
OH, OKAY... HE'S ADJUSTED TO ME.
FLOWING RED SCALE! HE'S FOCUSING THAT TECHNIQUE IN HIS EXTRAOCULAR MUSCLES TO RAISE HIS DYNAMIC VISUAL ACUITY!

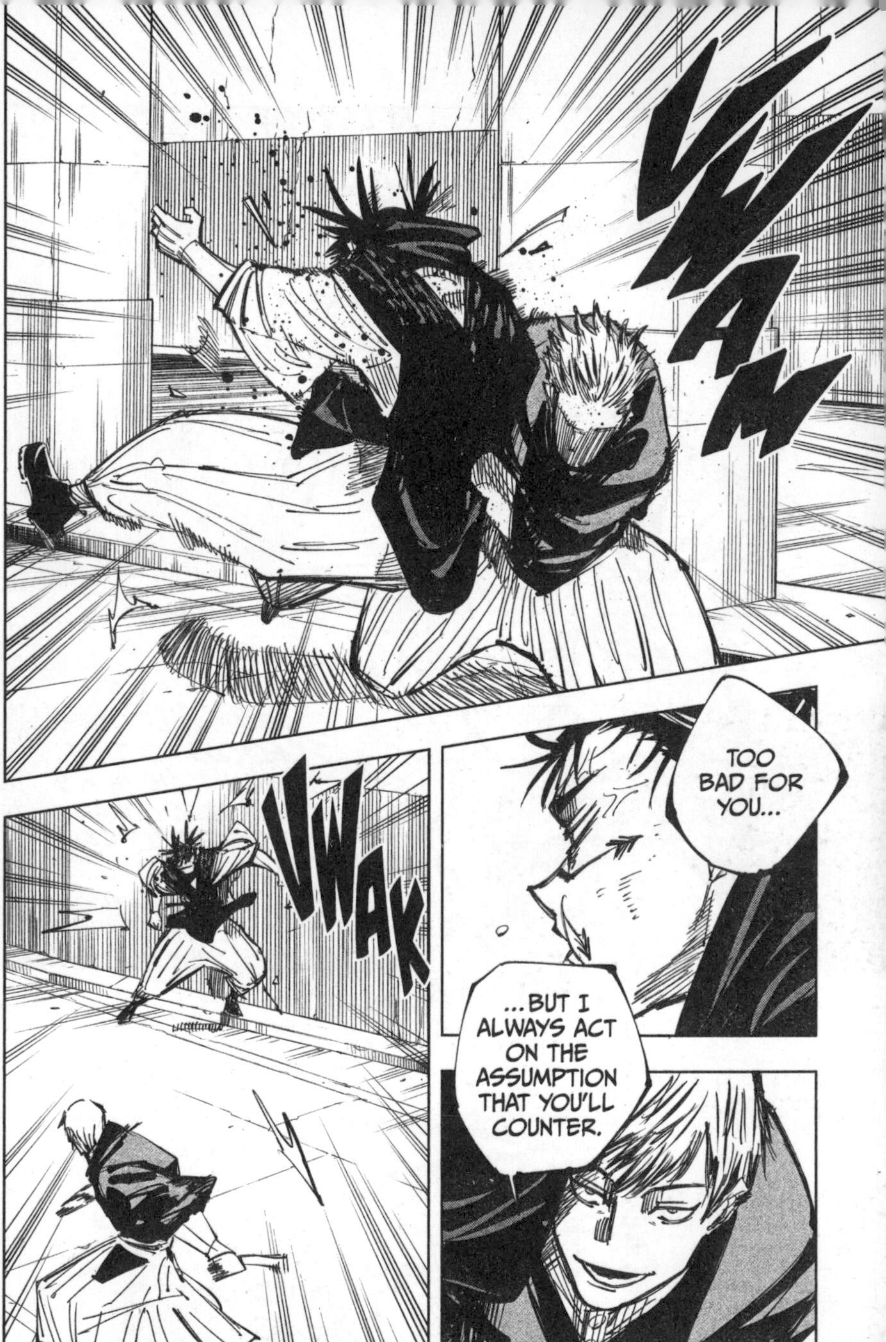
WHAM
TOO BAD FOR YOU...
...BUT I ALWAYS ACT ON THE ASSUMPTION THAT YOU'LL COUNTER.
VWAK

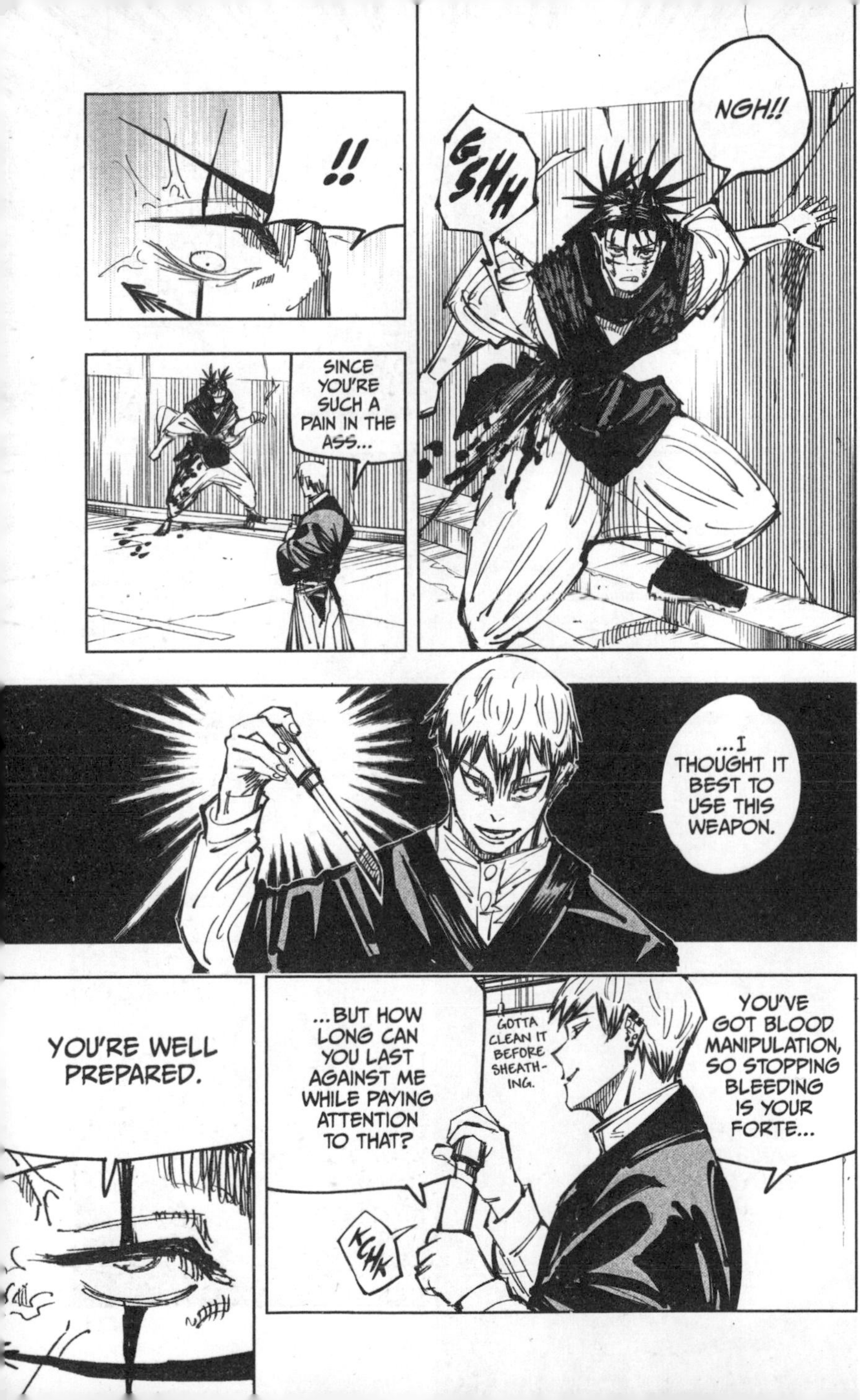
NGH!!
GSHH
!!
SINCE YOU'RE SUCH A PAIN IN THE ASS...
...I THOUGHT IT BEST TO USE THIS WEAPON.
YOU'VE GOT BLOOD MANIPULATION, SO STOPPING BLEEDING IS YOUR FORTE...
GOTTA CLEAN IT BEFORE SHEATH-ING.
...BUT HOW LONG CAN YOU LAST AGAINST ME WHILE PAYING ATTENTION TO THAT?
KCHK
YOU'RE WELL PREPARED.

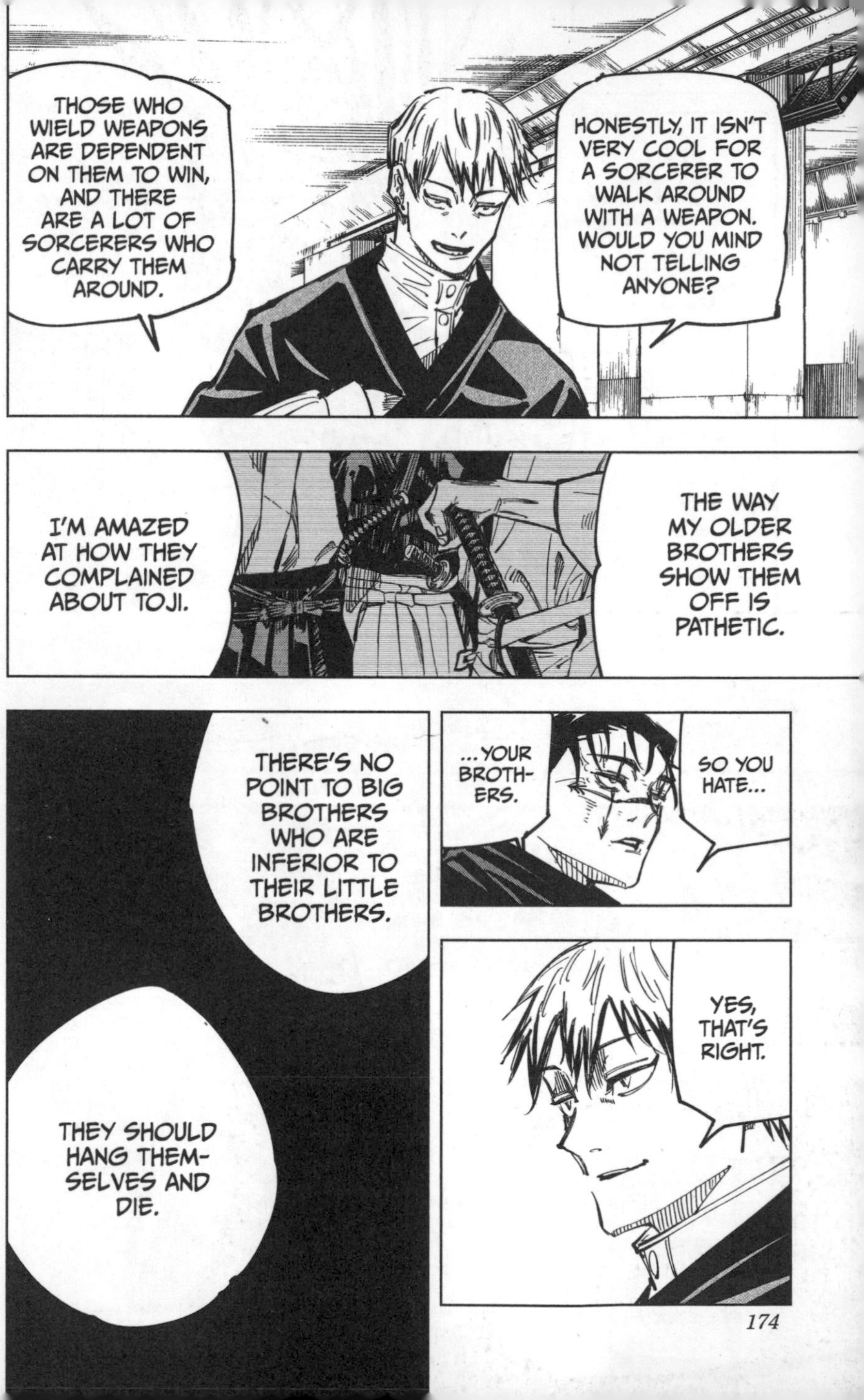
HONESTLY, IT ISN'T VERY COOL FOR A SORCERER TO WALK AROUND WITH A WEAPON. WOULD YOU MIND NOT TELLING ANYONE?
THOSE WHO WIELD WEAPONS ARE DEPENDENT ON THEM TO WIN, AND THERE ARE A LOT OF SORCERERS WHO CARRY THEM AROUND.
THE WAY MY OLDER BROTHERS SHOW THEM OFF IS PATHETIC.
I'M AMAZED AT HOW THEY COMPLAINED ABOUT TOJI.
SO YOU HATE...
...YOUR BROTH-ERS.
YES, THAT'S RIGHT.
THERE'S NO POINT TO BIG BROTHERS WHO ARE INFERIOR TO THEIR LITTLE BROTHERS.
THEY SHOULD HANG THEM-SELVES AND DIE.

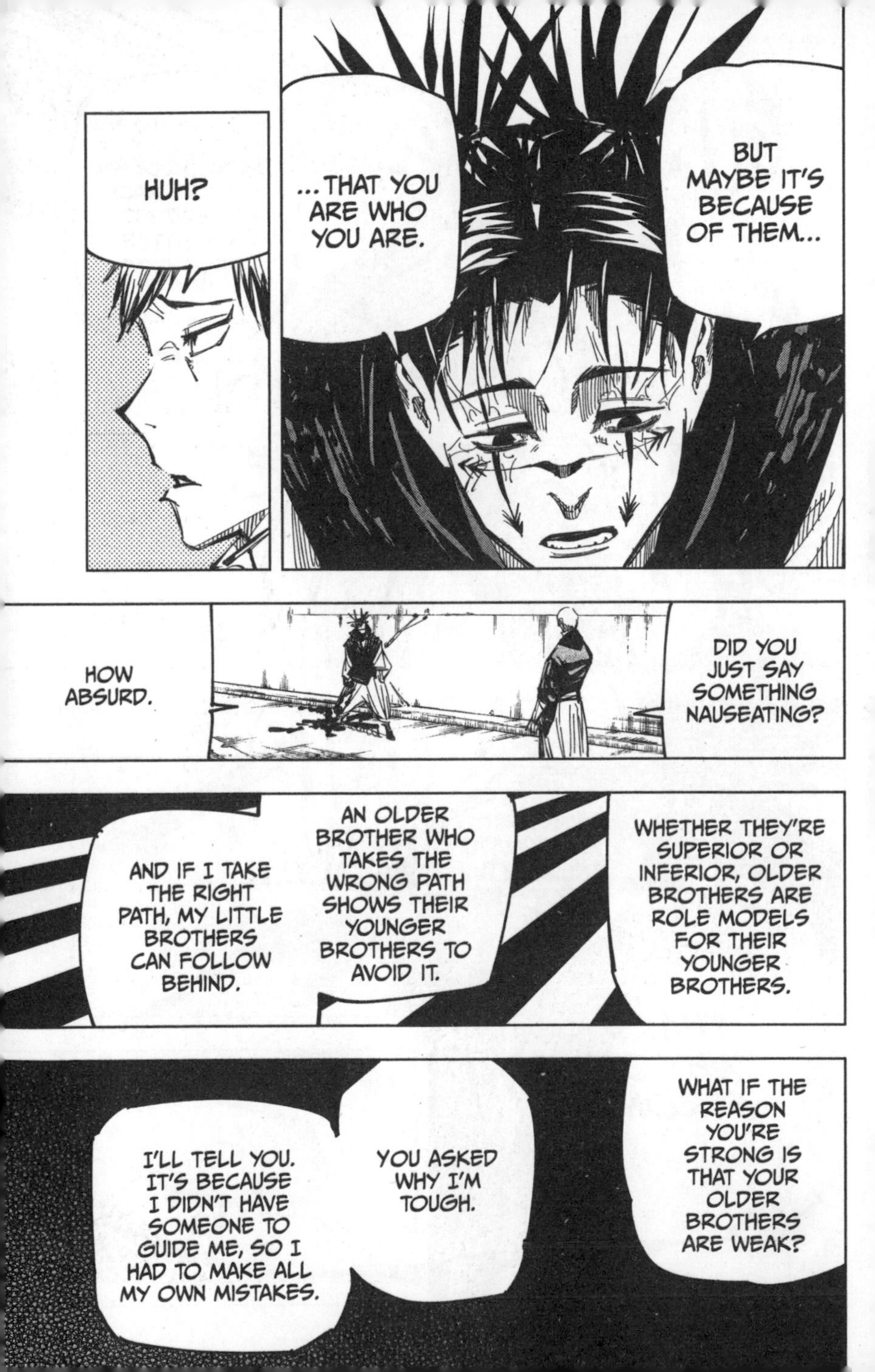
BUT MAYBE IT'S BECAUSE OF THEM...
...THAT YOU ARE WHO YOU ARE.
HUH?
DID YOU JUST SAY SOMETHING NAUSEATING?
HOW ABSURD.
WHETHER THEY'RE SUPERIOR OR INFERIOR, OLDER BROTHERS ARE ROLE MODELS FOR THEIR YOUNGER BROTHERS.
AN OLDER BROTHER WHO TAKES THE WRONG PATH SHOWS THEIR YOUNGER BROTHERS TO AVOID IT.
AND IF I TAKE THE RIGHT PATH, MY LITTLE BROTHERS CAN FOLLOW BEHIND.
WHAT IF THE REASON YOU'RE STRONG IS THAT YOUR OLDER BROTHERS ARE WEAK?
YOU ASKED WHY I'M TOUGH.
I'LL TELL YOU. IT'S BECAUSE I DIDN'T HAVE SOMEONE TO GUIDE ME, SO I HAD TO MAKE ALL MY OWN MISTAKES.

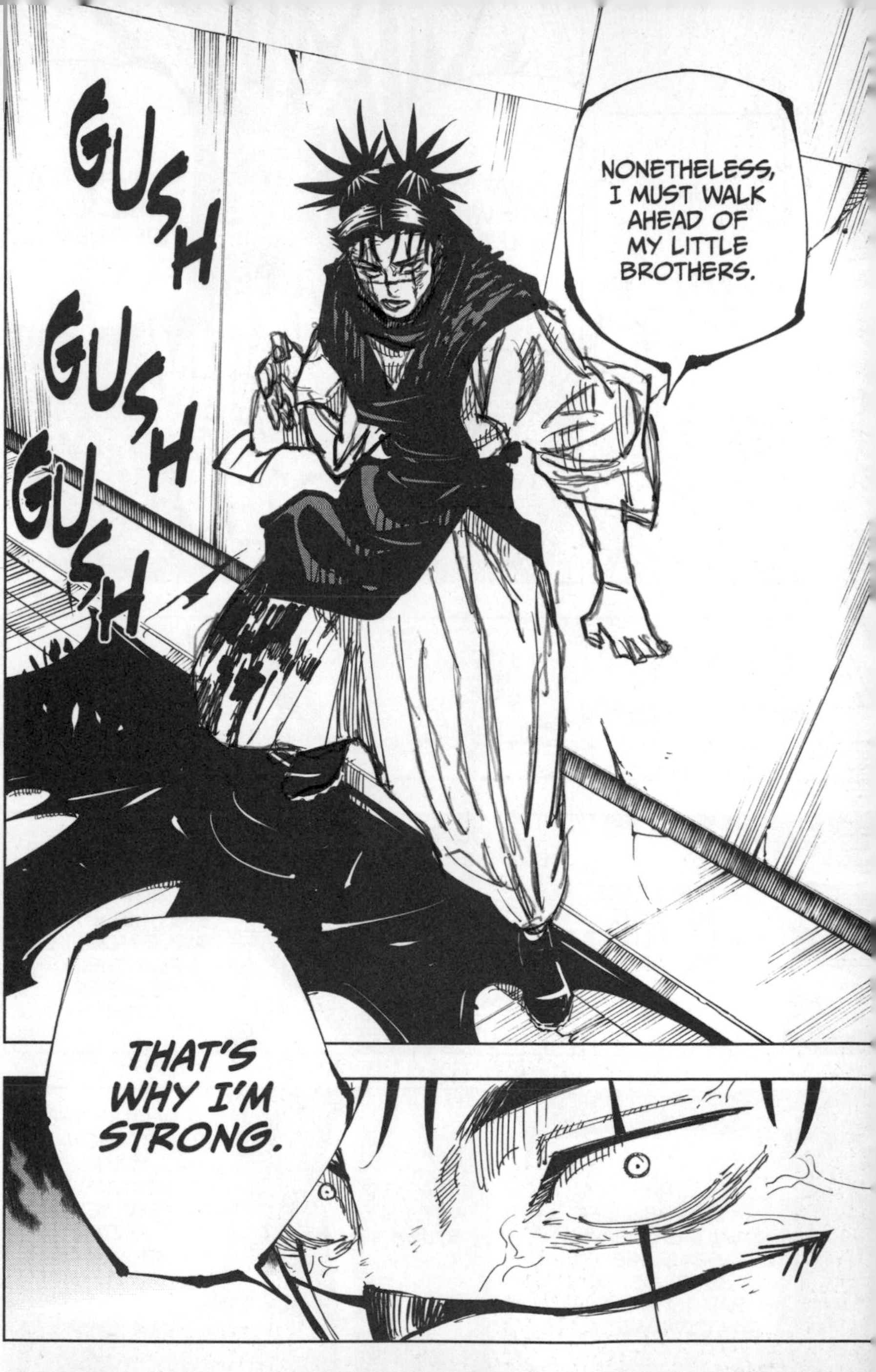
NONETHELESS, I MUST WALK AHEAD OF MY LITTLE BROTHERS.
GUSH
GUSH
GUSH
THAT'S WHY I'M STRONG.

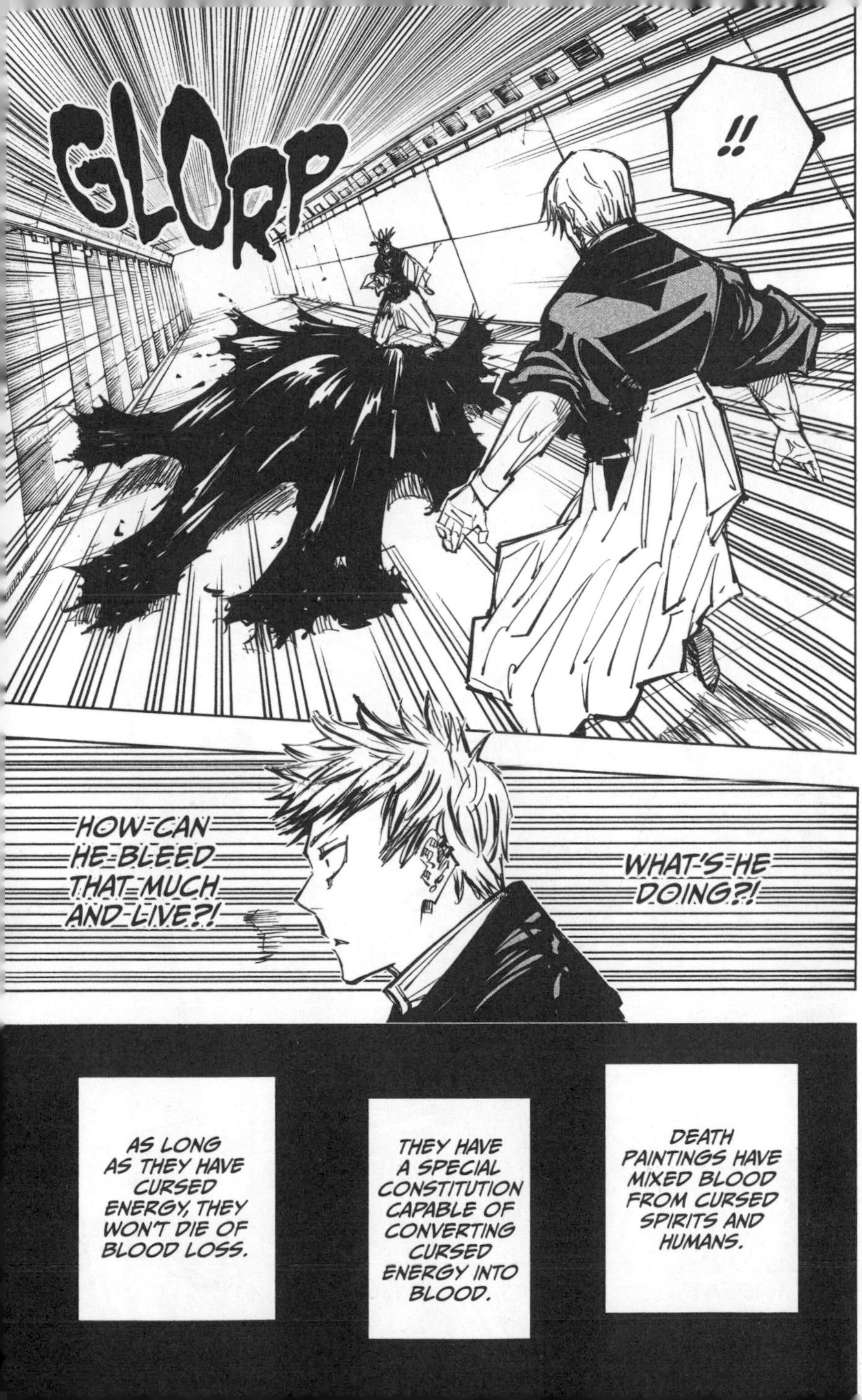
!!
GLORP
WHAT'S HE DOING?!
HOW CAN HE BLEED THAT MUCH AND LIVE?!
DEATH PAINTINGS HAVE MIXED BLOOD FROM CURSED SPIRITS AND HUMANS.
THEY HAVE A SPECIAL CONSTITUTION CAPABLE OF CONVERTING CURSED ENERGY INTO BLOOD.
AS LONG AS THEY HAVE CURSED ENERGY, THEY WON'T DIE OF BLOOD LOSS.

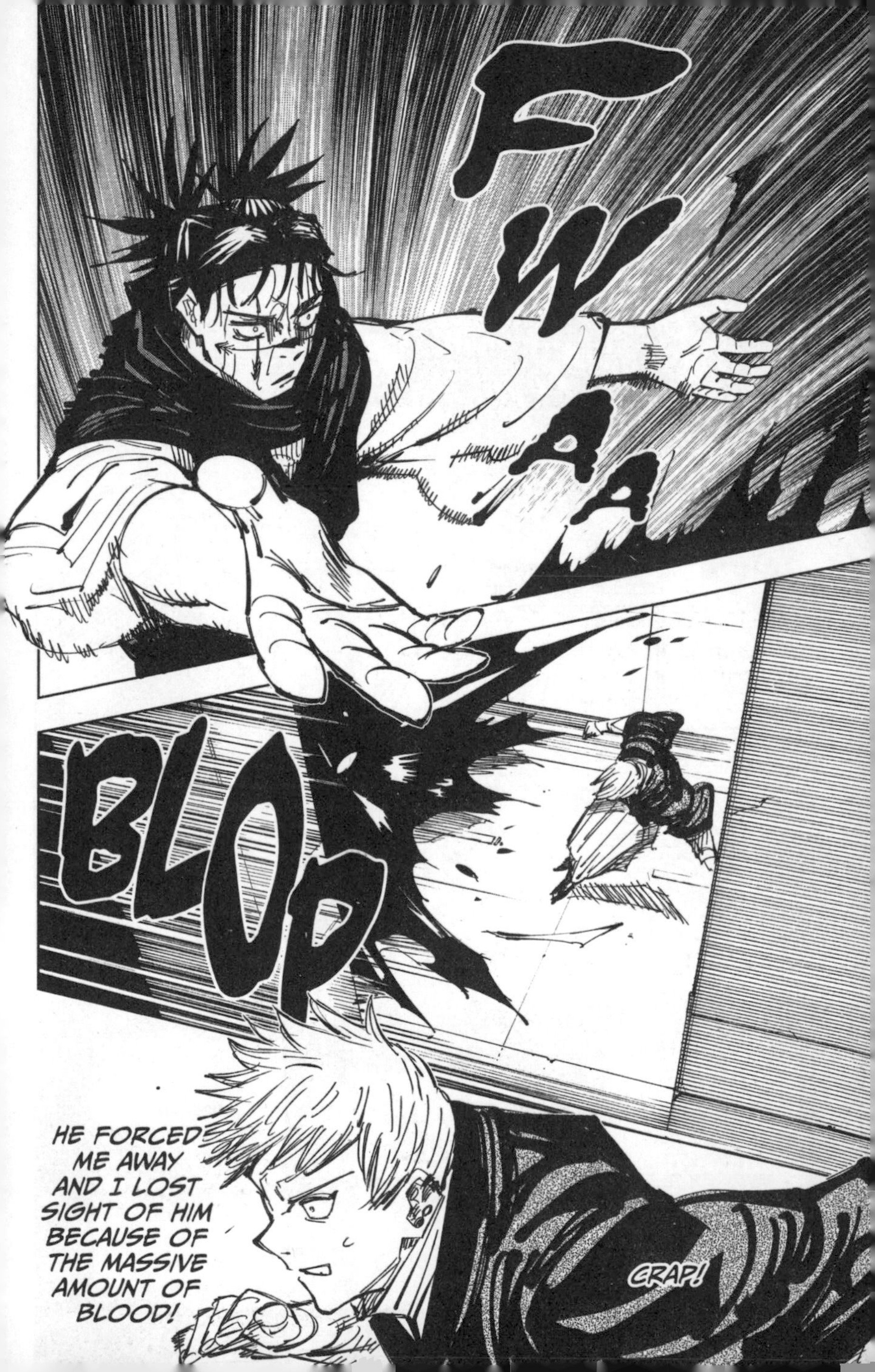
FWAA
BLOOD
CRAP!
HE FORCED ME AWAY AND I LOST SIGHT OF HIM BECAUSE OF THE MASSIVE AMOUNT OF BLOOD!

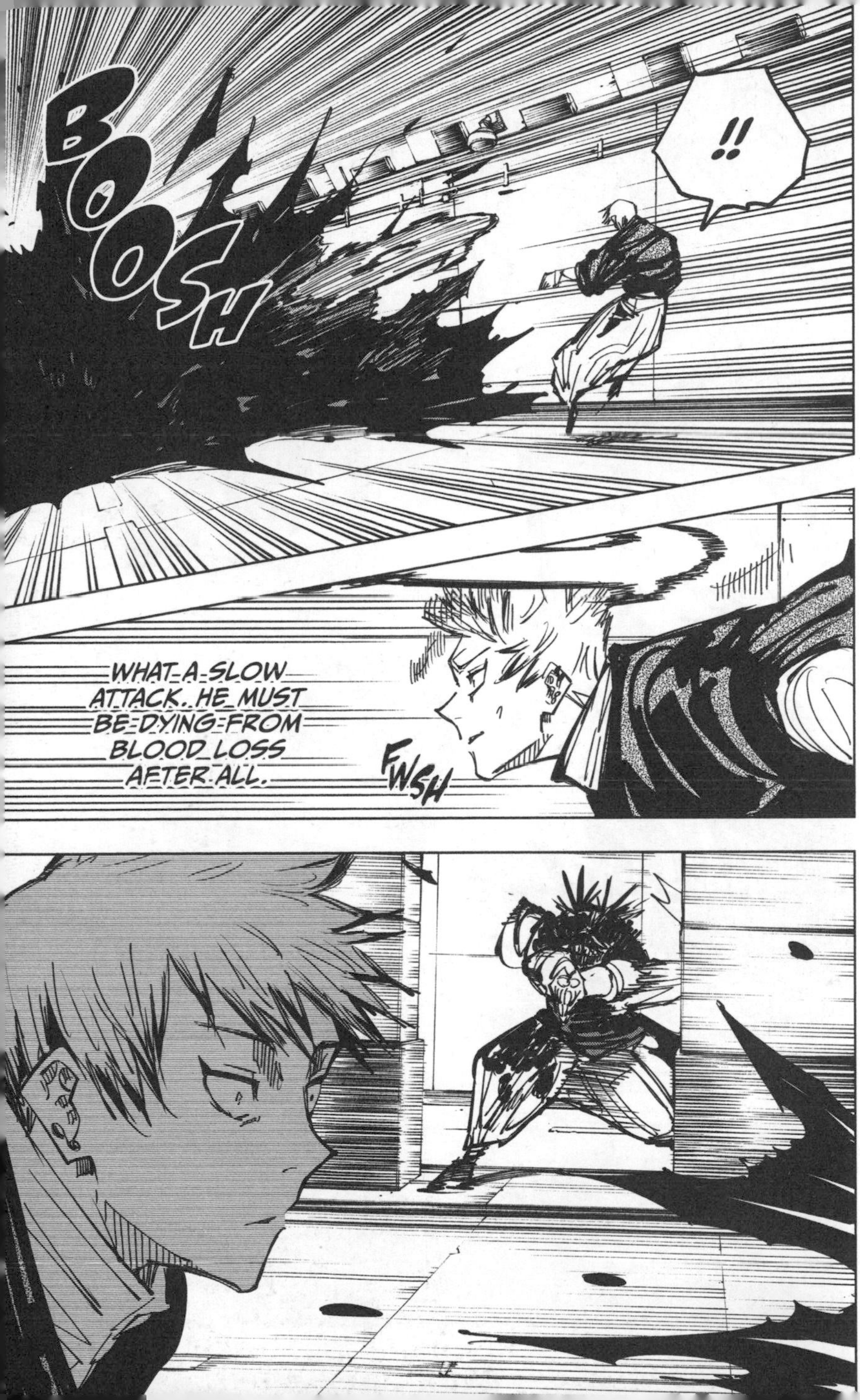
!!
BOOSH
WHAT A SLOW ATTACK. HE MUST BE DYING FROM BLOOD LOSS AFTER ALL.
FWSH

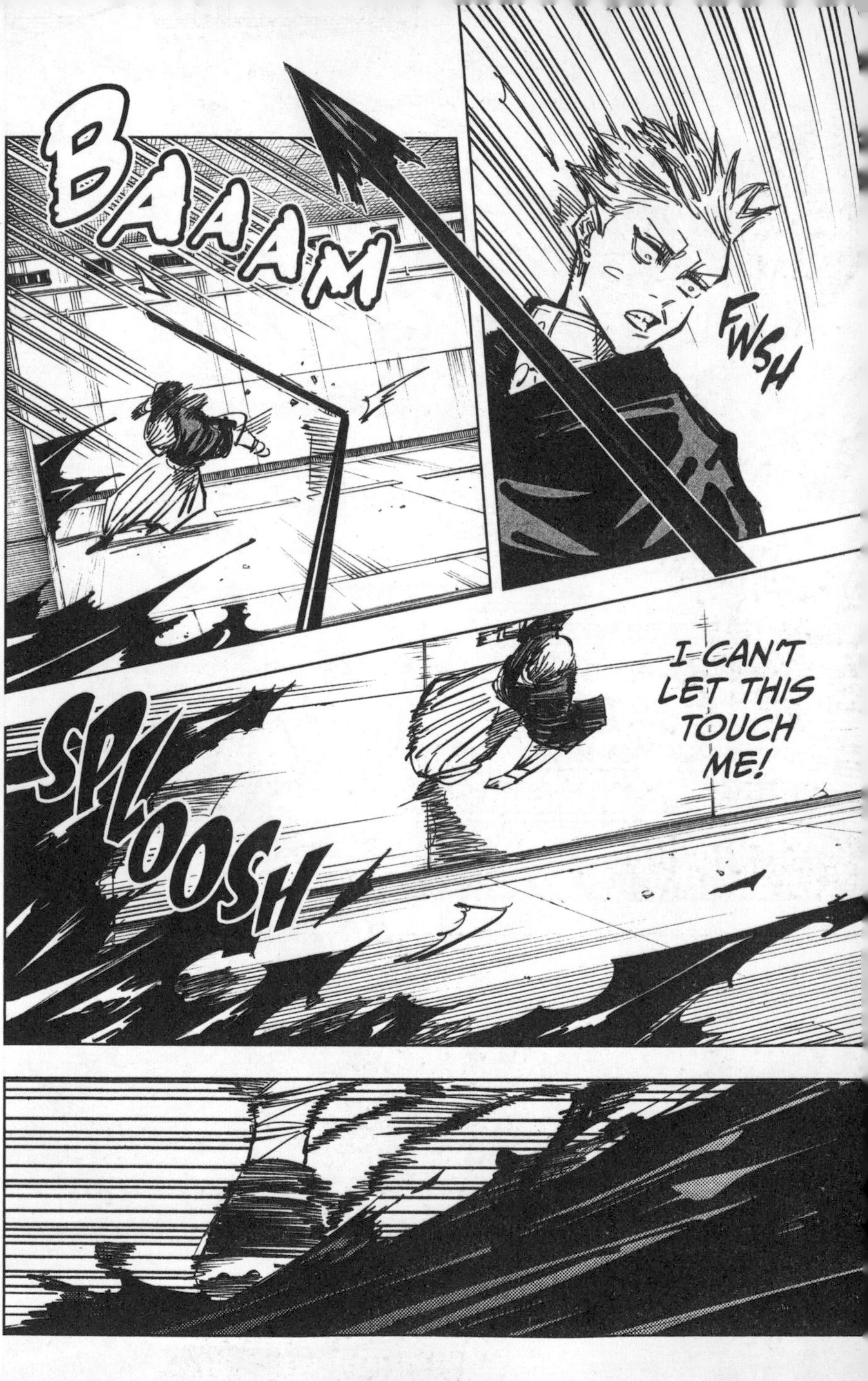
FWSH
BAAAM
I CAN'T LET THIS TOUCH ME!
SPLOOSH

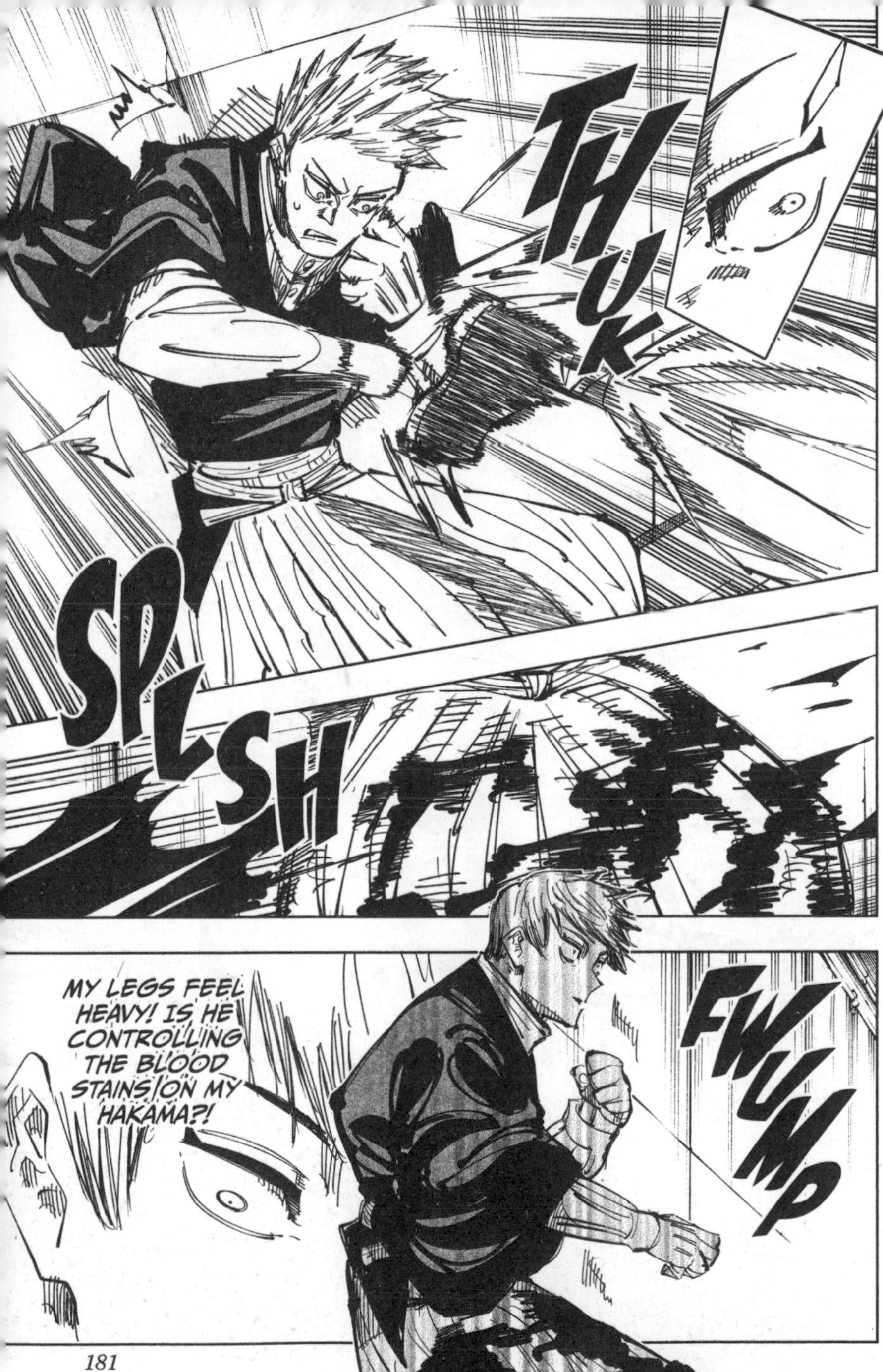
THUK
SPLSH
FWUMP
MY LEGS FEEL HEAVY! IS HE CONTROLLING THE BLOOD STAINS ON MY HAKAMA?!

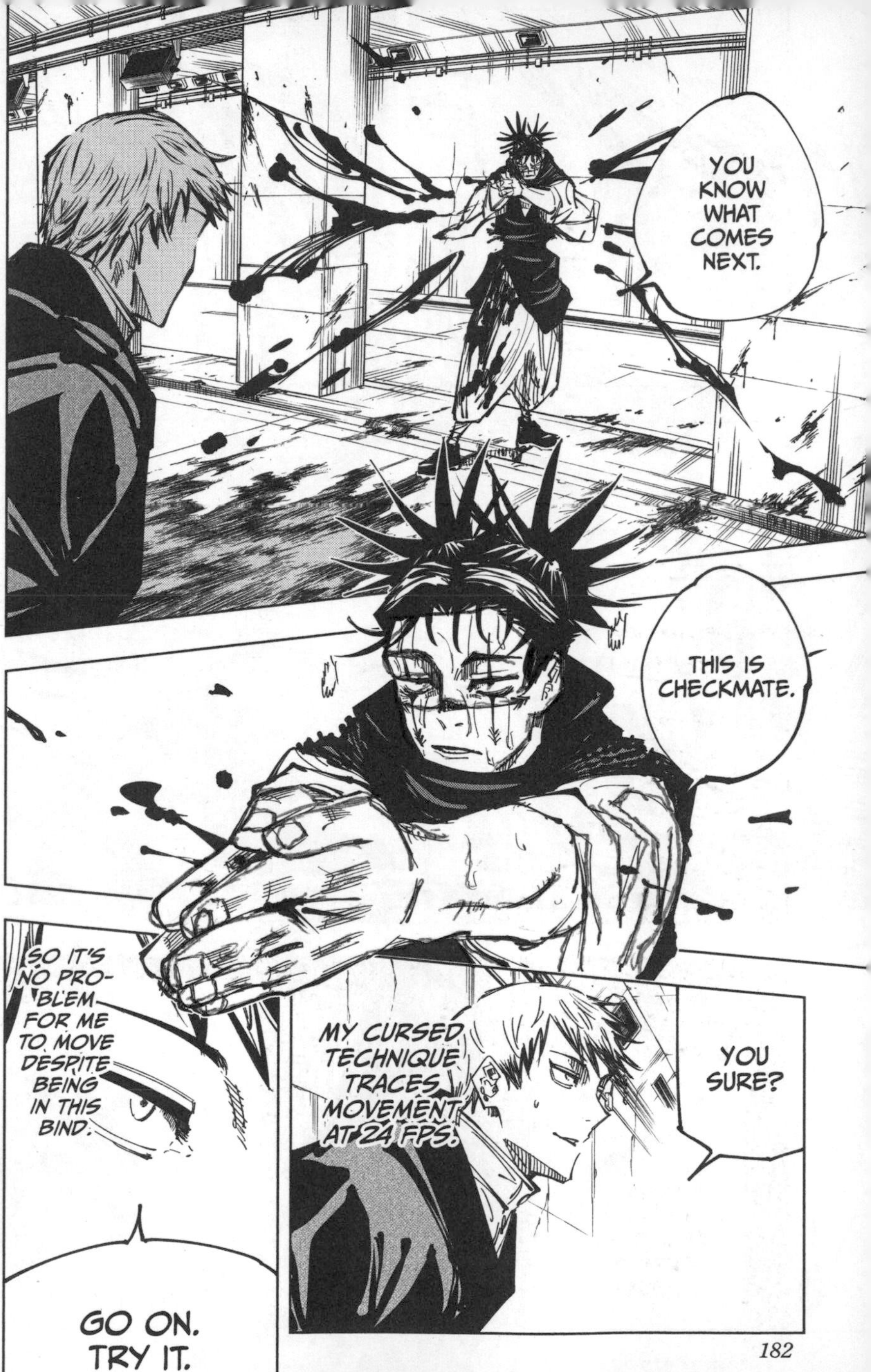
YOU KNOW WHAT COMES NEXT.
THIS IS CHECKMATE.
YOU SURE?
MY CURSED TECHNIQUE TRACES MOVEMENT AT 24 FPS.
SO IT'S NO PROBLEM FOR ME TO MOVE DESPITE BEING IN THIS BIND.
GO ON. TRY IT.

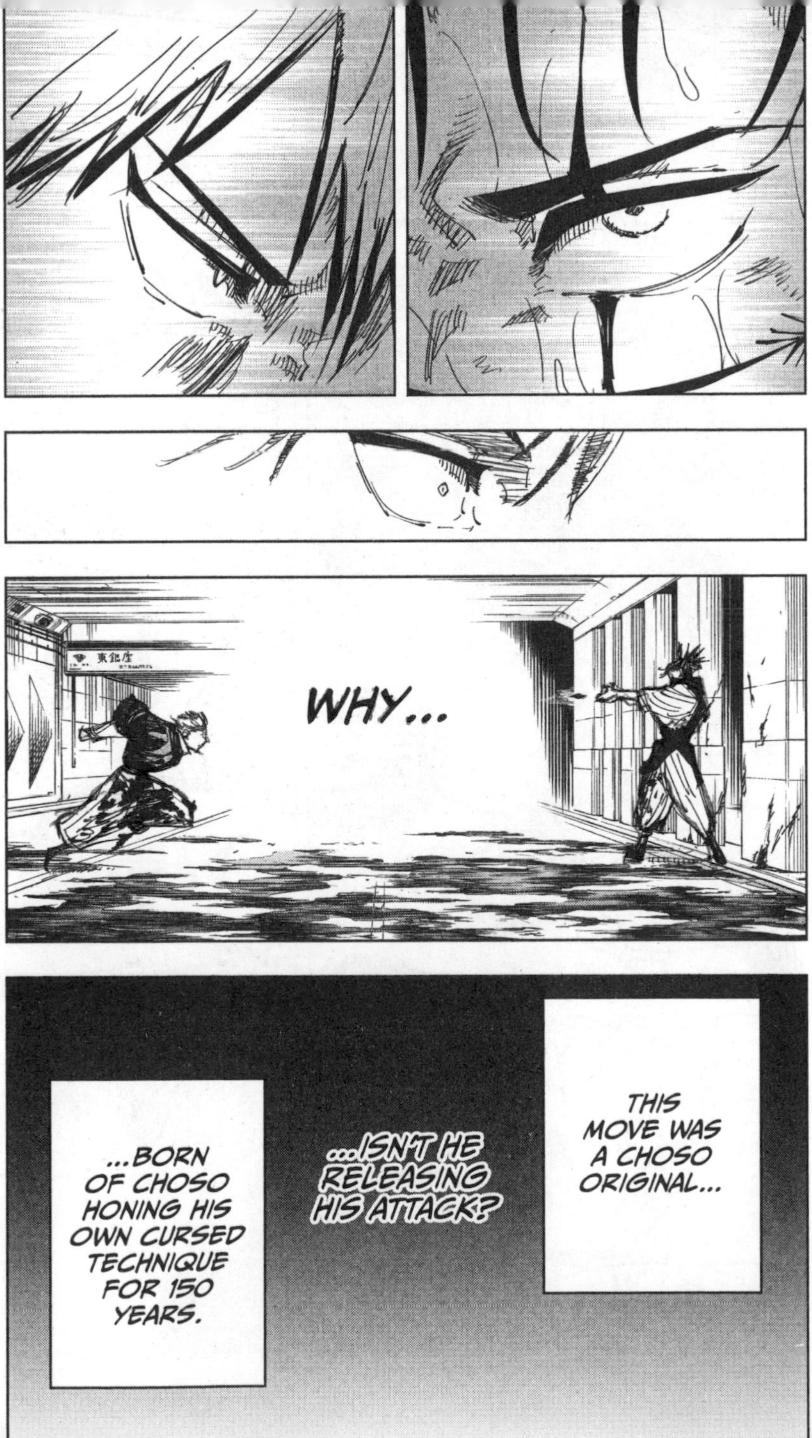
WHY...
東銀座
...ISN'T HE RELEASING HIS ATTACK?
THIS MOVE WAS A CHOSO ORIGINAL...
...BORN OF CHOSO HONING HIS OWN CURSED TECHNIQUE FOR 150 YEARS.

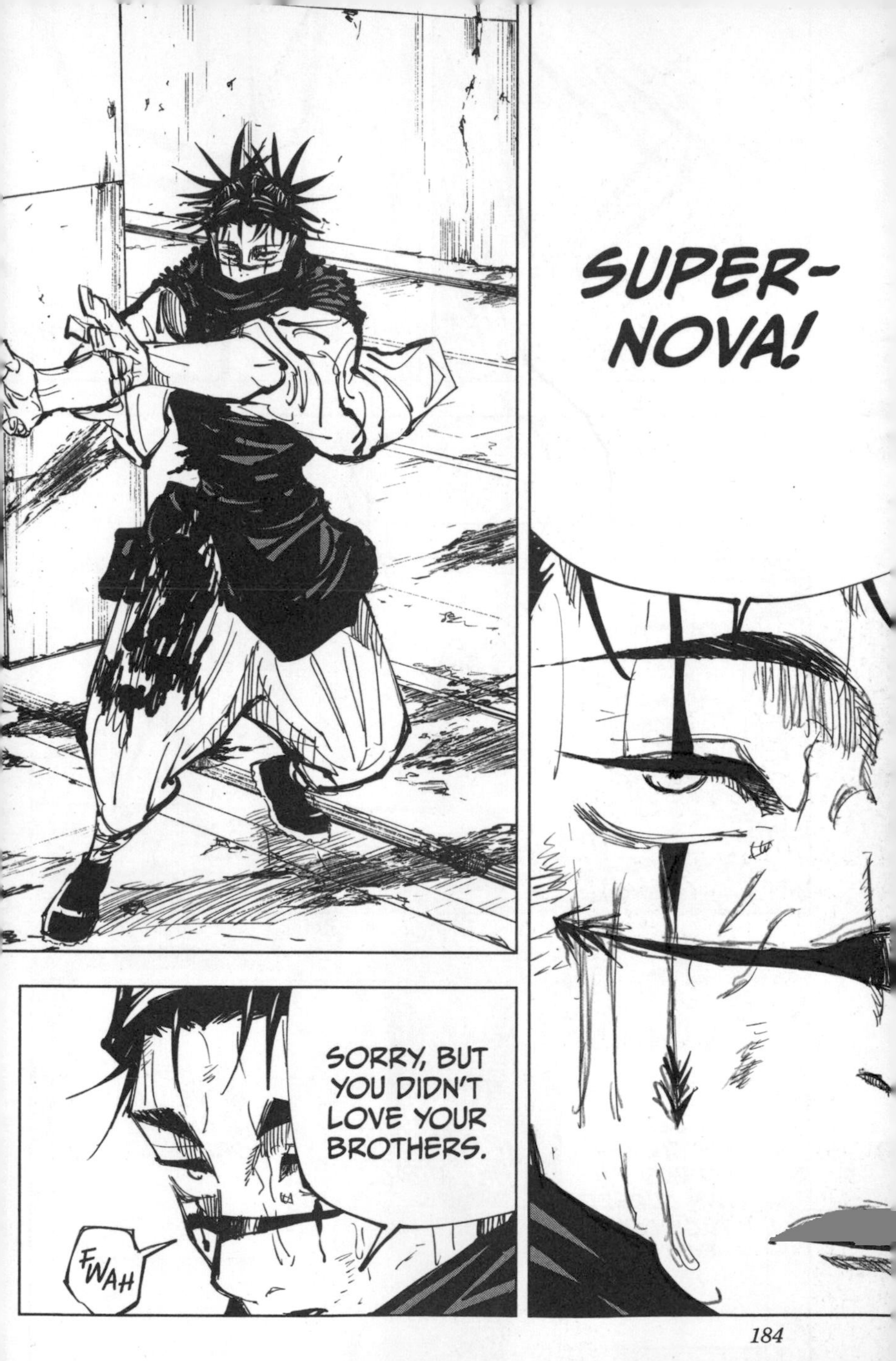
SUPER-NOVA!
SORRY, BUT YOU DIDN'T LOVE YOUR BROTHERS.
FWAH

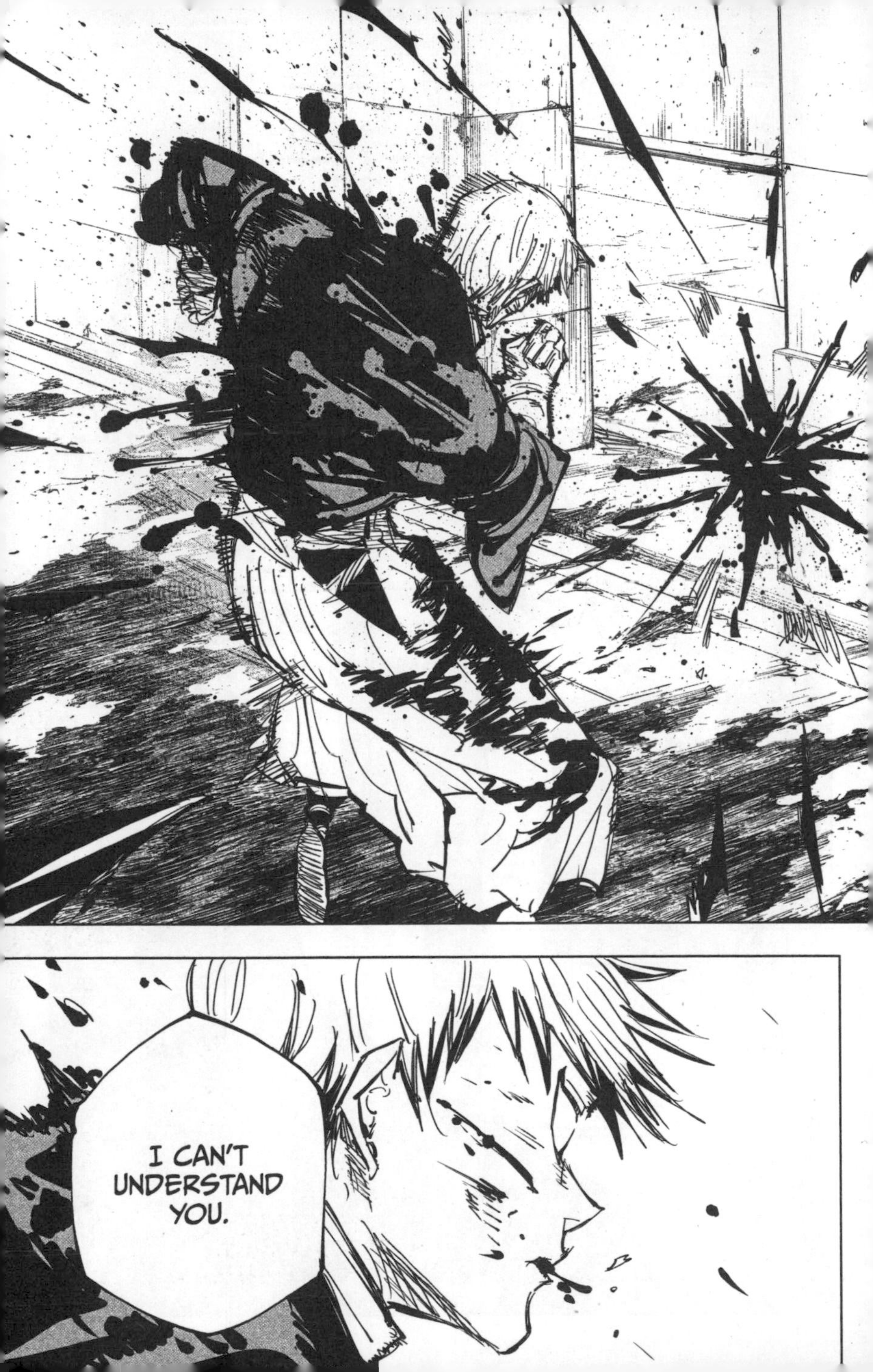
I CAN'T UNDERSTAND YOU.

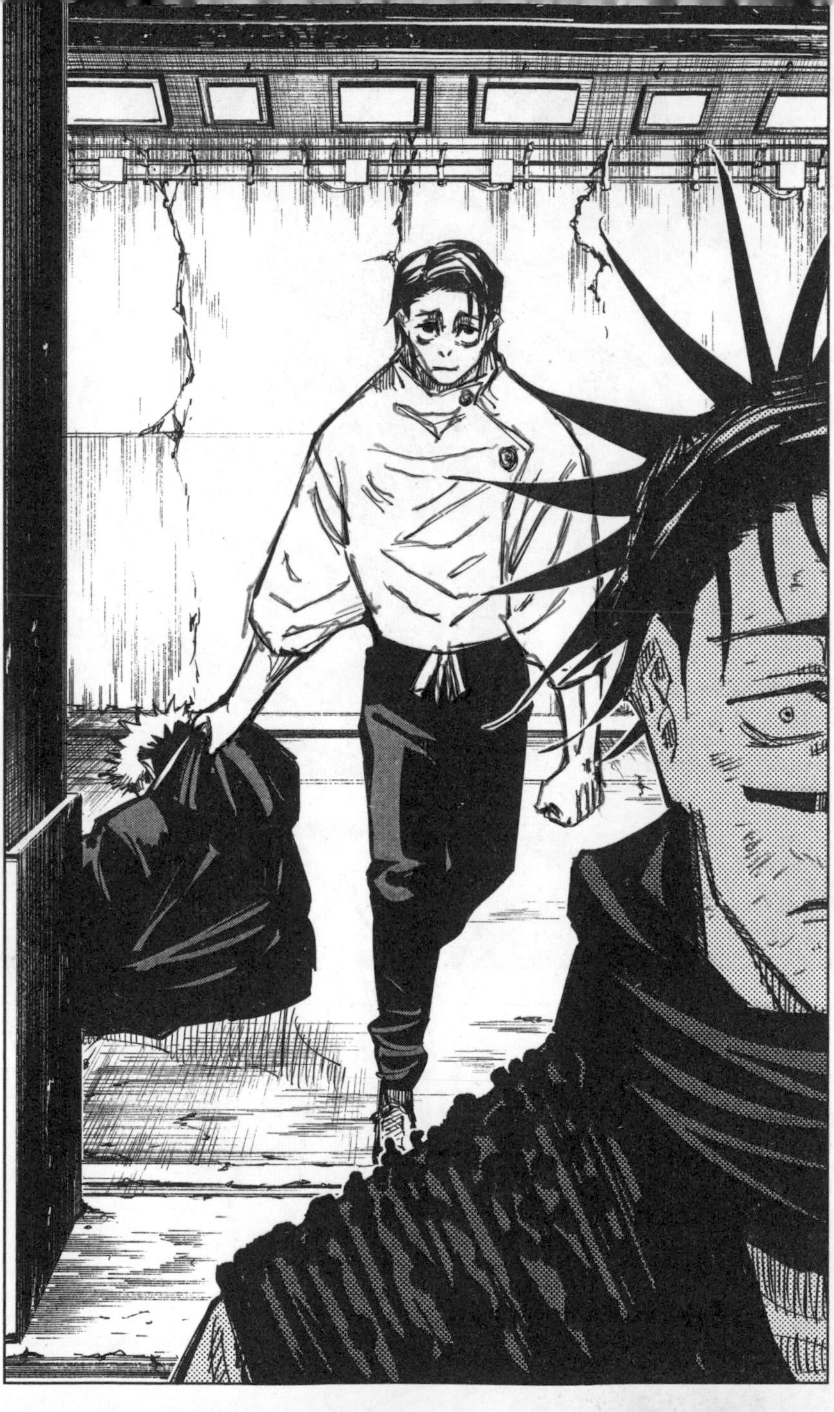

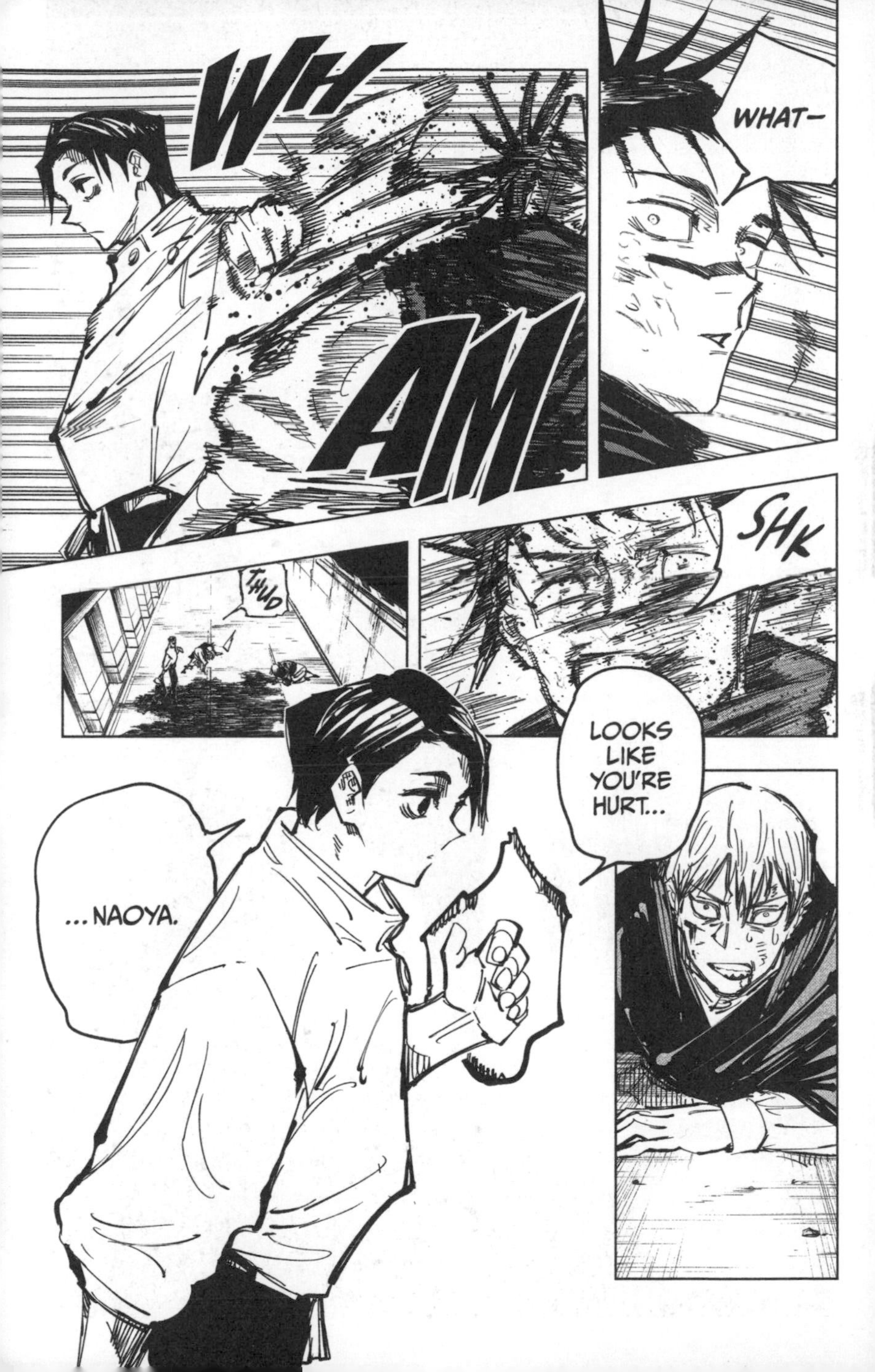
WHAT–
WHAM
SHK
THUD
LOOKS LIKE YOU'RE HURT...
...NAOYA.

GOJO

SUKUNA

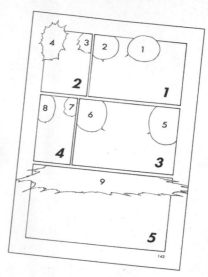

JUJUTSU KAISEN
reads from right to left,
starting in the upper-right
corner. Japanese is read
from right to left, meaning
that action, sound effects,
and word-balloon order
are completely reversed
from English order.